The Old Pubs of Deal and Walmer
(with Kingsdown and Mongeham)

by Steve Glover and Michael Rogers

Front cover photo: The Prince Albert,
Middle Street, Deal – 1906.
Back cover photo: The Berry,
Canada Road, Walmer – c1960.

Contents

The authors dedicate this book to

William, Georgia & Rose Glover,
Joanna & John Carey and Oliver Ling

Steve Glover

- and -

My father John Rogers & late mother Betty Rogers

Michael Rogers

The authors' local credentials

Steve Glover was born in Dover, the son of a Royal Marine Commando based in Deal. When he was only a few months old, the family decamped to north Surrey where his newly retired father bought and ran a pig and poultry farm. Steve continued to live in Surrey and south west London for most of his adult life but never cut his ties with Deal, holidaying there most years with his parents, Ralph – aka Bob – and Evelyn – aka Peggy, sister Angela and later with his wife and children. After being a DFL (Down from London) weekender for several years, he became a permanent resident in 2005. Steve is a musician, a Guinness drinker and a very keen local history enthusiast!

Michael Rogers is a Man of Kent, having been born and bred in – and a continual resident of – the county. Michael was also born in Dover and spent most of his early years living in North Street, Deal, where his parents, John and Betty, owned and ran a bakery, later moving to another in Church Path. They made bread from scratch on the premises and Michael would deliver it – "make it, bake it and take it" as he puts it! He later worked for many years at a distribution centre in Faversham, where he also lived, returning to Deal when he took early retirement. He is a great fan of Black Sheep beer and has spent many enjoyable holidays 'researching' its brewery in North Yorkshire! Michael is also a very enthusiastic local historian.

Introduction

While researching information for this book, we came across several different spellings of names for what appeared to be the same people or hostelries. On other occasions, unusual spellings of commonplace names were recorded. We have tried to be as accurate as possible and have either reproduced the spellings as they originally appeared in the research documentation (even if the same ones have appeared differently in various original documents) or, in places, where it was obvious that some earlier (but more up to date) document had merely been misspelt by previous researchers, we have amended the errors. This might be a good tip for those researching their genealogy – cast your nets wide when dealing with family names.

In particular, several pub names differ in their spellings (see, for example, the **Roxborough Castle** entry). This was not usually because the pubs had changed their names to something similar sounding but more often due to the illiteracy of much of the population in earlier times, so a general stab at a name when documenting it would probably have been considered good enough in most instances.

We have also deliberately not included apostrophes in the names of any of the hostelries simply because their use was inconsistent – even when documenting the same pub! Evidence was also found to show some pub keepers themselves apparently did not know whether or not to use an apostrophe either or, if they did, where to actually place it! Readers of books such as *'Eats Shoots and Leaves'* will know this conundrum is not just an historical problem relating to public houses (or greengrocers)! To give an example therefore, we have omitted an apostrophe when referring to the **'Dukes Head,'** even though it is hoped the Duke only had one head and therefore the apostrophe should appear after 'Duke' but before the 's' (and we won't even entertain the possibility of several Dukes sharing a single head!).

Frustratingly, the only information to be found on some of the old local watering holes has either been simply a mention of their names alone (sometimes without a location given) in, for example, a regional rate book or directory, or maybe just in a list of individual local innkeepers. Because of this it could be argued the contents of this book fall between two stools in that, while we hope it will be an interesting and definitive reference book about local public houses, we would also like it to be an entertaining and easy read wherever it has been possible to add a description, or a story or two, about a particular pub or its incumbents.

Despite the fact we have undertaken extensive research over a number of years (as will be seen in Acknowledgements & Bibliography), there are still a few known places that have managed to escape being documented in any shape or form. Local people often say: *"Deal used to have 365 pubs, one for every day of the year"*. The presumption being they were all operating at the same time. While this is probably an exaggeration, after the Beerhouse Act of 1830 any ratepayer was permitted to set up a beerhouse in their own home solely by purchasing an excise licence without the need to appear before magistrates. Unfortunately, no central register of beerhouses has survived. (In 1869, however, the act was changed again to bring beerhouses under the control of the magistrates).

Needless to say, the new act opened up the floodgates and thousands of beerhouses around the country proliferated. A description of what could be termed a beerhouse often differed from house to house and would frequently consist of just the downstairs front room with a simple wooden table and chairs and no bar counter – or even just a cellar – in the humblest of homes. Beerhouses also proved popular business ventures for former members of the armed forces after leaving the services with small pensions – many landlords at the time were ex military men. (Beerhouses were often nicknamed 'Tiddlywinks' or 'Tom & Jerry' houses).

There were also probably very many unlicensed houses in Deal and Walmer illegally selling alcohol. These places were known locally as 'Blind Pigs.'

We have endeavoured to include all licensed premises that were open to the general public and have mainly excluded those places where being a private member or a hotel resident was a requirement. (For example, the Fair Maid of Kent – see entry for **Royal Standard** – in Dover Road, Walmer, did hold a full licence although it has been excluded from this book. Its licence was accompanied by so many restrictions, it did not have an actual bar, there was no alcohol on display and one either had to be a resident or guest to be allowed to consume alcohol there).

Deal, Walmer, Kingsdown and Mongeham public houses

The original idea was to concentrate our research solely on the public houses of Deal and Walmer purely because there were so many of them, without any overspill into the surrounding hamlets or villages. However it was decided during production to include the pubs in Kingsdown and Mongeham. It is for this reason that they appear in a separate section of their own. We apologise to the innkeepers and residents of Sholden, Ringwould and other surrounding villages that owing to time constraints, their pubs have not been included. We hope to include them either in a reprint or in a separate publication – so watch this space!

Extremely brief history of the local area

The history of Deal and Walmer (not to mention Kingsdown and Mongeham) is already a fairly well documented one and it is therefore not our intention to delve into the same here at any length since many authoritative local history books are already available on the subject. For the first time visitor who has picked up this book and who has no prior knowledge of the area, a few paragraphs may assist.

According to the memorial stone on the beach at Walmer which marks the approximate spot, the Romans first set foot in England in 55BC and landed on a beach (now located somewhere inland) nearby.

Fast forwarding to the 1500s, after the Dissolution of the Monasteries, King Henry VIII built Deal, Walmer and Sandown Castles (the latter now a ruin) to protect the coastline from possible attacks by the French and the Spanish. It was not until after this time that Deal, as we now know it, gradually started to develop close to the beach. Until then, the old town had been situated further inland in the vicinity of the present day St Leonard's Church in what is now referred to as Upper Deal.

Deal became an important port (despite having no natural harbour) because of its position in the English Channel and the fact the waters of the Downs (the area of sea between the beach and the treacherous Goodwin Sands) provided sheltered anchorage for sailing ships in rough weather, sometimes up to 500 or more at a time. It was also to Deal's advantage that the larger port of nearby Sandwich had silted up by the 14th century and was therefore unusable by large craft. As more of the original Cinque Ports (of which Sandwich was one) gradually silted up, Deal rose to prominence and became a 'limb' of Sandwich and, in 1699, it was granted its own Royal Charter. Deal prospered and grew by providing for the needs of the ships and sailors, on and off shore – pilots, food and provisions, ship repairs, drinking establishments, boarding houses, public houses, music halls and brothels – and not least its own Naval yard. The arrival of steam tolled the death knell for Deal's seafaring economy.

Also, because of Deal's close proximity to the Continent, a lucrative smuggling trade built up throughout the 1600s and into the first half of the 1800s. It is said most people living in the area at the time, both rich and poor, had connections with it in some form, either by receiving, supplying or buying smuggled goods. It was dubbed: *"a sad, smuggling town"* in the 18th century and further: *"There are said to be in the town of Deal, not less than two hundred young men and seafaring people, who are known to have no visible way of getting a living, but by the infamous trade of smuggling … This smuggling has converted those employed in it, first from honest industrious fishermen, to lazy, drunken and profligate smugglers."*

Several inns were notorious safe houses for smugglers and their contraband, not least the *Jolly Sailor* and the *Noahs Ark* in Deal. By its very nature much smuggling activity remained secret and it is believed many local pubs were involved in the trade but were more discreet in their dealings and remained undetected from the authorities (and also the authors). Many of Deal's old buildings, especially those in Beach Street and Middle Street and the roads and alleyways leading off from them, still bear witness to those old smuggling days. In recent times, secret compartments, drops below floorboards, passageways, tunnels and roof runs have been discovered during renovation works. If householders were found guilty of involvement in the smuggling trade, one of the punishments often included the filling in of their cellars with shingle from the beach. By the mid 1800s, however, smuggling had largely died out.

By the Napoleonic Wars, military barracks had become well established in Deal and Walmer. The Royal Marines were a big presence in town from the 1800s and were installed in three local barracks, namely North, East and South (also called Cavalry). September 1989 saw the tragic deaths of 11 marines by an IRA bomb in the Royal Marines School of Music. In 1996, the last of the Royal Marines' units – the Musicians – moved to Portsmouth after 200 years in the town, the Commandos having left some years earlier. All three barracks have now been converted into private housing. This general area of Lower Walmer was known for a while as Bluetown because of the military presence from around 1798 to 1815.

William Cobbett wrote of his travels in 1823: *"Deal is a most villainous place. It is full of filthy looking people. Great desolation of abomination has been going on here; tremendous barracks, partly pulled down and partly tumbling down, and partly occupied by soldiers. Every thing seems upon the perish. I was glad to hurry along through it, and leave its inns and public houses to be occupied by the tarred, and trowsered, and blue-and-buff crew whose very vicinage I always detest."*

Deal and Kingsdown were also renowned for their fishing industries. Until the beginning of WWII, processing and canning factories were still in operation in Deal, mostly sited at the north end of the town. Although these factories have since been either converted into private housing or demolished altogether, northenders are sometimes still affectionately referred to as 'sprat wafflers'! Deal also boasted its own fish market which was in the vicinity of the present day Market Street. It was reported in 1710 that a cage was to be erected over the town stocks that were sited in the market place but, in 1811, the decision was taken to dismantle the cage and stocks since they were considered: *"greatly incommodious to the fish market."*

There were also very many breweries situated in Deal, Walmer and Mongeham over the years, including Oakley's, Iggulden's, Thompson's, and Hill's, to name but a few.

After coal was discovered in east Kent around 1890, various mines were opened up in the early 20th century, including Betteshanger, Tilmanstone, Chislet and Snowdown collieries. As local people had no previous experience of coal mining, many workers were drafted in from Wales, Scotland and the north of England at a time when the industry was booming there. High wages were offered as an incentive for the men and their families to uproot themselves from their home towns and to settle in Kent.

After the General Strike of 1926 and the years of depression that followed, many more miners came to East Kent looking for work and some were so poor they would walk hundreds of miles as they were could not afford the train fare. Some included militants who had been blacklisted at their former collieries during the General Strike and they would often sign on using false names. Many of the men, especially those working at Betteshanger, settled in Deal with their families and a thriving mining community built up around the Mill Hill area where all the different accents and dialects were thrown into the melting pot! Many former miners and their descendants live in the area to this day, even though the last of the east Kent mines (Betteshanger) closed down in 1989. Some of the men later helped to excavate the Channel Tunnel.

Nowadays, local jobs are mainly connected to the agricultural, catering, leisure or tourism industries but the biggest employers in the area are Pfizer UK, the pharmaceutical company in Sandwich, and Dover harbour. In December 2009 the high speed train service from Dover to London St Pancras commenced and it is hoped will make commuting further afield easier, bringing more wealth and tourism to the locality.

What's in a name?

Nowadays we tend to describe most drinking establishments collectively as being pubs or public houses (unless they are obviously hotels, private clubs or merely bars) but until Victorian times this was not the case. Although public houses were so called before this period, other names for them included alehouses, beerhouses and inns (names dating back to medieval times), not to mention taverns (which had ancient Roman origins). Each had their own specific identities.

For example, an alehouse originally only sold ale (fermented malted barley) and later, a beerhouse (also known as a beer shop or beer cellar) initially only sold beer (fermented malted barley and hops), both of which would sometimes also provide basic food and accommodation. Because the Government at the time was concerned at the nation's fondness for strong gin and its subsequent effects, the 1830 Beer Act was passed. This enabled any ratepayer to sell beer for a fee of two guineas a year as duty on beer had been abolished – although the duty on malt and hops remained. See also Introduction above.

Taverns could be found in larger towns that catered for the wealthy customer. They generally did not offer accommodation but expensive imported wines and elaborate meals would be available.

Inns were mostly sited on important highways and in towns where they provided refreshment and accommodation for travellers, together with stabling for their horses. Many offered a variety of rooms and parlours where business could be conducted or dining carried out privately. Because of this, they were often used to hold court sessions, inquests, concerts, theatrical performances while rooms were also hired to private clubs and societies for dinners, balls, concerts and lectures. A hostelry was just another name for a hotel or an inn with lodgings.

Throughout this book, where we have been unable to establish the type of long gone drinking establishment, we have usually used the generic term of pub or public house.

Within a public house, other internal divisions existed in the days when there were separate public rooms. There would be the comfortable saloon bars for the professional lower middle class customers and the basic, uncarpeted public bars for the working classes such as artisans and manual workers (where the prices would be cheaper), sometimes complete with spittoons on the floors. There might also be a tap room. This description latterly evolved into just another name for a public bar, although its origin appears to date from the 18th century, suggesting a separate room where liquor was drawn off. It would often be located away from the main serving area and sometimes be housed in a separate building altogether. A 'snug' bar was another drinking room and, as the name suggests, was very small in size, perhaps housing just one table, and ideal for private drinking.

A 'parlour' was usually the name of the sole public room in a simple beer or alehouse in someone's home, so it would literally be their front parlour. There might also be an in-house 'off licence' (sometimes called a 'jug and bottle') where alcohol to be consumed off the premises could be bought at lower prices. These facilities are now almost entirely extinct, their use fading away in the 1980s when off licence shops, completely unattached to any pubs and, of course, supermarkets, took over their trade.

Same pub, different names

All the pubs are listed alphabetically, and we have done away with prefixing the definite article before the names in the headings for this reason (and also because some of them were known without it anyway). Where the same pubs have traded under different names, we have entitled them by generally using their last known – or, occasionally, their most famous (or infamous!) – names, and have listed their other appellations beneath the titles.

Who's in charge?

It should be pointed out that we have taken a lot of our information concerning the names of licensees, especially from 1975 onwards, from the records held by Dover magistrates' licensing office. Until that year, many of these facts were otherwise gleaned from local newspapers and directories but after this date a change of landlord at a pub was no longer considered worthy of publication. Unfortunately, the records held by Dover magistrates only include a person's name – and not their role – beside each pub. On several occasions, therefore, where we have included lists of landlords during the past 35 years especially, some of the people named may, in fact, have only been licensees (the secretary of a brewery company, for example) or even managers, and not actual landlords, since we unfortunately have no way of knowing their distinct roles in connection with the pubs documented in those records.

Street renumbering

The three main streets of Deal, Beach Street, Middle Street and Lower Street – now High Street – along with others in Deal and Walmer, were renumbered during the 1890s to take account of building demolitions and erections that had taken place since the streets were originally numbered. As time passed, some buildings and streets were renumbered more than once. We have stated the current addresses of the building or site under the names of each pub and have added their previous addresses in brackets afterwards whenever possible. It is usually for this reason these other numbers appear and not because the pubs moved into different buildings in the same street, although, where this *is* the case, we have said so.

A large section of Middle Street, its tributary roads and alleyways were heavily bombed in WWII and subsequently demolished but, street renumbering did not take place. The Middle Street car park was created on the site and the old numbers remain unused to this day, which is why for example, there are no longer properties numbered 17 to 53 Middle Street.

Refusing to billet Dragoons

Occasionally, publicans' refusal to billet the military was simply a case of their not having the necessary accommodation or stabling required. Paul Jennings states in his book, 'The Local – A History of the English Pub', that:*"Billeting soldiers was a legal obligation, and although their keep was subsidised, its cost was very much resented by otherwise patriotic publicans"*. He adds that in 1741, it was: *"costing innkeepers £20 a week in hay alone, and nearly as much again for meat and drink"*. In 1759, several *"publicans … petitioned the government for troops not to be billeted* [at their pubs] *during the fair, as it took up much needed accommodation"*. A customer found it: *"'a plague to be at an inn with troops'. Public houses were also used for recruiting, either by volunteers or through impressment … Publicans disliked press gangs… They were supposed to inform landlords of their intention to search and, if requested, show a warrant. Proprieties, however, were not always observed. In 1744, a … publican was assaulted and coughed blood for days after remonstrating with a zealous lieutenant on the hunt for deserters. Others collaborated … acting as 'crimps', as the entrappers were called, through their use of credit for customers."*

Barrister, George Rowe of the Inner Temple in London, recorded the following on 18 November 1776: *"In the town and Borough of Deal are 30 Publick Houses including taverns and Inns, 18 whereof have stabling fit for the accommodation of Dragoons and horses and the other 12 have no stabling at all. These Dragoons (12 or 13 in all) were to assist the Officers of the Revenue at Deal. The following houses refused to billet the Dragoons for lack of suitable accommodation"*. (He then went on to list various local hostelries).
The Dragoons were not always well liked in Deal since, in 1781, they had raided the town searching for contraband and, acting under the orders of William Pitt the Younger in 1784, they set fire to all the boats pulled up on the beach to stamp out smuggling. It only temporarily stopped activities and merely helped the smugglers' cause since many law abiding residents turned on the Government, outraged that ordinary fishermen were no longer able to make a living or provide for their families.

Pubs on the beach

It should be mentioned that in between Deal Pier and the North End (ie Capstan Row), many fishermen's houses, pubs and boarding houses were built on what would then have been part of the beach (also known as the 'capstan ground' or the 'archbishop's waste'). The buildings were constructed of wood or brick and over the years, they gradually became more and more ramshackle owing to numerous high tides and gales. They were compulsorily purchased and eventually demolished for road widening and to make way for the wide concrete promenade and sea wall we see today.

In October 1869, it was reported that, out of the 79 buildings that once stood on the beach, only 42 remained. Buildings had started to be pulled down as early as the 1830s and this had been a gradual process until the final one was demolished in the 1950s, leaving only the **Royal Hotel** – formerly known as the **Three Kings** – still remaining.

Descriptions of pubs

Wherever possible we have attempted to describe the interiors (and sometimes their furnishings and contents) of closed down pubs to bring them temporarily back to life for the reader. Since this is not a 'good pub guide', we have not usually described at length the interiors of pubs which remain open or their current facilities but would respectfully suggest that a tipple or two in these places may enlighten the modern visitor.

The future of the pub

It is anyone's guess whether the pub as we know it can survive, not least since the introduction of the smoking ban and the competitively low prices charged for alcohol by supermarkets. It was originally envisaged by the Government (but not, perhaps, by landlords) that the smoking ban would encourage non pub goers into the pubs but now, unless a pub also has a restaurant, it appears the opposite is true. It seems a person is either a pub goer or they are not, irrespective of whether they smoke. Many smokers have stayed away from pubs altogether since, especially during the winter months, when they may be reluctant to smoke outside.

Since the ban and the recession which hit soon after, hundreds of pubs countrywide have closed and continue to do so at an alarming rate, although it is probably not for us to pontificate about all the whys and wherefores or to offer solutions. There is absolutely nothing like the traditional pub outside of Britain (and parts of Ireland) – no American bars or European cafés can compete. Whether or not you are a pub person yourself, it cannot be denied that pubs have formed a major part of the social fabric and traditions of this country over the past several hundred years. They can be a lifeline and the heart of communities for isolated villages especially, irrespective of whether or not alcohol is consumed within their walls, and not least when villagers may have already lost their corner shops, post offices and bus services.

Please do find the time to visit your local pubs (as well as the pubs mentioned in this book which remain open if they are not already your locals) to keep them, their histories and traditions alive since it will be a very sad day if and when they all closed forever.

We very much hope you enjoy reading this book (with or without a drink in hand!) and we will simply leave the last word to Hilaire Belloc who famously said: *"When you have lost your inns, drown your empty selves for you will have lost the last of England."*

Steve Glover and Michael Rogers
Deal – July 2010

Academy Sports Bar (Albys, Velvet Underground, Tube, MDs, Laughing Toad), 32-36 Queen Street, Deal

Mid 1930s.

The original buildings on or close to the site of the *Academy Sports Bar* included military barracks in the late 1700s, as well as the grounds of the old Admiralty House which was, until 1815, the home of the Admiral of Deal but demolished in the mid 1930s.

The present day *Academy Sports Bar* also includes Rivals, the nightclub, next door. (Up until 1985, the whole site consisted of, initially, the Odeon and then the Classic cinema. In 1986, the now defunct Flicks cinema took over the front part of the building).

A members only licensed club called the *Laughing Toad* operated there in 1989. It was later variously called *MDs, Velvet Underground, Tube* and *Albys*.

After a major refurbishment and the separation of the remaining site, it reopened in June 2003 as the *Academy Sports Bar* in one part (and Rivals nightclub taking over the other part). Its owners were Bill Flavell and John Stevens of FS Leisure.

The bar remains open to the present day.

Admiral Keppel (possibly also Farriers Arms) 90 Manor Road (Upper Deal Road), Upper Deal

Admiral Augustus Keppel, 1st Viscount Keppel PC (25 April 1725 – 2 October 1786), was an Officer of the Royal Navy during the Seven Years' War and the War of American Independence. (The Duchess of Cornwall, the former Camilla Parker Bowles, née Shand, is a direct descendant).

Upper Deal used to be the most important part of town at a time when the main area of present day Lower Deal remained largely undeveloped. The pub originally stood in its own 2½ acre orchard which in turn was surrounded by rich agricultural land.

The early history of the *Admiral Keppel* is veiled in obscurity but its origins are known to go back to at least the seventeenth century if not earlier. Parts of St Leonard's church opposite the pub are 850 years old, so perhaps the old maxim applies that

"When God builds His house, the devil builds one next door." According to a 'ghost hunt' held at the pub in 2006, several spirits walk the house at night. Local folklore has it that a tunnel used to lead from the cellar to the church, and the late local historian, David Collyer, mentioned in a Mercury article dated 15 February 2001 that another tunnel led from the pub into the cellars of an old cottage nearby.

The Sandwich Licensing Register showed the Goodson family running the pub from 1725 to 1804 and, prior to this time, St Leonard's baptismal records indicated that Steven Goodson and Hannah Ffasham (the Ffashams were a local brewing family) had a son, John Goodson, in 1678, who was also a landlord there in the 1730s.

The story goes that the pub was named following a visit from

c2000.

Admiral Keppel himself in 1778 (but what the pub was previously called is unknown although there is a slight possibility that it was the **Farriers Arms** – see separate entry - although no documentary evidence can be found to substantiate this). Admiral Keppel supposedly came ashore while his ship was anchored in the Downs and walked along Church Path to drown his sorrows at the pub, after being blamed for the escape of the French fleet at Ushant, an island off the coast of Brittany. He fell into conversation there with a gathering of retired Royal Naval officers who were sympathetic towards his situation. On the day news reached the pub that he had been given an honourable acquittal at his subsequent court martial, the landlord immediately changed its name to the **Admiral Keppel** and announced that the drinks were on the house! However, there is no evidence to suggest that Keppel ever revisited the pub that had been named in his honour.

c2006.

The Kentish Gazette reported in February 1779: "*Last night an elegant ball was given to the ladies and gentlemen of this town, by Admiral Drake and the captains of the navy, at Sandown Castle in honour of that truly patriotic Englishman Admiral Keppel, the whole was conducted with greatest regularity, every naval Briton there striving to out-vie each other in civility and pleasing occasion; a genteel collation was provided, after which the whole company drank the health of the noble Keppel; the gentlemen wore blue cockades in their hats...*" (Keppel was Admiral of the Blue).

Thomas Goodson was landlord in 1804, James Hall Powell in 1824, James Hammond in 1832, James Sutton in 1834, James Farrer in 1840, Stephen Reader White in 1848 and James Marsh in 1850. In 1864, Susannah Verrier Marsh took over the licence on her husband, James' death. During her time at the pub, she was granted a special licence to sell alcohol to farm labourers from as early as 5am during harvest time.

A Borough Police Court report from September 1865 stated: "*An old offender Maria Tringlove, a*

*miserable looking woman, was charged with being drunk and disorderly, creating a disturbance and smashing windows at the **Admiral Keppel**. So drunk that she could not walk she was taken to the police station in a wheelbarrow. She was sentenced to seven days in Sandwich Gaol.*"

In 1883, celebrations for the election of the Mayor of Deal were held at the **Admiral Keppel**: "*A numerous and merry party enjoyed a pleasant evening of good cheer with many a song and joke until the old church tower rang a warning that it was time to desist.*"

In 1903, Susannah Marsh's daughter, Mrs Emily May, a widow, was installed after her mother's departure that year. On 3 May 1916, a bomb from an enemy plane crashed through the roof of the **Admiral Keppel,** passing a first floor bedroom and landing in the bar on the ground floor. Although Mrs May and her daughter were present at the time, they were fortunately uninjured since the bomb itself had missed them and had miraculously failed to explode. The pub had been in the care of the Marsh family for almost 70 years by the time Mrs May left in January 1919.

1922 records showed AE Child as landlord, and he was succeeded by David Allen who remained at the pub until at least 1939. Mr J Pritchard arrived in 1947, having previously been landlord of the **Jolly Gardener**. Later landlords and licensees included N P Rooff from 1955 to at least 1966, Alex C Watkins in 1970, Arthur North in 1982, Sandra Crossland in 1992, C & J Forster in 1994, A McFadyen and Pamela White in 1997, John and Iris Butler in 1999, Matt and Sally Golding also in 1999, Patrick O'Connell and Terence Attle in 2001, Clair Hobson also in 2001, David Dadd (a former Deal Town FC manager), Emma Roberts and Brian Roberts in 2002 and Stewart Walters and Louise Dowle in 2003.

The present incumbents are Mr and Mrs Shakey who held a Grand reopening Day soon after taking over on 6 July 2008.

The pub remains open for business.

Admiral Owen (exact location unknown)
The Strand (Walmer Road), Walmer

Admiral Sir Edward Campbell Rich Owen (1771-1849) had a large house with land, roughly sited where the present day Deal Fire Station now stands. A letter from Deal by him addressed to Admiral Lord Keith dated 14 July 1818 discussed the navigation of Calais harbour and the advantages of developing a steam yacht, particularly for the benefit of the Prince Regent on the short journey from Deal to Calais.

The *Admiral Owen* pub was apparently situated somewhere in The Strand (formerly known as Walmer Road) in Walmer, according to a previous researcher's notes, but the authors have unfortunately been unable to find any other evidence at all to substantiate this.

Admiral Penn
(Rose & Crown Inn) 79 (122) Beach Street, Deal

The first mention of this property was in 1808 when it was described as being a *"dwellinghouse and shop"* (with no mention of the premises being either licensed or unlicensed), with Jonathan Read, *"Tailor and Draper"*, in residence, staying until at least 1839.

The property was leased in 1847 by Valentine Hoile, a brewer from Sandwich, even though the 1851 census still showed no indication that the house had yet become a pub. However, on 31 January 1854, James Munday Redman was named as *"Licensee and General Dealer"* of premises still described as a *"dwellinghouse and shop"* even though it appears that later that year the building was sub-divided, probably in readiness for the forthcoming pub to be used as a separate entity. The following year, Redman was listed as a *"Shopkeeper and Beerhouse Keeper"* and the building finally became registered in Melville's Directory in 1858 as a *"Beer Shop."* When Redman obtained a full licence and Valentine Hoile assigned the lease to him and his wife, Mary Elizabeth Redman, for £135 in 1860, he was described as being an *"Alehouse Keeper."* In May 1862, Redman secured the freehold of the property from its owners, the Archbishop of Canterbury and the Church Estates Commissioners, for the sum of £65. The legal document stated that the building *"is now used as a public house."*

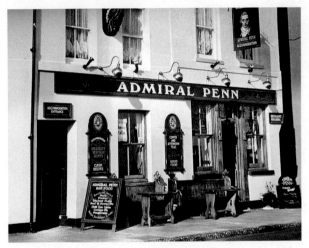

c2000.

By 1874, James Redman's son, Charles Redman, held the licence. In February 1883, a clipping from a local newspaper, headed *"Supper at the 'Rose & Crown' Inn"*, reported that: *"On Wednesday evening last, David Bell, Esq, invited a number of his friends to a supper at the Rose & Crown, Beach-street. The repast, a substantial one, was provided by Mr Charles Redman, and gave universal satisfaction. After supper, Mr Murry Larkins amused the company by playing several variations on the violin."*

In July of that year, an advertisement appeared, stating: *"For Sale. The well-built 4-oared Service Galley, 'Undaunted', with all her gear, fit for sea. Apply at the 'Rose & Crown' Inn, Beach-street, Deal."*

In 1887, James Munday Redman sold the freehold to Flint & Co, brewers of Canterbury, for £700, and Frederick Roberts was installed as landlord. He was soon in trouble, however, since a local newspaper report dated 28 January 1888 and headed *"Infringement of the Licensing Act"* stated: *"At the Borough Petty Sessions on Thursday, Frederick Roberts, of the 'Rose & Crown', Beach-street, was charged with serving during prohibited hours on Sunday, 22 January, and Robert Osborn, Henry Bayly and William Dadd were charged with being on the premises. PC Mercer proved the case, and fines, including costs, were inflicted, Roberts having to pay 20 shillings (£1) and the rest 7/6d (37½p) each."* Nevertheless, he remained at the pub until his death in 1910 when his son, Frederick Henry Alick Roberts (nicknamed 'Flint' Roberts), took over. 'Flint' was a reference to the brewery controlling the pub. (His father had also been known as 'Flint' but his son became the famous 'Flint' Roberts since he was to become Deal's longest-serving publican of his time). The pub was therefore sometimes informally referred to as 'Flint's' (as well as the 'Dark House' at some point during its history). By 1930, Fremlin's brewery owned the freehold and locals apparently still called the pub 'Flint's' up until the 1950s, which must have irked Fremlins somewhat!

Flint junior had apparently been born at the **Rose & Crown**, taking over the landlordship at the age of 21. He was a keen competitor in the annual Deal Regattas and Deal Rowing Club races, as well as being the undefeated sculling champion of Deal for over 20 years.

According to a 1957 Mercury article, Flint Roberts had recently advertised his motor boat, the Golden Spray, for sale since the crew who ran it for him had to seek their livelihoods elsewhere. The boat had previously been used on many rescue missions off the Deal coast, including the time it picked up survivors of the French cargo boat, the Dinard,

c2007.

after it had been accidentally rammed in a storm by a British ship on 9 December 1939. Once safely ashore, rescued mariners would be taken into the bar of the **Rose & Crown** where Flint would prescribe his own brand of alcoholic medicine, at the same time as being treated for their external wounds by attendant doctors and nurses!

Flint Roberts, together with his wife, Jenny, retired in the latter part of 1957 and he died on 14 February 1963, aged 74.

In the meantime, Harry Bruce had become landlord in September 1961. In July 1970, the Mercury reported that the **Rose & Crown** had walked away with all the trophies in the LVA Bar Billiards Championships that year.

Brian Speed was listed as landlord in June 1977, by which time the pub was owned by the Whitbread Fremlin's brewery. On 1 July 1982, the pub changed

its name to the **Admiral Penn**. Admiral Penn (1644-1718) was a Quaker who set sail from Deal for North America, and was the founder and first governor of Pennsylvania.

Brian Pickard took over as landlord in October 1988 and, on 10 November that year, the Mercury reported that: *"Actor Peter Howitt, Joey in BBC's Bread, will be in Deal next Monday to perform the opening of the **Admiral Penn** for new landlords, Brian and Donna Pickard, at 11.30am."*

In September 1990, Anthony Smith was installed as landlord, followed by Arthur and Christine Fay in August 1993 and Leslie and Janet Smith in January 1994. Mr and Mrs Smith were documented as saying at the time that there had been a pub on the site of the **Admiral Penn** since 1818 although unfortunately they did not reveal the source of this knowledge. While there may well have been a beerhouse of sorts there, as will be seen above, the authors have been unable to find any documentary evidence to support this claim.

Linda and Adrianus ('Artie') Ouwersloot owned and ran (with the assistance of their daughter, Natalie) the **Admiral Penn** as a free house from January 1998. By the time they had taken over, the separate bars that had previously divided the pub were no longer, and the interior had become open plan, with a bar along the left hand side. However, the pub's seafaring history had not been lost and the interior retained many original period features. The quirky décor included many nautical objects suspended from the ceiling, old beer barrels covered in carpets doubling as tables, and very dim lighting was created by suspended lampshades covered with brightly covered kerchiefs. Together with good background music, Linda and Artie created a wonderfully unique and cosy atmosphere that helped to make the **Admiral Penn** an extremely popular pub with customers of all ages.

The pub had two entrances, one in the front on Beach Street and the other around the side in Market Street. The Beach Street entrance was often locked during bad weather coming in off the sea and a sign used to hang in the window advising *"Hippies to use the side entrance."*

Sadly, the pub shut down in January 2005 and a party thrown for its regulars on its last night was captured on film. Shortly afterwards, the building was divided into two separate buildings (now individually known as nos 77 and 79 Beach Street) and the film was apparently hidden somewhere inside during renovation works, as a lasting time capsule for any future generations who may unearth it!

The pub's nautical figurehead remains on the front wall of no 77 Beach Street. The downstairs of the right hand building on the corner became a gift shop for a short while (also ran by the Ouwersloots) but, after closure, the whole of that building was also converted into a private house and the Ouwersloots moved out.

The old pub building now comprises two separate private houses.

Admiral Rodney
(40) Beach Street, Deal

The pub's location was described in 1804 as being set on the eastern side of Beach Street (actually on the beach), and *"eleven houses south of the Crown and three houses north of the Pelican"*, and was named after Admiral Lord George Brydges Rodney (1719-1792). His name became a *"bye-word for hard drinkers who were dubbed 'Utter Rodneys'"*, perhaps because of his fearlessness in battle or maybe instead because of his fondness for the bottle!

Richard Cook was landlord in 1804, and, at the time, the pub had its own landing stage on the beach onto which important passengers *"could disembark from boats without distress and be borne straight to the establishment."*

James Tomlin was landlord in 1821 and was still resident in 1828, by which time the pub had ceased trading. The property was included in the sale of the Manor of Chamberlain's fee, along with a number of other local pubs (including the *Hoop & Griffin*), and it was purchased by Edward Iggulden, a local brewer. The sales' particulars described it as being: *"A messuage lately called the Sign of the Rodney with buildings, ground and appurtenances containing about 2½ perches"* and continued: *"All that messuage or tenement no 40 in Beach Street, lately used as, and known by the name of the Rodney public house with the buildings, ground and appurtenances thereunto belonging and now in the occupation of James Tomlin. These premises are subject to a Lease granted to John Iggulden Esq for 21 years from the 29th September 1814 at the yearly rent of £1 15s 6d (£1.77½) and to a Covenant therein contained for renewal thereof for a like term of 21 years at the end of 18 years of the existing term upon payment of a fine of £17 17s (£1.85)."* It was later sold to Deal Pavement Commission in 1836 for £300.

The property was one of many buildings demolished on the beach in the mid 1830s and its site on the present day promenade lies somewhere between Oak and Brewer Streets.

Report from the Kentish Post – February 5th 1725

"We hear from Deal that Wednesday last . . . a certain merry seafaring person tumbled into a well – he is supposed to be an enemy to the ladies drinking tea ... he being in liquor, let down his breeches with an intent, it is thought, to befoul the well, but fell into it about 20 feet deep and remained three hours in a deplorable condition . . ."

Albion (Globe)
167 (166) Beach Street, Deal

The *Albion* was named after two local luggers of the same name. 'Albion' is also the ancient and literary name for Britain, although it usually refers just to England. It probably derives from the Latin 'Albus' meaning 'white' from the white cliffs which form such a feature of the south eastern coastline and which would, of course, have been the first landing stage of the initial invading Roman army.

On 26 November 1694, Sussana Wood took a lease of and occupied the property/land. (On the same day, she also leased the whole or part of another property, which is now known as the *Ship* public house in Middle Street). There is no definite evidence of the property in Beach Street ever being used as licensed premises until 1845 when it was recorded in the Post Office Directory of that year, showing Philip John Finnis in residence and listing his occupation as landlord of an unnamed pub. Finnis was still there in 1851 and his profession was given as '*Sail-maker*' as he also had a sail loft in Farrier Street. In Melville's Street

c1922.

Directory of 1858, he was residing at what had by then become known as the *Albion* Beer Shop.

(The *Deal Cutter* pub was next door (north), with Mary Finnis as landlady – see separate entry).

In 1861, the census noted the property as being called the *Globe* Beerhouse, still with Finnis as landlord but, in 1862, the name had changed to the *Albion* Beerhouse. By 1863, the landlord, Edward Galley Grigg, held a full licence, including one for music.

John Roberts was listed as landlord in 1878 and the licence was transferred to Lydia Roberts in 1883. By 1887, William Finnis was landlord and the licence was then transferred back again to Edward Galley Grigg, who served until at least 1898. By 1904, Philip George Grigg was mine host and he was still there at the outbreak of WWII in 1939.

Other landlords included J Peters in 1948, F Tobin in the early 1950s, HF Paige in 1966 and Mr Sloper who was the very last licensee of the pub when it closed on Derby Day, 2 June 1971. The property is now a private dwelling called Albion House.

Albys

See entry for the *Academy Sports Bar*.

Alcazar

See entry for the *Rink*.

Alhambra, 4 (11) Robert Street, Deal

Alhambra is an Arabic word meaning "Red Castle" or "Gate." It was reported in 1863 that an as yet unnamed music hall had been built, and local magistrates grudgingly granted the house a full licence in 1864. It was listed as the *Alhambra* Music Hall in an 1865 street directory.

George Friend was the landlord in August 1866 when he got into trouble for assaulting 83 year old George Warder who lived in Robert Street. He was

fined 40 shillings (£2) or one month's imprisonment. Magistrates warned him to be careful of his future conduct since his licence would not be renewed, the same having been reluctantly granted two years previously.

In 1870, Friend was listed as a "*Publican/Carpenter*."

The *Alhambra* closed in 1877. The property is now a private house called Cherry Tree Cottage.

Alma (Tavern)
126 West Street (8 Portland Terrace), Deal

The pub's name commemorates the Battle of Alma of the Crimean War in 1854. This pub opened on 13 September 1855 when Henry Shipley was landlord. An advert in 1858 stated: *"**Alma Tavern**, Portland Terrace, Deal. Visitors to this neighbourhood & Commercial Gentlemen, can enjoy the cleanliest and comforts of home, at very reasonable charges at the above Tavern. Beds equal to the first Hotels, 1s. (5p) per night. Proprietor, Henry Shipley."*

A later advert in 1860 read, *"Shipley's **Alma Tavern** – Ales, Beers, Wines, Tea, Coffee, Chips, Steaks and Other Refreshments Prepared at Short Notice – Good Beds – Open at 6am"*

By 1862, G Hinds was landlord, followed by Charles Cobb in 1865, John Nethersole and FA Chanel (owners/brewers) in 1872, William Kelsey in 1874 and Mrs Harriet Small from 1882 to 1891. The Alma Gun Club used the pub as their HQ in 1888, with a monthly subscription of 1 shilling (5p), advertising, *"To be Skilled in the Use of Firearms means more than Mere Success in Bringing Down a Bird."*

Around 1890, the entertainments hall at the rear was built, measuring 54 feet x 36 feet, capable of holding around 100 people for dining and dancing purposes.

Later landlords included James Smallbones in 1899

c1917.

2009.

and Walter Wingate (described as a *'Lathe Renderer'*) in 1902. His widow, Jessie, took over after his death and was still serving in 1911. She was followed by Stewart Reading in 1912, George Howland in 1913 and, on his death, his widow, Louise, stayed there until around 1929/30 when Frank Charles Smith took over. Frederick J Meadows was landlord in 1936 and Jim and Lil Read in 1939. They stayed at the *Alma* for the next 27 years, retiring from the pub trade in 1966 when J Read took over. He was followed by Alfred James Perry in 1968 (when the pub was a Fremlins outlet) and Ian Birchell in 1977. Sydney Grout was landlord in 1984, Ronald Shaw in 1987, Adrian Pepin and Brian Jones in April 1991, Margaret and Stephen Finnis in October 1991 and Douglas and Audrey Vickers in 1995. Sometime during the 1990s, the hall at the rear was extended.

Andrew and Henry Miller were landlords in 2001, Andrew and Renee Miller in 2002, Gary and Jane May in May 2006 (following a temporary closure due to refurbishment) and Michael Newell in 2008.

The *Alma* continues to be run as a pub with bars, restaurant and hall for music.

Alma (Tavern/Hotel)
25 (19) The Strand (Walmer Road), Walmer

As with the *Alma* pub in Deal, this tavern's name commemorates the Battle of Alma in 1854 fought as part of the Crimean War.

The records of the Leith family (who owned the property) show that the *Alma Tavern* was leased in 1855 to Joseph Ran and then to Stephen Hinds in 1857. George Hinds was recorded as the landlord in 1861 and also in 1870, his occupation being noted as a *"Plumber and Victualler."* Later in 1870, Mary Ann Webb was landlady (having previously been at the *Bricklayers Arms* in 1867) and she remained there until 1882. George Band was landlord in 1891, followed by FE Russell in 1898 and George Dawkins in 1902.

Sometime prior to 1901, the pub also encompassed the building next door to the south (and perhaps afterwards as well since the *Alma* later boasted as many as 14 bedrooms).

In March 1904, a local newspaper reported that landlord, James W Skinner, was assaulted by James

c1904.

Mokon, who was fined £2/8d (£2.40). In December 1905, Mrs S Reeves, landlady of what was now called the *Alma Hotel*, was charged with selling gin *"not of the substance demanded"* and fined 5 shillings (25p), with 8/6d (42½p) costs. In 1906, an application was granted to extend the premises to form a clubhouse for the accommodation of the Walmer Oddfellows' Society.

M Shrubb was mine host in 1911, followed by Matthew Edward Shrubb in 1914 who stayed until 1945 when Herbert Sokell took over, followed by William Orgill in the mid 1950s and PJ Powell MBE in March 1957. The property was sold to Lloyds Bank on 3 December that year but the pub remained open until August 1963 when it was noted at the time that the landlord unceremoniously put down the keys, shut the door behind him and left.

The property became a branch of Lloyds Bank, remaining open until the 1970s, but it is now a private house.

Amsterdam (exact location unknown), Beach Street, Deal

The *Amsterdam* may possibly have been named to commemorate the Battle of the Goodwin Sands that took place between the English and the Dutch in 1652.

Details are sketchy as to when the pub opened for business but, in 1680, goldsmith, John Travis, was in residence, the premises having formerly been leased to Richard Estes in 1662. Later occupants included

a boatbuilder in 1744, a ropemaker in 1756, a tallow chandler and one William Hulke, a surgeon, in 1787 and 1795.

Carpenter, Francis Oldfield, was resident in 1808 and had joint use of a pump with a nearby wash house and privy to the west.

In 1837, the premises, excluding the capstan ground, were sold to the Pavement Committee.

Anchor & Cable (location unknown), 'Deale'

A cable was a mooring rope or chain attached to an anchor. This pub appears on the 'Payments for Signs' lists for Deal in 1662

with its landlord, William Warner, owing three shillings and sixpence (17½p), but its location is unknown.

Anchor & Rose (location unknown) 'Deale'

This pub was mentioned in the 'Lycence' Book for Deal in 1680 but its location is unknown.

Anchor (Blue Anchor and Blew Anker)
46/48 West Street, Deal

This building was situated on what was once an 'anchor field', ie a field where salvaged anchors were stored. The road still exists (Anchor Lane) that once ran down the north side of the pub.

There is a 1714 reference to *"snode at Blew Anker"* although its meaning or significance has been lost in the mists of time! In 1804, the pub was situated *"at back of chapel"* with the *"Widow Carden"* listed as landlady.

By 1821, AT Curling was licensee and Thomas Curling (possibly one and the same person) was listed in 1826 and 1832 respectively. Blacksmith, Simon Marsh, was resident from 1839 until 1864 when Thomas Langley, an auctioneer, took over the licence. It was in 1864 that novelist, William Makepeace Thackeray, died. He was writing a story at the time, called *Denis Duval*, about smugglers on the Kent and Sussex coasts, which unfortunately he did not complete. The main character was staying at the *Blue Anchor* in Deal where he met with his mother to be fitted out in a naval uniform. The fictional landlord is referred to as *'Mr Boniface'* who invites Duval to *"step into the bar and take a glass of wine"* before setting off to sea.

In 1865, William Goodchild was landlord, followed by Richard Garrett, who gave his occupation as shoemaker, in 1872.

Later landlords included Henry Miles in 1882, Joshua Gammon and DJ Curling in 1894 and Edward Friday Hall in 1905. Plans submitted for the possible rebuilding of the pub that year showed the premises to be set back in line with the next door coachbuilders. However, Friday Hall died before the procedure was put into action when he became an early casualty of a road traffic accident. A newspaper article reported in July 1905: *"Edward John Friday Hall killed in a motor accident at Strood Hill.*

c1920.

The solid rubber tyre came off the rear wheel throwing 3 men from the car. He was dead on arrival at St Bartholomew's, Rochester. He leaves a widow and 4 children." His widow, Emily, subsequently took over the licence.

A 1909 Licensing Magistrates' report stated: *"the premises old and obsolete ... having to go down 3 steps to get in ... they are ill adapted"*, adding that there were another five pubs nearby. It goes on to describe the pub as having a long bar, a fairly large tap room with adjoining small *"snuggery"*, stables accessed through a door at the rear and a bedroom at street level. It further commented that the *Anchor* was over 300 years old and had previously stood at street level until the road outside was raised.

In 1913, another Licensing report stated that there were seven public houses within 253 yards of the *Anchor*, and that its annual rent was £14 and rateable value £14/5s (£14.25). The property was considered to be *"old-fashioned with steps down from street into the bar"* and was under threat of closure. However, Mrs Hall was granted a new licence after throwing herself at the mercy of the magistrates, stating that she and her *"3 children"* were dependent upon the pub for a living, even though she subsequently transferred it the following year to Percy Baston.

By 1915, the pub was owned by Thompson's brewery and its rent was £25 per annum and rateable value £14/10s (£14.50). It was described as having stabling for nine horses and a large garden where teas were served in the summer. The pub's customers were principally labourers and porters, it was noted at the time, although trade had been somewhat reduced because many of its clientele were away in the Army.

There was also something called a *"Nick Club"* attached

c1920.

to the house which consisted of 20 members.

As can be seen by all of these reports, the *Anchor* had been under threat of closure for many years. The pub closed in 1915 and the building was demolished some years later.

Adamson's garage now stands on the site, and the former Deal station goods yard – now Sainsbury's car park – was built on the 'anchor field'.

Angel (location unknown) 'Deale'

This pub was mentioned in the 1680 'Lycence' Book for Deal but otherwise remains untraceable.

Angel & Trumpett (location unknown) 'Deale'

This pub appeared on the 1677 'Payment for Signs' list for Deal in name only but its location is unknown.

Antwerp

See entry for the *Bohemian*.

Army & Navy
68 (65, 66 and 64) The Strand, Walmer

The *Army & Navy* was a beerhouse, variously numbered 65, 66 and 64 The Strand, on the corner of Cheriton Road.

The Walmer Poor Rate book of 1857 stated that Thomas Richard Baker was in residence. In 1858, according to the County Magistrates' Office, Charles Brown, a fish salesman, was charged with assaulting landlord, Richard Baker, and with using threatening language. In court, Brown accused Baker of being drunk *"morning, noon and night"* and was consequently half mad, adding that he had a reputation for taking out warrants against respectable people! Brown, however, was fined nine shillings (45p) costs and bound over for six months.

The following year, landlord, *Thomas* Baker, unlawfully opened the pub until midnight. He pleaded that he had got married on the day in question and had invited guests to celebrate at the pub with him afterwards. The case was adjourned.

2009.

By 1862, David Axon was landlord and he was still serving in 1881, followed by Edward Sutton in 1889 and Morris Wellard in 1898. Landlord, Benjamin Horner, was listed as a Beer Retailer and Umbrella Maker in 1899 and continued trading until 1908 when the premises were delicensed. (Horner had previously owned a fried fish shop and umbrella 'hospital' business in Deal High Street in the early 1890s before moving to Walmer).

The *Army & Navy* premises were described in March 1907 as comprising a *"small beerhouse, some parts old, with some additions. Although near the Barracks, it is not used by the Royal Marines. Both landlord and wife have other trades. The property has a sign 'Umbrella Hospital' outside. Too many public houses in the area. Description of property: the general room in the Army & Navy is fairly spacious. It is weather-boarded outside and not a substantial* building. A small house, probably originally a cottage with some additions. The tap room is an addition. Licence to be expunged. Provisional licence to be provided."

Mrs Horner was still running the Umbrella Hospital on the premises in 1929.

The property, now numbered 68 The Strand, houses Bank House estate agency. An enquiring eye can still spot the original pub doorway blocked up in the middle of the front of the building.

Arrow (Harrow)
(location unknown) 'Deale'

The only mention of this pub appeared in the Sandwich Licences Recognizances register on several occasions during the mid 1700s but no location was indicated.

It was variously referred to as the *Arrow* and, at other times, the *Harrow*. As these names were shown together on the register, we have assumed that the *Arrow*'s name had been misheard when verbally communicated. For the purposes of this book, therefore, we have supposed the correct name to be the *Arrow* and that the *Harrow* pub was one and the same establishment as opposed to being a separate entity altogether.

The register recorded George Smith as landlord of the *Arrow* in July 1759 and landlord of the *Harrow* in September 1759. Again, in January 1760, he was down as landlord of the *Arrow* in the January and then of the *Harrow* in April.

The last mention of the pub was in November 1762 when John Stokes was listed as landlord of the *Harrow*.

Local newspaper report dated 24th June 1865 headed:

"Death of a Private in the Royal Marines. About a fortnight since, a picquet of four men under the orders of an MCO, proceeded to a house in Duke-street, to apprehend a Marine who was there drunk. It appears that the man in question, after being got from the house, resisted a good deal, and a pair of handcuffs were procured from the police station.

"He was then laid hold of by the arms and legs by the four men and carried through the principal streets in the town, with his face downwards, a proceeding which he resisted violently, and begged to be allowed to walk, a request which was not complied with, and he was so conveyed to the Marine Barracks.

"As far as we have been able to learn the man received a severe shock to his system from the rough manner in which he had been handled, and it was found necessary to put him under the care of the surgeon, and he died on Monday or Tuesday last. The man was tiresome, as drunken men usually are, but nothing could have justified the brutal handling he received from the hands of his comrades, which was witnessed with disgust by many of the inhabitants. We recollect a similar circumstance occurring at Dover about three years since, when a soldier died immediately on his arrival at the barracks, from being treated in a similar manner."

Bathing House Tavern
The Beach, Walmer

The tavern was situated on the northern corner of Clarence Road at the junction with The Beach. John Francis was recorded as landlord of the *Bathing House Tavern* in the Alehouse Keepers' Book for Walmer in 1809, 1810 and 1811. (He had previously been listed in 1805 as licensee of the *Royal Canteen*, Walmer).

After its closure, the Tavern became a Reading Room and later an establishment called Sharpe's Bathing Rooms (which were unlicensed) run by Elizabeth Sharpe. She was still resident there in 1857 when the building was described as being *"in front of village"*. (This referred to the model 'village' which Alexander Tod had built comprising of cottages and stables. He was a retired Egyptian merchant and lived in some opulent style at nearby Walmer Lodge, complete with cook, general servants, two housemaids, kitchen maid, footmen, etc).

In his book entitled Records of Walmer, Charles Elvin described the *Bathing House Tavern* building in 1890: *"... until recently, stood the low wooden erection, which once served the purpose of a Reading Room, but latterly was known as Sharpe's Bathing Establishment. It ... has been gone these three years past."*

The building was demolished around 1887 and a large Edwardian property now stands on its site.

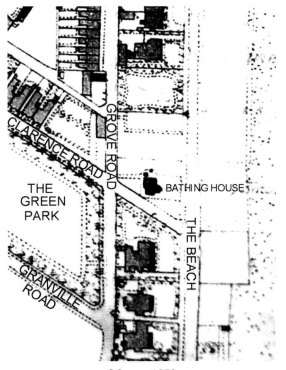

OS map 1872.

Beachbrow
29 (94) Beach Street, Deal

Despite its prominent position on the seafront, the history of the *Beachbrow* is unfortunately a rather sketchy one since it falls sadly short on documentary evidence.

According to the hotel's own website, the *Beachbrow* was founded in the late 1700s when Lord Nelson's flag officers apparently stayed there.

The first evidence of the building found by the authors appeared in a 1767 indenture between the Archbishop of Canterbury and Magdalene Fisher,

2010.

followed by a mention in 1808 when the property was rebuilt.

Frederick R May was registered as residing at both nos 29 (now the *Beachbrow*) and 31 (next door north) Beach Street during the same period in the early 1890s, and his occupation was given as *"Private Tutor"* (he being a Fellow of the Royal Geographic Society). The *Beachbrow* was first documented by name, however, in 1895 and it is possible that no 31 was used as some sort of annexe – see over.

Interestingly, the building next door south of the **Beachbrow** - ie no 27, now Wellington's Café - was also apparently used as an annexe of the hotel at some point. By 1904, no 29 was not registered as being run either as a hotel or a guesthouse in any of the street directories for that year, although this was possibly an oversight.

By 1915, the property was listed as a boarding house. May died in 1925 and, in 1932, Mrs Jane B May (presumably his widow) advertised that the *"private hotel"* was celebrating *"41 years of unchanged proprietorship."* Another advertisement later that decade declared that the *"Beachbrow has been established for nearly 50 years"*. This was placed by Mr and Mrs John Roger Tucker who took over in 1932. Mrs Phyllis Tucker sold the property to Deal Corporation in 1964 and they, in turn, leased it to Mr and Mrs JFS Wyatt (known as Ken and Kate) in 1966. The Wyatts retired from the business on 29 August 1997.

Ken and Lynn Hill took over the **Beachbrow** in 1998 and continue there until the present day (having obtained a full licence in the interim).

An old icehouse is situated at the rear of no 31 Beach

Old ice house at rear of Beachbrow, 2010.

Street (as seen from Middle Street car park), although the building is actually owned by the **Beachbrow**. Icehouses were a popular way of keeping fish, meats and other provisions fresh before the invention of refrigeration, and blocks of ice would be shipped over from Scandinavia and stored inside to keep the temperature cold. This small building was later divided up into four separate rooms where the live in staff used to sleep, before being converted into the hotel's kitchen (which was formerly housed in the basement).

The **Beachbrow**'s vast cellars comprise several rooms, including some smaller ones that are hidden behind original wooden doors which are believed to have been used as lock-ups in earlier days. Another door, now permanently bolted, leads into the basement of no 31 Beach Street next door - see above.

The **Beachbrow** remains a hotel to this day and is housed in the same imposing double fronted building overlooking the beach. The accommodation comprises letting rooms, bar and the Waterfront restaurant (the latter two being open to the general public).

Bear Pump
High Street (Lower Street), Deal

The **Bear Pump** was situated on the corner of the present day High Street and St George's Road. The pump in question was in the vicinity of the pub and its water was non-brackish and renowned for being particularly clean. (Nearby Oak Street was formerly known as Bear Pump Lane).

The first mention of this pub was in 1674 when it was referred to in a legal document as comprising *"1 messuage called the Bear Pump and 12 perches of land [from] Geoffrey Safrey by will to his daughter Mary Brown."*

Another document from 1744 records *"Sarah Gilbert holds 1 messuage and yard purchased from Richard Maundy who purchased from Mary Brown."*

According to 1757 deeds concerning the **Black Horse** pub in Deal, the **Bear Pump** also gets a mention: *"Sarah Friend mortgages (inter alia) The Bear Pump to Thomas Rammell of Eastry yeoman*

Map c1770.

LAND BELONGING TO THE HEIRS OF PETER BRIDGER

SITE OF BEAR PUMP INN LATE 1700S

BEAR PUMP LANE

SPRING GARDEN LANE

LOWER STREET

CHAPEL

with the kitchen, outhouse, brewhouse, yard, garden grass platts, land and ground in Lower Deal within the liberty of the town and borough of Deal in or near the Lower Street near the Chapel, abutting to the King's highway there East and South and to the lands belonging to the heirs of Peter Bridger north and west."

Other deeds record in 1759 that *"Sarah Gilbert died seised of 1 messuage and yard formerly the estate of Mary Brown called the* **Bear Pump** *and the premises descended to her daughter Sarah Friend widow..*

There are no records in existence of when the pub closed down or the building was demolished.

Deal Town Hall now stands on the site. Interestingly, a drinking fountain donated by Earl Granville in 1875 is still in existence on the corner. It no longer works, unfortunately, but it could possibly have been the location of the original pump.

2009.

Beare

See entry for the **Fountain** (south) (2).

Beehive

See entry for the **Eagle**.

Bell
(89) Beach Street, Lower Deal

The **Bell** was situated on the north east corner of the present day Sharpe's Alley at the junction with Beach Street. It got its name from the pilots' bell that hung in a lane running from Middle Street eastwards towards the beach. (The narrow lane divided the **Three Kings** - now called the **Royal Hotel** - from the **Fountain Hotel** immediately next door south, which was

c1900.

sited on the present day car park next to the **Royal Hotel**. The western part of the lane between Middle Street and Beach Street can still be traversed behind the **Royal Hotel**).

It is a possibility that the **Bell** served as a tap room for the **Three Kings** (not least since the two places were linked together in a lease dated 1720).

William Woodman leased the **Bell** in 1661, together with two other pubs, the **Hamborrow Arms** and the **Lyon & Whelp**. When he died, all three

leases were transferred to his widow, Constant. (By 1672, she was licensed to hold Presbyterian meetings at her house in Upper Deal).

Title deeds dated 1698 stated *"Michael Guppy Read: tenement known by the name or sign of the* **Bell** *in Lower Deale, part of the Archbishop's waste, abutting to the Beach Street towards the east, to Val Bowles to the north, to Peter Eaton to the west and to a lane to the Middle Street to the south."*

It had become AM Jennings butcher's shop by the early 1900s, if not earlier. The house next door (north) was an incarnation of the **Watermans Arms** for a period – see separate entry - and which later became a branch of Wedgwood Dairies.

Both properties were demolished in 1954 for road-widening purposes. Nothing further was built on the site and the road as it is today remains slightly wider here behind the **Royal Hotel**.

Bell (Inn)
1-11 (1) Robert Street, Deal

The first mention found of the house was in the 1841 census showing George Ludford and his wife, Mary, both 65 years of age, in residence, followed by an entry in the 1845 Post Office Directory when Ludford gave his occupation as *"beer seller"*. By 1847, Stephen Foster Mockett was landlord. In 1850, he gained a full licence and remained there until 1878, although, in the interim, Joshua Mockett was at the helm in 1852. The *Bell* was auctioned in 1859 when the sales particulars described it as having *"a good bowling green and wheelwright's shop."*

Sarah Elizabeth Bennett Mockett took over in 1890, transferring the licence to Harry Foster in 1893. He was still listed as landlord there in 1899, followed by Mary Ann Foster on her husband's death in 1903. In 1907, Edward Chandler became landlord. He made the news the same year when he committed suicide by slashing his throat with a razor. The verdict was recorded as temporary insanity. Hugh Crawford Hunter took over immediately thereafter. No doubt keen to publicise the inn as being under new management, he placed an advertisement in a local newspaper as follows: *"The 'Bell' Inn, Robert Street, Deal. Proprietor … HC Hunter. LALOOF Lodge. Good Bowling Green. Also Three-Quarter Billiard Table."*

John Edward Hobday was there from 1911. During his landlordship, it was reported that Mr and Mrs Crump (who were outside caterers) served 100 people at the Annual Butchers' Dinner held at the pub on 2 March 1912. At the start of WWI, Hobday was called up but, because he ran the *Bell Inn* single handedly (his wife suffering from a debilitating long-term illness), his conscription was deferred and he did not actually enlist until 1916, the year his name last appeared in any directories. Leonard Bussey took over the licence the same year. He was its final landlord, staying until the *Bell* rang last orders on 31 December 1919.

In 1920, the forthcoming sale of the pub's contents appeared in a local newspaper: *"Ex 'Bell Inn', Robert Street, Deal. Sale of Trade Furniture, Utensils, Etc. Messrs. West, Usher & Co. are instructed by Mr L. Bussey, to Sell by Auction, on Wednesday, 11th February, 1920, the Useful Surplus Utensils and Business Furniture. Mahogany top bar counter, cabinettes with shelves and mirror panels, fittings, five-pull beer engine, with pipes & taps, mahogany framed slate bed billiard table, marking boards, racks, cues, rests and ivory balls, 32 Windsor chairs, 7 long stained Deal tables, 4 ditto forms, music stool, painted cupboard and ditto meat safe, coat racks, drainer tray, beer stillon, spring game machines, mahogany*

Chippendale tables, mantel glasses, and pictures in gilt and ebonised frames, mahogany frame billiard table with leaf cover, forming dining table, oak and china wine and spirit barrels, and ditto glass urn with brass taps, copper kettle, wine funnels, pewter beer and spirit measures, decanters, flasks, ale and stout glasses, iron fenders and spittoons, garden seat, lawn mower, stone roller, 25 lignum vitae lawn bowls and jacks, and other useful articles. On View the Day Previous to the Sale, from 10 till 4 o'clock. Sale at Eleven o'clock. Further particulars and Catalogues may be had of the Auctioneers, at the Deal Estate & House Agency, Victoria Town, Deal; and Cliffe Road, Kingsdown."

The auction sale for the pub itself was advertised in a 1921 catalogue of auctioneers, West & Usher & Co: *"1 Robert Street – with large store and bowls lawn, formerly the Bell Inn"*. The property later became a private residential property known as "Belle House" and was supposedly haunted, according to one of its residents.

In January 1944, the late local historian, David G Collyer, noted in his book, *Deal & District at War*, that a WWII shell demolished one of a pair of brick built shelters in Robert Street close to the old *Bell Inn*. All the men went into one shelter so that they could smoke and the women and children into the other one. As David Collyer related it: *"Unfortunately the blast of the explosion killed all the women and children – there was not a mark on the bodies – but the men were untouched."*

Belle House was demolished in 1977, and the site of the old *Bell Inn* is now occupied by a row of modern houses numbered 1 to 11 Robert Street. The land lying between Nos 11 and 13 Robert Street used to form part of the pub's bowling green.

OS map 1872.

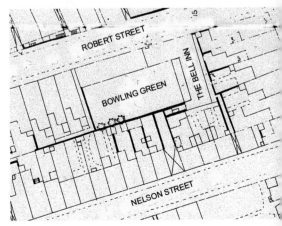

Berry (Green Beret, Green Berry, Royal Arms, Royal Marines)
23 (1) (8) Canada Road (Military Road), Walmer

c1960.

This pub is situated at the entrance to the former Royal Marines' Cavalry Barracks (also known as South Barracks), and a green beret is the distinctive headwear worn by the Royal Marine Commandos. The pub changed its name from the *Green Beret* to the *Green Berry* in 1996 since all the Royal Marines' units (Musicians, as well as Commandos) formerly based in Deal had by then moved on to their new depot in Portsmouth and the military name was no longer relevant. Since 2004, it has simply been known as the *Berry*.

According to a 1795 map, no road existed at all on the site of the present day Canada Road, although North and South (Cavalry) Barracks had already been built (the latter with stabling for 63 horses). With the exception of Walmer Road (now called The Strand), Lower Walmer was practically non-existent at the time.

An 1861 map shows the presence of 'Military Road' (latterly Canada Road) but, apart from the Barracks and a school, no other buildings can seen.

In October 1865, Richard Hobbs was registered lessee of the pub, transferring the lease to John Young, an Army pensioner, the following year. The brewery company was Tomson & Wotton of Margate.

In 1867, John Young was charged with the "*house being open on a Sunday*". However, the case was dismissed since it was argued that the drinks that day had been paid for by a woman who actually lodged on the premises. In the same year, the pub was recorded in the Walmer Poor Rate book as the *Royal Marines* but this was either a very brief name change for that year alone or it was an error, since this is the only example of the pub being called by that name. In 1871, John Foulkes was registered landlord of the *Royal Arms*.

Other landlords included John Jordan in 1873,

Joseph Mercer in 1874, George Johnson in 1878, Cornelius Dillon in 1881 (when the pub's address was given as no 8 Canada Road), James Dillon in 1889, Rebecca Dillon *"widow"* in 1891 (when the address had changed to no 1 Canada Road) until 1903, WHD Phillips in 1904 and Thomas Bell in 1904 to 1912. By 1910, according to a contemporary street directory, Canada Road had been renumbered again and the **Royal Arms'** address was now no 23 Canada Road and, in 1913, plans were approved for improvements to be carried out to the premises.

Later landlords included William Evans in 1913, Henry Leggett in 1915, John Henry Harris in 1918, G Harris in 1921, John G Harris in 1926, John Harris in 1931, Thomas Taylor in 1934 to 1938, Alice S Upton in 1948, JW Watt in 1956, L Upton also in 1956 and William Davison from November 1958.

In or around the early 1960s, one of the horses from Cavalry Barracks was famously photographed attempting to buy a drink at the bar, surrounded by servicemen and members of the public.

The **Royal Arms** was often colloquially referred to as the *'Thatch'* or the *'Old Thatch'* because of an advertisement for 'Thatch's Nut Brown Ale' that used to be displayed on the outside wall of the pub. However, it did not officially change its name until the mid 1960s when it became known as the **Green Beret**.

Davison remained until 1975 when Barry Eason took over the new licence. Local sources state that the pub temporarily closed down around this time but the authors have unfortunately been unable to find any documentation to back up this information.

John G Howe took over as landlord in 1981 and, in July 1982, the pub was granted a special licence allowing its basement bar to be used as the Babalou Club.

Michael O'Grady became landlord in 1984. On 22 September 1989, 11 musicians from the Royal Marines' School of Music were tragically killed as a result of an IRA bomb exploding in their barracks. Mr O'Grady heard the explosion while still in bed that morning and related scenes of its aftermath to the national and international press, which made for harrowing reading.

Gavin O'Grady was landlord in 1996, followed by John and Sue Leeson the same year. They remained until 2005 when Chris Barnes and his father Malcolm took over in the February.

The pub is now a free house specialising in real ales. Chris with his new wife Harriet and father Malcolm hold an annual beer festival, and the Berry was awarded CAMRA Branch Pub of the Year in 2008, 2009, and 2010.

2009.

Bird In Hand (location unknown) Deal

Richard Ayler, pilot, stated in his Will of 1676 that he was leaving the premises in Deal known as the *Bird in Hand* to Jane Hodges, and to his brother, Nicholas Goughe, he left part of his great boat and capstan lying southwards from the house. In a 1686 document, Peter Whiteacre mentions "*one tenement [being] the Bird in Hand.*"

Black Bull
115 High Street (30 Lower Street), Deal

c1960.

The *Black Bull* was located in the building immediately next door and north of the Town Hall and both were erected in 1803.

Stephen Elgar was documented as being landlord of the "*Black Bull with Town Hall wine vaults*" in 1804. According to the 1821 Poor Rate book, the pub also had "*stables and room over*" when Henry White was in charge. James Rigglesford followed in 1832, with Thomas Leach in 1839, Thomas Jelly in 1847 and Thomas Castle in 1851 until his death in 1877 when his widow, Mary, took over. The pub was owned by Hill's Brewery at the time. Mr Evans became licensee in 1881 and Edward Chittendon by 1888. He successfully applied for an extension of opening hours on the occasion of a 'smoking concert' held at the pub that year.

Samuel Ingram took over in 1898 and, round about 1901, the pub became a Thompson house. G Palmer was mine host in 1915, James Joseph Delahaye in 1924, George Knight in 1925 and WA Mory in 1930. According to a Mercury article dated April 1930, 65 year old Albert Edwin Chandler pleaded guilty to breaking a window and he asked to be sent to jail since he was tired of walking about all day! He was sentenced to two months imprisonment, without hard labour, which was considered to be a lenient judgment at the time.

In 1940, the licence was transferred from Richard Frederick Thompson to Charles Brailsford, followed by George Dale in 1945. By 1965 when the pub shut its doors for the last time, the *Black Bull* had become a Charrington's house.

c1960.   *2009.*

An article appeared on 21 January 1965 in the Mercury concerning the fate of the pub: *"Situated beside the Council Chamber in the Town Hall, in which its future will be discussed, is the **Black Bull**. Present licensee of the house is Mr George H. Wilding, who has been the "landlord" for the past* six months. *Previous licensee was Mr George Dale, who died recently after 19 years behind the bar."*

Peppers Health Food shop took over in 1979 and remains open to this day. Some of the old Charrington's bar fittings can still be seen inside, on the right hand wall of the shop.

Black Dog(g) (exact location unknown) Deal

The **Black Dog(g)** was mentioned in the 1680 Payments for Signs List for Deal. On 22 April 1719, a local Vestry Meeting book reported that the **Black Dog(g)** was bought for the use of the poor (and, one might assume, would no longer function as a pub) and ordered that the adjoining messuage, tenement, land and stable be sold and that the monies be used for part payment in the purchase of the main building. However, an advertisement in the Kentish Post dated 15 October 1727 read: *"Daffy's Elixir. The said Elixir is appointed to be sold at Mr Samuel Simmons, a baker, over against the **Black Dog** at Deal"* which seems to indicate that perhaps the premises remained licensed as a pub (or had changed location).

According to late local historian, Les Cozens, the **Black Dog(g)** was located somewhere on the beach, and that the property was used as a Military Hospital at some point for sailors with infectious diseases.

Black Horse (exact location unknown) Broad Street, Deal

This pub was situated somewhere near the north-eastern corner of Middle Street and Broad Street. It was leased to John Gardner from the Archbishop of Canterbury in 1661. The only mention of it being a pub was in a 1679 lease: *"Anthony Berry of Sandwich, gentleman, and Jane, his wife, [at] the **Black Horse Inn**."*

However, local brewer, Samuel Ffasham resided at the property in 1720, as well as John May and William Mackeson, brewers of Hythe, in 1815.

Elizabeth Sole was listed as resident between 1822 and 1851 and this was the last found documentary evidence of the building when the leases came to an end.

Black Horse 36 High Street, Deal

See entry for the *Strand*.

Blacksmiths Arms, 149 (73) Middle Street, Deal

See entry for the *Hope*.

Blakes Head

See entry for the *New Inn*.

Blew Anker, Deal

See entry for the *Anchor*.

Blewbore, Deal

See entry for the *Royal Oak*.

Blue Anchor, Deal

See entry for the *Anchor*.

Bluebell, Deal

See entry for the *Red Lion*.

Blue Boar, Deal

See entry for the *Royal Oak*.

Boatswain, Deal

See entry for the *Providence*.

Bohemian (Antwerp and Lord Keith) 47 (105) Beach Street, Deal

Old leases showed that the original building dates back to 1680 when it was described as *"a tenement used as a storehouse and shop"*. However, it did not become licensed until around 1805 when it became known as the **Lord Keith**. The pub was named after Admiral Lord Keith (1746-1823). He was a frequent visitor to Deal and, according to local legend, used to drink in the *India Arms*, alongside other seafaring luminaries of the day.

John and Sarah Carey were listed as landlords of the pub in 1813 to 1836. The 1821 rate book stated that they also leased the house next door (what is now known as Guildford House). They were followed by John Jarman in 1839 and John Clayson in 1847.

The Deal Pavement Committee purchased *"the Lord Keith Stage* (a boat jetty) *and capstan ground"* (on the beach) opposite the pub in 1836, the same year as it changed its name to the **Antwerp**.

In 1859, a soldier was charged with stealing a decanter of rum from the pub. A Mercury report from 1869 stated that boatman, William Irvine, was summonsed by landlord, George Forth, for being drunk and riotous and refusing to leave the pub on 6 and 7 September. Irvine was bound over for three

2009.

The fire in 1909.

months to keep the peace. He was soon in trouble again, however, when he was charged with once more being drunk and abusive at the *Antwerp* and for assaulting PC Horton. He was sentenced to one month's imprisonment in Sandwich Gaol or a fine of £2/05 (£2.25). The fine was paid.

In November 1877, contemporary reports noted that the *Antwerp* took in survivors of the Great Storm at sea that year. Henry Spears was landlord in 1878. The pub was rebuilt in the late 1800s but was badly damaged by fire in 1909 and rebuilt yet again into the construction that stands today.

WG Wareham was listed as landlord in 1936. In September 1944, during WWII, a shell fell at the rear of the house, almost on the same spot of the 1940 blast that destroyed ye *Olde Victory* pub.

According to Dover Magistrates'

Upstairs c1960.

Licensing records, later landlords included C Holden in the early 1950s, FC Pygall in 1966, H Bagnall in the late 1960s, J Jones in 1971, Stanley Dale in 1975, Stewart Workman in January 1979, Arthur and Gary Tilbury in December 1979 and Colin and Margaret Brown in 1982. They were still listed there as landlords in 1994, and then Clifford and Irene Salmon took over in 1995, followed by Michael Ormston and Roy Richards in 1999. They were joined on the licence by Angela Riley in 2000. The *Antwerp* changed its name to the *Bohemian* on 12 December 2003 during the landlordship of Jonathan Brown and Carleen Cooke.

The pub was sold on 12 November 2008, although Jonathan Brown remained licensee. The *Bohemian* is still open for business as a public house, complete with modern ground floor bar, garden and first floor restaurant.

Bowling Green Tavern (Gun Inn)
164 Church Path (Bowling Green Lane/Road, Stony Path, Gravel Walk, Gun Lane), Deal

As will be seen from the address above, Church Path has, over the centuries, been known by several different names, the pub being situated on a road junction with different entrances.

In 1845, the cost of licensing a bowling green had reduced from £100 (a not inconsiderable sum at the time) since the 1541 statute had finally been repealed under the new Gaming Act. Pubs were attempting to attract more customers and bowling was considered to be one of England's longest established and most popular sports at the time.

Undated records of Fremlin's Brewery held at the East Kent Archives described the pub: *"Bowling Green Tavern, formerly the Gun, and grounds south-west side of Gun Lane."*

The first mention of the tavern was in 1847 when Richard Verrier junior was landlord of what was then an unnamed beerhouse. The following year, it became a fully licensed alehouse known as the *Bowling Green Tavern.* Verrier was followed by Thomas Kite Parker in 1863, John Stills in 1872, Richard Percy in 1874, Frederick George Curling in 1876, Harry Francis in 1880, Henry Gunner in July 1887 and George Divers in November 1887.

Ezra Harold Foulser followed in 1889, staying until 1893. During his time at the tavern, he placed the following advertisement in a local newspaper: *"Bowling Green Tavern, Upper Deal (Under entire new management). H. Foulser (late of 'Station Hotel', Martin Mill, near Dover), having taken the above Tavern and Tea Gardens, begs to announce to the public generally that he has provided, as far as possible, everything for comfort and amusement. Lawn Tennis, Bowls, Quoits, Target Shooting, and various other sports. Large and Small Parties Accommodated. Luncheons, Dinners, Teas, &c., Private apartments. Bicyclists, &c., accommodated. Stabling. Lawn Tennis from 10am to 5pm. Bowls from 5pm. Special arrangements made."*

After Foulser left in 1893, John Rennie took over, followed by Charles Quinton in 1894, Joseph Taylor in January 1896, William Henry Lamburn in August 1896, James Ford in 1897 and HJ Sayers from 1904 until at least 1915. In 1923, George Wearmouth

c1920.

transferred the licence to William James Barty, followed by William Austin in 1928, H Lewis from 1932 and Walter A Kebell from 1942 until his death in January, 1964. His widow, Ruby, temporarily took over until July that year when, the Mercury reported, Cyril Turner, on behalf of the regulars, presented her with a wall clock to mark her 22 years at the pub.

SA Chamberlain was landlord in 1966, William and Lydia Barty in 1987, followed by Paul and Julie Kematon in 1988.

During the Kematons' time at the tavern, the Mercury reported that the building dated back to 1502 and that it was licensed as the *Gun Inn*, Gun Lane in 1721. The authors have unfortunately been unable to discover any licensing records or directories concerning its time as the *Gun Inn* (apart from the initial Fremlin's reference above) so are not able to provide any further information. According to Licensing Magistrates' records, Michael and Susan Barnes took over the tavern in 1994, although the Mercury referred to *"Mike and Penny Barnes"* in a 1996 article, mentioning that they were also simultaneously running the *Stag* in Walmer.

By 1997, the pub's restaurant had been renamed the Garden Room. In 2002, Brian and Eunice Pitchford took over, followed by David Styles in 2004.

The pub remains open for business.

Bricklayers Arms, 69 West Street, Deal

2009.

This pub was situated a short way north of the *Swan* (now the *Hole in the Roof*), on the eastern side of West Street. According to the 1841 census, John Macey was landlord and, in 1845, the property was described as a beerhouse, and was a rough and notorious place by all accounts. In 1858, Mary Banks complained in court of *"rough and cowardly treatment by John Tandy at the house."*

In 1859, landlady, Anne Macey, charged Mary Banks with assault, and for creating a disturbance and fighting with one Sarah Cooper. Banks claimed Macey and her mother *"flew at her like serpents"* and threw her out *"in an indecent manner."*

In 1868, landlord, John Robert Macey, was summonsed to court for encouraging drunkenness and disorderly conduct. The house was evidently *"one that gave the military a great deal of trouble."*

In 1869, Mrs Macey was charged with allowing persons of *"notoriously bad character to assemble in her house"*. She was fined 20 shillings (£1) or 14 days' hard labour. In 1873, three complaints to the authorities put the licence in jeopardy but it was renewed after adjournment. The Maceys were fined 10 shillings (50p) for serving drinks after hours.

In 1875, there was a relicence application from *"the Brickmakers"* (sic) which was opposed by the good people of St George's Parish on the grounds of the '*immoral character of the house*'. The pub closed the same year and the property was put up for auction at the *Black Horse*.

The building, which stood on the site of the current entrance to Somerfield's car park, was subsequently demolished.

Bricklayers Arms, 26 Dover Road, Walmer

Unfortunately, the early history of this pub is rather sketchy, although, given its close proximity to the barracks, it was known to be a very popular watering hole with the Royal Marines.

In 1852, George Webb was listed as *'Gardener and Beer Retailer'* living and selling alcohol from un-named premises. By 1855, he was living in Dour Cottages, in what is now Cambridge Road, as a *'Beer Retailer'*. An 1858 street directory had him registered at the *Bricklayers Arms*, although no location was given.

The 1861 census showed three pubs in a row: the *Bricklayers Arms*, the *Cambridge Arms* and the *Wellesley Arms*. In 1867, by

c2009.

which time the pub had moved a few houses north to new premises in the building mentioned below, Mary Anne Webb was landlady until 1871.

Other landlords included William Worsley in 1882, R Pageter in 1898 and John H Cleve in 1906 when the premises were delicensed. A number of other pubs were also delicensed around this time owing to the strict 1902 Licensing Act which aimed to get rid of small beerhouses.

The property is now occupied by John's Tackle Shop, and the *Bricklayers Arms* sign bearing William Worsley's name can still be seen at the top of the building.

Brickmakers Arms
9 (5) Mill Road, Deal

The pub's premises were built around 1882 by George Henry Denne of 8A Queen Street, Deal and they were then sold on to George Henry Cotton Stapleton, a brewer from Sandwich. The *Brickmakers* was so-called since, at the time the property was built, it was surrounded by brick fields. Immediately upon opening, it was described as the *"Brickmakers Arms and shop"* in all local street directories and rate books (and remained to be so described until around the 1930s). When *The Brickmakers* first opened in 1883, it was originally only allowed to sell beer for consumption off the premises, although its first licensee, William Wyborn, was fined for serving beer on the

c2000.

premises that same year.

Mrs Gunnor, the landlady in 1898, was fined one shilling (5p), with 7/6d (37½p) costs, *"for allowing intoxicating liquor to be drunk on the premises while only having an off-licence"*. On 3 June 1899, East Kent Brewery bought the pub. The same year, John Batt Annall, a retired police officer, was installed as landlord and the licence was changed in order to allow the consumption of beer on, as well as off, the premises. By 1903, Nathan Everett was in charge, followed by RT Wakerell in 1911, who had previously been landlord of the *Lifeboat* in Walmer which had just closed down. He stayed at the *Brickmakers* until at least 1916.

1918 saw Frederick

Cox in charge. In 1920, brewers, Jude Hanbury & Co, acquired the property. E Cox was landlord from 1931 to 1937 and, during his time as mine host, Mackeson brewery took over in 1934. Erroll Carlisle Cox was at the helm from 1945. In 1948, the pub was granted a wine licence due to shortage of beer at the time (following the war years). A full licence (to include spirits) was granted on 30 March 1950.

Former boxer and ex-miner, Ernie Kemp was a longstanding landlord, serving from January 1953 until December 1976. A former customer recalled cricketer, Freddie Trueman, being an occasional visitor to the pub when playing in Canterbury, as he was apparently an old friend of Kemp's.

Later landlords included Martin Burgess in 1979, followed by Malcolm Formoy and then former miner, Alan Garton, in 1991 until 2002.

The pub shut down in early 2010 and owners Punch Taverns put the property up for sale. At the time of writing, it was rumoured the building was being converted into two residential dwellings.

British Fair (location unknown) Deal

This pub appeared on a list of public houses owned in Deal by the Cobb Brewery of Margate between 1808 and 1818 but unfortunately no location was given and nothing more is known about the place.

British Tar, Deal

See entry for the *Queens Head*.

Bull(s) Head
(location unknown), Deal

In his book regarding the history of Deal, Laker talks about "the *Bulls Head*" being mentioned on a 1680 list of local public houses but unfortunately no location was given so the authors are unable to ascertain whether or not it was a mistaken reference to the *Bull Head* or a separate entity altogether.

The first mention of this pub was in a legal paper dated 1732 documenting the purchase of *"The Bull Head and ½ acre land"* by Josiah Lane from John Walker. Walker also held *"1 messuage, 1 stable, 1 granary and ½ acre of land in Middle Deal"*. By 1771, the *Bull Head* was described in Walker's will as being in two separate dwellings, divided by ½ acre of land, and was to be left to his grand-daughter, *"Elizabeth Bromsall, wife of John Baker esquire."*

An abstract of title dated 30 September 1776 read: *"Indenture of Lease between the Archbishop of Canterbury and the executors of the wills of Elizabeth Rentone and Thomazine Norwood, on surrender of former lease of messuage or tenement … the Bull Head and the outhouse building stable yard … in Lower Deal abutting to Middle Street and a tenement demised by John Iggulden to East, to a lane between Middle Street and Lower Street to West, to a tenement demised to Mary Shave widow and John Iggulden and a lane leading from Middle Street to Lower Street to North and to a tenement demised to Robert Stringer and Thomas Wilkins and Mary his wife to South, then or late in the tenure or occupation of John Goodchild, Thomas Gillet and Elizabeth Shrewsbury."*

The *Bull(s) Head* was probably located in the Griffin Street area of Deal although this cannot be confirmed.

Cambridge Arms
(Drum Major) 42 Dover Road, Walmer

c1970.

The original pub dates from the early 1800s and was a popular hostelry with the military, situated as it was opposite the barracks.

In 1840, Mr ETS Reader took a 63-year lease from the Leith Estate and ran the property for a while before later moving on to look after several other pubs in the area. In 1841, Benjamin Verrier was proprietor of an unnamed beerhouse and shop there and, by 1851, Mr Stephenson had taken over the running of the beerhouse.

The first mention of the *Cambridge Arms* by name was in 1858 under the landlordship of George Barnes (who was also listed as a *"Grocer and Cheesemonger"*). In 1861, Harry Levy, an eccentric *"Buffalo Singer"*, performed there, apparently amidst much merriment and laughter, as the pub held a music hall licence for some time.

In 1882, Thomas Barnes, a *"Fly Proprietor"* by trade, took over. In May 1892, Mrs Godfrey was landlady when a fire broke out early one morning, resulting in the destruction of the building and damage to neighbouring properties. After the pub had been rebuilt on the same site, ironically perhaps, it was announced in November 1894 that *"Smoking Concerts"* were to be held every Saturday, with Musician Brown at the piano and Mr J Coutts in the chair. In October 1895, it was advertised that the *"first of a new series of smoking concerts will be held fortnightly … from October 19th at 8.30."*

In 1905, landlord, Albert Ashby (who had formerly been at the *Crispin Inn*), was unfortunately found drowned in the sea but no evidence was put forward as to how he came to be there.

Henry N Wraight was landlord from 1913, followed by Edward Fletcher Davison from 1915 (when his application for improvements was agreed) to 1932, James Spooner in 1933 and RS Edgecombe in 1948. Mr Edgecombe died in 1949 and Edith Edgecombe took over the running of the pub until at least 1955. Tom Lenham was landlord in 1966. (His son, Jeffrey, later became licensee of the *Deal Hoy* for many years). According to Dover Magistrates' records, Peter Stevens and former Royal Marine, Clarence Bolder, took over in 1970.

Bill Pierce, Bass Charrington's local artist, painted Drum Major Charles Bowden for the pub sign and Bowden performed the reopening ceremony of the newly named *Drum Major* in April 1971. The two bars were christened Gibraltar and Zeebrugge in commemoration of earlier Royal Marines' campaigns. By 1977, the house had become somewhat dilapidated, but new landlords, Arthur and Joan North, who took over that year, arranged for the total refurbishment of the pub with the brewery owners, Bass Charrington, to create a more family orientated environment. They reassured prospective customers that the updated *Drum Major* would offer *"A new scene, live bands, bar billiards, pool, disco, 2 dart boards, bar snacks, a friendly atmosphere and a first-class pint"*. The Norths also came up with the idea of creating a restaurant in a large upstairs room and installing its own kitchen. The restaurant, called the Cambridge Room, was opened in 1978 by Kent cricket captain, Alan Ealham. Between 1979 and 1981, Ian Dunkerley (now owner of **Dunkerleys** – see separate entry) ran the restaurant. The Mercury referred to him in 1981 as being *"the 27 year old proprietor"* who declared the establishment to be *"Walmer's Finer Diner"*. By the time the Norths gave notice to the brewery in 1980, the fortunes of the pub had been turned around. (Interestingly, Arthur North was one-time Chairman of the Deal & Walmer Licensed Victuallers Association). In 1982, Ray Tyrell was listed as landlord, with Diane Tyrell installed as the new restaurant manager. The Cambridge Room was reopened later that year by former Indian test cricketer, Dr Carl P Maras, "a regular customer and an interesting character" by all accounts! Later landlords included Gareth Jones in October 1984, Peter Watts in December 1984, Clifford Salmon and Mark Netherclifft in May 1989, Shaun Wright in October 1989, Leonard Dye and Theresa Donnelly in March 1992, Ian Sparshott and Margaret Hawkins in November 1992 and Susan Dobson in 1994. It is believed that the pub reverted to its former name of the **Cambridge Arms** in 1994. Now back under its old name, landlords included Brian Johnson and

2009.

Kevin Deverill in February 1995, Paul Leach later that year, Paul Leach and Richard Baker in 1998, John Kemp in May 2000, John Kemp and Angela Jones in July 2000 and Charles and Sharon Bramhall in 2002. The **Cambridge Arms**, with its two bars, remains open to this day, although there is no longer a public restaurant on the first floor. Live music is a regular feature of the pub, as well as pool table, Sky Sports, real ales and good pizzas. Colin and Julie Roberts are the pub's current landlords.

Castle Inn

See entry for the **Sandown Castle**.

Chequers
1 & 2 Primrose Hill, Middle Street, Deal

Primrose Hill is an alleyway that partially still exists, linking Beach Street to the Middle Street car park. The **Chequers** would have stood on the junction with what was then Middle Street, although the car park now stands on the site. Many of the alleyways and buildings that stood there were heavily bombed during WWII and were later demolished.

Primrose Hill and nearby Primrose Alley were both named after Dr Primrose who was an eminent citizen of Deal and a friend of Elizabeth Carter's father in the 18th century.

According to author, Barbara Collins, there was a beerhouse called the **Chequers** on the site in 1824 but we have been unable to find any early records to confirm this date.

What we do know is that George Hills Mackins resided at the property, and, at the Petty Sessions held on 5 September 1868, he was refused a

licence, although he was listed as landlord from 1869 to 1871 when the **Chequers** was a beerhouse. At the Petty Sessions held on 30 April 1870, *"Maria Tringrove, an occasional visitor at this court, was brought up and charged with breaking 8 squares of glass at the **Chequers** beerhouse, 1 Primrose Hill, Middle Street, kept by George Hills Mackins. Sentenced to 6 weeks' hard labour"* (in Sandwich Gaol). Tringrove was also a known troublemaker at the **Admiral Keppel** pub and was described as being *"a miserable looking woman."*

The pub closed in 1871 when Magistrates again refused to renew Mackins' licence, and, by 1897, it had become a slaughterhouse.

The site of the **Chequers** is on the right hand side of Middle Street car park as approached from the entrance in Broad Street, and lies opposite the side of the rear section of Deal library.

Chequers Inn (Halfway House)
Golf Road (Sandhills, Ancient Highway), Deal

Although the **Chequers Inn** is technically situated in Sholden, it has always been considered to be a Deal pub since its main access route is via Deal.

The **Chequers Inn**, also called the **Halfway House** in an earlier ancient building on the site, is set in an isolated location behind the beach, on the low lying coastal land in the Lydden Valley, between Deal and Sandwich. Because of its secluded position, it was a well known watering hole for local smugglers who often used to hide their contraband in the nearby sandhills. Pottery dating between 1250 and 1350 has also been found on the site.

Early records going back to the 1500s indicate that the tavern was a stopping off place for travellers along what was then the busy Ancient Highway.

In August 1648, contemporary reports describe a battle on the sandhills between Parliamentarians and Royalists during the Civil War, ending in the death of eight or nine soldiers. Two of the soldiers had previously been guarding "*two halfway houses*" situated between Sandown Castle and Sandwich, and it is probable that one of these houses was the **Halfway House** inn. (If this is indeed the case, the other "halfway house" referred to finished life as a farmhouse, collapsing in a fire in the 1930s. Later excavations unearthed original footings dating back to around 1650 under four feet of earth).

In 1740, Mark Jones was listed as landlord of the **Chequers**. Not far away from the inn, the body of Mary Bax was found in 1782. She had been walking from Deal to Sandwich when she was attacked and killed by a Swedish sailor. A headstone at the site reads: "*On this spot, August the 25th, 1782, Mary Bax was murdered by Martin Lash, a foreigner, who was executed for the same.*"

In 1830, according to the late local historian, David Collyer, the landlord, George Marsh, was suspected by Customs and Excise of being in league with smugglers who frequented his pub. The shed belonging to the farmhouse next door was often used as a temporary mortuary. The bodies of drowned victims found on the beach would be stored under tarpaulin, and it seems that the smugglers took full advantage of this by making sure that a few tubs of brandy were also placed under the sheet for safekeeping until the coast was clear!

Edward Marsh became landlord in 1912. Nearly 50 years later, the Mercury reported, in December 1961: "*5 men entered the **Chequers Inn**, tied up the octogenarian landlord and his spinster daughter, locked them in a bedroom and ransacked the pub. They were later discovered by the landlord's son. Edward Marsh, 81, who has lived at the pub since he was 2, was once a dairyman as well as landlord. His daughter, Irene Caroline Marsh, is manager of the pub.*"

In February 1962, the Mercury reported that "*Deal's oldest landlord*", Edward Marsh, had died and that his son in law would temporarily hold the licence until the pub was sold. (The paper did not comment on whether or not Mr Marsh's death could have been caused as a direct result of the incident three months earlier). Mr Marsh was apparently the fourth generation of his family to hold a licence at the **Chequers**. He had also owned nearby Walnut Tree Farm for many years where he kept a large herd of cattle. With a van and two horsedrawn carts, he delivered milk locally, originally straight from the churn. The grazing land was eventually sold and much of it was used by the **Chequers** as a caravan park for holidaymakers in the summer.

THE CHEQUERES SITUATED ON THE FAMOUS ROYAL CINQUE PORTS, GOLF LINKS, DEAL.

c1930.

Michael Rogers, one of the authors of this book, recalls supplying bread to the **Chequers** in his younger days and the small sharp lumps in the road re-arranging the neatly laid-out cakes on the trays in the back of his van! He also recalls Mr Marsh delivering milk to the Rogers' family home and bakery in North Street during the 1950s.

Probably due to its isolated location and lack of passing trade, subsequent owners sought many different ways to try and boost the wavering fortunes of the **Chequers**.

By March 1964, Helen and George Wakeham had bought the inn. They also owned nearby Wakeham's Farm. With the assistance of family members, Lionel and Sylvia Eddy, they ran the pub until September 1973 when it was sold at auction to a company called Leisurescope who planned to turn it into a country club.

In January 1974, the **Chequers** was relaunched with a new Highwayman's bar and Saddle Room restaurant, and boasting "*Wine, Dine & Dance to 2am, live entertainment Fridays and Saturdays.*"

The manager was Michael Griggs who had previously been landlord of the Coastguard at St Margaret's Bay and manager of the **Queens Hotel** in Deal. In the March, it was reported that that there had been local protest over Leisurescope's plans to replace the caravans with chalets and to build a large open-air swimming pool, squash courts and changing rooms.

In March 1976, Bob and Olive Humphreys took over. They stated that the ghost of a man evading a press gang haunted the pub. In 1978, the Mercury reported that eight people took refuge on the roof of the pub following the worst local flooding seen in years. As a result, in February 1979, the pub only opened on Fridays and Saturdays since Southern Water was working on sea defences close by the rest of the time. The company subsequently compensated the Humphreys for its closure. The pub returned to its usual licensing hours on 10 March that year.

By 1983, John and Claire Radford, in partnership with Tom Clift, were in charge. John Radford had previously been at the Crown in Finglesham. After modernising and enlarging the bar, they organised a grand reopening at "*6pm, Saturday, July 23rd – Food from Sunday*". In November, they advertised their "*Early Winter Programme*" which included an American Thanksgiving Evening on 24 November, as well as a "*Christmas Oompah Party*" on 19 December with "*Gluwein and thigh slapping*", as well as a New Year's Eve party to include a four course meal while listening to Henry Chan and His Steel Band. In July 1984, they announced the opening of 10 double motel style rooms and, in July 1985, Tom Clift (by then described as the owner of the **Chequers Inn** and **Lord Nelson**) announced the introduction of Pastor Ale to both his pubs. By February 1988, he had a new partner, Cliff King, who had previously been the chef at the **Hare & Hounds** in Northbourne. Many more local newspaper adverts and publicity articles followed, one of which mentioning, in June 1988, that there had apparently been an inn on the site since Henry V's time in 1422 and that it had become known as the **Chequers Inn** in 1600. The inn was put up for sale in December 1990 but it was still unsold when it was reported in October 1993 that the Radfords had twice been burgled in two days, the thieves having got away with £700 in cash, together with a stereo, alcohol and cigarettes.

In November 1994, the inn was put up for auction and, a year later, it was reported that it had been empty for two years and that Dover District Council had approved changes to the bar, restaurant and holiday accommodation. It reopened for business in April 1996 but, by the August, no landlord's name appeared on the registers.

In February 2001, the Mercury stated recent heavy rain had left water kneedeep in the bar of the **Chequers**, and, in the March, the late Les Cozens writing for the Mercury related that "*low tides had again uncovered elephant bones at the end of a footpath from the **Chequers Inn** to the sea.*"

The **Chequers** remains open for business and comprises a modern bar and stylish restaurant run under the successful ownership of Gary Rose and Pieter van Zyl.

c1920.

Cherry Tree
(location unknown) "Deale"

In 1680, Edward Taylor was listed as landlord of the *Cherry Tree*, "Deale" but, other than this entry, no other record can be found of the pub.

Cinque Ports Arms, Deal

See entry for the *Druids Arms*.

Cinque Ports Arms, possibly 3-4 The Strand (Walmer Road), Walmer

The *Cinque Port Arms* was a beerhouse situated two or three buildings in from the northern end of The Strand. This part of Walmer Road was re-named The Strand between 1839 and 1841.

In 1832, William Claris was landlord, followed by William Pearce in 1839, 1840 and 1841, who gave his occupation as "*Publican*".

Unfortunately, no later documentary evidence can be found about this pub.

2009. Possible location of Cinque Port Arms, The Strand.

Cinque Ports Arms (location unknown) Walmer

According to an undated 1830s street directory for Walmer, Stephen Chapman was registered as being a Boot and Shoemaker at the *Cinque Port Arms*. Unfortunately, there is no evidence to suggest that he was ever at the *Cinque Port Arms* in The Strand. It is possible, however, that this pub was an earlier incarnation of the *Cinque Ports Volunteer* since a later landlord there shared the same surname (Chapman).

Cinque Ports Arms (location unknown) Upper Walmer

John James Flower was listed in an 1876 directory as being landlord of the *Cinque Port Arms* in Walmer. However, the Poor Rate book for the same year lists a John Flower as living next door to the *Cinque Ports Volunteer* (and continued to do so until the 1890s).

It is therefore possible that this may just be a case where the pub's name was incorrectly recorded in the 1876 directory.

Cinque Ports Volunteer (Volunteer)
287 Dover Road, Walmer

c1900.

This pub was also referred to as the **Volunteer**. Frederick Chapman was resident at the above address in 1857 and he appeared again in the 1861 census, giving his occupation as "*Carpenter and Beerhouse Keeper.*"

In 1863, the pub was owned by Morris Thompson, brewer. In April of that year, a Telegram report stated: "*The four-year-old daughter of Mr Frederick Chapman, landlord of The **Volunteer**, Walmer was run over by a dog cart containing three men. Little hope is given of the girl's recovery*". (It is not known whether the poor child survived).

By 1871, Henry Adolphus Martin (who, as well as being an inn keeper, was also a fly proprietor) was in charge, and an 1886 report noted him as being fined £1 for serving liquor out of hours. His long stay at the pub ended in 1906 when George Kennet was installed, followed by Henry Wraight in 1907. The pub became vacant in 1909.

In 1910, when the renewal of the licence was applied for by Jessie William Lewis, the premises were described as being "*an old house, in fairly good repair, the tap room measuring 10-feet by 20-feet*". At the time, Walmer had 20 alehouses, one 'on' and one 'off' beerhouse and three grocers. The licence was eventually renewed, after a certain amount of kerfuffle.

On 9 September 1944, Lewis applied for a protection order to BC Dredge of Thompson's brewery, and he was still shown as living on the premises in 1948. In March 1949, the licence was transferred to the **Jolly Gardener** in Deal, which, up until that time, had only been licensed to sell beer and wine.

The house is now a private residence called Cinque Ports House.

2009.

Clarendon (Royal Clarendon, Seagull, Ship), 51-55 (107-109) (107) Beach Street, Deal

The original building was erected around 1743, according to the hotel's own potted history. The Poole family rang a shop there from the 1820s to the 1840s.

An 1849 street directory documented William Baker, shopkeeper, as residing at 107 Beach Street. In 1851, the census showed Samuel Baker (together with his wife, Ann) listed as a coach driver and beerhouse keeper living at the property. According to the Deal Licensing Register, he obtained a full licence on 13 September 1855 when the house officially became known as the *Ship*.

On 28 March or 20 April 1857 (records differ), Samuel Baker apparently took exception to an insult directed at his wife by Edward McCarroll, an ensign stationed at Walmer barracks, who had been drinking in the *Ship* that night. Brandishing a poker, Baker chased McCarroll out of the pub, caught up with him near Deal Castle and killed him in the street. Accordingly, in July of that year, Baker, who was 36 at the time, was found guilty of manslaughter at the Maidstone Assizes and transported for life. He was taken to the West Indies on a convict ship called the True Briton, but ended his days as a proprietor of a small pub in New

Zealand, having lived to a ripe old age. (His wife, Ann, took over the running of the *South Foreland*).

Accordingly, on 7 May 1857, the licence was transferred to Edmund Hadlow and the pub was renamed the *Seagull*, no doubt in an attempt to distance itself from its recent bad reputation. On 5 September that year, it was listed as being unlicensed. However, a local newspaper article in 1858 recorded Mrs Rogers breaking a window at the *Seagull*.

By November 1859, the property had been rebuilt and changed its name yet again to the *Clarendon*, with Edward Hammond as landlord. John Thomas Outwin became landlord in 1860 and also in 1865 when the Poor Rate book for that year described the pub as being called *"The Clarendon, coach house and tap"*. (The tap was situated away from the house, in a building that in 1866 had become a separate pub called the *Clarendon Tap* - see separate entry for ye *Old(e) Victory*).

By 1868, Outwin had renamed the hotel the *Royal Clarendon*, much to the annoyance of its neighbour, the *Royal Hotel*, since they had apparently objected to the *Clarendon* prefixing its name with the word "Royal". More controversy ensued in 1870 when Mercer Taylor, landlord of the *Clarendon Tap*,

c1930.

Members of the Pioneer Corps wait outside the Clarendon for their lunch. c1940.

embarked on a legal battle with Outwin. Outwin had opened licensed premises called **Wine Shades**, without a licence, next door to the **Royal Clarendon**'s premises (at no 108, now numbered 53 Beach Street and forming the middle part of the present day **Clarendon** building). The ownership of the **Royal Clarendon** was also called into question at the time. The upshot of the dispute was that the **Royal Clarendon** closed down in 1870 and Outwin continued running **Wine Shades** while Taylor remained as landlord of the **Clarendon Tap**. (See also separate entry for **Wine Shades**). During the **Royal Clarendon**'s closure, the building was leased to the *"Trustees of the Union Club"*, and its accommodation was also used as a meeting place for other clubs, according to the 1881 census.

In 1886, the building reopened as the **Clarendon Hotel**, it having lost its "Royal" moniker in the interim, and which included the former **Wine Shades** building next door. The landlord at the time was William Henry Collins. In 1891, Anna Walker was licensee, followed by Frank Fryatt in 1904 until at least 1910, JW Pinder in 1914 and HC Stacey from 1922 until 1937 when Percy Booker took over. During his time, Stacey presented plans for the extension of the hotel into the recently purchased building known as St Olaf's.

On 4 October 1940, an air raid destroyed four houses on the south side of Short Street, (as well as ye *Old(e) Victory*). Several members of the Harris family who resided at no 36 Middle Street (which stood on the corner of Short Street and Middle Street, the site now forming part of Middle Street car park) were tragically killed. The following spring, the body of a soldier was found on the roof of the

Clarendon while repairs were being carried out. He was identified as the son-in-law of the Harris family who had been present at the house on the day of the bombing the previous year.

According to a local newspaper report on 2 January 1969, a Royal Marine called Brian Reed was unfortunately killed in the lounge bar of the **Clarendon** in the early hours of New Year's Day.

In June 1969, it was reported that Molly Broadbent, wife of the landlord of the **Clarendon** who had been there for two years, had become the new Chairwoman of the DLVA's Ladies Auxillary.

Henry Brown was landlord from 1970 to 1977, during which time he was lauded for having created a first-class establishment and for running a most successful hotel and restaurant. (He retired to Rhodes where he died in 1992). Harry and Vera Fairclough, together with Frances Thorneycroft, were at the **Clarendon** from 1977, followed by Bernard Windsor in 1980, Joseph Quinn and Frances Thorneycroft in 1983, Anita Law later that year, Keith Davis in 1986, John Thompson and Colin Jones later the same year, John Thompson and Michael Ridley in 1987, John Thompson and Gaynor McHayle later that year, Frank Embleton and James Lewis in 1988 and Frank Embleton, James Lewis and William Flavell in 2001. Phil Bailey and Stephanie Eldridge became licensees in 2004 when they oversaw a £600,000 refit of the hotel, and they remained at the **Clarendon** until early 2010.

At the time of going to press, the 20 year lease was being offered by Shepherd Neame for £40,000 per year. However, the hotel remains open and boasts two bars, two restaurants and ensuite letting rooms. Live music is also a regular feature of this attractive establishment overlooking the beach.

Clarendon Tap

See entry for ye *Old(e) Victory*.

Clifton Hotel
(Clifton Inn, Redan), 102 (153) Middle Street, Deal

In 1851, no 153 Middle Street was leased to George Claringbold, and in 1857 the property was referred to as merely being a (residential) 'house'. However, by 1858, it had become a fully licensed alehouse called the **Redan**. It is thought to have been a public house before this date but no documentary evidence can be found to confirm this. It was also rumoured to have been a temperance hotel at some point but, again, nothing can be found to substantiate this.

William Peckham was landlord from 1858 until 1878. According to a Telegram report dated 1 June 1859, Edward Mummery, aged 14, was found guilty of robbing the landlord's till, and was sentenced to 14 days' hard labour in Sandwich Gaol.

In 1879, James White Parrett bought the property and re-fronted the outside wall. A local newspaper reported at the time: "*Anything that tends to be to the improvement of our town, we are pleased to notice, and the resuscitation of the old 'Redan' in its*

2009.

new form of the 'Clifton', in Middle-street, has arrested our attention. Mr Parrett, with an eye to the future, has rendered this place not only worthy of our passing notice, but by laying out the grounds at a great expense and has provided a place that our visitors will no doubt be quick to recognize".

Parrett placed the following advertisement in a local newspaper dated 22 July 1882: "*The Clifton Hotel. Broadway, Middle Street, Deal. Superior Accommodation for Visitors. Modern Prices. First Class Cuisine. Proprietor – J W Parrett.*"

Parrett later sold the **Clifton Hotel** to Messrs Nadler and Collyer, a Croydon based brewery (who remained the owners until at least 1921).

Charles Berringer was landlord in 1887 when an advert appeared in a local newspaper: "*Important Notice – Clifton Hotel & Gardens, Beach Street, Deal – Al Fresco Concerts. Prof Seammons begs to inform the public generally that he will open the above Gardens with a Company of London Artistes, on Monday next, July 31st, at 8 o'clock. For particulars, see bills.*"

In 1888, the premises were referred to in a local street directory as the "*Clifton Inn.*"

Other landlords included Frederick Wilson Hawkins in 1890, Frederick Coucher in 1891 and Harry Roper Russell from 1892 to 1893, by which time the property appears to have been referred to by its previous name once more. Russell placed the following advert in a local newspaper: "*H R Russell, Clifton Hotel, Middle Street and Beach Street, Deal. Family and Commercial House (Private Entrance in Beach Street). Lawn Tennis Court at the Disposal of Visitors. Spacious Hall for Public Dinners, Picnic Parties, Concerts, etc. Special Attention and Every Comfort. Dancing Saloon reopened. Good Stabling. H R Russell, Proprietor.*"

Later landlords included John Frederick Wright in January 1894, Annie Wright (Frederick's wife) in August 1894 until at least 1897, Henry Arthur Chappell in 1910 and William Robert Maker in 1911 to 1921 when the pub closed.

In 1922, the Mercury carried a lengthy article, entitled "*An Old Hostelry*", reminiscing about times at the **Clifton** which had "*closed at the end of last year*". It stated that: "*The Clifton, when Middle Street was a residential thoroughfare of importance, was one of the most commodious of residences in the* street. Townspeople of importance trod its sound old floorboards, and sunned themselves in its sizeable garden. Thick walls, plentiful wainscoting, ceilings with substantial beams, woodwork mouldings, cupboards like small rooms in all sorts of unexpected places, flooring of irregular widths but sound and seasoned timber, tell of a time long before the age of the jerry building, and when machine-made joinery was unknown."

The article continued: "Disused entrances lead from Coppen [sic] Street and from Beach Street into the grounds, where classic figures, a bandstand and a pavilion tell of a former proprietor's endeavours to provide for the entertainment and amusement of the visitors to this healthy and attractive watering place."

Further, that: "The **Clifton Hotel**, in pre-war (WWI) times, was the headquarters of the St George's Army Veterans' Association. In halcyon weather, heroes of sturdy fights foregathered on the lawn, and with a glass of pre-war brew as refresher, recounted deeds of derring do. Annually, on St George's Day, the veterans assembled around the festive board, with worthy Mr Ben Whitaker and the yet vigorous Mr Joseph Knight, of Indian Mutiny renown, as

c1900.

guests of honour, keeping up the comradeship of Service days, generally with Alderman Hayward, keen on the associations of St. George's Day, in the chair. Who, that was present on these occasions, will forget the gallant veteran Mr Knight singing of those far-off days of the Mutiny, when 60 years earlier he was helping to maintain the beneficent power of Britain in India. On the formation of the National Reserve the Clifton became the headquarters of the Deal Battalion, and many times the green in summer time, or the floor of the pavilion when daylight no longer served, were trodden by 'the feet of the men wot drill'. With the stirring day of August, 1914, the Clifton became busy as men of the National Reserve took once more the oath of service to the King, and enrolled for the defence of his dominions, menaced by a worse peril

than when the glint of the sun on the bayonets of Napoleon could be seen from our shores."

In 1921, Colin Rich and Sidney Leger bought the **Clifton Inn** and ran an antiques shop called the Old Redan there for the next three years. Together with mortgagee, Elizabeth Marshall, they sold the building in 1924 to Ernest Bruce Charles for £1,350. At the time of his purchase, Charles agreed a covenant with the vendors to prohibit a hotel, tavern or other place from selling intoxicating liquor on the premises. The document also showed a plan of the large garden to the rear that at the time contained a concert room and a right of way between nos 133 and 135 Beach Street. At some later date, Charles also bought these properties. The majority of the garden now belongs to Bruce House on Beach Street.

An Indenture dated 24 July 1924 stated that the brewery's four gentlemen tenants were partially released from the temperance order by Charles in order to allow the premises to be used by the British Legion as a club and that an excise licence should be held solely for their purposes. One of the tenants went by the splendid name of "*Edward Stanislaus Bulfin of Walmer, Kent, KCB, Lieut General in His Majesty's Army.*"

In 1928, Charles became "The Hon Sir Ernest Bruce Charles, CBE KStJ, resident of Bruce House."

In the 28 October 1999 edition of the Mercury, the late local historian, David Collyer, reported that, while workmen were carrying out alterations to the staircase of the property in June 1905, they saw an apparition of a lady, dressed in what appeared to be 18th century milkmaid apparel, walking through a blocked up doorway. The workmen fled and refused to return.

According to a recent owner, there is obvious evidence of an underground passageway in the cellar of the premises. She believes it led to a property in Coppin Street but that it was cemented up by HM Customs & Excise some time before her ownership.

The hotel is now a private house.

Cock (location unknown) "Deale"

This pub was mentioned in a 1680 list of "Deale" pubs. No location was given and information is untraceable.

Compasses (location unknown) "Deale"

As well as being for nautical use, compasses were also an heraldic symbol of carpenters. This pub was mentioned in the 1662 "Deale" Payments for Signs list, but no location was given. For this reason, it cannot be connected to the *Three*

Compasses in Beach Street since that was a much later establishment.

It is, however, possible that it was another name for the *Carpenters Arms* – later the *New Inn* – in the High Street – see separate entry.

Countries/Countreys/Countryes (location unknown) "Deale"

In Laker's History of Deal, he made mention of a letter from Admiral Byng to Mr Nicolas who was *"Secretary to the Duke"*. Part of it read: *"3 Julii 1626 – Deall Castle. I, understanding some of the campanye of that ship were at Countryes, an hostelry, sent them a civill message"*. This apparently referred to a Dutch ship in the Downs not saluting by lowering its flag when passing Walmer Castle.

In the Sandwich Borough Licensed Victuallers Recognizances list dated 26 May 1635, Richard Countrie was listed as *"Victualler of Deale"* at the premises known as '*Countryes*'. (Spellings of the surname and pub differed – see title above – as well as being spelt without an 'o' on other occasions).

In 1636, there were three unnamed wine taverns operating in Deal, one run by Mary Countrey, another by Susan Woodland and the third by Judith Hudson.

The last found mention of this name was in the 'Sea Valley of Deal': *"On September 6th, 1644, the Archbishop required one Mary Countrey, a widow (one of the squatters) to attorn tenant to him and accept a lease of a messuage and 18 perches of land being part of ye sea beach or Sea Valley situate and being upon ye sea beach of Lower Deale and part or parcel of ye waste belonging to ye Arch Bishopp of Canterbury, ye said messuage and premises being within ye Royalty of ye Mannors of Deale Prebend and Court Ash which belong to ye See of Canterbury."*

Crispin Inn
(28, 28a, 195) Middle Street, Deal

The first mention of this property when the address was known as no 195 Middle Street appeared in an 1847 local street directory, listing it as an unnamed beerhouse run by James Tuck. He was mentioned again in 1851 when his profession was given as *"Cordwainer"* (being an old fashioned term for a shoemaker). In 1862, he gave his occupation as *"Beer Retailer and Shopkeeper"*.

The property was sold to brewer, Morris Bowles Thompson, in February 1865 for £110, although James Tuck was still landlord there in 1869 when it was known as the *Crispin Inn* for the first time, St Crispin being the Patron Saint of shoemakers. In 1872, Elizabeth Tuck was registered as innkeeper and by 1878 her occupation was given as *"China Dealer."*

In 1879, the licence was transferred from Elizabeth Tuck to Alfred Goslett, followed in 1885 by James Henry Graves who gave his occupation as

"Wood and Coal Dealer". He was fined 20 shillings (£1), with 13 shillings (65p) costs, for *"unlawfully selling intoxicating liquor during prohibited hours."*

An Indenture dated 27 July 1894 was made between brewer *"John Matthews of Walmer Esq and Thompson & Son of Walmer"* in return for shares. Matthews agreed to sell property to include the freehold of *"all that messuage or tenement and public house known as the Crispin Inn in Middle Street."*

C Chapman was landlord between 1895 and 1898.

Albert Ashby became landlord in 1899 when he placed the following advertisement in a local newspaper: *"'Crispin', Middle Street. Noted House for Thompson's Ales and Stout. Splendid Burton on Draught. Bottled Ales and Stout 2/6 (12½p) per dozen. Families waited on daily for orders. Superior Vinegar 3d (1p) per quart. For pickling, 10d (4p) per gallon. Lovely Ketchup 3½d (1½p) per quarten.*

A Ashby, Proprietor". Ashby had left by 1903.

In November 1902, Daniel Smith was fined 2/6d (12½p) and 2 shillings (10p) compensatory costs for damaging a glass, a mantel board, an iron fender and a windowpane belonging to landlord, William Stacey. In February 1903, it was the landlord's turn to appear before the Court. Stacey was charged with permitting drunkenness on the premises and was fined 15 shillings (75p), with 10/6d (52½p) costs.

The pub closed on 28 December 1907. Thompson's sold to printer and stationer, Samuel Thomas Northey, of 35 High Street, Deal for £200 *"all that messuage formerly a public house known as the* **Crispin Inn** *but now known as 28 Middle Street"* (due to street renumbering). Northey died in 1929 and the property was left to his widow and son. It was then divided into two tenements, respectively known as nos 28 and 28A Middle Street, together with a garage and other building in Tucks Alley.

On 20 April 1959, Samuel Northey's son, JH Northey, sold to Deal Corporation for the sum of £450 *"all that piece of land being the site of two former tenements known as 28 and 28A Middle Street ... formerly described as the* **Crispin Inn.**"

That part of Middle Street came under heavy enemy attack during WWII so it is likely the buildings were damaged and demolished after the war, along with many other nearby properties, to create the Middle Street car park.

The inn stood on the south western corner of Middle Street and Tucks Alley. From looking at old plans, Tucks Alley appears to have been a fairly long and winding one and it is just possible (but cannot be confirmed) that part of it may still exist in the form of the alleyway running alongside the present day **Bohemian** public house in Beach Street. The site of the **Crispin Inn** consequently lies roughly behind the Quarterdeck, towards the centre of the Middle Street car park. Where other sections of Middle Street remain, situated at opposite ends of the car park (off Broad Street and King Street), it is still possible to determine the old line of Middle Street where it used to run past the site where the **Crispin Inn** once stood.

Crosskeys (location unknown) "Deale"

The only mention of this pub appeared in the 1668 Will of Joan Mumbray of Deal who left *"my part of the house called* **Crosskeys** *and £20 to my daughter Susan."*

The pub remains otherwise untraceable (although it is possible that it was the one which later became known as the **Watermans Arms**, 41 Beach Street – see separate entry).

Crown, Blenheim Road, Deal

See entry for the *Oak and Ivy*.

Crown, 236 & 238 Church Path
(1 & 2 Ivy Cottages, Stony Path/Gravel Walk), Deal

This pub was located close to the present-day junction with London Road in what had formerly been two cottages. Unfortunately, the **Crown** does not appear by name on any licensing records and therefore very little is known about it.

Exactly how long it was a pub is uncertain but it was one of four pubs called the **Crown** in Deal and Walmer. The earliest reference found about it was when it was mentioned in 1678 deeds as *"now and lately known as the* **Crown.**"

It seems that the property was sold by Thomas Woodruff in 1768 to *"William Gurney of Deal, Yeoman, heretofore known as the* **Crown** *and now untenanted"*. It was also registered as being untenanted in 1789.

The buildings are now private houses.   *2009.*

Crown (location unknown) Walmer

The only mention of this pub was in the Walmer Alehouse Keepers book of 1810 when Samuel Baker was landlord of *"the Crown in Walmer"* but no precise location was given.

Crown Inn, 138 (29) Beach Street, Deal

The **Crown Inn** was situated on the eastern side of Beach Street.

The pub was mentioned in documents dating back to 1680 and again in 1683 when Stephen Norrington, Carpenter, included his property *"near the sign of the Crown, North Deal"* in his Will.

c1900.

Esau Griffiths was installed in 1727 when he gave his occupation as *"Victualler"*. In 1746, John Wyborn was landlord of *"a messuage commonly called the Crown with outhouses and buildings"*. Alex Viles was listed as landlord in 1776 when his name appeared on the *"Refused to Billet Dragoons"* list.

Other landlords included Trevor Shrewsbury in 1823, Thomas Snoswell in 1826, Thomas Leach in 1828, Joseph Marsh in 1831, George Tanton in 1836 and William Singer in 1837. According to Hancock's Journal, in September 1838 there had been a *"very bad storm this past night. Many ships slipped to North. Erridge and Bailey in fair wind brought six from Jamaican to Crown"*. He also noted on 23 December 1838 that *"Crown full, beach full of coal."*

Hancock also wrote In 1838, *"Mr Elverly with Erridge and the two galley punts of the Crown stage took 140 casks of salted to transport."*

Later landlords included spinsters, Sophie and Ann Stupples in 1841, James Buttress later in 1841, Richard Thomas Adams in 1845, John Brown from 1847 to 1855, Charles Denne in 1856 and Richard Sharp in 1864. In 1875, the Mercury reported that the Apollo Harmonic Club held their first meeting at the **Crown**.

Edward Erridge was landlord in 1878, followed by Charles Redman in the late 1800s, RA Bullock in 1904 and JP Fish in 1908. The following year the pub was de-licensed and, in 1910 it was put up for auction but possibly did not sell at the time since it was eventually purchased by Deal Council in 1912 and later demolished.

The 1910 auction was advertised in the Mercury as follows: *"'The Crown' Inn, Deal. Messrs. West, Usher & Co. are instructed to Sell by Auction on Monday, 21st March, 1910, a quantity of Surplus House Furniture, Bar Fittings and Utensils, including iron French bedsteads, pilliasser, mattresses, feather beds, bolsters and pillows, dressing tables, mahogany and walnut marble-top washstands, chamberware, decorated bedroom suite, dressing tables, chests of drawers, and wardrobes, Windsor, cane, stuffed and spring-seat easy, and other chairs, couches, Kidder, Brussels and tapestry carpets, floorcloths, curtains, and curtain poles, pictures, and mantel glasses, in walnut and gilt frames, upright pianoforte in walnut case, antique mahogany sideboard, ditto dining, side and stand tables, Ping-Pong table top, mahogany bureau, walnut ditto with enclosure over, barometer in rosewood case, old pewter, hot water plates, and ditto well dish, china, glass, and earthenware, fenders and firesets, mahogany knee-hole pedestal writing table with 9 drawers, match-boarded cupboard, zinc panel meat safes, grained panel front return bar counter, sets of shelving, a quantity of stoneware bottles, ditto and china spirit barrels with brass taps, several spare ditto taps, pewter spirit and beer measures, corking machine, timber stillons, the usual kitchen utensils in tin, iron and earthenware, and numerous other articles. On View the Morning of Sale. Sale at Eleven o'clock. Further particulars may be had of the Auctioneers at the Deal Estates and House. Agency, Victoria Town, Deal."*

After its sale, the pub briefly became the Liberal Men's Reading Rooms before the building's demolition.

The site of the pub lies on the present day beach promenade, practically opposite the turning for Coppin Street.

Cutter Tavern

See entry for the **Deal Cutter**.

Dane John/Danejohn

See entry for the *Jolly Butcher*.

Deal Castle Inn
31 Victoria Road (7, 17 Prospect Place), Deal

The building would probably have been erected around 1750 as a private house initially. At the time, Victoria Road (or Prospect Place as it was known then) was a very busy thoroughfare and the main route into Deal from Dover.

According to the 1786 Poor Rate book relating to that part of Deal, Simon Amis was resident at *"Deal Castle"* but no actual address accompanied the entry. However, it is thought more likely that the record did indeed refer to the **Deal Castle Inn** rather than to Deal Castle itself, not least because he was mentioned there again, together with Joseph Cobb (probably from the local brewing company of the same name), paying £1 in rates in 1791. Also around this time, another directory notes he was resident at a property on the north-eastern corner of Gladstone Road (which may possibly have been a forerunner of the later **Deal Castle Inn**).

That being said, the first conclusive mention of the building being an inn was found in the 1803 Poor Rate book, as well as in a register belonging to Cobb's brewery for the same year which recorded landlord, Richard Piper,

c1897.

paying £10 per annum rent. In 1818, it was reported that The Lodge of Union no 44 and part of The Grand Lodge of Ancient Free and Accepted Masons of England held a meeting there with 15 members in attendance.

The inn was opposite the old naval dockyard and would have been a popular watering hole with its high-ranking employees, as well as with the local military. (The dockyard covered a large area in between the present day South Street, Prince of Wales Terrace, Deal Castle Road and the eastern side of Victoria Road. The dockyard was dismantled in the 1860s and large houses were erected and new roads laid out on its site, the area afterwards becoming known as Victoria Town).

Henry Appleton was landlord in 1821 and Elizabeth Appleton in 1824. By 1826, Stephen Watts was in charge, with Elizabeth Watts taking over by 1845, Mary

Elizabeth Parker in 1858, HC Solley in 1865 and Robert Redman in the early 1870s.

In 1874, a local newspaper reported George Pearce, landlord of the **Deal Castle Inn**, was charged with late opening, being caught out by the sharp eye of PC Shelvey Cox. By 1881, Pearce's registered occupation was given as '*Wheelwright and Licensed Victualler.*.

In 1886 Mr Fry, on behalf of Hills' brewery, exhibited a plan and elevation of what was described as a *"New Gin Palace"* to be constructed on the southern side of the **Deal Castle Inn**, in Castle Row (now Beaconsfield Road). Plans were approved, and a lengthy extension was subsequently built along the side of the house but no evidence can be found that it ever operated as a 'gin palace' as such. Indeed, it appears the extension was merely used as an extra bar area, at least latterly, for the existing inn.

In 1903, the licence was transferred from Frederick Bond Horncastle to T Valentine Hookham (who stayed until at least 1948). At around 1.30 one afternoon in 1944, a bomb fell in the back garden of the pub, partially demolishing nearby 6A Beaconsfield Road, with one fatality. A 1956 street directory for that year showed ALA Brooks as licensee.

A former customer described the pub in its latter years as being *"a lively, youngsters' place, with two bars on different levels."*

It is believed that the inn closed down in the first half of the 1960s since, in 1964, Thompson's brewery offered to sell the property to Deal Borough Council for road widening purposes (which were never carried out) and certainly, by 1966, no landlord was registered at the property.

The premises were converted into a private house. In more recent times, the old inn briefly found national fame when included as one of a number of properties available for sale in the East Kent area, featured in the Channel 4 television programme,

A Place in the Sun: Home or Away, in 2006. According to the presenter, the interior of the ***Deal Castle Inn*** once included a theatre.

Indeed, the authors were fortunate to see inside the property at the beginning of 2010. The current owners stated earlier visitors to the house some years before confirmed, that when they were children, the inn did indeed house a theatre. The authors were also shown a large bedroom on the first floor that could well have been the auditorium, while another room directly behind it was thought to house the stage and dressing room. The original landing door into this room intriguingly has a small square wooden peephole in the centre at eye level that can be pulled across to open or close it from the inside!

The downstairs hallway used to extend the whole length of the house and, of the many rooms (or former bars) that ran off it, there still remains intact a stripped wood panelled private snug bar, complete with period fireplace. This is sectioned off from the hallway behind a 'stable' door with original wood-panelled and glass partitions either side. The owners think this may have been a 'ladies only' bar since an internal window is set in the wall dividing the snug and the room behind it from where drinks could discreetly be served, without the need for the ladies to step out into the hallway. It may also have been used as a payments kiosk, not only because of its stable door but the fact that the room is located near the bottom of the staircase.

The property is still a private home and retains many of the old inn's fine original features.

Deal Cutter (Cutter Tavern) 169 (167) Beach Street, Deal

According to the Valuation List, William Marsh was the first known proprietor in 1804. In 1821, landlord, Richard Ladd Canney, and wife, Pleasant, were at the property and he was still listed there in 1828 (and 1832) when the premises were described in sales' particulars as *"all that messuage, tenement, outhouses, buildings, yard and ground as described in the sale of the Manor of Chamberlain's fee"*. Edward Iggulden bought the pub that year (after initially leasing the same in 1817), along with several other public houses in Beach Street. (Iggulden ran breweries in Lower Street – now the High Street).

In 1839 and then again in 1859, Mary Finnis was registered as landlady. A transfer of the licence from

Deal Cutter is to the left in this 2009 view.

the estate of the late Thomas Parker to John Miles took place in November 1876. In 1878, Charles Langley was described as being the *"Licensee of the **Cutter Tavern**, Upholsterer and Paper Hanger."*

Thomas Hornsby Finnis was resident in 1892 and listed as a *"Bathing Machine Proprietor"* and he was still there in 1906 when the house was delicensed. It later became known as the Selby Dairy. The pub is now a private house.

NB It should be mentioned that the house next door to the old pub currently bears the name of the 'Deal Cutter' but no evidence can be found to suggest that this building did, in fact, ever form part of the pub. (It was, however, registered as being an early incarnation of 'Catt's Restaurant', according to a 1915 street directory).

Deal Hoy, 16 Duke Street, Deal

A 'hoy' was a small boat, often rigged out as a sloop, which carried passengers and goods on fairly short journeys. The route of the Deal Hoy (after which the pub was named) was between Deal and London.

The very early origins of the pub are sketchy. The creation of Duke Street was completed by 1811, having been built on the gardens bought around 1798 from its former owner, "Duke Hayman and Basden", and the road having been stumped out in 1803. There were however already buildings in the surrounding area, including the nearby assembly hall which had been there since at least 1723 and which was unfortunately demolished in the 1960s.

An early map, circa 1804, showed the area in the hands of Samuel Ffasham Roby who also owned a brewery in Lower Street (now High Street) facing the turning for Farrier Street (later the site of the **Phoenix/Queens Arms**). There was another short-lived brewery on the same site owned by the Hayman brothers around the turn of that century (but which was only in existence for about seven years).

The first mention of the property by name was in 1836 when "*J Hayman of the **Deal Hoy***" (then a beerhouse) appeared on the Jury List, and his name was on it again in 1847. The pub was granted a full licence in 1848. In 1863, a local newspaper reported: "*Police Court – A soldier was charged with being found concealed in the house of Mr John Hayman, the "**Deal Hoy**", in Duke St, on the previous night, for an unlawful purpose. [Hayman was] Sentenced to 14 days' hard labour in Sandwich Gaol*". John Hayman appeared on the 1861 census as being aged 79, a widower and licensed victualler, living at the premises with his unmarried daughters, Sarah, 34, Caroline, 28, and Charlotte, 25.

In 1864, the licence was transferred to Charles Robert French and, in 1866, it was reported that: "*A fire broke out on the premises of Mr French, "**Deal Hoy**", Duke street, on Monday evening last. The cause of the conflagration is unknown, but it is supposed to have originated by some tobacco ashes having been dropped in the skittle alley, and, as that building is composed entirely of wood, which is coal-tarred, the fire quickly assumed alarming proportions. Assistance was soon on the spot, and the flames were got under control before much damage was done.*"

The description of the building being comprised entirely out of wood is probably misleading since it

seems more likely that the article was referring to the skittle alley alone (which was in a separate building at the rear of the premises).

In 1867, the unusually named Rattery Brown was landlord, having formerly been in charge at the **Maxton Arms** and the **Fawn** public houses. Later that same year, the licence was transferred to John Langley Cory who appears to have stayed until at least 1878. During the early 1870s, the pub was shown on an Ordnance Survey map as encompassing the next door property (now a private residence called Duke House), which was also occupied by the Hayman family.

Around this period, several changes of brewery ownership occurred, with Tomson & Wotton in 1868, Gillow & Wareham in 1871 and Baxter & Stapleton of Sandwich in 1883.

William Finnis was landlord in 1887, William J Grant in 1891 (whose occupation was given as a bricklayer's labourer), Frederick K William Coleman in 1898 and, later that year, George T Norris. In November 1905, landlord, John Edward Devereux was charged with stealing two gallons of whisky worth £1/17/6 (£1.87½). Devereux duly exited the pub and George T Norris returned as landlord later that year. By 1924, the brewery company had again changed to Gardner's Cask Ales. On George Norris' death in 1933, the licence was temporarily transferred to his son, William Worthington Hadley James Norris. Later that same year, it was again transferred to Mrs Maud Norris and, in 1935, she passed it on to Frederick Jackson. In 1938, JW Oates was landlord, followed in 1941 by Miss May Elizabeth Abbot.

Pictured – The Deal Hoy in 2010.

A protection order in favour of Roger Thomas Jones of Gardner's Ales was granted later that year when the pub closed. It reopened on 21 April 1944 with the advert: *"Old and new friends will be welcome. Proprietor: Roger T Jones, Gardner's Ales."*

Like so many other pubs, the **Deal Hoy** used to have a separate off sales bar – otherwise known as a 'jug and bottle' which was accessed via a door on the left of the building (and which probably closed down in the 1970s).

The landlord in 1955 was CE Curling and, from 1962 through to 1987, Eric Oatridge was in charge. According to Dover Magistrates' records, he was followed by Trevor Brett in 1987, Charles and Josephine Johnson in 1992, Stephen Williams in May 1993, Jeffrey M Lenham, Christopher Ball and Michelle Holmes in November 1993, SH Williams in 1994 and Jonathan Brown from 1995 to 1999. During this period, Jonathan Brown (who is currently landlord of the **Bohemian**) was ably assisted behind the bar by Lyn Clay (now Nicholls).

Michael Ormston appeared on the licence in September 2000, together with Bryan Mulhern in the October, B Mulhern and M Ormston in February 2001, Jeffrey M Lenham and ML Callaghan in March 2001 and Jeffrey M Lenham and Christopher J Ball from May 2001 to the beginning of 2009.

The pub is still open and is owned by Shepherd Neame. It is run by Gill Hawkes, a descendant of former landlord, John Hayman. Nowadays, the **Deal Hoy** comprises one modern openplan bar and award winning garden and terrace area, and is a very popular live music venue.

Deal Lugger
(possibly Grove Inn) 201 (183) Beach Street, Deal

A lugger was a very large boat that was built for strength, speed and seaworthiness. The **Deal Lugger** was a beerhouse, situated on the junction with North Street. The building was first mentioned in 1851, with Charles Spears in residence, although no pub name was given.

Daniel Jarvis was licensee in 1855, succeeded by Elizabeth Jarvis in 1858, Miss Finnis in 1862, James Norris in 1867 and George Edward Norris in 1866.

A local report from 1869 stated that Norris applied for a spirits licence on the grounds that he frequently had to get up in the middle of the night to serve men who had just come ashore, rendering it necessary for him to have some spirits in the house. However, the application was refused and, later that year, he was cautioned for opening during prohibited hours on a Sunday.

The 1871 census showed *"Harriet Norris, widow"* as landlady, with Robert Dawes Smith in 1874, followed by Grove Ralph Norris in 1876. An 1880 Mercury report stated: *"Harry Meredith, 13, stole 12 shillings* (60p) *from Grove Ralph Norris of the **Deal Lugger**. He pleaded guilty to stealing 7/6d* (37½p) *but not 12/-* (60p)". 21 days' hard labour and 12 strokes of the birch rod ensued.

On 24 1886, the following advert appeared in a local newspaper: *"Notice to Brewers and others. To be sold at Auction, by George West – A very eligible Leasehold Ale or Public House called The **Deal Lugger** at the North end of Beach Street Deal in the occupation of Mr Norris. The property is held under lease from His Grace, the Archbishop of Canterbury for 21 years commencing September 1851 at the rent of 1/7d (8p)."*

During its later years, the pub's customers were described as being *"labouring classes and boatmen"*. Other landlords included William Browning in 1888, James Folwell in 1889, Margaret Folwell in 1890 and Richard Petty Brown also in 1890. 1891 saw a licence transfer from William Greenstreet to Amos Allen, followed by Thomas Selth in 1901, Richard Thompson in 1905 and GR Erridge in 1906 when the house was de-licensed. (Erridge then went on to become a long-serving landlord at the **Prince Albert**).

The **Deal Lugger** was another casualty of the strict licensing laws brought into force in the early 1900s.

See also entry for **Grove Inn**.

The pub is now a private house.

2009.

Deal Lugger
6 (19,10) Farrier Street, Deal

The *Deal Lugger* beer shop was the first house south side, situated east of the junction with Middle Street.

The first mention of the property was probably in 1832 when Richard Robinson, *"Retailer of Beer"*, was registered as living at an unknown address in the vicinity. Interestingly, the house always held just a beer 'off' licence, despite many applications for an 'on' licence.

In 1841 and 1849, Stephen Thompson was listed as being resident of no 10 Farrier Street and in 1851 and 1855, his address was given as 19 Farrier Street, the change of numbers being due to street renumbering.

c1960.

2010.

Numerous other proprietors followed and, by 1898, the aptly named Miss Firkins was in residence.

Around 1922, the *Deal Lugger* beerhouse appeared by name at that address for the first time, with William Frederick Chinnock in occupation. Before then, it was locally known as "the beer shop without a sign". William Allaway followed in 1924. It was still trading as the *Deal Lugger* beerhouse (despite still not being able to sell beer 'on' the premises) in 1935 and, two years later, it was called the *Deal Lugger* Off Licence and General Store, still with William Allaway as proprietor. The licence was transferred from Mrs M Crawford to landlord of the *Mill Inn*, Andrew Morgan, in June 1952. He continued at the *Mill Inn* and his son and daughter-in-law managed and lived at the *Deal Lugger*. The business carried on until 1966 when Mr H Sissons was registered at the premises.

The property is now a private house.

Deal Shallop, Deal

See entry for the *Red Lion*, Deal.

Dogg, Deal

See entry for the *Poor Dog*.

Dolphin (exact location unknown) Beach Street, Deal

There are several explanations as to why this pub was so called (as well as all the other pubs of the same name in the area). Most obvious, of course, was in celebration of the friendly sea creature beloved of mariners over the centuries.

Another possibility is that it was called after a ship of that name. Other explanations include the fact that a figure of a dolphin appeared on the coats of arms of (among others) both the Company of Watermen and Lightermen, as well as the Fishmongers' Company (so the pub could have been a place where they met); also, that Dauphin (French for 'dolphin') was once a common surname in both France and England (as well as being the title for the heir to the French throne); not to mention that a dolphin was also a battering ram, as well as a wooden breakwater, a mooring post on a beach and furthermore a type of harbour buoy. It really is a case of take your pick!

Very little is known of this pub but it first appeared in the *'Refused to Billet Dragoons'* (see page 10) List of 1776 when T Mackney was landlord. Despite this, he was made a Freeman of Deal on 21 November of that year. The *Dolphin* was likely to have been a very small pub and probably run by Mackney as a secondary occupation.

Dolphin, 36 High Street (Lower Street), Deal

See entry for the *Strand*.

Dolphin (Good Woman)
97-105 Gladstone Road (Rope Walk), Walmer

The *Dolphin* was situated on the corner of Gladstone Road (formerly called 'Rope Walk') and North Barrack Road.

A map of 1810 showed a brewery on the site. According to the Alehouse Keepers' Book (1805-1825), Thomas Baker was landlord at the *Good Woman* in 1811. (A 'good woman' at the time was considered by men to be one who kept quiet, especially where the exploits of local smugglers perhaps were concerned).

In 1835, Jessie Smith (landlord of the *Royal Standard*) was found drowned in a well at the *Good Woman*.

According to a report in the early 1860s, two soldiers robbed Mark Dixon, a vendor of faggots, near the *Good Woman*, at the back of the North Barracks.

In 1862, James Coleman was landlord and cowkeeper at the pub.

c1950.

In February 1864, William Rose, 31, an itinerant singer, was charged with stealing a sheet and blanket from Mrs Collis at the *Fountain Inn*. The ever-vigilant PC Shelvey Cox found him in possession of the items at the *Good Woman*. Rose was given one month's hard labour at Sandwich Gaol.

The *Good Woman* changed its name in 1866 to the *Dolphin*, with Charles Read taking over until at least 1876. By 1878, William Bullen was landlord until 1908 when he retired to Cheltenham and his son, Victor A Bullen, took over. William died in 1912 and local solicitors, Brown & Brown, placed an advert in the Mercury on 30 October inviting any of his creditors and claimants to come forward. The *Dolphin* was advertised for auction the same year, giving an interesting description of the premises:

"The Dolphin Inn – old-established and fully-licensed free public house – together with the

adjoining extensive stores, stabling and garden ground. *The house is substantially brick and tile built, and contains 3 bedrooms, sitting room, smoking room, private and public bars, bar-parlour, the usual domestic offices and cellar, together with two large stores. Three-stall stable and coach-house and excellent enclosed garden which has a building frontage to Gladstone Road of about 54-feet, and a depth of 115-feet, more or less … at the exceedingly low rental of £30 per annum."*

No evidence of a sale can be found but, in 1913, the inn was mentioned in Pain's Directory as having W Hayden (Sergeant KCC) as landlord. Other later landlords included Robert Ernest Grace throughout the 1920s, Percy Jackson in 1934, Sidney George Rook in the 1940s, CR Barnes in 1956 and W Heaton in 1966.

Mr John Rogers, the father of author, Michael Rogers, recalls that, in the 1920s when Mr and Mrs Grace were in charge, the private bar was just a narrow passage, with a bench seat either side. The large public bar was to the left which was always well patronised. There were large and gruesome pictures hanging on the wall showing Chinese bandits on their knees with their hands tied behind their backs, together with other ones showing the bandits decapitated with their heads beside them!

On 15 January 1970, the Mercury reported that landlords, Edith and Kenneth Southam, had pulled their last pints the previous week. They retired after having served at the pub for 10 years, three as managers and seven as tenants. A very popular place with young people, it had unfortunately attracted a certain amount of trouble in its latter years, probably not helped by the fact that the pub had been famed for serving very strong Scrumpy cider. (At one point, it was locally dubbed "the Cider House"). Regulars were apparently not told in advance of its closure and only found out the news when they saw the pub boarded up. Charrington's, the owners, took the opportunity to close the pub for good and the building was subsequently demolished.

Private houses now mark the site.

Dover Castle
177-178 (176) Middle Street, Deal

Edward Robinson was landlord of an unnamed beerhouse at 176 Middle Street in 1847, with James Redsull, beerhouse keeper, in 1851.

By 1858, the first known reference to the house as the *Dover Castle* appeared when two women were charged with fighting in the pub.

A court report dated 9 February 1859 stated that landlady, Sarah Selth, appeared in court to give evidence against the theft by some soldiers. It appears that a *"Mrs Wately of 5 Market Street charged a soldier with being found in her house in the middle of the night. The back of her house opened into a shared passageway leading to Sharp's Alley, and the back gate of a public house called the Dover Castle opened into the same alley, very close to hers."*

In 1861, Thomas Sutton was fined 10 shillings (50p) and 4/6d (12½p) costs for opening during the hours of divine service.

Due to street renumbering, it is hard to place the *Dover Castle*'s exact location. However, it was situated somewhere south of Sharps Alley, among the terrace of houses numbered between 60 and 66 Middle Street that we see today.

2009.

Druids Arms
(Cinque Port Arms) 2/4 (12-13) Market Street, Deal

Site of Druid's Arms in 2009.

Formerly known as the **Cinque Port Arms** in 1866, the Order of Druids regularly met there and, in 1867, it became known as the **Druids Arms** on a licence transfer to Stephen Reader.

1869 saw William Browning, "**Druids Arms and Ginger Beer Manufacturer**" resident at 12 Market Street. His stay would be a lengthy one – until 1901 – when, according to Julie Deller in her article in Bygone Kent, Volume 15 – 'Death at The **Druids Arms**'- "*he became ill with worry and depression, having broken his leg two years previously, and was unable to carry on his boat business and money was short. Regrettably, he was found dead in the outside water closet of the pub, having hanged himself*". The inquest recorded a verdict of suicide while temporarily insane.

Thereafter, the pub had numerous landlords including JR Hayward in 1904 and a Mr Jennings in 1908. The pub was under the ownership of Thompson's brewery when it closed down on 2 May 1908.

The building later enjoyed a period as The Druids Supper Rooms. In 1923, Mr JP Catt was listed as owner. The rear of the property was damaged by shelling in WWII and in 1948 the premises were demolished and the business had moved to nearby premises on the corner of King Street and Middle Street until the 1960s. In the 1950s an extension to the restaurant was built on the Druids Arms site, the top floor of which is now home to the Royal British Legion.

Drum
(203) Dover Road (Drum Hill), Walmer

The first documentation of an inn being found on this site dates back to 1541. The earlier inn would have been rebuilt and added to over the ensuing years. According to local legend, the pub (and, indeed, the earlier road name) eventually acquired its name as a reminder of the days when from a drum was pounded along the road every morning, summoning workers to nearby Walmer Castle which was then in the process of being constructed (in between 1540 and 1542).

c1960.

In 1643, Thomas Willington and/or Ben Couper were resident at the address, followed by Jacobus Neale in 1664 (when the property was owned by local brewer, Thomas Ffasham), Julia Cranbrooke in 1674, Ursula Cranbrooke in 1681, Mary Parsons in 1685 and Robert Burnville from 1705 to 1724 (during whose time the **Drum** had apparently acquired its name, although Sandwich Licensing records are unfortunately sketchy, often not mentioning pubs by name at all).

c1920.

Later landlords included John Rickman from 1766 until 1797, Charles Holbrook from 1797 to 1803, Jessie Smith in 1804, Charles Marsh junior in 1807, John Raynor in 1839, Elizabeth Raynor until 1860 when Stephen Huxstep took over, followed by Henry Huxstep in 1866.

In 1867, William Robert Minter, a *"Fly Proprietor"*, became landlord. In 1881, he was charged with assaulting William Browning Lumley and was fined £2 plus costs. The pub was rebuilt and then relicensed in 1897. Lumley remained at the **Drum** until 1898, although the pub stayed in the Minter family until its closure.

It was reported on May 1 1969 that William Minter, the former landlord of the **Drum** who had retired the previous year when the pub shut prior to demolition, died at his home in William Pitt Avenue. He had taken over the place from his mother during WW2 and ran it with his wife, Florence, together with Minter's Taxis which also operated from the pub. WE Minter took over the licence of The Drum in September 1951 following the death of Mrs EJ Minter. He commented at the time of closure he was glad the pub was *"coming down"* since it would not have been the same without a Minter in charge!

The site of the pub lies roughly opposite Walmer Castle Road. Local people still describe that part of Dover Road, in between Salisbury and Walmer Castle Roads, as "Drum Hill."

c1920.

c1960.

Drum Major, Deal

See entry for the *Cambridge Arms*.

Dukes Head, Deal

See entry for the *Lord Nelson*, Deal.

Duke of Norfolk, Norfolk House
67 Cornwall Road (Cornwell Road, New Road), Walmer (Hamilton Road) (Cemetery Road), Deal

The *Duke of Norfolk* enjoyed a very brief, yet somewhat confusing, history! According to 1874 and 1878 directories, Patrick Harris, fresh from his comings and goings at the nearby *Duke of York* pub which was located in Cemetery Road, opened a new pub called the *Duke of Norfolk* (not to be confused with the *Norfolk Arms* in Deal where another landlord called Harris was installed) also in Cemetery Road (now known as Hamilton Road), Deal.

The boundaries between Deal and Walmer changed slightly with the coming of the railway, and, in 1879, the *Duke of Norfolk* was recorded as being situated at a new address in New Road/Cornwell Road (now known as no 67 Cornwall Road), Walmer. The last mention of the *Duke of Norfolk* was recorded in 1883.

It is either just a case of the address for the same building altering after the boundary changes (which could well be the case given that the present day Cornwall and Hamilton Roads run into one another,

Most recently the building has been a shop called Methuen & Son. 2009.

divided as they are by the railway bridge), or, alternatively, that the pub did actually move locations.

The following appeared in a local newspaper dated 9 August 1884: *"John Shelvey, now residing at Norfolk House, situated in the New Road in the parish of Walmer, grocer and bricklayer, do hereby give notice that it is my intention to apply at the general annual meeting to be held at Guildhall, Sandwich for the Parish of Walmer, on the 1st September next for a licence to hold an excise licence to sell by retail beer to be consumed of the house, shop and premises, known as Norfolk House, of which Mary Jane Smith was the present owner".* It is not documented whether or not his application was successful.

The exact location of the first *Duke of Norfolk* pub in Hamilton Road is unknown (if, indeed, it ever was on a different site). The pub's second address is now a shop called Methuen & Son situated at Norfolk House, Norfolk Terrace, 67 Cornwall Road, Walmer.

Duke of Wellington, 11 Water Street, Deal

Arthur Wellesley, the Duke of Wellington, held the post of Lord Warden of the Cinque Ports, and died at Walmer Castle in 1852.

In 1847 John Reynolds was resident at an unnamed beerhouse in Water Street. By 1851 (when the property was owned by Thomas Brown), Reynolds' occupation was listed as *"Cordwainer"* and by 1862 he was registered as *"Beer Retailer and Shoemaker"*. He was still serving there in 1875, by which time the beerhouse was known as the *Duke of Wellington*. Charles William Spears was landlord in 1877, followed by William Robert Betts in 1878, Robert Batchell in 1880 when local brewer, John Hatton, owned the house, Charles Scovell in 1886, Alfred Philpott in March 1887 and James Elson later that year.

2009.

The *Duke of Wellington* was granted a licence to sell wine and beer in 1893. In 1897, Edward Chandler was landlord, Frederick Russell, who was listed as a *"Wine and Beer Retailer"*, in 1905 and 1909 (when the brewery company was Leney & Sons), Francis James White in 1910, William Upton in 1913, and Mrs M Upton up until 1932 when the licence was transferred to Richard Marsh, a former First Class Petty Officer in the Royal Navy. W Soole was landlord from 1944 when the pub gained a full licence owing to the post war grain shortage, followed by Harry Dean in 1949 (around which time

the 'Winkle Club' operated from the premises – see below), Mrs K Dean in 1953, J Wheland in 1955, Stanley Wells in 1960 and FW Greatorex in 1966.

(The 'Winkle Club' advertised a *"A Day Flight from Lympne Airfield"* in September 1950, to include lunch at Hythe and tea in Rye. The flight was to leave Deal at 8.30am, returning home at 11.30pm).

The *Duke of Wellington* was by all accounts a small but lively pub, especially on a Saturday night when the pianist started playing. It closed down around 1971 and is now a private house.

Duke of Wellington

See entry for the *Stag*.

Duke of York (exact location unknown)
The Strand(Walmer Road), Walmer

This pub is mentioned as being situated *"in the Parish of Walmer"* with Thomas Carter as landlord in 1807. James Hoile was registered as landlord in 1823, followed by Sarah Hoyle (different spelling) in 1829 when the location of the pub was given as Walmer Road.

Duke of York
80 Hamilton Road (Cemetery Road), Deal

The first mention of this building was in 1865 with Elizabeth Parsons in residence, and, although it was owned by the executors of local brewer, Mr C J Hills, it did not appear to have become a pub by that time.

In 1867, John Weston was successful in applying for a full licence on the understanding that the house must be properly conducted or the licence would not be renewed.

2008.

He died later that year and, in January 1868 his widow transferred the licence to Patrick Harris who in turn transferred it to William Crofts in 1869. In September that year, the licence was withheld following complaints of the house being badly conducted.

The 1871 saw Patrick Harris resident again, listed

as *"Manager of Music Hall"*, aged 41. In January 1873, Harris then transferred the licence to auctioneer, Morris Langley. In 1875, Langley transferred the licence back to Harris again.

By 1877, the house was reported as having been *"empty for one year"* and was refused a licence by magistrates. However, in September 1878, an off licence was granted for the purpose of serving railway workmen, with a Mr Horton in charge. In July 1879, John Thomas, foreman of a gang under Mr Walker, a railway contractor, was proprietor.

By the 1890s, a row of houses attached to the former pub building had been called Duke of York Cottages. Cemetery Road was renamed Hamilton Road in 1952. The building is now a private house.

Dunkerleys (Pier Hotel, Sandwich Arms, Fairfax)
9 (21, 73, 90) Beach Street, Deal

c1920.

The present day *Dunkerleys* comprises two originally separate buildings now brought together under one roof.

A pub called the *Fairfax* stood on the site from round about 1661 to 1698.

The right hand side of the building was originally a grocer's shop (as well as probably being an unnamed beer shop), according to the 1841 and 1851 censuses. It later became a public house called the *Sandwich Arms* and was fully licensed by 1861. In 1871, the pub changed its name to the *Pier Hotel*. Numerous landlords included John Edward Lawrence in 1861 to 1870 (as the *Sandwich Arms*), and, (after name change to the *Pier Hotel*), William Harry Hayman in 1870.

In June 1878, Daniel Frederick Kirkaldie and Simon Pritchard, boatmen, were fined £5 each for annoying, and using threatening language towards, the landlord, William Hayman.

There followed John William Spicer in 1880, George Edwardes Startup in 1886, Maria Louisa Abbott in 1889, James Holbrook in 1891, Edward

Walter Chittenden in 1891, Thomas Nash from 1904 to at least 1910, WG Parmenter in 1915 and MA Collins in 1924. That same year, Ellen Charlotte Mercer, a *"regular customer"*, was ejected from the pub for being drunk and disorderly.

Louis William Welton took over in 1924 (until 1944) and it was during his landlordship there that the hotel was rebuilt in 1926. He also held a licence in the 1930s for the nearby *Roxborough Castle* pub – see separate entry – which he often used as an annexe for the *Pier Hotel* (which was owned by Thompson's brewery at the time).

Other landlords included H Hargreaves in 1948, P Sitton in 1953, HF Brookes in 1955 and JE Stewart in 1966. According to Dover Magistrates' records, there followed Richard H Neale in 1971, Alan Evans in 1980, Kenneth Attfield in April 1982, Petros and Catherine Kavrazoni in December 1982, Jean Ivy Radcliffe and Margaret Ann Branch in 1985 who were joined on the licence in 1989 by James Branch, John and Jean Ivy Morgan from 1992 together with Catherine Corbett and Michael Reilly in 1994.

In June 1987, Ian Dunkerley (who had previously been the proprietor of the restaurant above the *Cambridge Arms* – see separate entry) bought the building in Beach Street (which now comprises the restaurant of *Dunkerleys*) when it was called the Pegasus restaurant/café. Jim and Margaret Branch, landlords of the *Pier Hotel*, opened a steakhouse and restaurant on their premises.

2010.

On 2 May 1997, Ian Dunkerley reopened the *Pier Hotel* as the Bistro Bar and announced that the hotel would include an additional 10 bedrooms by the following year, bringing the total up to 16. The old

Pier Hotel now houses *Dunkerleys'* front bar and that part of the building siding onto Broad Street.

Now all under the same roof, *Dunkerleys* today remains one of Deal's finest dining establishments, specialising as it does in fresh fish and seafood dishes and overseen by Ian and his wife Linda.

The bar is a comfortable one for those just wishing to pop in for a drink before or instead of their meal in the restaurant next door. It also boasts occasional live piano or other music, but never so loud as to spoil the enjoyment of the diners or indeed the overnight guests in the bedrooms upstairs.

Local newspaper report of Petty Sessions held in May 1884 headed:

"Drunk While in Charge of a Horse and Cart. William Perrin appeared to answer the charge of being found drunk in Queen-street while in charge of a horse and cart. Perrin said he could not have been very drunk as he had only drunk three half pints of beer besides what he had had for breakfast. He had been in the habit of coming to Deal … for 50 years, and hoped to be leniently dealt with. Discharged on payment of 10/- (50p)."

Eagle (Beehive) 52 Queen Street (4) (Upper Queen Street/Queen Street West), Deal

c1920.

Previously called the *Beehive*, the *Eagle* is situated on the approach road to Deal railway station and is supposedly haunted by two ghosts. It could have also previously been the location of one of the many 'lost' pubs of Deal where precise addresses are unknown and that are mentioned by name only throughout this book. The *Beehive* was previously sited on the *White Horse* site a few doors away before moving along when the *White Horse* opened in 1849. It was in this particular part of town that many old malt houses were sited.

It has been suggested by the *Eagle*'s own potted history that the date of the present building is 1704 but the authors are unable to confirm this one way or the other.

Originally an unnamed beerhouse in the 1830s and in 1847 when Mr Redman was resident, it was known as the *Beehive* beerhouse by 1851 according to the census of that year, having moved along and occupying the site which would soon become known as the *Eagle*.

The first known landlord of what had by then become the *Eagle* was Stephen Pritchard in 1854, the same year the pub became fully licensed. Pritchard also owned many of the aforementioned malt houses. (He remained at the pub until around 1882).

According to a contemporary local newspaper report, the 74th Anniversary Dinner of the Society of Enlightened Cottagers was held at the *Eagle* on 27 January 1868. *"This excellent institution is the only one we are aware of now in existence, and is of very ancient origin. Several of the present members have been connected with this society upwards of 40 years, and from the increase of its members, it will continue to exist for many years longer.".*

Edward Law Bridger was

c2006.

landlord from 1882. In December 1886, thanks to *"the liberality of the Tradesmen and gentry of Deal and Walmer"*, the employees of Deal Railway Station were wined, dined and entertained at their Annual Supper held at the *Eagle*. *"The manner in which the supper was served reflects great credit upon the worthy hostess (Miss Hubble) and also upon our friend, Capt. Spicer"* (a former landlord of the *Pier Hotel* – see entry for *Dunkerleys*).

Thomas White Collard took over in May 1886, followed by Esther Hubble in August 1886, Charles Maltby in 1887, Jonathan Coleman in 1890, Walter Padbury in May 1891, Julia Ann Hollands in July 1891, Julia Ann Groombridge to Edwin Groombridge in 1894, Charles Edward Gray from 1897 to at least 1915, John Mockett in 1922, Alfred Thomas Tyler from 1934 to 1938, Wilfred Martin (of George Beer & Rigden) in 1941 and Ethel A Fittall from 1944 (until 1974). On 8 January 1970, the Mercury reported that Hungarian, Andras Ofscak, was sentenced to four years in jail for breaking into three public houses in the local area, including the *Eagle* (the other two being the *Rising Sun*, Kingsdown and the *Swan*).

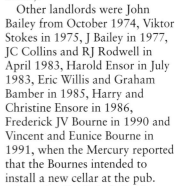

Other landlords were John Bailey from October 1974, Viktor Stokes in 1975, J Bailey in 1977, JC Collins and RJ Rodwell in April 1983, Harold Ensor in July 1983, Eric Willis and Graham Bamber in 1985, Harry and Christine Ensore in 1986, Frederick JV Bourne in 1990 and Vincent and Eunice Bourne in 1991, when the Mercury reported that the Bournes intended to install a new cellar at the pub.

Later landlords included J Walsh and S Morkan in 1999, JA Wardle and AE Ferris in 2001, and James and Rosemary Collins from 2005 until the present.

The *Eagle* remains open to this day, complete with cosy open plan bar and rear patio area.

Eagle (location unknown) Deal

There was an Eagle public house in Deal mentioned in Laker's list of inns in 1680 but, other than this reference, nothing more can be found about the pub.

Eagle & Child (location unknown) Deal

The only mention of this pub by name was in the 1677 Sandwich Recognizances records for Deal, but otherwise remains untraceable.

East India Arms

See entry for the *India Arms*.

Empire (Paragon, Star, Two Brewers) 164 (80) Middle Street, Deal

Originally a pub called the *Two Brewers*, it publicised its cock fighting in a 1770 edition of the Kentish Gazette. William Hubbard was licensee between 1797 and 1804 and it was around this time that the pub was renamed the *Star*. Henry and Mary Hubbard were landlords in 1815 and 1817, followed by William Kennett in 1828, Ann Kennett from 1832 to 1840, Thomas and Edward Kennett in 1846, Henry Philip Kennett in 1847, Thomas Castle in 1848, George Hinds in 1849, Robert Harvey in 1853, Frederick Mills in 1859, Edmund Ashdown in 1860, Alfred Howe in January 1863, Thomas Parker in September 1863 and John Weston in 1865.

2006.

According to the late Les Cozens in his regular *Not a Lot of People Know That* column of the Mercury dated 27 November 1997: *"It was always of dubious character, and the Royal Marines were, at one time, banned from it. In 1866, the landlord of the 'Star' appeared before the Bench to answer the complaint of an 'unfortunate' who said she had been unable to obtain possession of articles given to her. She was accompanied by one or two 'frail sisters'. The landlord said the girls were his servants."*

According to Les Cozens, James Elson applied for and was granted a licence in 1871, despite the fact that he had brought with him four or five known prostitutes from Ramsgate.

However, he denied this and said two of the girls would be performing on stage and the other three would be house servants. The pub had become known as the *Paragon* Music Hall by 1876 and Elson remained there until at least 1882.

A local advertisement of the time publicised: *"Paragon Music Hall, Middle Street, Deal, Proprietor ... Mr J Elson. The only place in Deal to enjoy an Evening's Entertainment. Grand Shadow Pantomime, Monday next and during the Week. Pantomimists: Clown, Mr JO Keef. Pantaloon, Mr H Bernard. Harlequin, Mr Patrick Gill. Columbine, Miss Ada Graham. Harlequina, Miss Sarah Elson. First appearance of Miss Nellie Courtney, Serio-Comic Singer and Dancer. Manager ... Mr H. Bernard. Pianist ... Miss Corie. Hall Keeper ... Mr W. Parker. No boys under 16 admitted. Strict attention to Garrison time. Doors open at 6; commence at Half-past. Admission, 2d (1p). Front seats, 4d (2p). Balcony, 6d (2½p). Boxes, 1s (5p). A Private Box to accommodate Eight Persons, 5s (25p); apply before Six o'clock."*

Joseph Owen took over in 1877, followed by Henry Cracknell in 1878, James Elson (again) in

1886, Henry Pearce in January 1888 and Sarah Eyres in September 1888 until 1899, by which time the *Paragon* had changed its name to the *Empire* Theatre of Varieties. John Owen became landlord in July 1899 and, in March 1900, the *Empire* was refused an extension to raise money for the Unemployed Artists Benevolent Fund.

The *Empire* closed its doors for the last time in 1903 under the landlordship of Mr May. Magistrates ordered Thompson's brewery to give up its licence that year on the *Empire*, together with that of another of its pubs, the *Lord Nelson* in Short Street, so that a new licence could be granted in advance for the prospective construction of Thompson's new pub, the *Telegraph* in Cemetery Road (now Hamilton Road).

The building was later used as leisure and reading rooms in 1908, McLuskie's Billiards Hall in 1928 and a social and billiards club in 1934 and 1935. Throughout WWII, the building was empty, after which it was briefly a dairy and is now a private house.

Endeavour
Dover Road, Walmer

This pub was fleetingly mentioned in Langridge's researches in 1977 but the authors have unfortunately been unable to find out any other information about it.

Exchange
(exact location unknown) Beach Street, Deal

The Exchange Beer Shop was located on the eastern side of Beach Street, close to the present-day pier. Leases for the property ran from 1768. 1840 saw Charles Minter resident and his occupation was given as 'pork butcher and milkman.'

The only mention of the property ever being licensed premises was in an 1841 lease: *"Henry Trott, Exchange Beer Shop. A slaughterhouse and kitchen adjoining and communicating in brick, weatherboard and tile, etc."*

In 1845, the powers that be decided to widen Beach Street along this stretch since the road was considered to be *'narrow and dangerous'* there and the premises were therefore demolished.

The site has since been covered by the beach promenade.

Local newspaper report from June 1865 headed:

"Drunk and Stupid. As PC Horton was on duty in Broad Street two or three evenings since, he fell in with a soldier nearly in a nude state, having neither shoes, stockings, trousers, cap or belt – his only covering being a shirt upside down with the sleeves hanging down behind, and a jacket, through the sleeves of which he had thrust his legs."

Fairfax, 19 Beach Street, Deal

This pub was situated on the site of the present day **Dunkerleys**. In 1661, the property was leased to Ann Bowen. By 1680, she had died and John Bowen was lessee. The **Fairfax** was mentioned in the Deal Tenements book of 1698.

See also entry for **Dunkerleys**.

Farrier, "Deale"

Only two mentions of this pub could be found, the first appearing in the 1662 "Deale" Payments for Signs list with Finnigan Waltham as landlord and the second in the records of St Leonard's which read: "*Account spent at the Farrier, marrying Ann Cook and Lester, stayed up all night. 5/6d* " (27½p). These references could possibly relate to the **Farriers Arms** – see entry for the **Admiral Keppel**.

Farriers Arms

See entry for the **Admiral Keppel**.

Fawn (White Posts Inn) 33 College Road (74 Lower Street), Deal

The **Fawn** public house was probably so called after the loss of four boatmen and a Deal lugger by the same name in 1864. Certainly the pub was called the **Fawn** by the following year. 'The Fawn' was run down by a colliery steamer called Biddjet that had been on its way home to Sunderland from a delivery to Bordeaux. It was rumoured that 'The Fawn' had been taking part in a smuggling trip at the time of the tragedy.

c1955.

Money for the boatmen's widows and orphans was subsequently raised by means of a grand concert held at the Assembly Rooms in Deal.

The title deeds apparently refer to this property as previously being called the **White Posts Inn** in 1645 but the authors have unfortunately been unable to have sight of the deeds themselves.

The next documentation of the property being licensed premises was when Rattery Brown was landlord in 1862. His occupation was listed as "*Beer Retailer and Pig Dealer*" and he had previously been landlord at the **Maxton Arms**. In 1869, Brown was summonsed for opening on a Sunday. He told the court that the pub's clock was wrong and, anyway, he was not at home at the time of the incident. Nevertheless, he was found guilty and fined 2/6d (12½p) with 7/-

(35p) costs. Brown remained at the pub until at least 1875 since James Bentley appeared on the registers from 1876 to 1879.

Later on in 1879, Joseph Redsull took over as landlord. This heralded a long stay for the Redsull family at the **Fawn**. He was followed by Elizabeth Angela Redsull in 1895, Mrs A Redsull in 1904 and William Ashby Redsull in 1915. The pub was a Thompson's house at the time.

In February 1916, William Redsull found himself in trouble concerning new regulations issued by the Central Board of Liquor Control since his niece, Ada Jordan, had been delivering bottles of ales and stout without the appropriate delivery book or invoice and was also making deliveries "*out of permitted time*". However, the case was eventually dismissed.

Frederick Avery took over from William Redsull in 1938. According to Pain's street directory, WE Atkins was registered landlord at the pub in 1948 and 1955. (It became fully licensed during this period when the **Fawn** was owned by Charrington's). In August 1963, the Mercury reported that the pub had recently closed.

The **Fawn** is now a private house.

Field Marshal Blucher

See entry for the *Shield of Marshall Blucher.*

Fishing Boat

See entry for the *Shah.*

Five Bells, Golf Road, Deal

See entries for the *Hare & Hounds, Deal.*

Five Bells, Middle Deal Road, Deal

See entries for the *Five Ringers.*

Five Bells, Queen Street, Deal

See entries for the *Swan.*

Five Bells Inn, 75 (39) Middle Street, Deal

c1955.

The first mention of this inn was in 1847 when William H Finnis was registered landlord of an unnamed beerhouse. By 1858, it was known as the *Five Bells Inn* and, in 1860, it was auctioned (together with the *Rose*) and described as an *"old established beerhouse."*

In 1862, Charles Langley, an auctioneer, was the licensee. He held a full licence and, in 1864, Richard Verrier was landlord, followed by Richard Collins in 1872. The inn was owned by Hills & Co brewery at the time. On Collins' death, his widow, Elizabeth, continued the running of the inn until 1893 when William Johnson and H Capeling took over, followed by Thomas Valentine Randall in 1896.

Randall made the news in September 1898 when he was accused of threatening his wife, Eliza. The court heard that after closing he had raised a table knife and threatened to murder her. He was bound over and fined £10 and a surety, or £10 to keep the peace for six months, plus costs of 8/- (40p) and solicitors' fees of one guinea (£1.05). Eliza had apparently been ill treated throughout the two years of their marriage.

By December 1898, George Redman was installed at the inn. He was followed by James Wratten in 1901, James T Watson in 1904, George Charles Payne in 1910 and George Marsh from 1911 to 1939. KT Morgan was landlord in 1953, WC Roberts in 1955, GW Hawkins and FO Robinson in 1957 and Kenneth Robert Southam in September 1958.

He rang last orders when it closed in 1959 and the licence transferred to the Archer at Whitfield. The property is now a private house.

Five Ringers (Five Bells) 345 Middle Deal Road (Back Road) (formerly Church Path), Deal

Original building c1900.

Later building c2000.

According to a contemporary newspaper report from 1887, a new bell, together with the five existing bells, were recast at the expense of Captain Coleman and subsequently re-hung in St Leonard's Church. It may be assumed therefore that the pub's name originated from the first casting of the five original bells.

Confusingly, throughout the 1830s especially, the pub was also referred to as the *Five Bells* in various forms of documentation.

Early records showed J Watts resident at the house that was situated somewhere near Church Path in 1725, as well as various other family members up until around the mid 1770s. Henry Cavell was landlord in 1776 when the *Five Ringers* appeared on the 'Refused to Billet Dragoons' list. He was followed by Widow Holman in 1785 and 1790, John Read in 1795 and 1804, Robert Spinner in 1828, Mary Spinner in 1836 until at least 1847, Henry Marsh in 1850, George Bethel Wyborn in 1858, George Driver in 1862, John Springhall in 1866, John Clements in 1867, Thomas Kemp from the early 1870s to July 1905 when H Gilbert took over. (Thompson's brewery owned the pub at this time).

The attractive thatched pub, which faced onto Church Path, was destroyed by fire around 1906 and rebuilt soon afterwards in a slightly different location, ie at the address in Middle Deal Road (previously known as Back Road).

W Halford was licensee from 1908 to 1922. During his time at the pub, an article in the Mercury dated 22 April 1911 reported: *"The Upper Deal Bowling Club was reopened on Easter Monday afternoon. The Club is in a sheltered little nook by the Five Ringers abutting Church Path."*

A further list of landlords included G Sainsbury in 1921, Ernest Wallace in 1925, Frederick KJ Castle and HN McKinnon in 1929, Sydney Haggar in 1934, Robert James Brown in 1938, GW Neeve in 1939, TG Larkin in 1948 and James and Doris Dry from 1964 to 1970. On 22 January 1970, the Mercury reported that they were moving to Malmö in Sweden to become the first English landlords of a Bass-owned pub there called the 'William Shakespeare.'

The Drys had served at the *Five Ringers* for six years (during which time it was a Charrington's outlet) and the Mercury noted that Edith had been born at the *Jolly Sailor* in Deal.

K Cecelin was landlord in 1974, and Ken and Rita Saggs took over in February 1983. During their time at the pub, they sold the large adjoining car park, and bungalows were built on its site. The Saggs remained on the licence until they retired in 2005 and the pub closed down.

The *Five Ringers* was subsequently demolished and new housing was erected on the site of the old pub.

Fleece

See entry for the *Pelican (2)*.

Fleur de Lis/Luce (later British Tar and Queens Head)
Alfred Row, The Drene/The Drain/Devils Row

Three Fleurs de Luce (later Providence)
Market Place, 5-11 King Street

Fleur de Luce/Lys/Lis, 19 Union Road
(12 Union Row, later known as Union Street)

Fleur de Lys (also Flower de Luce)
7 & 9 (5 & 6) King Street, Deal

Prior to 1803, the *Fleur de Luce* was situated in a road called The Drene/The Drain (sometimes referred to as Devils Row but now Alfred Row), with Henry Wood as landlord. In 1803, it had become known as the *British Tar* with Henry Wood still registered as licensee.

Also in 1803, William Cullen appeared as landlord of the *Three Fleurs de Luce* at a site in Market Place, King Street. (This inn would, by 1854, be known as the *Providence*). The 1804 Valuation List named the pub as the *Three Fleurs de Luce* with stable located in the *"next building north of King Street"*, with William Cullen still in charge. Cullen was also listed later that year as being landlord of the *Fleur de Lys* at 12 Union Row.

An 1810 Conveyance relating to a new street called 'Union Row' mentions *"premises and messuages, formerly of John Pettit, late of Thomas Parker Oakley, now belonging to Frances Cobb, called by the name Flower De Luce and passageway to the west, in the tenure of James Hutch. Consideration £400."*

By 1818, the *Fleur de Lys* had settled at 12 Union Row under the landlordship of John Ferry (who was still there in 1824). The pub was documented again

19 Union Road 2010.

in 1821 under the name of the *Fleur de Lis*.

In 1823, the owner of the *Flower De Luce* was Edward Iggulden (of the Iggulden brewery in Lower Street). In 1825, the pub was registered again as the *Fleur de Lys*, as it was also known in 1826 and 1827 when Henry Saffery became landlord. In 1828, Joseph Whitall was registered as being landlord of the *Three Fleurs de Luce* and also the *Fleur de Lys* (the name varied according to the document) and he enjoyed a long stay until 1864.

By 1854, Edward Iggulden had died and the premises were bought by Charles Thomas Hills of another local brewing family, Hills & Son.

In 1864, the licence was transferred to Thomas Langley and then again to Samuel Steed later that year. However, a new licence was refused the following year since it seems the pub was not doing very well by that point. (Langley also ran a carpentry and paperhanging business from the premises). The Mercury reported a transfer of licence from Langley in 1870 to a Mr Myhill. It was again transferred from Myhill to a BF Foster in 1871, from Foster to Richard Sharp in 1872 and from Sharp to Morris Langley in 1875.

A new licence was applied for in August 1875 by

Hills & Son since they wished to close the *Fleur de Lys* in Union Street and transfer the licence to 5 & 6 King Street. They bought up the two old houses there and had them demolished, and, perhaps in anticipation of gaining the licence, built new premises in which they envisaged a *"first rate hotel"*. The new building was situated on the corner of King Street and Middle Street and boasted a 44 feet frontage in King Street, with 20 feet depth into Middle Street. It had three rooms downstairs and three bedrooms. (Another storey was added at a later date). However, the licence was opposed by a Mr Laundy and it was subsequently refused on the grounds that, first, there were too many pubs nearby (15 within 200 yards) and, secondly, the building was supposedly built as a hotel but only had three bedrooms.

In September 1875, another application was made to relicence the old premises at 12 Union Row but this was also refused.

The building now numbered 7 and 9 King Street stands on the site of the original numbers 5 and 6 (part of which currently houses Play It games shop), and a keen eye will notice that it still looks like an old pub. It had many uses in living memory, the most famous of which probably being Catt's Restaurant during the post WWII years.

The original pub building in The Drene/The Drain (ie the *British Tar*, which later became the *Queens Head* – see separate entry) was sited on the present day corner of Alfred Row and Bridge Road (formerly known as Bridge Row).

The second pub building situated in Market Place later became known as the *Providence* in 1854 – see separate entry). Public conveniences now stand there. In the 1950s 23 Union Road was a guest house called The Fleur de Lys, but is now a private house.

Flying Horse
(location unknown) Lower Deal

The term 'flying horse' has several possible origins. The most obvious perhaps could be a reference to Pegasus, the winged horse from Greek mythology that carries the thunderbolt of Zeus and which sprang from the blood of Medusa; this, in turn, could relate in astrological terms to Pegasus, the star in the northern constellation; or, alternatively, it could also refer to the heraldic device used by the Knights Templar. Perhaps more likely, however, is that the name referred to the fast-moving 'flying horses' that pulled the messenger stagecoaches during the early days of travel.

Elizabeth Rentone, together with Stribblehill and Thomazine Norwood, were known to own property in Griffin Street (then called Tea Street) in the 1730s when legal documents included descriptions of four tenements with brewhouses, yards and gardens. In the 1739 Church Wardens Overseers book, the orchard of the *Flying Horse* gets a mention but, again, no location is given.

In an Indenture of a Lease dated 30 September 1776 made between the Archbishop of Canterbury and the executors of the wills of Elizabeth Rentone and Thomazine Norwood, the *Flying Horse* is described as having an *"outhouse stable yard ... and a small tenement thereunto adjoining and belonging in Lower Deal abutting to Middle Street and a small tenement ... in a lane leading from Beach Street to Middle Street to North ..."*.

Unfortunately, apart from other several fleeting mentions of the *Flying Horse* by name in old legal documents (see entry for the *Red Crosse*) very little is known about the pub, save that it was located somewhere in "Lower Deal" and possibly near to Griffin Street.

See also entry for *Pooles*.

Forester
15 The Marina (185a Beach Street), Deal

The Ancient Order of Foresters was founded in 1834, originating from the Royal Foresters dating back to the 1700s. However, in this instance, the *Forester* pub was named after one of the old luggers that used to be beached opposite the house.

The pub is situated on the north-eastern corner of Dibdin Road (previously informally called 'Foresters Opening').

Title deeds for this property began in 1859. The pub's first landlord was William Henry Hayman who applied for and was granted a full spirits' licence on 26 September 1861. He was a carpenter by trade and ran the pub as a secondary occupation. It was not uncommon for tradesmen of the time to run pubs in order to attract extra business customers, as well as to supplement their often meagre incomes when times were hard.

By 1873, George Ralph, an ex county policeman

formerly stationed at Walmer, was in charge, under the ownership of W Denne, brewer of Sandwich. The Mercury reported in 1881 that Thomas Obree, a boatman, was charged and found guilty of assaulting Susan Ralph at the pub. He was ordered to pay 20/- (£1) plus 15/- (75p) costs or 14 days' hard labour. It later reported the sudden death of George Ralph at the *Forester* in 1886 and the fact that his widow, Charlotte Ralph, would take over the licence. She remained there until Susan Faucheux was installed in 1891. Interestingly, she was married to Felix Humanter Marianne Francouis Faucheux, who was manager of a sprat factory that was located in the north end of Deal.

Stephen Roberts was there from 1898 to 1911, followed by Frederick Redsull until his death in 1922 when his widow, Mary Annie Sarah Redsull, took over until 1944. In the early 1950s, NF Redsull was the resident host.

Around 1966 when I Bolt was licensee, the house was described in Tubbs' Book of Kent pubs as being very popular with sea rowers, rugby and soccer players, as well as with oyster addicts. The latter would telephone the pub with their requirements from far and wide and consume the oysters at the

2009.

bar, together with Guinness, Champagne or Black Velvet.

An advert in a local newspaper dated 9 October 1969 read: *"Pam & Arthur, late of the **Rising Sun**, Kingsdown, welcome you to their new house, the **Forester**, The Marina, Deal. Fresh cut sandwiches always available. Whitstable oysters to order."*

Arthur Silbury was landlord in 1971, followed by Thomas Palmer in 1974 (at which time the pub was owned by Charrington & Co). John Joseph Spallin took over in 1978 and, to mark his 12 months at the helm, the pub was given a relaunch in 1979, with the popular singing duo of the time, Peters and Lee, attending the ceremony of the newly refurbished pub, amidst great celebrations.

In January 1980, the Mercury reported that, since John Burton, aged 82, had been using the pub since 1916, he was officially its most longstanding customer!

The pub remains open to this day and is a free house comprising one through lounge bar, together with pool table. Following the sad death of John Spallin in 2008, his effervescent wife, Margaret, now runs the *Forester* with much verve and enthusiasm.

Fountain (1)

See entry for the *Pelican*.

Fountain (south) (2) (Row Barge, Monks Head, Beare) (82, 53, 54) Beach Street, Deal

The origins of this pub date back to 1661 and it was by all accounts a weather boarded building that used to stand immediately south of the present day *Royal Hotel* – so close, in fact, that just a narrow passageway leading to the beach separated the two buildings.

It was originally called the *Beare*, followed by the *Monks Head*, then the *Row Barge* and the *Beare* again, before eventually becoming the *Fountain*.

The pub was first mentioned in a 1675 lease between Gilbert, Archbishop of Canterbury and George Hodgson, a mariner, of Deal, and his wife, Mary *"on*

consideration of surrender of a former lease made to Humphrey Bigglestone of Deal, mariner (father of said Mary, and Robena, his then wife) for 40 shillings (£2) of a tenement or dwellinghouse in Lower Deal lately erected on the sea valley there being called or known as the Beare ..."*

By 1680, the pub had changed its name to *"the sign of the **Monks Head"*** and comprised part of the Archbishop's Waste. Archbishop Thomas leased the pub to William Conning, a brewer, in 1698.

In 1710, Elizabeth and Joseph Clark mortgaged the property to Samuel Ffasham, brewer, for £100.

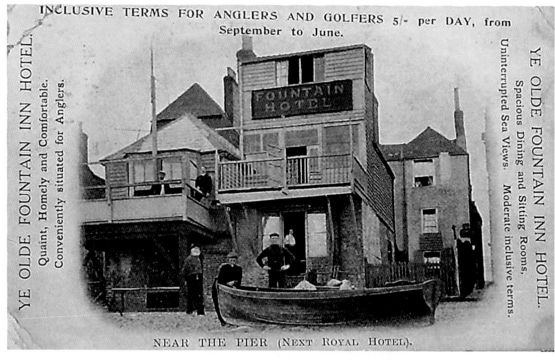

YE OLDE FOUNTAIN INN HOTEL.
Quaint, Homely and Comfortable.
Conveniently situated for Anglers.

INCLUSIVE TERMS FOR ANGLERS AND GOLFERS 5/- per DAY, from September to June.

YE OLDE FOUNTAIN INN HOTEL.
Spacious Dining and Sitting Rooms,
Uninterrupted Sea Views. Moderate inclusive terms.

NEAR THE PIER (NEXT ROYAL HOTEL).

c1900.

By 1719, the pub had changed its name when Archbishop William leased to William and Elizabeth Ashton *"all that tenement known as the Row Barge … for 21 years at 2/- (10p) per annum … the greater part of the buildings fallen down."*

In 1747, the pub was described as being *"called by the Beare and now the sign of the Fountain a part whereof lately erected and built with brick"* and was also similarly described in 1751 when Elizabeth Dehane sold it to John Iggulden, a bricklayer, for £60. By 1770, it was recorded as the *"late Row Barge and now the Fountain"* when it was still in the hands of Iggulden.

Later licensees included Edward Batby in 1776 (when the pub was documented as *'refusing to billet dragoons'*), and the widow Coller in 1804. The pub reputedly had a tunnel, as well as a concealed staircase and secret panels. These must have been in existence in the days when press gangs were roaming the streets so escape routes and hidey-holes would have been vital, not to mention convenient stores for smugglers' contraband.

According to the 1821 Rate book, William Thompsett was landlord of the pub which included *"dwellinghouse, stable, long room and capstan"*. He was followed later that year by Giles Morgan, William and Mary Baker in 1828, Henry Burrows in 1832, Gilbert Wood also in 1832 and Henry North in 1836. By 1845, the pub had become known as *"The Fountain Tavern and Commercial Inn"* Later

landlords included Josiah (or Joshua) Ludwig in 1849 to 1850, William Denne in 1851, Catherine Philpot in 1861, followed by Samuel Sherlock Collis later that year (until at least 1865).

The Deal Telegram in January 1862 reported: *"The annual Punch and Cake Festival was held at Mrs Philpot's Fountain Inn on Monday last, having originated in this house. This was a highly respectable gathering consisting of nearly 40 of the town's principal tradesmen"*. Later on that year, Samuel S Collis took over as licensee. An advert from June 1869 announced: *"Billiards Pyramids and Pool. Every evening at the Fountain Inn. Pleasantist room in Deal. Marker always in attendance. J Ottaway, Proprietor."*

The *Fountain* was, by all accounts, somewhat of a rowdy house since its name cropped up in several local newspaper articles reporting from the Petty Sessions. The first one was dated 20 April 1871 and headed *"A Scandalous Affair"*. *"A Mrs Marsh was charged with having been drunk and disorderly on the previous night. She was without a bonnet and her dress was very much torn. She stated she had been violently thrown out of the door of the Fountain public house, that she was not drunk, having had only some beer and two glasses of gin, but that she was very much excited at the time. The case was dismissed with a severe caution"*. George Edward Porter was registered landlord in 1872.

The second article was dated 15 October 1874.

*"Simon Pritchard and Albert Cannaway, boatmen, were charged with being drunk and disorderly, creating a disturbance near the **Fountain** Inn, Beach-street, about a quarter to eleven on Monday night, also with being stripped for fighting, and threatening the policeman if he dared to interfere. Both young men pleaded guilty to the charge and excused themselves by saying that it being holiday time they had indulged in a little extra to drink. The Bench ordered the defendants to pay 10/- (50p) each, including costs, which was immediately paid."* George Edward Porter would probably have been landlord at the time. He was followed in 1877 by Edward Rea.

The third report was dated October 1882 and headed "Rea Against Erridge". *"This was a charge against Edward Erridge for refusing to leave the* **Fountain** *Inn when requested by the landlord to do so. It appeared that the accused, after he had recovered from his fit of intoxication, called on the landlord and apologised, which induced him to withdraw the charge after he had taken out the summons, but this being a public offence, the Magistrates declined to allow the charge to be withdrawn. Both parties were now in attendance, and Erridge ordered to pay the costs, 5/6d (27½p)."*

Godfrey Flynn was licensee in 1884, followed by Frederick William Cullen in August 1889, Caroline Almond in November 1889, Jane Mary Evans in 1890, Mrs Caroline Almond in 1891, John Friend in 1894, John Friers in 1896 to1903 and Robert William Pearce in June 1905. On Sunday, 10 December 1905, Police were called to the **Fountain** at 00.15 hours. Pearce had been murdered by his potman, Percy John Murray, aged 21, who was described as a slight young man.

According to the Kent Mercury, the landlord *"had been done to death"* and was found *"lying on his back in a pool of blood"*. Murray was quoted as saying *"I have done it with that knife. I shall have to suffer for it"* before being taken into custody. The newspaper continued: *"Pearce was violently stabbed in the breast with a chef's kitchen knife, a formidable looking weapon with a firm blade, 7 inches in length and an inch or two in width at the handle and tapering to a sharp point."*

While awaiting sentence in Maidstone gaol, Murray wrote a letter to his brother giving his version of events. It appeared that Pearce had heard him talking to his wife, Hetty, and, noticing a hole in the partition of her bedroom wall, accused Murray of making the hole and spying on her (the landlord and his wife having separate bedrooms). Murray denied the accusation and Mrs Pearce told her husband that she had made the hole herself. Despite this, Pearce struck Murray, who then blindly retaliated with the knife, seemingly without meaning to kill him. In February 1906, Murray was found

c1890.

An old-world nook, DEAL – KENT.

guilty and sentenced to death, but with a recommendation for mercy because of his age. He was granted a reprieve in the March and sentenced to penal servitude for life.

Immediately after the murder, Hetty Pearce transferred the licence to her late husband's cousin, Robert John Pearce, in 1905. A Nicholls was in charge in 1907 and he, together with Thompson's brewery, applied for a licence renewal. The pub was described at the time as having *"rooms overlooking the Downs and attracted visitors. 4 other pubs within 90 yards, nearest Royal, 4 yards away. Inn is one of only two having a verandah directly overlooking the Downs, and is a hotel rather than just a pub"*. The licence was duly renewed.

It was transferred from W Hicks to Mary Ann Jennings in 1909. The pub was threatened with closure that year when its trade was described as: *"Medium, well conducted pub. 13 pubs within 200 yards. Carpenters' & Joiners' Union (100*

members), Bricklayers' Union (50) & Workmen's Union all hold their meetings there, in one of the finest clubrooms in town. Good 2nd class hotel, landlord made good living letting 10 bedrooms."*

The pub remained open for a few years longer, eventually closing on 30 December 1922. It was acquired by Deal Corporation in 1924 for £1,200 and later demolished.

In an article dated 14 October 1965, the East Kent Mercury described the old *Fountain* as being *"much patronised by smugglers, pilots and seafarers of all sorts ... right on the beach, and very convenient for all maritime travellers, this inn was surrounded by a wooden stage and boarded walls. There used to be displayed an old sign which read, 'Downs pilots' night bell"* (in the narrow alleyway which divided the *Fountain* and the *Three Kings* – now the *Royal* – next door) *"and many of the proprietors were themselves engaged in nautical affairs."* The car park next to the *Royal Hotel* now stands on its site.

Fox
(182, 10, 11) Beach Street, Deal

Although fox-hunting origins would appear to be obvious in more rural locations, in coastal areas, the term is usually nautical, referring to the name for a twisted rope used on boats. However, this particular *Fox* was possibly named after a cutter called 'The Fox' that was used by the Revenue

The Fox Inn is to the right in this c1910 view.

service along the Deal coastline, even though it is uncertain when the name was actually adopted. In 1815, 'The Fox' apprehended a smuggling boat, but the smugglers overthrew the crew of 'The Fox', beating and wounding the Revenue officers. Those that were not thrown overboard were left for dead inside the cutter. According to a modern-day article in the Mercury: *"The Commissioners of Excise offered a reward of £500 for anyone who could give evidence which would convict people involved"*. An alternative explanation is that it was named after a galley punt called 'The Fox' that was owned by Deal pilot, William Stanton, in 1832.

The first documentation found of the property

operating as licensed premises was when it was sold to Alfred Kingsford, a brewer from Dover, sometime between 1843 and 1846, the resident/landlady at the time being Mary Powell. Richard William Robinson, *"Beerhouse Keeper"*, took over in 1847 and served until 1877, followed by William Finnis in 1878 and Thomas Hornsey Finnis in 1885 who applied for, but was refused, a full licence. The pub was then owned by the Dover Brewery Company.

George Henley was landlord from 1887 to 1891. The brewery company had changed to George Beer & Co and the pub's address was registered as no 11 Beach Street. A contemporary report described it as: *"Beer shop, the Fox, containing 3½ perches."*

In 1893, Pamela Harris was listed as holding a wine and beer licence at the *Fox* and she remained there until 1898 when Henry James Wells took over. In 1903, he was fined 10/- (50p) with 7/6d (37½p) costs for *"having his premises open to other than bona fide travellers during prohibited time"*. The licence was transferred to John Roberts one month later. Around this time, many beerhouses were being closed down by magistrates as it was considered that there were too many of them about. Their report stated: *"The tap room upstairs not good from the point of view of police supervision; mostly boatmen customers; 8 public houses within 240 yards; landlord Mr Roberts commented the tap room was used by visitors because of the view"*. The house was referred to the compensation committee and a temporary licence was issued.

In 1914, the pub and several adjoining houses were used as billeting quarters for Belgian refugees and Scottish troops. The pub closed in 1915 but Roberts remained living there at least until 1916. It was sold to Deal District Council on 29 June 1920 for £550 and plans for its demolition were approved in November 1925.

The *Fox* used to stand on the eastern side of Beach Street, slightly north of the junction with Griffin Street, and the site is now covered by the wide concrete promenade running alongside the beach.

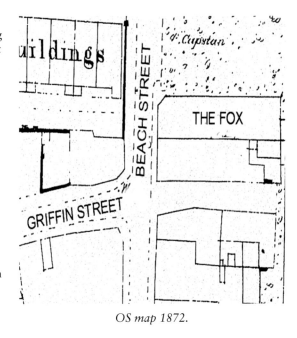

OS map 1872.

Frederick William

See entry for the *Tally Ho*.

French Arms (location unknown) "Deale"

The only mention of this pub appeared on a 1680 list of "Deale" inns but is otherwise untraceable.

Friendly Port (Oddfellows Arms, Silver Lion and possibly Salutation), 6 (2) New Street, Deal

The term 'friendly port' may have referred to Deal since it was used in a contemporary report about the burning of an East Indiaman, 'The Kent', in 1825 in the Bay of Biscay since prior to that, the ship had been anchored in the Downs awaiting good weather.

There were also a number of friendly societies around at the time (such as the Oddfellows) that could have met at, and described the pub as, a friendly port. (The pub did, in fact, later change its name to the *Oddfellows Arms* – see below).

By 1820, New Street was so named. The first mention found of the *Friendly Port* was in 1843 when landlord, John Charles Weston, was ordered to make a late payment of rates of 1/6d (7½p) with 1/6d costs. He was also recorded as running a beerhouse on the premises in 1847. By 1855, William H Shelvey had been installed as licensee.

The pub briefly changed its name to the *Oddfellows Arms* in 1865. In 1866, the local

c1960s.

Nuisances Book records stated: "*Unable to empty cesspit at the rear of the house, which was covered but quite full*". By 1868, the pub's name had reverted to the **Friendly Port**. In 1872, it was again described as a beerhouse, with Freeman George Thompson as licensee, followed by Morris Langley in 1873.

Landlord, John Bax, closed the house down for three months in 1875. He was later fined in 1877 for selling 'schiedam' (gin), "*being ex-flotsam or wreckage*" without a spirits' licence, and Edward Snoswell took over as licensee later that year until 1879. He was followed for a very short term by Jason Charles Joseph Plumridge, and then Amos Augustus Sparks took over in 1880, Thomas Henry Jarvis Bing in 1891 and Patrick John Harris from 1893 to 1896. In January of that year, Harris (who also played piano at the **Rose** in Deal on Thursday nights), was fined £1, with 11/7d (58p) costs, for allowing gambling on the premises.

George Robert Harris took over in 1897 but, by 1907, the licence was in jeopardy when Harris complained that he had to seek other work as the trade was "*rather rough*", the house being described as "*very old and out of repair*". The rent was 4/- (20p) a week and the pub's rateable value was £11/10d (£11.50) at the time. There were also five other public houses within 136 yards of the **Friendly Port**. In March of that year, the pub was granted a provisional licence while being referred for compensation on closure, and it eventually shut down on 28 December 1907, its licence expiring on 21 January 1908.

As indicated by a recent former resident of the house, the deeds showed that the property was once called the **Silver Lion** beerhouse but the authors have been unable to find any further evidence of this.

2009.

However, the current owners have stuck to this name, as indicated on a modern day plaque attached to the wall outside.

It appears that the pub may also have been called the **Salutation** at some point in its history, according to a previous researcher's notes, but, again, the authors' findings have come up with nothing to confirm this. The building is now a private house.

Fullers (location unknown) Deal

S amuel Pepys wrote in his diary in 1660 that "**Fullers**" in Deal had "*no ale*". Thomas Fuller was registered as "*Victualler*" at the time, according to the Sandwich Recognizances list.

In 1679, William Fuller's occupation was given as "*Brewer*". He was also mentioned in the 1695 will of widow, Mary Miles, together with another brewer by the name of William Conning.

John Fuller was described as being a "*Part Owner*

and Brewer" in later deeds belonging to the **Phoenix** (later known as the **Queens Arms**) in Lower Street (later High Street).

It can only be speculated whether all these Fullers were connected in any way. Likewise, it is not clear if **Fullers** was actually the name of a pub or a brewery and, if the former, whether or not it was an early incarnation of the **Phoenix** and the **Queens Arms**!

Garibaldi (1) Market Street, Deal

Giuseppe Garibaldi, born 1807, was a leading military and political figure, as well as a popular hero during the age of Italian unification known as the Risorgimento. It was said that the famous Garibaldi biscuit named after him was so-called because he would make sure his marching troops were fed on raisin bread to keep up their stamina. He died in 1882. It is presumed that the *Garibaldi* was named in his honour.

The *Garibaldi* was a beerhouse situated in Market Street, on the corner of Lower Street (now High Street). In 1861, William Wheatley, *"Landlord and Shoemaker"*, was fined £1 for selling beer between 1 and 2 o'clock in the morning. He was also summonsed that year for *"insulting professional singer, Virginia Bell, at the Park Tavern and calling her 'a whore'"*. It was recorded at the time that his wife, Fanny, was a shoebinder and they had six children.

The beerhouse appeared to be a short-lived affair since no other records have been located.

The Original Factory Shop (74-80 High Street) now covers the site of the *Garibaldi*.

Site of Garibaldi 2009.

General Wolfe, 149 (155) Beach Street, Deal

General Wolfe was born in Westerham, Kent in 1727 and died in 1759. He was mortally wounded in the battle of Quebec and, as he lay dying, on hearing that the French were being defeated, his last words were *"Now, God be praised, I will die in peace."*

The *General Wolfe* was listed as a beerhouse in 1847 when James Snoswell was landlord. The following year, new landlord, Charles Spears found himself in trouble for opening after 11pm and for keeping a disorderly house, although the charges were later dropped.

There was no more documentary evidence found about the *General Wolfe* so it is impossible to say when it closed down. It is now a private house.

2009.

George & Dragon, Deal

See entry for the *Jolly Butcher.*

George & Dragon, Walmer

See entry for the *Thompson(s) Bell*.

Globe, 167 (166) Beach Street, Deal

See entry for the *Albion*.

Globe (location unknown) Deal

This particular pub was *"sometimes called the Globe"* between 1674 and 1853 but, other than its location being at the "south end" of Deal, very little is known about the house.

The pub was in the ownership of the Mullet family in the early 1700s. They also owned houses that are now known as the **Kings Head** and the **Port Arms** around this time.

The **Globe** was one of many local pubs advertised in the Kentish Post in 1730 for sale by auction, and which named Stephen Norris as the landlord at the time.

Globe (Scarborough Cat)
199 (182) Beach Street, Deal

The name *Scarborough Cat* might suggest a cat-rigged boat that was traditionally fitted with a rigged sail on a single mast, set up high on the boat, between 16 and 26 feet long. A 'cat' was also an old name for a coal and timber vessel on the north east coast of England (Scarborough, perhaps?). In this instance, however, the Scarborough Cat was probably the name of a local 'cat lugger' used for ferrying heavy goods to and from the ships anchored in the Downs.

1772 title deeds refer to Shadrack White as landlord of the *Scarborough Cat*, with the property comprising *"8½ perches in sea valley"*, together with stable, cow house, capstan ground opposite, garden and a plot of land.

In 1804, Stephen White was licensee, followed by Joshua Mockett in 1819 who was known to be a *"notorious smuggler"*, so much so that, on 18 June 1816, a 'Wanted' poster offered a reward for the *"Recapture of Joshua Mockett, landlord, Scarborough Cat"* for his smuggling activities. It seems that he had originally been arrested by Samuel and William Hawkes but had been freed *"by hovellers."*

2009.

William Powell was landlord in 1821 and 1829 and was succeeded by Mary Elizabeth Powell until at least 1847. The curiously named Onesiphorus Sneller (later to become builder and landlord of the **Napier Tavern** – see separate entry – which he erected almost opposite the **Globe** in 1855) took over from 1850 to 1852, followed by Isaac Brown, "Butcher", from 1862 to 1867. Hills brewery of Deal ran the house and, in May 1869, it advertised for *"Persons willing to contract for sundry alterations and additions to a public house known as the Scarborough Cat."*

John Bingham took over the licence in 1869, being declared bankrupt the following year, as well as being accused of beating and ill-treating his wife. He was sentenced to three weeks' hard labour at Sandwich Gaol, and, his wife and children being destitute, were admitted to the Eastry workhouse. By 1873, the pub had been renamed the **Globe**. Sarah Bishop took over in 1897 and remained there until it closed in 1906 when the pub was referred to the compensation committee.

The **Globe** is now a private house.

Globe, 191 (179), Beach Street, Deal

William Brown was landlord in 1804 (until at least 1811) when the house was described as being *"next on south to Yarmouth Packet"*. John Lawrence was licensee there in 1821. The *Globe* is described in 1828 in *"the sale of the Manor of Chamberlain's Fee"* as *"All that messuage or tenement no 179 Beach Street, lately called or commonly known by the name or sign of the 'Globe' with the cellar, outhouses, edifices, buildings, yards, ground and appurtenances thereunto belonging, and the backway or passage to the same, and now used therewith late in the occupation of John Lawrence and now unoccupied. These premises are subject to a lease granted to Francis Cobb Esq. For 21 years from Michaelmas 1811 at the yearly rent of £3 15s (£3.75) and to a Covenant therein contained for renewal thereof for a like term of 21 years at the end of 18 years of the existing term, upon payment of a fine of £37 7s (£37.35)"*. The *Globe* was sold to *"Mr Iggulden"* and, despite Iggulden being a brewer, the pub appears to have closed down that year, probably due to the 1828 Alehouse Act that had just come into force.

By the 1860s, street directories indicated that the *Globe* had become a boarding house (presumably unlicensed).

The former pub is now a private home called Globe House.

2009.

Golden Ball (location unknown) "Deale"

Other than a mention in the Deale Payments for Signs list of 1694, this pub has proved untraceable.

Golden Fleece

See entry for the *Pelican (2)*.

Golden Lion/Lyon (location unknown) "Deale'

This pub was only mentioned once – in the Sandwich Lycence Booke for Deale of 1677 – with no location recorded.

Good Intent

See entry for the *Sandown Castle*.

Good Intent (location unknown) Walmer

According to the Alehouse Keepers book for Walmer of 1805, James Hoile was landlord, followed by William Beal in 1814. (Beal moved onto the *Duke of Wellington*, later known as the *Stag*, in 1815). Unfortunately, the location of the *Good Intent* remains untraceable.

Goodwins (Pier Refreshment Rooms)
Pier, Beach Street, Deal

2008.

The ***Pier Refreshment Rooms/Goodwins*** is included in this book since, according to Dover magistrates, they were considered to be in the same category for licensing purposes as a public house, inn or tavern. JT Outwin applied for, and successfully obtained, a licence for what was originally known as the ***Pier Refreshment Rooms*** in September 1866. This was shortly after the building of the 'new' pier (pier 2) had been completed, and the rooms themselves were housed in a building at the seaward end.

They were thereafter managed by various landlords who, as a condition of employment, had to have had previous experience and knowledge of the business. Until 1937, when they were taken over by Deal Borough Council, prospective landlords would bid for three year leases. In March 1957, shortly after the building of pier three, the licence which had, up to that point, been

2003.

suspended, was transferred to JC Bodker, the Entertainments Manager of Deal Borough Council. After some refurbishment to the premises, Mercury readers were invited in November 1961, to name the new pier bar, the successful entrant winning two guineas (£2.10) in prize money. The following month, the Entertainments Committee chose the name ***Goodwins*** from the 70 entries. The licensed bar itself was situated on the north side of the building, separate from the snack bar in the other part. The two eventually merged into one in an effort to cut costs some years later.

The original ***Goodwins*** building was demolished and a new award winning construction was erected and officially opened to the public in November 2008. I currently contains an eating establishment called Jasin's Restaurant.

Good Woman

See entry for the ***Dolphin***, Walmer.

Granville Arms
13 Cambridge Road, Walmer

1878.

The name of this pub was inspired by the installation of Earl Granville as Lord Warden of the Cinque Ports at nearby Walmer Castle, until his death on 31 March 1891. An advertisement at the time read:

"Patronised by The Right Hon Earl Granville, KG, WJ Miller, (late coachman to Miss Bird) – Granville Arms and Mews, Walmer. Closed and Open carriages, by the Day, Hour or Journey. Good Stabling and Lock-up Coach-Houses. Clipping and Singeing in all its branches. Foreign and British Spirits, Bottled Ale and Stout."

William Romney was registered landlord in 1866, followed by William John Miller from 1870 to 1874 and Gilbert Laurence in 1878. This was the year when a hurricane hit Walmer, damaging many properties including the *Granville Arms* which had its roof lifted. John James Lownds was licensee in 1882.

The pub was put up for sale in 1888 and advertised thus: *"The Granville Estate: a fully licensed corner house comprising Granville Arms, Granville Mews and Granville House"*. An amusing anecdote printed in the Mercury that year concerned the Earl Granville's eldest son and the fact that he *"still suffers severe inconvenience from the half-crown he swallowed which has not been removed."* (For younger readers, the 'half-crown' was a large coin, approximately 1½ inches [3cms] wide).

In 1889, landlord, Thomas Luther, was fined 17/6d (87½p) for opening after hours. Later that year, W Adamson was landlord (as well as a blacksmith) until at least 1903, and, in February 1904, alterations for the pub were approved. Later landlords included AW Fox in 1908, CH Ambrose from 1914 to 1922, Mrs Ambrose, widow, in 1924, Mrs A Finnis in 1925, Walter Henry Lumley in 1929, Horace Cecil Laming in 1934 and 1938, Percival John Tidy and John H Hewitt in 1942, Rose

Maud Hewitt in 1944, EA Sinden in 1956, TG Meaning in 1966, Elaine Meaning in 1969, Eric Cousins in 1972 and Denis Moore in 1976. According to the Mercury in July 1988, Denis and Iris Moore did not recognise their new pub sign which erroneously showed the painting of a ship called 'The Earl Granville' rather than of the Second Earl Granville, Lord Warden of the Cinque Ports!

John Walton became landlord in 1994, followed by Sandra Crossland in May 1995 until the present date.

The pub remains open for business and is a free house.

2009.

Green Dragon (location unknown) "Deale"

A green dragon appears on the coat of arms of the Earl of Pembroke. According to the Sandwich Recognizances list of 1662, 6/8d (33p) was paid for a new inn sign, together with £5 surety, by licensee, Mary Bedlove.

This pub was mentioned again when important meetings were held there between 1770 and 1776. Because of this, the pub would have been a prominent one and situated in a central location since the *Hoop & Griffin*, *India Arms*, *Black Horse* and *Three Kings* were all similarly placed and also known to be important meeting places in the same era as each other.

Greyhound (exact location unknown) possibly Middle Street, Deal

A s well as being a breed of dog, a 'greyhound' was a type of fast ocean-going ship. 'The Greyhound' was also a name given to various British ships throughout the centuries.

According to a 1661 lease, there was *"a tenement called the Greyhound and piece of beachy ground, part of which is in Lower Street"* (now High Street). The lease showed Nicholas Whetstone resident there in 1661, and, in 1679, although the same name appeared, it is probably that of his son.

The premises are described as being a *"tenement or dwelling house, stable backside and premises in Lower Deal, commonly called the sign of The Greyhound, abutting to the Middle Street east to lands and housing demised to William Mullett senior* *and assigned to Nicholas Whetstone west to a land leading from Middle Street to Lower Street north to housing and ground demised to William Mullett and Nicholas Safry south, now in occupation of Nicholas Whetstone. For 21 years at 2/- [10p] pa. Witness: R Snowe".* (Nicholas Whetstone was recorded as being Deal's first Postmaster, and Whestone Street – an early name for King Street – was named in his honour).

From contemporary descriptions, the *Greyhound* was possibly situated somewhere in between Lower Street (now High Street) and the section of Middle Street that lays behind the present day *Kings Head* and *Port Arms* (the Mullett family owning both of these pubs in the 1700s).

Greyhound (Seven Stars) 142 (133) Middle Street, Deal

S hortly before its closure, the *Greyhound* pub was described as being a *"very small house"*, despite the fact that the existing building appears comparatively large. When the authors were fortunate enough to visit the property, it certainly had the feeling of having once been a tavern or an inn.

One has to assume that possibly only part of the large downstairs room was used for the purpose. Interestingly, the house backs directly on to what would have been the yard and stables of the old *Hoop & Griffin* pub in the 1700s.

John Clynch Payne was landlord from 1866 to 1874. It was during his time at the pub that the name changed from the *Seven Stars* (which had a full licence by 1872) to the *Greyhound* in 1873. Mr Worth was there in 1880, transferring the licence to Mr Copland

in November of that year, followed by John Capeling in July 1881, James Goldup in October 1881, Thomas Appleton in 1882, Frederick William Sands in November 1886, George John Weller in 1887, Horace Small in 1888, Frederick Small in 1889, Esther Annie Sparkes in 1892 and Ernest William Stride from 1893 to 1913, when the house was referred to the Compensation Committee for closure.

The pub was owned by Croydon brewery, Nadler and Collyer, at the time. The licensing magistrates' findings were that the *Greyhound* was *"A well-conducted house, with largely working class trade; 4 public houses within 100 yards which were larger and offered better accommodation."*

The pub is now a private house.

2009.

Griffin & Trumpet (location unknown) "Deale"

The *Griffin & Trumpet* appeared on the Deale Payments for Signs list of 1662 and an amount of 6/8d (33p) was shown. Other than this entry, nothing more is known about the pub but it could possibly have been a forerunner of the *Hoop & Griffin* – see separate entry.

Grove Inn (possibly Deal Lugger)
(exact location unknown) Beach Street, Deal

The only record of this pub was found in an 1880s' street directory but its name does not appear in any licensing records so the *Grove Inn* unfortunately remains something of a mystery.

(Grove Ralph Norris was landlord of the *Deal Lugger*, Beach Street around this time, although whether or not the *Grove Inn* was a nickname for that pub is unknown).

Gun Inn

See entry for the *Bowling Green Tavern.*

Letter addressed to the editor of a local newspaper dated 1 November 1862:
Sir, Are there any policemen in Deal? I am induced to ask you this question from the fact of residing in Middle St, a few doors from Short St, and almost nightly I, as well as the rest of my neighbours, are awakened by the loud kicking of doors and blasphemous language, which continues sometimes for an hour or two at a time. These noises come from a well-known establishment in Short St, known to the police, who must be wilfully deaf and blind, or else they would put a stop to it. Now, if these disturbances are to continue, what is the use of paying policemen?
(signed) A Ratepayer – who finds it very difficult to get a night's rest.

Half Moon (Hut/Hutte), 124 Beach Street, Deal

This pub was mentioned on the Deal List of Inns dated 1678 and again in 1680 in a Payment for Signs receipt book - 6/8d (38p) was paid, plus £5 surety. Yet another List recorded that it was latterly known as the **Hut** or Ye **Hutte**.

The building was demolished in November 1912.

Halfway House

See entry for the *Chequers.*

Hamborough Castle, Beach Street, Deal

See entry for the *Watermans Arms.*

Hamborough Flag

See entry for the *Hamburg Flag.*

Hamborrow Arms

See entry for the *Watermans Arms*, 41 Beach Street.

Hamburg Ensign

See entry for the *Watermans Arms*, 41 Beach Street.

Hamburg Flag (Hamborough Flag)
47-49 Queen Street (Five Bells Lane), Deal

This pub was located at the junction of the present day Blenheim Road and Queen Street on the south-east corner.

In 1732, according to the Poor Rate Assessment book, the property was owned by Mr Hulke. In 1739, Anthony Ffasham purchased the "*house, garden, brew house, malt house, store house, hop ground and Hamburg Flag*". It was also mentioned in the 1739 Church Wardens' Overseers book as - probably erroneously - the *Hamborough Flag.*

Site of Hamburg Flag 2009.

From 1783 to 1786, Joseph Cobb, among other people, was named in leases relating to the property. Cobb's, brewers from Margate, were rumoured to have a branch of their brewery company in Deal so maybe this was it, although it cannot be proved. This was the last known recording of the premises as a public house. A garage has stood on the site since the 1920s, and the showroom frontage can still be seen.

Kwik-Fit auto repairs now occupies the spot.

Hand & Copper Pot (location unknown) Deal

These premises were mentioned in a local List of Inns in 1680 but, other than this entry, nothing more is known.

Hare & Hounds, 13 Golf Road (Western Road/Sandy Lane North), Deal

It is possible that the *Hare & Hounds* started off life as a beerhouse before a full licence was applied for and granted to landlord, William Jordan, in September 1865. The pub held a special licence, perhaps because of its proximity to the market gardens, whereby licensees would be permitted to sell alcohol to early morning workers from 5am, especially during harvest time.

Licensing documentation from the 1860s suggests that the *Jolly Gardener* – see separate entry - could possibly have been a forerunner of the *Hare & Hounds* in this building, but the authors have been unable to find any other evidence to substantiate this. Richard Grant took over in 1875 and, during his time as landlord, it was reported that John Bax, a pieman, had attempted suicide by cutting his own throat in one of the pub's outhouses. He was taken to the dispensary where he eventually recovered.

In 1881, the pub's early morning opening licence was renewed. Grant left the *Hare & Hounds* in 1887 and Frederick Thomas Shelvey took over from 1887 to 1900 when he died at the age of 36. His widow, Mary Anne, then ran the pub until April 1902 when she was charged with opening during prohibited hours and fined £1 plus 7/6d (37½p) costs, and the licence was transferred to John Batt Annall.

In 1903, the pub was rebuilt, with the proviso that a 7-foot high fence be erected at the rear in order to control access to

1887.

c1960.

the pub. Annall remained at the *Hare & Hounds* until at least 1905 and George Skinner took over from 1910. He was charged with serving three cases of adulterated spirits (but remained at the pub until around 1948). The case was dismissed on payment of costs. In 1935, the brewery company changed from Leney's to Fremlin's. According to the late local historian, David Collyer, George Skinner's son, Victor, recalled the pub as being a very lively one, with lots of music and singing and he would play piano there for locally based soldiers during WWII. He also remembered that workers on the night shift at the nearby gas works would throw a basket attached to a rope over the pub wall. Inside would be a note of their orders, together with some money. His father would place the order inside the basket and, with a tug on the rope, it would disappear back over the wall again to the other side!

During WWII, the pub enjoyed the local accolade of being known as the 'Cleanest Pub in Deal', according to a former resident. She went to live there at the age of 8, together with her mother, after her father died. Her grandmother, the landlady, would awake every morning at 6 o'clock in order to clean down and scrub the entrance and polish the brasses. Soldiers billeted at the nearby Royal Cinque Ports Club House frequented the pub. She recalled that, if her grandmother thought they had consumed too much beer, she would not hesitate to take them to one side and tell them that she would not serve them anything stronger than shandy.

HO Letts was landlord in 1955, followed by David Allen in 1956, P McLernon in 1958 (transferring to the **Albion** in 1962), George Kitchener Harmsworth in 1962 and RG Thornhill in 1966. The pub closed down on Thursday, 11 February 1971 and the licence was transferred from George Wint to John Coomber of Whitbread Fremlins who considered the pub to be *"surplus to the requirements of the area."*

On January 24 1980, the Mercury reported that planning permission had been sought by David and Philip O'Sullivan in order to convert the former **Hare & Hounds** into a new pub, which would possibly be called the **Golden Hind**. On 14 February, the application was opposed by the Deal & Walmer Licensed Victuallers Association, stating that there would be no demand for a new pub in the area.

The **Hare & Hounds** building now comprises two private homes.

Hare & Hounds
363 Dover Road (High Street), Walmer

At the time the pub was built, barracks dating back to the late 1700s were located on the site of the present day St Margaret's Drive close to the **Hare & Hounds**. They housed the Third Royal Hussars of the King's German Legion and the pub would have been ideally situated for their custom.

c1910.

1891 to 1906, C Kenward in 1907, W 'Nobby' Leach in 1908, his wife, Mrs Leach, in 1922 and JF Turner from 1923 to 1933.

Widow, Mrs Sarah Turner was the last landlady on the premises when they were de-licensed in 1936 after the Brewster Sessions which were held on 5 March

Although an ancient building, the first reference found was in 1841 with Henry Bushell, aged 45, residing at the **Hare & Hounds** Beer Shop (later known as an alehouse). He was still there in 1851 and had added *'Brewer's Servant'* to his credentials.

This could have been a reference to the Thompson's brewery which had been situated opposite the premises since 1816, replacing an earlier brewery on the same site. By 1861, William Bushell was shown as *"Victualler and Beerhouse Keeper."*

Other later landlords included William Jordan in 1865, Edward Bentley in 1866 and 1874, Susannah Moat in 1878, George Spears from

2009.

that year. The Licensing Magistrates' report described the property thus: *"Five licensed rooms on the ground floor and two small bedrooms in the original building, together with a bed-sitting room which had been added and was permanently let. The rest of the living accommodation was constructed of corrugated iron. A lawn and summer house were for use of customers. Last public house in the borough owned by Thompsons. Old structure, with low-pitched rooms. Fair sanitary arrangements (no bathroom)."*

The following advertisement appeared in the 6 January 1937 edition of the East Kent Mercury under the heading 'Redundancy':- 'The **Hare & Hounds**,

Dover Road, Upper Walmer. *RA Howland, FAI is favoured with instructions to Sell by Auction, on the Premises as above, on Thursday, 7th January, 1937, at 11am, the household furniture and trade effects, comprising: Chest of Drawers, Mahogany Sofa, Overmantels, Carpets, Lino and Matting, Windsor Chairs, Mahogany and other Tables and Forms, Engravings and Pictures, Mahogany and Deal Shelving, Bagatelle Table and Accessories and various Games,* *Trade Glasses, Cutlery and Crockery, Mahogany Top Counter, 5-Pull Beer Engine, Pewter Tankards and Measures, Stilling, Perforated Zinc Blinds, Pine Seating, Mahogany Case Clock, Carpenter's Bench, Slate Rain Water Tank, Fowl House, Kitchen and Culinary Utensils. Goods on View Day prior to Sale from 11am. to 3pm. Catalogues and further particulars of the Auctioneer, 22 Watling Street, Canterbury. Tel 106."*

The property is now a private house.

Harp, 78 (167) Middle Street, Deal

In 1855, George Hinds was listed as "*beer retailer, painter and plumber*". By 1858, Thomas Joseph Hume Turner was landlord when he was refused a spirits licence. He applied again in 1860 and this time it was granted. By 1862, he was also listed as a "*tailor.*"

A story from the 25 January 1860 edition of the Deal & Walmer Telegram headed "*Local Intelligence*" stated: "*An excellent supper was given by Mr T. Turner, the landlord of the 'Harp' Inn, on Tuesday evening, when between 40 and 50 of the friends of Mr Turner assembled to partake of the excellent repast which was provided. The chair was taken by Mr Henry Thompson, and a most agreeable and happy evening was spent, enlivened by sentiment and song to a late hour.*"

Stephen Huxstep took over in 1873, having previously been at the **Drum** in Walmer. Thomas Walter Desormeaux was resident in 1878 and reports showed him still to be in residence in the 1890s. It appears he could cut hair and supply a beer on a Sunday morning all for 4d (2p)! However, in 1895, he was fined 10 shillings (50p) and 8/6d (42½p) costs for selling spirits "*not of the substance demanded.*"

JW Lusted was mine host in 1897, swiftly followed by Harry Thomas in 1898. In February 1899, he was fined for selling gin below strength. He pleaded guilty as he thought the offence had occurred "*due to evaporation as so little gin was sold*". He was fined 5 shillings (25p) and 8/6d (42½p) costs.

Rowland Henry Wallis took over the licence later in 1899 and, in 1905, Joseph Cole was the licensee.

According to a local report of 31 October 1908, landlord, Frederick Sawkins, was summonsed for "*serving ale by retail, not in a cask or bottle known as a two of ale*" and was fined 10 shillings (50p), with 13 shillings costs (65p). Later that year, Cyril Higgins took over as landlord.

In March 1909, a report stated: "*the building is old and, with the exception of the club room and tap*

2009.

at rear, rooms are small and it is recommended that the house should be closed". The East Kent Brewery was the beer supplier at the time.

The following year, the premises became a pork butcher's shop and, by 1915, they belonged to F Hammond – Fried Fish Shop but, more recently, Skardon's.

The Middle Street fish restaurant now occupies the building.

Harp

See entry for the **Pelican (2)**

Harrow

See entry for the *Arrow.*

Hole In The Roof
(Swans, (Old) Swan Hotel and Five Bells), 42-44 Queen Street, (Five Bells Lane), Deal

Original building c1900.

In 1890, workmen carrying out repair work to the original building found a stone dated 1694 that may suggest a build date for the house. In past centuries, Queen Street was called Five Bells Lane, named after the pub and brewery that stood close to the site of the present pub.

The Poor Rate book of 1776 stated: "*Thomas Oakley, and garden, Five Bells Brew House, water works, brew house, new malt house and brew house.*"

There was yet another brew house opposite the pub (now Kwik-Fit) as well as several others in Deal, in what was then a busy, thriving area.

Five Bells Lane was apparently barely wide enough for a hay cart to pass through and, in 1797, after an Act of Parliament was passed allowing tolls to be collected, it was decided to demolish properties on the south side and, after road widening, the Lane was renamed Queen Street. The tollgate was situated close to the pub.

In 1804, William Ladd was landlord of the *Five Bells* until at least 1824. By 1828, Brockman Beal was licensee and, around this time, records showed a name change to the *Swan*.

In 1838, the *Swan*'s outbuildings and yard could accommodate 20 horses and 6 wagons. Later records showed stabling for 35 horses, yet, when an agricultural show was held in nearby Victoria Park, room was made for 101 horses to be tethered at the premises.

Local legend has it that Charles Dickens stayed at the hotel during the summer of 1847 (when John Pockett was landlord) and joined in the celebrations of the opening of the Deal to Minster railway that year, and he is rumoured to have written a part of one of his novels there.

In September 1881 when Mrs Garner was landlady and the owners were Hills & Sons, brewers, a fire broke out at the rear of the hotel and a horse worth 200 guineas belonging to Sanger's Circus had to be destroyed.

In 1908, Mr Rothwell began a long stay at the house until 1937 when Thompson's brewery reluctantly agreed to re-build the pub in order that the council could widen Queen Street. On re-building, the pub was set back a few feet away from the original site and its address became known as 42-44 Queen Street. The reopening took

Current building c2009.

place in June 1937 with new landlords, Mr and Mrs Green, being installed and serving throughout the 1940s.

During the 50s and 60s, CW Foster was in charge. Several landlords followed and the pub initially changed its name to **Swans** on 1 May 1985 and then to the ***Hole in the Roof*** on 10 September 1997. A £160,000 refit followed in 1999.

The ***Hole in the Roof*** is still open for business and comprises two modern bars, one called the Soul Bar, which is a popular weekend venue for live music. It also encompasses a restaurant and hotel, and is currently in the capable hands of Paul and Kathleen Lynch.

Holland Arms (location unknown) Deal

This pub was mentioned in the Sandwich Licensed Victuallers' 'Payments For Signs List' of 1662 but otherwise remains untraceable.

Hoop & Griffin Inn
(possibly Griffin & Trumpet), Beach Street, Deal

This inn was situated between Griffin Street and Exchange Street, two houses south of the ***Royal Exchange*** pub (according to the 1804 rate book).

In 1739, the 'Friendly Society in Deal' "*meet (at the pub) forenoon to inspect accounts and do usual business of the day.*"

A reference in a 1768 edition of the Kentish Express mentioned a "*sale of furniture at Canterbury; catalogues to be had at the **Hoop & Griffin**, Deal*". A 1775 report stated that the premises are "*recommended as being in every respect superior to the **Three Kings**.*"

In 1776, the pub "*refused to billet dragoons.*" The following year, the landlord was D Pilcher and the inn was described as being "*where coaches and*

post chaises could be had". In common with many of the local pubs, the ***Hoop & Griffin*** had its own landing stage where important persons could be "*borne ashore safely and without distress.*"

In 1793, Prince Adolphus, Duke of Cambridge, landed at the ***Hoop & Griffin*** where he "*took refreshment before posting to London*". J Tomlin was landlord at the time. In 1804 James Parnell was in charge of the pub "*and tap*" and, in 1821, Harry Pluckall was landlord.

In 1828, the house was sold in the "sale of the Manor of Chamberlain's fee", along with a number of other seafront properties, and the ***Hoop & Griffin*** was one of a number of inns (including the ***Admiral Rodney***) mentioned in the sales catalogue: "*All that capital messuage or tenement lately called or*

Site of Hoop & Griffin 2009.

commonly known by the name or sign of the **Hoop & Griffin** Inn situate in Beach Street, together with the tap adjoining, with the extensive outhouses, buildings, coach-houses, stables, yards, grounds and premises thereunto respectively belonging and used therewith, lately in the occupation of Erasmus Sympson and his under-tenants and now untenanted. The Lease of a moiety of these premises has expired – and the other moiety is subject to a Lease granted to Edward Iggulden Esq., for 21 years from Michaelmas last, at the rent of £4/16s (£4.80)."
(Mr Iggulden was a wealthy brewer from Lower Street (now High Street), Deal).

In an auction at the **Royal Exchange** pub in 1853, the catalogue states that it is "well known as the site of the **Hoop & Griffin**, extending at the front 57 feet, with a depth of 149 feet."

There is unconfirmed evidence to suggest that the **Hoop & Griffin** was one and the same as the **Griffin & Trumpett**.

The name '**Hoop & Griffin**' suggests a hoop around an old wooden beer barrel and a griffin was a mythical hybrid of the offspring of a lion and an eagle, being the king of beasts and the most majestic of birds.

There was also a Mr Griffin living in Griffin Street, according to the 1841 census, but whether or not he had connections with the pub is unknown.

Coastguard cottages were built on the site and, later, Mary Hougham's Almhouses which remain to the present day.

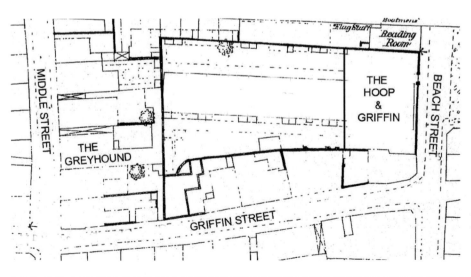

Map showing Hoop & Griffin (and later the Greyhound).

Hope (Blacksmiths Arms)
149 & 149a (73) Middle Street, Deal

The pub was originally called the **Blacksmiths Arms** when John Foffey was landlord in 1738. (It was also mentioned in an auction sale held there in 1768 when the property being auctioned at the time was the nearby **Ship** inn).

According to a recent resident, the cellar probably dates back to the reign of King Charles II since this is the age of the round fireplace in a ground floor room. There is an old doorway leading to what was a snug bar in the next door corner property as the pub was originally situated in the two buildings which have since been separated. Old maps do indeed show the pub to be situated on a corner plot. Both buildings are situated north of Portobello Court (a thoroughfare then containing brothels and nicknamed 'Blood Alley') which itself was built around 1755.

The pub was still known as the **Blacksmiths Arms** in 1821 with Thomas Buttress, but the first mention

2009.

of it as the **Hope** was in 1823 with Thomas Redsull as landlord.

It is likely that the pub was christened the **Hope** after a local lugger of the same name that went down with all hands lost.

Other landlords included John Smith who was mentioned in 1832 and 1840, James C Roberts in 1845 and 1855, and a licence transfer of 1868 showed Eliza Shepherd Roberts in charge.

William Cavell Durban was resident in 1872 and 1881, Charles Durban in 1888, Frederick Charles Spicer in 1893 and 1902 and William Robert Chapman in 1905 who transferred to Henry Thomas later that year.

The pub closed around 1908 when Henry Thomas took over the **Ship** in Middle Street. Charrington's brewery held onto the property until 1956 when it was sold and divided into two separate residential properties. The old pub premises are now private houses.

Horse & Farrier
19 (8)(9) Farrier Street, Deal

The 1804 Valuation List records the pub's location as being the *"fifth on the north side of Farrier Street"* (as approaching from Middle Street), with landlord, James Larkins, who was still resident in 1821. Mary Larkins was shown in 1824. Samuel Mourilyan the younger was in occupation in 1828 when the premises were shown as being at no 8 Farrier Street.

Other later licensees included John Marden shown listed in 1839, Mary Marden from 1845 to 1852, Richard R Canney in 1855, Robert M Mackie in 1859 and Henry Mackie in 1873.

On 2 August 1884, a local newspaper advertised: *"To be*

*disposed of with immediate possession of an old established public house in a good position in Farrier Street now in full trade the **Horse & Farrier**. A good skittle ground. Apply to John Norris on the premises"* (no 9).

In March 1897, landlady, Anna Maria Diggerson, was found be open out of hours and accordingly fined 10 shillings (50p) with 7/6d (37½p) costs. The following year, the premises held a music and singing licence when Mrs Ellen Harris took over (and she was still listed as being there in 1910).

In November 1906, John *2009.*

Drummond of Lowestoft was remanded in custody after stealing 16 shillings (80p) in coppers, 14 ounce packets of tea and about 40 cigars while staying at the premises.

In 1908, Henry Wilson was listed as landlord.

The pub closed on 31 December 1911 and it is now a private house.

Horseshoe
(exact location unknown) North End, Deal

In 1662, John Poole sold to Thomas Swaine, husbandman, *"a messuage, malthouse and the **Horseshoe** at or near north end now or late in the tenure of Thomas White."*

Horseshoe, Middle Street, Deal

See entry for the *Shah*.

Hovelling Boat
11 Silver Street, Deal

Hovelling is most usually associated with smuggling, although the word roughly means the supplying of provisions to ships, in this case to the Downs. Hovellers would also sweep for anchors and salvage wrecks.

The *Hovelling Boat* was a beerhouse run by Henry Epsley between 1845 and 1847. Luke Penn (or Pain) was the licensee in 1851 and 1852.

By 1861, the premises had become a lodging house The pub is now a private house.

From the police court – 8 October 1887: Edward Williams was fined 7/6d (37½p) or 7 days, for being drunk and disorderly in the High street, and William Frost was ordered to pay the same amount for being drunk and incapable in a public passage leading from King street to Custom House lane.

The Hovelling Boat 2009.

Hut(te)

See entry for the *Half Moon*.

India Arms (East India Arms)
71 (118) Beach Street, Deal

This pub was formerly called the *East India Arms* and was situated on the north western corner of Beach Street and King Street. The East India Company was established in 1600 to challenge the Dutch-Portuguese monopoly of the spice trade with India and the East.

c1860. From a painting by S Willey.

The company's ships would anchor in the Downs to unload goods or to take shelter.

The first mention of this hostelry appeared in 1680. King Street was called Whetstone Street in the 1600s (named after Deal's first postmaster, Nicholas Whetstone) and thereafter became known as East India Arms Lane. It later became King's Street and various other names in the interim before settling on the present day 'King Street'.

Deal Mayor, Thomas Powell, known to be a *"God-fearing man"*, noted in his diary for 1703 that he advised a coach driver waiting outside the *East India Arms* not to travel to Canterbury because it was the Lord's Day. Powell was famous for walking around Deal and closing down any pubs that he found to be open on a Sunday.

An advertisement in the 7 July 1750 edition of the Kentish Post read: *"To let or for sale, old accustom tavern, East India Arms. Inquiries to Rob Cudden, Draper."*

In October 1753, it was announced that: *"John Dixon of Deal has taken up the East India Arms which is now fitted out as an inn and tavern."*

During the 1770s, meetings of the Justices were held at the *India Arms* to discuss parish business, with William Read being the landlord in 1773, followed by Stephen Long in 1788 and George Noakes (and later Isabel Noakes) from 1788 (to 1824). A local newspaper reported that the Deal Lodge of 'The Free and Easy Johns' met at the pub on Thursday, 21 February 1794. The *East India Arms* was considered to be a *"noted hostelry"* and used by many important townspeople and naval luminaries, not least by Lord Horatio Nelson himself.

George Curling took over the licence in 1824, followed by Robert Neal, *"Licensed Victualler and Brewer"* in 1838 and Mary Neal from 1851 to 1852 when the house was noted as the *India Arms* tavern and, in 1855, as the *India Arms* hotel when it became the property of Alexander Frederick Samuel Bird (later Alderman and three times Mayor of Deal, a Justice of the Peace and an agent for the East India Company).

The premises were described in 1867 licensing records as: *"The India Arms and Wine and Spirits Merchants ... vaults and a counting house in King Street"*. It was probably around this time the *India Arms* closed down, with Bird turning the premises into a private residence for himself and family, and the wine vaults continuing to operate in King Street as a separate entity as they still retained an alehouse licence. The old pub now forms part of an arcade.

2009.

Jolly Butcher (George & Dragon, Danejohn, Dane John) 73 (119), Beach Street, Deal

The *Dane John* beer shop was mentioned only once by name – in Melville's Directory of 1858 – with John Belsey Finnis as landlord. He was still registered at the address as a beer retailer in 1862. The 'Danejohn' brewery belonged to Ash & Co of Watling Street, Canterbury at the time so this would have been the connection.

By 1866, George Lawrence was shown as a *"Beer Retailer and Grocer"*. According to the Poor Rate books in 1867 and 1868, the premises were then known as the *George & Dragon*. By the following year, they had become known as the *Jolly Butcher* with Richard Fox as *"Beerhouse Keeper"*. According to the Mercury, the pub ceased trading round about 1870/1871.

By 1875 the property was known as a "refreshments room" with Stephen Pain Job as landlord. Job was fined 5 shillings (25p) for being open during prohibited hours. According to Pike's Directory of 1904, he was still at the premises running a "dining room."

Pains Directory also refers to the premises as being a "refreshments room" in 1913, with Mrs E Wedge as proprietor. The façade at the front of the house remains but the interior has been incorporated into the amusement arcade on the corner of King Street.

2009.

Jolly Gardener, 37 (14) Golf Road (Western Road, North Sandy Lane), Deal

This pub is situated at the North End of Deal. When the house originally opened, it was surrounded by market gardens, a fact which is reflected in the pub's name.

John Taylor, *"Labourer and Publican"* was landlord from 1841 until 1875. According to licensing documentation from the 1860s, the *Jolly Gardener* was noted as being *"formerly the Hare & Hounds"* – see separate entry – which causes confusion as to its early history. According to Ordnance Survey maps, the pub had been rebuilt in the late 1800s on the corner plot which it now occupies, having seemingly been previously sited slightly further south (in what was

c1920.

possibly the *Hare & Hounds* premises at no 13 Golf Road before its rebuild).

Taylor transferred the licence to Edward Redsull, followed by John Thomas Skinner in 1879, WH Skinner in 1906 and Francis Joseph Wyatt in 1911. In May of that year, he was summonsed for installing an illegal *"automatic gaming machine that only had an element of chance and skill involved"* at the pub. He was fined 9/- (45p) with costs.

Edward Fletcher Davison was landlord in 1914, FS Adams in 1921, Albert Charles Pilcher and C Swinyard both in 1933, James Henry Fisher in 1934, SJ Day in 1948, EJ Gutteridge in 1957, Cecil James

2009.

in 1965 until at least 1974 (when the house was recorded as being owned by brewers, Charrington), Anthony Tweed in 1982 and Clive Burrell and Janice Evans in 1994.

The pub closed down in 1997, and, on 23 December 1999, the Mercury announced the District Council's intention of turning it into a community centre for the people of North Deal. However, on 5 October 2000, it was reported that tenders for conversion works were higher than had been originally anticipated. In the event, the council eventually withdrew its plans and, by 2003, the building was under threat of demolition.

However, William "Billy" Lee Smith bought the empty freehold property at a sealed bid auction, having formerly been manager of the *Lord Nelson* in Walmer for five years, and the Mercury reported in May 2004 that the *Jolly Gardener* was due to reopen on 20 May for the first time in seven years.

The pub, a free house, remains open to this day.

Mid 1950s.

Jolly Sailor, east side of Beach Street, Deal

The *Jolly Sailor* was located near the Customs House which once stood on the beach, opposite the current turning into King Street. An advertisement in the Kentish Post dated 31 January 1750 read: *"Deal – Sale at Jolly Sailor of large* *house facing sea near custom house; Jolly Sailor, capstan and ground. Inquiries to Wm Iggulden, Plumber"*. The sale of the *Jolly Sailor* was to be held on the premises themselves.

No further mention of the pub could be found.

Jolly Sailor
(Norfolk Arms) (440 Western Road), Deal

c1960.

The building was recorded as being a malthouse in 1700, 1751 and 1754 when it was noted as being the *"Jolly Sailor late of Theophilus Carter"*, even though the late local historian, Les Cozens, suggested a build of 1778 for the house.

The pub was a known "receiving house" used by smugglers. With the landlord's knowledge, contraband would be safely hidden away until a time when it could be sorted in readiness for transportation to places such as London in order to be sold on.

From 1804 until 1839, Matthew Brown was listed as landlord. In those days, the pub was much frequented by vagrants and itinerant travellers passing along the Ancient Highway in between Deal and Sandwich, and it was known as a doss-house that provided cheap lodgings. Those who were unable to afford a bed would be offered the use of a line that was secured on the wall from one side of a room and stretched tightly across to the opposite wall. They could then hook their arms over the line while standing up and leaning against it in the hope of getting a little sleep (all depending on how much alcohol they had previously consumed presumably!). In 1861, it was documented that 37 people had stayed overnight on the premises.

In July 1858, landlord, Alexander Harvey, charged Ellen Miller with assault. After serving her beer, he advised her to seek lodgings elsewhere since the hour was late and all of his beds had already been taken for the night. She apparently became abusive, scratched his face and threw stones at the windows. PC James Shelvey Cox said in evidence she had been very drunk when he had taken her into custody. He had seen her an hour earlier fighting with another woman at the *Ship & Castle*. Miller admitted she had been drunk but denied the assault, claiming she had only been defending herself. She was found guilty and was told to pay a fine of 14/- (70p) or spend seven days in Sandwich Gaol.

The pub must have been a very squalid place in the mid 1800s since, in 1831, there was an outbreak of cholera at the house and, in September 1858, it was reported that a lady had fainted from the smell of *"night soil"* that had been deposited next to the *Jolly Sailor*. Further, in July 1865, a nearby ditch had been causing a nuisance, running off from the farm next door and, in August 1866, cholera once again broke out at the pub resulting in the deaths of five people. Part of a letter, signed *"A Rambler"*, addressed to the editor of the local newspaper in September that year stated: *"I walked until my olfactory nerves warned me of my approach towards a market garden in North Sandy Lane, where I saw about three or four dozen pigs playing round a large heap of manure; these pig-styes join the road, and a few yards from them stands the 'Jolly Sailor', where five persons recently died from cholera in the short space of two weeks.*

A gentleman visitor has just told me that Deal people are very dirty, and, if visited with cholera, it would be their own fault". (Although the contents of the ditch would have been used as manure for the nearby fields and orchards, it is also believed that smuggled goods were sometimes secreted in the mire).

The pub was renamed the Norfolk Arms later that year in an obvious attempt to distance itself from its recent bad publicity, and, on 7 August 1868, compensation was paid to the landlord following the *"destruction of materials after cholera deaths."*

In 1871, a licence change from George Weaver to William Forester took place and, in February 1873, landlord, Edward Austin was summonsed for selling beer without a licence and for exhibiting a sign inferring that the premises were licensed when they were not. Owners, Hills & Son, brewers, applied for and were granted an order allowing them to eject Austin from the premises after he had refused to leave. The pub's licence was temporarily placed in the name of auctioneer, M Langley, who transferred

it to Patrick Harris who, in 1878, was summonsed for keeping prostitutes on the premises. He was fined £1 with 10/6d (57½p) costs or, in default, 14 days' imprisonment.

According to the 1881 Census, the following people were resident at the pub: *"Patrick Harris, widow, aged 50, born in Ireland, head, licensed victualler; Patrick Harris, unmarried, aged 15, born in Canterbury, son, assistant licensed victualler."*

The following local newspaper article, headed *"A Child Scalded"*, appeared in the 23 October 1886 edition: *"On Monday last, a little girl named Mary Connor, 7 years of age, daughter of a tramp who was staying at the Norfolk Arms, was badly scalded. When near the fire in the kitchen, she ran against a kettle of boiling water, upsetting it over her face and head. She sustained very severe injuries to the right side of her face and eyes. The little sufferer was attended to by a chemist in the town, and afterwards proceeded with her parents to Folkestone."*

On 5 September 1889, the pub reverted to its original name, the *Jolly Sailor*, with William Hanger as landlord. During his time at the pub, he advertised: *"Fine Deep Sea Herrings. A large quantity of fine bloaters (well-cured, and fit for keeping), in large or small quantities; also sprats, hams and tongues, smoked with the best materials. Apply William Hanger, 'Jolly Sailor', Deal. Letters Answered."*

Landlord George Neeve oustide the pub c1930.

In October that year, Hanger was fined £1 including costs for opening during prohibited hours.

George Neeve and his family took over the pub in 1903 until the mid 1940s, followed by William Frederick John Foat in 1948 and Mrs E Foat in 1955 who was the last licensee.

The *Jolly Sailor* closed its doors for the last time in 1966. Evidently, the underground workings of Betteshanger Colliery had caused subsidence that had affected the pub's foundations. The building was demolished in 1969. Residential housing now stands on the site.

Kings Arms (1)
185 (176) Beach Street, Deal

The **Kings Arms** was located next door to the **Royal Exchange** pub. The first reference found of this pub was in relation to John Wyborn, *"late Master of the Kings Arms"* who died after a lingering illness in 1794.

James White was registered landlord in 1804 until 1824. During his time at the pub, John Nelson was shot in the doorway in 1818, having been involved in some sort of smuggling dispute.

John Petty took over in 1824, followed by Mary Ann Petty in 1848, Richard John Boakes in 1856 and widow, Eliza Ann Boakes, in 1863. The pub was put up for auction in 1870 and advertised thus:-

"Deal – Important to Brewers, or other Persons Requiring an old Established Freehold Inn. Mr George West has received instructions to sell by auction, on Tuesday, July 5th, 1870, all that convenient Freehold Inn known as the 'Kings Arms', pleasantly situated in the Beach Street, commanding an uninterrupted view of the Downs, Goodwin Sands, Coast of France, &c. A good Trade has for many years been carried on and the Buildings are in an excellent state of repair, there having been a considerable sum expended on them within the last few years. The House contains 7 Bed Rooms, WC, 3 Sitting Rooms, Bar, Bar Parlour, good Domestic Offices, large Yard, and an extensive range of Buildings in the rear, with back entrance into Middle Street, and an excellent supply of good water. Time of Sale 2 for 3 o'clock in the Afternoon, on the Premises as above. The Old Established Business to be Disposed of, offering an excellent opportunity to any Person requiring a good and respectable trade. The Stock, Furniture, Trade Fittings, &c., to be taken at a valuation in the usual way. For further Particulars and Conditions of Sale enquire of the Auctioneer, or of Mr J.C. Martin, Solicitor, Deal and Sandwich."

"All that messuage, tenement or public house, no

2009.

176 in Beach Street, commonly called or known by the name or sign of the 'Kings Arms' and the outhouses, edifices, buildings, stable, yard and ground thereunto belonging, and now in the occupation of John Petty; together with a small messuage or tenement at the back of the last-mentioned premises in a passage leading from Middle Street, in the occupation of Thomas Beach and also a piece of land or ground now used as a way or passage leading as well from the last described premises as from other premises to the Middle Street there. These premises are subject to a Lease granted to Matthew William Sankey for 21 years from 29th September 1812 at the yearly rent of £3/13s. (£3.65) and to a Covenant therein contained for a renewal thereof for a like term of 21 years at the end of 18 years of the existing term upon payment of a fine of £3/9s (£3.45)." (The passage referred to used to link Middle Street and Beach Street. A commemorative sign bearing the name 'Kings Arms Alley' can be seen on the side wall of no 154 Middle Street marking the start of the passage which has since been blocked off).

Eliza Ann Boakes transferred the licence to Robert Fleming in February 1872 but he died shortly afterwards so it reverted to her in October 1873. In 1877, the renewal of the licence was refused but no reason for this was given and the pub shut down.

By the early 1900s, the building had become part of the Enfield boarding house, along with other neighbouring houses to the north along Beach Street.

Fast forwarding to the mid 20th century, the **Kings Arms** was a private members' club in the 1960s, 70s and 80s, variously known as the Pink Shell, Oasis, North Beach, Beach and the Baron's clubs, with several different owners including Arthur Fuller, Baron Browning and Peter and Ann Young.

The pub now rests as a private house.

Kings Arms (2) Beach Street, Deal

See entry for the *Royal Hotel.*

Kings Head
(Olde Kings Head) 9 (8, 83, 85, 84) Beach Street, Deal

The first mention of the *Kings Head* tavern was found in 'The Calendar of State Papers Domestic' in the reign of King Charles I in 1643.

William Matthews, linen-draper, bought a shop on waste ground *"near the Kings Head tavern in Deal."* He wanted to build a property three storeys high but was legally prevented from doing so as it would *"interrupt light from the tavern"*. The location was confirmed in the Deal Tenements Book of 1673 when Matthews was stated as having two tenements next door (north) of landlord, William Rand's pub, the *Kings Head*. Rand himself owned eight properties also described as being situated north of the pub. Further confirmation of their location was found in the deeds of the *Fairfax* (now part of *Dunkerleys*) stating that he owned housing to the south and to the west of the *Fairfax*.

By 1720, William Mullett was resident (followed by Susannah Mullett in 1740). Some time during that decade, William Mullett sold the pub to Hercules Baker. (The Baker family owned a large mansion, later known as the Beach House Hotel, which overshadowed that part of Beach Street. It was used as a 'block house' during World War II, but was demolished, with some difficulty, in 1953. It occupied the site of the current sea front seating area used by customers of the *Kings Head,* the *Port Arms* and *Dunkerleys*).

The *Kings Head* was sited close to the entrance of the large Naval Yard that dated back to Elizabethan times and which covered the area between the Timeball Tower and Deal Castle, and inland as far as the present day Victoria Road.

2009.

The pub was variously addressed as no 84 Beach Street in 1836, no 85 in 1878 and, later, no 83, and then, mysteriously, no 8, until the main streets of Deal were renumbered in 1893 when it settled on no 9 Beach Street. (Interestingly, the 1872 Ordnance Survey map indicates that the pub was merely half its size at that time and only occupied the northern part of the current building).

An article, headed, *"The Late Thomas Spears"*, appeared in the Mercury sometime in the 1860s: *"The body of this poor fellow, who was drowned at the Goodwin, on the 10th February, has not yet been recovered, and a reward of £2 has been offered therefor. The following description of the deceased is given: Blue jacket and trowsers, blue Guernsey, blue cotton shirt, white flannel shirt and drawers, marked TWS, half Wellington boots. The age of the deceased is stated to be 22 years. Information is to be forwarded to Mrs Moat, 'Kings Head', Beach-st."*

A look at the list below of landlords, owners and licensees shows an abundance of different tavern keepers. Perhaps most interesting of all is the lady named "Sarah Anne" and "Sarah Annie", assuming she is one and the same person. Installed in 1866, she appears to have to seen off a fair number of husbands during her time at the pub – five in all – until her eventual departure in 1893!

The licensees included William Rand in 1673, William Mullett in 1720, Hercules Baker in the 1720s, Susannah Mullett in 1740, Richard Dawes in 1776, John Iggulden, brewer, in 1777, Widow Cavell in 1804, Edward Iggulden, brewer, in 1817, Stephen Gosby in 1821, William Ralph in 1834, John Gough in January 1846, Margaret Prescott in 1846, Hills brewery in 1851, George Manger Moat in 1855, Sarah Anne Moat, widow, in 1866, Edward Charles Trott in 1867, Sarah Anne Trott, widow, in 1871, William Stephen Collard Lambert in 1872, Sarah Anne Lambert, widow, in 1874, Campbell Cleary in 1877, Thomas Kitchen in 1878, William Robert West Meakins in 1880, James Holland in 1881, Sarah Annie Holland, widow, in 1883, Sarah Annie Rock in 1885, Esther Annie Sparks in 1893, Walter Francis Padbury in 1894, Arthur Bassington also in 1894, Edward John Miles in 1895 until 1935 (during which time Thompson's brewery became the owners circa 1901), Rosetta Miles, widow, in November 1935, Nora Daw-Miles in 1937 until 1963 (during which period Charrington's brewery took ownership from Thompson's around 1951), Frank and Rose Kitchen in 1963 and Rose Kitchen, widow, in 1971, when the pub closed.

In 1975, Charrington's decided to sell the *Kings Head* as a private house. Major James Corke bought the building in 1979 with the intention of renewing the licence and reopening the pub. Despite some opposition, the new licence was granted and the *Kings Head* once more opened for business. According to Dover Magistrates' Licensing records, Thomas Clift and Timothy Corbett were landlords in 1979. Graham Stiles became mine host in October 1980 and continues to run the pub to the present date, together with Shirley and James Stiles.

Although the interior of the modern day *Kings Head* has changed in recent years, it still retains a rustic décor. It has a circular counter with an open plan bar that is partially sectioned off to create three separate areas, together with an outside terrace overlooking the beach. The pub serves meals, and shows regular televised championship football matches, as well as other sporting events. Bed and breakfast is available at the pub, as well as at the Channel View Guest House, owned by the pub, a couple of doors away. The *Kings Head* is famous for its award winning floral displays that adorn the front of the building throughout the summer months.

Kings Head, Upper Deal

See entry for the *Liverpool Arms*.

Kings Head, Walmer

See entry for the *Queens Head, Walmer*

Kurn

See entry for the *Quern*.

From Deal Police Court – 1887:

Henry Kirkaldie was charged with being drunk and disorderly in Beach-street, Deal, on the 6th inst, and also assaulting Supt Capps while in the execution of his duty. After evidence, the defendant expressed his sorrow for what had occurred, and was fined 7/6d (37½p) for the assault, together with 4/10d (24p), or in default, 7 days hard labour for each offence.

Labour in Vaine (location unknown) "Deale"

Pubs bearing this name were considered to be a mis-translation of old Norman inn signs either called Laboureur Vanne (ploughman's gate) or Laboureur Vin (ploughman's wine).

In less politically correct times, pub signs would sometimes depict a white woman endeavouring to scrub a black baby white in a bath. Another possible explanation is that the name was meant to imply that any attempts to find ale of the same high quality in any other pub or indeed to brew one's own as excellent as that for sale inside the pub would be considered to be a complete 'labour in vain'!

The *Labour in Vaine* was mentioned briefly on a 1662 Payments for Signs list showing John Cranbrooke as landlord.

The pub's exact location is unknown but it is thought to have been situated somewhere on Deal beach.

Laughing Toad, 32-36 Queen Street, Deal

See entry for the *Academy Sports Bar.*

Laurel Tree

See entry for the *Phoenix.*

Lifeboat, 14 The Marina (Beach Street), Deal

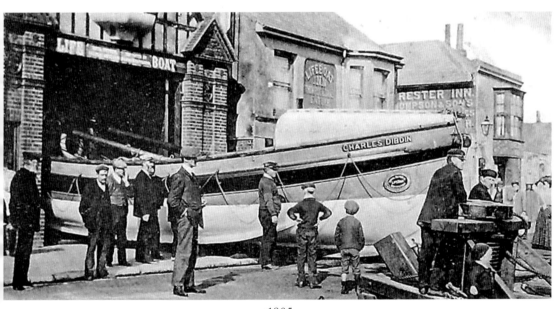

c1905.

The *Lifeboat* was located on the south eastern corner of Dibdin Road and opened as a beerhouse in 1870 after considerable difficulty in obtaining a licence following the Licensing Act of 1869 which was designed to reduce the number of pubs and to put beerhouses under the control of local magistrates. (The *Lifeboat* was situated next door to the North Deal Lifeboat Station – which was built in 1883 – and was located between the *Forester* and *North Star* pubs). Despite a later application for a full licence (which was rejected), the *Lifeboat* remained solely a beerhouse throughout.

Sarah Hannah Bowbyes was listed as licensee in 1870, Charles Phillip Bowbyes in 1871, Sarah Bowbyes (again) in 1873, William Nicholas in 1876, Rebecca Nicholas in 1878, Edmund Joshua Pain in 1888 and 1895, William Francis Partridge Stanton in 1902 and William Henry Marsh from December 1905 until the pub closed on 28 December 1907.

The property became a private house but it was demolished in 1972 to make way for the Dibdin House flats that now stand on the site.

Lifeboat Inn
28 & 28a (5) Campbell Road, Walmer

This pub was situated midway between the North and South Barracks.

The property was registered in the name of Edward Leith prior to the 1850s. He was a member of the prosperous Leith family who owned much property and land in Walmer at the time.

The *Lifeboat Inn* already had its name by 1857 when part of it was let to WJ Green for 13 shillings (65p) and another part to WJ Green and E Norris for 12/6d (62½p).

A Mercury article of 1885 reported that "*William Cullen Norris, landlord of The Lifeboat Inn, died suddenly. He had been out on the beach the previous evening in his usual good health.*"

2006.

Frederick Wingfield Leith was registered as owner in 1893 and, by 1898, William Daniel Bloyce was landlord.

An elderly Deal resident, in the course of documenting his childhood memories, described the character of the pub around the early 1900s. The habitués were mostly boatmen and fishermen who, sitting around hand-turned iron-legged tables, enjoyed their pints (which cost three old pennies – 1½p) in front of roaring fires while playing crib or dominoes for two old pennies (1p) a game (and sometimes sharing out their takings from the day's catch). The atmosphere was happy and casual and just the sort of place where the men could sup without the need to change out of their heavy weather clothing.

Bloyce remained landlord until 1908. He was followed by Richard Thomas Wakerell who remained at the pub until it shut down on 31 December 1909 (before moving on to the *Brickmakers Arms*) after magistrates had refused to renew its licence. Their report described the pub as being situated "*...midway between North and South Barracks. Cellar, public and private bars with modern fittings. Separate entrance from Canada Road. Tap room, good back yard, kitchen and scullery, upper floors with 8 good bedrooms, some with fireplaces. Gas and water laid on.*"

By 1913, the property had become a fishmongers run by Mr F Adams, and, by 1915, it was also selling fried fish. In 1924, the property was sold by Frederick Leith to WT Hunter and, a year later, it was split into two properties. In 1927, no 28 was sold for £385 and then again later, in 1961, for £1,500.

The pub now comprises private housing.

Lifeboat
(True Briton, Little Briton, Briton, Two Brittons, True Britain, True Britannia)
16 The Strand (Walmer Road), Walmer

The first mention of this house was in 1787 when Morris Wellard was listed as landlord of an unnamed pub (remaining there until at least 1823). However, the house (or possibly an earlier one on the site) is believed to be older since it was described in the early 1700s as being the last building on Walmer Road (now The Strand) before coming across the *Drum* on Drum Hill (now Dover Road).

In 1799, it was documented as being called the *True Briton*, followed by the *True Britannia* in 1807, the *Little Briton* in 1817, followed by various other variations including the *Two Brittons*, *True Briton*, *True Britain* and the *Briton*!

The True Briton was the name of an East Indiaman built at Deptford in 1790 and a picture of it used to hang in the bar. A ship bearing this name

c1904.

1989.

(possibly the same one) floundered on the Goodwin Sands in 1798 and, in 1857, it was the name of the convict ship which transported the landlord of the **Ship** in Beach Street to the West Indies (see separate entry).

William Wellard was mine host from 1829 until 1855, followed by Edward Wyborn in 1866, Samuel Thomas Pearson in 1870 until at least 1876, George Steadman in 1889 (under the ownership of Hill's brewery), George Redman in 1898, E Brooking in 1904, Frederick George Roser in 1908, George Edward Solley in 1911 and Walter Frederick Taylor in 1912. The pub came under threat of closure by the Compensation Committee in 1911, but remained open. Magistrates' report at the time described the pub as including *"Public bar, passage, bar parlour, private bar and large room which could be used as a tap room or parlour. A smoking room to the right of the front door. In the summer, 10 or 12 people might be staying there. Accommodation about same as **Stag** and better than **Alma**. Also tea and luncheon trade. Bar trade mix of lifeboat men, boatmen, RMs and tradesmen."*

In 1936, J Barlett was licensee, followed later that year by his widow, Alice, who in turn transferred the licence to Charles Douglas Miles.

The pub changed its named on 3 September 1976 to the *Lifeboat*, taking its name from Walmer Lifeboat Station that stands in front of the building on Walmer Green. The pub's sign was repainted every time the coxswain changed, the first one showing Harry Brown, coxswain of the Walmer Lifeboat called the Hampshire Rose (which was launched by round the World yachtsman, Sir Alec Rose).

The pub closed down in 2004. An article, entitled *"Pub Closes After Landlady Retires"* in the Mercury on 14 October of that year reported: *"The Lifeboat pub on The Strand, Walmer, has closed. Owner Margaret Renihan, 60, has retired after being at the pub for 16 years. 'I wanted to retire when I was 60 and just enjoy the time to do all the things I want to do', she said. 'I read a lot – and I can also now go on holidays without having to get someone to run the pub. But I will miss meeting the people and having a chat.'"*

After closure, when the pub was being converted into residential accommodation, the authors were invited to look inside the gutted building. From the few original fittings that remained, the property did not appear to be of any great antiquity beyond the Victorian era.

Little Briton

See entry for the *Lifeboat,* The Strand, Walmer.

Lion (location unknown) "Deale"

This pub appeared by name in a 1680 Deale List of Inns but otherwise remains untraceable although it could possibly relate to the **Red Lion, White Lion** or any of the other *"Lyon"* pubs in the area.

Liverpool Arms (partly Kings Head, Three Kings, Three Horseshoes) 96 (92) Manor Road (Upper Deal Street), Upper Deal

c1900.

In 1682, part of the inn was commonly known by 'the name or sign of the **Kings Head**' when in the ownership of the May family whose name appeared on documents from 1725, although the landlords at the time (from 1725 until 1785) included various members of the Hayman family. During this period (June 1769), the pub was described thus: "... *And all that other messuage or tenement there called or commonly known by the name of the **Kings Head** next adjoining to the said messuage or tenement last above mentioned with the garden yard and backside to the same belonging at Upper Deal and then in the tenure or occupation of John Brett ...*". Later that year, the pub had become known as the **Three Horseshoes**.

William Pope was installed in 1785, followed by Thomas Stokes in 1804 and Henry Stokes in 1824.

The pub was mentioned in an 1803 document thus: "*Court Leet of Henry Esq (Trustee), Lord of the Leet and the Manor of Court Ash holden at the Accustomed Place the **Three Horseshoes** in Upper Deal on Monday, 31st October 1803, followed by a meeting of the Court Baron, Lord Cooper, Lord of the Manor.*"

It was run as an alehouse by Richard Arnold in 1828 when its name was changed to the **Liverpool Arms**. Robert Banks Jenkinson (aka Lord Hawksbury, later the Earl of Liverpool and latterly Prime Minister from 1812 until 1827), died that year, having also held the position of Lord Warden of the Cinque Ports from 1805.

The pub remained in the ownership of the May family and, an Indenture dated 20 May 1829, stated: "*All that messuage public house or tenement formerly known as the **Kings Head**, lately by the name of the **Three Kings** and now by the name of the **Liverpool Arms** and the stable, outhouses, yard, backside and ground hereunto belonging at Upper Deal near the Church there lately in occupation of Henry Stokes, since of Richard Hayman and now or lately Richard Arnold abutting to Upper Deal Street South-west ...*". (The name **Three Kings** was probably written in error since no documentation exists to prove that the pub was ever called this. It should probably have referred to the **Three Horseshoes** instead).

William Hookham was landlord in 1830, followed by his widow, Elizabeth, in 1845. By 1847, Charles Davies, was innkeeper at the pub together with his wife, also called Elizabeth. He was listed as a carpenter by trade with five men in his employ.

Other landlords included Robert Gibbs in 1858, William Colley from 1878 until 1883 and George R Burton from 1885 to 1898.

Several local newspaper clippings reported as follows:-

"22 September 1883: Harvest Supper at Upper Deal – A harvest supper was held on Wednesday evening last at the **Liverpool Arms**, *Upper Deal, when about 40 guests were present. After ample justice had been done at the festive board, a most enjoyable evening was spent, interspersed with songs, recitations, etc. An extension of time was granted for the occasion. Great credit is due to Mrs Colley, the worthy hostess."*

"21 February 1885: A sparrow shoot will take place at the **Liverpool Arms**, *Upper Deal, on Thursday next, when a Good Supply of Birds will be provided. Luncheon at 12.30 pm. Shooting to commence at 1.30 pm. George Burton, Proprietor."*

"7 January 1888: The Upper Deal Bell-ringers had their annual supper at Mr George Burton's The **Liverpool Arms** *on Tuesday evening. After enjoying a well served and substantial hot spread, the cloth was cleared and the singing began ... While on this subject, we would congratulate the ringers on the advances they have made in their ringing; they are now enrolled as Members of the Kent County Association of Change Ringers."*

AJ Skinner was landlord from 1903 until June 1913 when the pub closed down and the licence was transferred to Edward Lidbury of Thompson's brewery. The property was later put up for auction, the sales particulars for which giving a fascinating glimpse into the fashionable Edwardian pub and home furnishings of the day:

*"Ex-***Liverpool Arms***, Upper Deal: Messrs West,*

2009.

Usher & Co are instructed to Sell by Auction, on Tuesday, 29th January, 1914, a Quantity of Useful Household Furniture, Bar Counter, Engine Fittings and other effects comprising: Iron and wood bedsteads and bedding, iron child's cot, painted dressing tables, washstands and chests of drawers, mahogany toilet glasses, chamberware, antique tall back rush and cane-seat chairs, easy, Austrian bentwood and Windsor ditto, hall seat, Deal carpenter's and linen chests, folding mahogany portable bagatelle table, upright pianoforte in rosewood case by WH Wilkie, violin in case, auto harp, sofas and couches, upholstered tapestry and American cloth, pictures in oak, maple and ebonised frames, bamboo and rosewood frame overmantels, china and glass ornaments, capital grandfather's mantel and dial clocks in antique, oak and inland mahogany cases, antique mahogany and oak tables including Cromwellian centre, Pembroke kneehold writing and side ditto, carpets, floorcloths and mats, three-pull metal lined beer engine and fittings, mahogany top and grained return front bar counter, mahogany glazed screens with Muranese and mirror panels, shelving and other fittings, stoneware spirit barrels, pewter measures, beer, wine and spirit glasses, balance scales, automatic game machines, kitchen utensils in tin, iron and earthenware, and numerous other useful articles. On view the Morning of Sale. Sale at Eleven o'clock. Further particulars may be had of the Auctioneers at the Deal Estate and House Agency, Victoria Town, Deal and Cliff Road, Kingsdown."

The property is now a private home called The Old House (previously known as the Old House Tormore).

Liverpool Arms (location unknown) Walmer

This pub was mentioned in the Walmer Alehouse Keepers' book for 1824, showing Andrew Wright Baker as landlord.

Unfortunately, no other documentation has been found to pinpoint its exact whereabouts.

Locomotive, 104-106 West Street
(3 Glanville Cottages, Portland Terrace), Deal

c1955.

The railway first came to Deal in 1847 and the pub was undoubtedly named in celebration of this event since the railway station was very close by.

The earliest found record of the pub was in 1855 when Henry Stewart Coleman was landlord and, in 1861, it was referred to as being a *"halfway house"*. An 1865 advert declared *"H.S. Coleman, dealer in spirits and compounds, draught and bottled ales and stouts, cigars, carpenter, wheeler, etc"*. In 1870, Coleman was registered as *"Licensee and Builder"* and, in April 1878, the licence was transferred from Mary Jane Coleman to John Pott and then later to Henry Francis.

In 1890, landlord, Henry Smith, was fined five shillings (25p) with one shilling (5p) costs for selling liquor out of hours. By 1898, Henry Taylor was licensee when the pub's address was given as 3 Glanville Cottages. The licence was transferred to George Newing Spicer in 1900 and, during his time as landlord (until 1922), the pub was enlarged to take in the adjoining property. A local advert mentioned *"Deal Pram Hospital and Exchange. Perambulator Repairers, Mr & Mrs Spicer at The Locomotive."*

Other landlords included Mrs Spicer, James Leslie Sykes from 1929 to 1930, Richard G Harris in 1935, A Diffey in 1938, Lewis Wolwill in 1956 and finally E Southall in 1959 (when the pub was owned by Charringtons).

The pub closed in March 1963.

The property has been converted back into two separate dwellings, both now private houses.

Lord Clyde
61 (56, 59 & 60) The Strand, Walmer

c1955.

Lord Clyde (1792 to 1863) was previously known as Sir Colin Campbell. He was a distinguished Field Marshall, mainly remembered for the relief of Lucknow in India. It was in 1858 that he became Baron Clyde of Clydesdale.

The pub seemingly started life round about 1860. According to the 1861 census, William Bushell ran an unnamed beerhouse at no 56 The Strand. In 1870, the landlord of the *Lord Clyde*, William Romney, was charged with unlawfully assaulting and beating his wife, Rachel, and was sentenced to six months' hard labour in Sandwich Gaol.

By 1874, William T Bullen was installed as landlord. Other hosts included W Petters in 1898, William Frederick Peaks in 1901, Alfred Clarke in 1903, Henry Thomas also in 1903, PA Cavell from 1910 to 1921 and Thomas Hilson in 1923 when the East Kent Brewery advertised the premises as including a "*beerhouse and stabling.*"

From 1924 through to the 1940s, it was considered to be a "cosy family pub", with ex Royal Marine bandsman, Billy Monckton, in charge. Mrs Monckton, with help from her sister and brother in law, ran a 'fish supper saloon' in York Road from around 1924

through to the Second World War and access to it could also be gained via the backyard of the *Lord Clyde*. The father of one of the authors fondly remembers the generous portions served there!

In January 1941, there was a protection order made in favour of the brewery, Mackeson's. By 1947, Monckton had been serving for 23½ years, the same year as he was granted a wine licence. In February 1950, the pub gained a full licence.

According to the Mercury, Billy Monckton transferred the licence to Ernest Reynolds in March 1960. (Mr Monckton died in January 1963 aged 79 years). In 1964, AF Jolly was landlord, as well as being Chairman of the Deal and Walmer Licensed Victuallers' Association.

In the early 1970s saw Ellen Pickford as landlady, with brewer Shepherd Neame acquiring the pub in 1971. Ellen was a lifelong fan of comedian Max Wall and he would pop in for a drink when in the area. Philip Bailey was landlord in 1983, Vernon Toms in 1990, John and Susan Leeson circa 2004 and Steven Curd took over in 2009. The *Lord Clyde* remains open, and consists of one open plan bar and beer garden to the rear.

Lord Keith

See entry for the *Bohemian.*

Lord Napier Tavern

See entry for the *Napier Tavern.*

Lord Nelson
50 The Strand (Walmer Road), Walmer

Horatio Nelson (1758-1805) died on board The Victory at Trafalgar. *"England expects that every man will do his duty"*, he proclaimed as he galvanised his troops ready for the battle of Trafalgar. He had visited Deal in 1801 when he commented that *"Deal must be the coldest place in England, most assuredly"* and, no doubt, this pub was named in the great man's honour. The **Lord Nelson** is the oldest pub in Walmer still retaining its original name. Interestingly, Lord Nelson has more pub names associated with him, either directly or indirectly (eg the Victory, the Trafalgar, the Emma Hamilton, etc) than any other individual in the whole of England.

William Bunce Simmonds became the first landlord in 1801. In 1811, William Holton was in charge, swiftly followed by John Sturges in 1812, James Graves in 1815, Francis Scott in 1816 and James Coulder in 1819. By 1821, Thomas Ellen was licensee, succeeded by his wife, Sarah, who served until the 1840s. Around this time, Walmer Road was re-named The Strand, as shown on the 1841 census.

The house would have attracted a mix of customers, including the military (from the nearby barracks), fishermen and local tradesmen.

John, and then William, Hookham ran the pub in the mid 1840s, followed by Benjamin Smith in 1847, Henry Marsh in 1854, Silas Foord in 1862 and John Hanbrook in 1866 who was in residence when a serious fire gutted the building in 1870. It was then rebuilt as the house that stands today.

Later landlords included Simon Willey in 1874,

2009.

Henry Barrett in 1878, William Wellard in 1889, NS Williams in 1898, James Randall Doughty in 1899 and Charles Gladwell in 1904. In June of that year, the Mercury reported: *"The five-year old daughter of landlord, Charles Gladwell, was playing outside the public house when she was run over by a milk cart as she crossed the road and suffered severe grazing to her ear and face as the wheel passed over her."*

Arthur White took over from Gladwell in 1913 but died later that year and the licence was transferred to his wife, Minnie. Alice Phillips served from 1918 to at least 1932, followed by Arthur William White in 1934 when the pub was known as the **Lord Nelson** Hotel. The late 1940s to mid 1950s showed A Harding at the helm, followed in the 1960s by the charmingly named AF Jolly.

In early 1970, Bob Goodman took over, the pub having recently been shut up for a month following the death of the previous landlord. An advert appeared in the local newspaper stating: *"**Lord Nelson** Public House, Strand, Walmer, reopens today, Thursday, 12 February. The new landlord invites all old and new patrons to visit the Horatio Bar and the Hamilton Bar during licensed hours."*

Later licensees included James Austen in 1972, Thomas Clift and Lesley Stapleton in 1985 and Christopher Lunn in 1994.

The pub, together with its hotel and restaurant, remains open for business. The pub is currently run by Richard and Bernadette Burnett, and Stefan Godden is owner of the Nelson Galley restaurant.

Lord Nelson
(Dukes Head) (2) (8) (10) Short Street, Deal

Richard Wildes took a lease on the building at Short Street in 1661 although there is no evidence to show the premises were being used as a pub at the time. In 1675 and 1734, they were registered as being used as a blacksmiths and, in 1795, as a butchers.

The building is mentioned by name, the *Dukes Head*, in lists of pubs owned by Cobb's brewery of Margate between 1808 and 1817, with Edward Iggulden, brewer, becoming the owner later that year, and William Scott registered as landlord in 1821. By 1824 at least, the pub had become known as the *Lord Nelson*, becoming yet another local watering hole to be named in his honour. Nelson was, of course, a frequent visitor to Deal and the Downs.

Between 1824 and 1847, John Holness was landlord and 1851 saw Elizabeth Holness listed as licensee at "*no 10 Short Street*". Reports from the 1850s suggested the beerhouse was mainly patronised by soldiers, with an Army Major reportedly saying the house was "*a great nuisance to the neighbourhood*", and from the evidence one can understand why!

Reports stated that landlord, Edward Cooper, was in constant fear of his life because of his wife, Sarah's drunkenness and continual threats, having once hit him over the head with a bottle. Police were apparently called out at least twice a week to the premises and Sarah appeared in court four times.

By 1858, Edward and Ann Beasley (or Beazley) had taken over and it appears they were in some way involved in the smuggling trade since a contemporary diary entry, written in code, was translated to read: "*January 7 1858: Of 38 barrels sunk for recovery later, only 27 were found, the rest*

having broken adrift. Each barrel was worth £4. Four barrels were taken to the Lord Nelson in Short Street, the landlord's name being Edward Beasley."

Around the same time, it seems that Sarah Cooper was still at large and creating havoc since she was charged with kicking the door in and throwing two large stones through the windows while drunk.

In August 1864, landlord, John Garrett, was sentenced to one month's hard labour in Sandwich Gaol for unlawfully assaulting Jimima Gisby and breaking her arm.

In August 1896, the licence was transferred from Harry Thomas Hayward to Harry John Mills.

Charles Hearn was landlord there in 1902 and, by 1903, it was advertised as a "*freehold drinking house and premises, until lately known as the Lord Nelson; brick, tile and slate; 4 bedrooms, 2 sitting rooms, kitchen, wash house and loft over 2 WCs, and yard with back entrance.*"

In October 1902, an application to renew the licence was opposed by the Police as well as Mr Hookham of Beach Street. It was known to be a rowdy house, with frequent fights and raucous arguments. For this reason, the pub shut down and its licence (together with the one for the *Empire* Theatre of Varieties – see separate entry) was 'sacrificed' so that Thompsons could open its proposed new pub, the *Telegraph* – see separate entry). After it closed, it became a billiards hall for some while.

The pub was situated on the south side of Short Street, a road that was sited beside the modern day Guildford House in Beach Street. The building was bombed during World War II and subsequently demolished, along with many other properties in Short Street and parts of Middle Street. The site now forms part of the Middle Street car park.

Map locating Lord Nelson c1900.

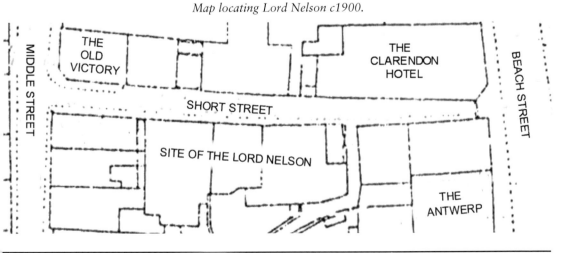

Lord Warden
(Sydenham Green) 185 Mill Road, Deal

This pub was situated on the corner of Mill Road and Hamilton Road (previously called Cemetery Road), and was originally known as the *Sydenham Green* pub, with ES Parker as landlord, in 1855. Parker was a native of Sydenham in south London and presumably named the pub after his home town. Joseph Maxted took over in 1859 and, in 1861 when James White Estes was in charge, there was a change of name to the *Lord Warden*, although, confusingly, it was still mentioned in the 1866 licensing records as the *Sydenham Green*.

The pub's new name was, of course, taken from the ancient title of 'The Lord Warden and Admiral of the Cinque Ports and Constable of Dover Castle' whose official residence was, and remains, at nearby Walmer Castle. The incumbent in 1861 was Viscount Palmerston.

In 1864, George Mackins, 58, a waterman, was charged with stealing cabbages from a field near the *Lord Warden* inn and was sentenced to 14 days hard labour. In 1867, J Smith was landlord, followed by Charles Alfred Smith in 1871. He was accused of opening during prohibited hours but the case was dismissed, with 6/6d (32½p) costs. Charles Smith was still there in 1883 when he accidentally cut the tops off two fingers on his left hand while chopping wood! In 1880, he was charged with selling alcohol at 9.45 am on a Sunday (9 November) and fined £1 and 1 shilling (5p) costs. He was still at the pub in 1891 but, by 1898, Mrs Smith was listed as licensee and "*Grocer at 1 Cemetery Road*" following her husband's death.

Other landlords included George Egbert Dunn from 1899 to1936 when WA Morey took over until at least 1948, followed by J Bilton from 1956 to at least 1966, James McLennan in 1968, Ivan Foster in 1978, Charles Pope in 1987, Ian Sparshott in 1993, David Gadd also in 1993 and Brian Johnson and

c1955.

John Kemp in 1994 until 1996 when the pub closed down and was delicensed despite public protest.

An article in the 27 February 1997 edition of the Mercury, entitled *Demolition Can Go Ahead*, reads as follows: "*Protestors have lost their fight to stop the* **Lord Warden** *pub being demolished to make way for shops. The district council backed the objectors and refused permission for the pub to be knocked down and replaced by two shops, three flats and a roof garden. But the applicants appealed against the decision and the Secretary of State for the Environment has decided the development can go ahead. An inspector considered the new building would not be inappropriate for the junction of Hamilton Road and Mill Road, or cause significant traffic problems. The inspector was concerned about late night use of the shops and insisted opening times be restricted to no later than 11pm and no earlier than 6am. He noted the 'considerable local opposition' but said many of the objections were not valid planning reasons for turning down the development.*"

The old building was subsequently demolished and the Co-op food store now stands in its place, although the pub's name still appears on a nearby bus stop.

Lord Warden
3, 5 and 5a North Barrack Road, Walmer

The *Lord Warden* was situated close to the entrance to North Barracks and was accordingly a popular watering hole for the military.

In 1863, Simon White took a 63 year lease on the property from the Leith Estate but transferred it over to E Rands in 1868. An 1869 advert mentioned "*all that newly-built and convenient hotel, three excellent billiards rooms, bar, bar parlour, coffee and sitting rooms, 5 bedrooms, coach house, stable, and other conveniences…*".

The property later went to auction and was advertised thus: "*Walmer, Kent. Leasehold Estate (fully licensed tavern, hotel, and billiards rooms) for investment. Mr Wymer, in conjunction with Messrs Gairdner & Son, will sell by auction, at the Guildhall Coffee House, Gresham Street, in the City of London, on Tuesday, July 21st, at Twelve o'clock (unless previously disposed of by Private Treaty), the Ground Lease of the Capital Premises known as the 'Lord Warden', situated in Lower Walmer, near the beach and barracks, Held for a term of 58 years at a low Ground Rent, and Let on lease terminable in 1875 at Fifty-five Pounds per annum. May be Viewed by permission of the Tenant; and Particulars and Conditions of Sale may be obtained of R.J. Emmerson, Esq., Solicitor, Sandwich and Deal; of T.C. Hall, Esq., Solicitor, Deal; of Mr Wymer, 203, Grays Inn Road, and Messrs. Gairdner & Son, 12, University Street, Tottenham Court Road, London, WC*". (The billiards rooms were eventually separated from the main property and became known as the Foresters Hall and later the Ace Ballroom).

George Rolfe was landlord in 1878, followed by J Christy in the early years of the 1900s, WH Rogers in 1910, Harry Arthur Snoswell in 1913, Percy F Grey from 1918 to 1922, FT Setterfield in 1924, PC Stevens from 1928 to 1930, FE Simpin in 1936, William Davis and BC Dredge (Secretary of Thompson's brewery) in 1938 and Anthony Frank Williams in 1945.

Interestingly, landlord, Tony (Anthony) Williams, was a friend of Noel Coward who had bought a house overlooking the beach at St Margaret's Bay shortly after WWII and who became a frequent customer at the *Lord Warden*. Before taking on the pub, Williams worked as a comedian after being demobbed from the Army following WWI. He appeared with Coward in his first revue, 'London Calling', at the Duke of York theatre in London in 1923. He later performed in several other revues and toured the halls with Charles Heslop in a golfing sketch, as well as being principal comedian with the Fols-de-Rols and appearing in several films and pantomimes. Williams met his wife, Ivy, a renowned soloist, at Leigh-on-Sea, and they toured with ENSA during WWII before settling in Walmer and running the pub. He died aged 61, in August 1953, two years after suffering a brain haemorrhage. Ivy continued running the pub until 1956.

In April 1956, the licence was transferred to Stuart Clarke, followed by LWFE Simkins and William Milne, both in 1959.

During the latter years of the pub's life, a local resident recalls having dancing lessons in the Ace Ballroom, followed by drinks at the *Lord Warden* pub afterwards.

Thompson's brewery sold the freehold on 4 July 1961 for £3,050. In August 1963, the Mercury reported that the *Lord Warden* had been closed for "*the last few years.*"

The original *Lord Warden* building has since been converted into two private houses and one retail outlet – no 3 is the original pub building, and nos 5 (now Keith Chadwick barber's shop) & 5A housed the pub's billiards rooms (later on becoming, first, the Foresters Hall and, latterly, the Ace Ballroom).

c1955.

Loyal Subject
(exact location unknown) Beach Street, Deal

The *Loyal Subject* was located on the eastern side of Beach Street, its site having presumably now been covered by the present day promenade.

The only documentation found for this pub appeared in a 1686 will made by John Laurence who left: *"to my daughter Mary Kingsland wife of John Kingsland the messuage where I now dwell called the* **Loyal Subject** *on Deal beach and all my other messuages against that called the* **Loyal Subject** *now occupied by Robert Hutton and the shop adjoining to my son John."*

Loyon & Whelp

See entry for the *Margate Hoy*.

Lyon & Castle (location unknown) "Deale"

The *Lyon & Castle* was mentioned in the Deale Payments for Signs list of 1662 but otherwise remains untraceable.

Lyon & Griffin (location unknown) "Deale"

The *Lyon & Griffin* was another pub mentioned in the Deale Payments for Signs list of 1662 but again remains untraceable.

Lyon & Whelp

See entry for the *Margate Hoy*.

From the Police Court – 1862:

Henry Walker, beerhouse keeper, was brought up in custody charged by PC Shelvey Cox with being found drunk and incapable, in Duke St on Saturday afternoon. He was bleeding from his face, and had a horse and cart with him, which he was unable to take care of; consequently Cox conveyed him to the lock-up, and took charge of the horse and cart. Walker was fined 10/- (50p) including costs, which was immediately paid, and the prisoner tripped lightly out of court, evidently well-satisfied with the decision of the bench.

Magnet
267 London Road (Church Path, Upper Deal Road, 62 Turnpike Road, Stony Path, Gravel Walk), Deal

1918.

A recent potted history stated that the **Magnet** had been an alehouse/shop in the 1700s and early 1800s although the authors have unfortunately been unable to find any documentary evidence to confirm it being a pub before 1845.

The first mention of a building called Magnet House appeared in 1784 when its location was given as 'Church Path'. By 1845, Richard Verrier junior was shown resident of the **Magnet** pub *"and garden"*. In 1847, it was described as a *"beerhouse"* and an *"alehouse"* (ie fully licensed) in 1850, with William P Verrier registered as landlord in 1851. A graveyard belonging to St Leonard's church backed on to the pub and, during the Victorian era, the story goes that the Verrier family was paid a fee by the parish to keep guard over it at night. This was probably done in an effort to prevent body snatchers from removing fresh corpses from their graves and sold on for medical science, as well as deterring other ne'er-do-wells and smugglers from using the graveyard for their own purposes. Indeed, a member of the family would, by all accounts, take up vigil every night at one of the pub's windows, shotgun at the ready!

An old headstone propped up against the wall in the now disued graveyard belongs to the Verrier family, who were apparently related by marriage to another family of local innkeepers, the Marshes.

A local newspaper article from 1863 headed *"Annual Tea Party at **Magnet**, Upper Deal"* reported: *"On the green attached to the premises, a very pleasant evening was spent, the time being occupied playing bowls and other rustic sports."*

In 1886, the **Magnet** was put up for sale. The sales' notice read: *"To Brewers and Others. Fully licensed Free public house – The **Magnet** – at Upper Deal. To be sold 19 August at 3pm in one Lot – All that eligible and very desirable Freehold Inn or Public House called the '**Magnet**' at Upper Deal, adjoining the main road from Deal to Sandwich, with about ½ acre of excellent Garden Ground, in the occupation of the owner Mr George Verrier. Possession at Michaelmas on completion of purchase."*

The pub went up for sale again in August 1888 and the auction was held at the Bull & George Hotel in Ramsgate. The particulars describe the **Magnet** as having *"an excellent enclosed garden, containing about a quarter of an acre, no 125 on Tithe Map, the whole having a frontage to the Main Road from Deal to Sandwich of about 80 feet. The House contains tap parlour, living room, kitchen, and wash-house, on the ground floor; four bedrooms and a dressing room on the next floor. The commodious basement comprises 3 large cellars and a coal cellar. There is a good supply of spring and rain water, and the fixtures will be included in the sale. The garden is very suitable for a tea garden. Possession will be given on completion of the purchase,* *or sooner by arrangement with the owner and occupier, Mr George Albert Verrier. May be viewed before the Sale, and Particulars and Conditions of Sale had of Messrs Mercer, Edwards and Williamson, Solicitors, Deal; or at the Office of the Auctioneers, 57, Queen-street, Ramsgate."*

By the late 1800s, the pub had been extended at the front, the original building remaining at the rear.

2009.

In May 1889, a probate sale was held at the pub where possessions of the late Richard Verrier junior were auctioned off, including furniture, books, valuables, coins, china and silver watches. (His father, Richard Verrier senior, had died in 1850).

By 1903, the *Magnet* was advertising its own bowling club on the green attached to the house (but which has since been built on and is now occupied by Haywards Close).

In October 1914, John Mockett, was charged with supplying water that he had previously received from the Town Council, on to George Curling through a *"pipe on his tenement"*. Ernest Verrier Mockett being manager at the time was also charged. They were found not guilty but had to pay costs of 13

shillings (65p).

Other landlords included S Partridge in 1898, Frederick William Holland in 1902, Alfred Bear in 1905, R Currie in 1906, LM Verrier in 1921, Mrs Berry and Albert George Powell in 1929, GW Neeve in 1948, J Ryan in 1955, Reginald Thomson in 1969 and, according to Dover Magistrates' records, William Knott in 1976, Peter Foxhall in 1987, Stanley Richards, David Smith, John Watkins and John Carraher in 1994, Malcolm Cameron and Dee Anne Jordan in 1995 and Bryan Mulhern in 1996. (It is known that Cobb's brewery owned the *Magnet* from at least 1918 to 1968, although the period could have been longer either side of those years).

The *Magnet* made the local news in October 1994 when the pub was hit by a truck causing £20,000 worth of damage (shortly after refurbishment!).

The present day *Magnet* is a lively place owned by Shepherd Neame and run by Mr and Mrs Judd. It advertises itself as an internet pub, complete with darts, billiards, pool, patio and outside children's play area. The pub is also home to the Deal and District Motor Cycle Club.

Man of Kent (exact location unknown)
High Street (Lower Street), Deal

The **Man of Kent** was a beerhouse under the landlordship of Richard Dixon when it was put up for auction at the **Walmer Castle** hotel on 20 June 1850. The house had apparently been the former long term residence of Mr George Joad, a respected and eminent townsman of Deal. On leaving the **Man of Kent**, Dixon became landlord of the **Ship & Castle** in 1851.

The exact location of the beerhouse remains something of a mystery, as does its earlier history.

Margate Hoy
(Loyon & Whelp, Lyon & Whelp, Tangier Arms)
Market Street/Middle Street, Deal

The **Margate Hoy** consisted of two tenements situated on the corner of Middle Street and Market Street.

In 1699, James Neale, *"innkeeper"* of the **Margate Hoy** took over *"part of premises leased to Constant Woodman formerly called the* **Loyon & Whelp** *[and* **Tangier Arms**] *and now the* **Margate Hoy**.*"

In 1720, Katherine Dale, widow, was registered landlady, followed by John Wyborn, *"Victualler"*, in 1740.

It is not clear whether or not the whole of the building remained a pub for much longer since later residents included William Cramp, a joiner, who was paying 2/6d (12½p) to rent the *"shop"* in 1757, followed by his widow, Mary, in 1774 and their son, Enoch, in 1787. In 1789, he assigned the *"newly erected tenement to William Brett and Margaret, his wife"* and, in 1795, *"John Iggulden Esq"*, brewer, took over the premises *"excluding the tenement previous assigned."*

According to the late local historian, Gertrude Nunns, a boatbuilder called Mr Saffery owned buildings and land to the north and west of these tenements around the same time. The pub was on the corner of Market Street and Middle Street, now occupied by the rear part of the Original Factory Shop.

Site of Margate Hoy 2009.

Below: Map showing position of Margate Hoy and later nearby pubs.

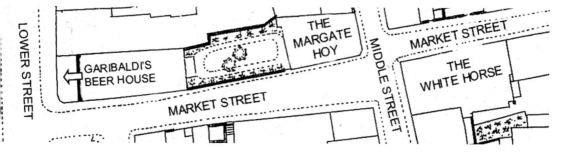

Marine Hotel (exact location unknown)
The Beach/Alexandra Road, Walmer

According to lists of Alehouse Keepers, John Francis was registered as landlord of the **Marine Hotel** in 1812, followed by Richard Hayman junior in 1813 (when The 3rd Royal Hussars, also known as The King's German Legion, were billeted there) and Edward Sharpe in 1818.

According to the Reverend Charles Elvin in *"Records of Walmer"*, the **Marine Hotel** was demolished in order to make way for the erection of Mr Tod's residence, Walmer Lodge, which, together with Walmer Place, occupied the land between Liverpool Road and The Beach, south from Alexandra Road.

Unfortunately, no other documentary evidence has been found for this hotel.

Mariners Arms (location unknown) Deal

According to AJ Langridge's research from 1977, this pub existed in Deal in 1725 but the authors have unfortunately been unable to find any other documentation.

Maxton Arms
Western Road, Deal

The *Maxton Arms* was situated next door south of the *Jolly Sailor* pub and, like the *Jolly Sailor*, was a rather down-at-heel and notorious lodging house.

The first mention of the pub appeared in 1855 when Rattery Brown was registered as landlord, followed by William Spicer in 1859, John Church/Clinch/Clynch Payne in 1862 and Thomas Stickells in 1863.

An 1863 local newspaper article, reporting from the Petty Sessions, stated that *"Two soldiers were charged by Thos. Stickles [sic], landlord of the **Maxton Arms**, with breaking nine squares of glass and taking off the tiles from an outhouse. Stickles, on being called, said he did not intend to press the charge. Both men were discharged."*

The pub was advertised for sale in the Deal & Walmer Telegram in January 1864 as a *"Freehold Public House – 'Maxton Arms' near the Railway Station. Frontage to road 54'-0", with Garden Ground and Stabling let to George Chamer, Brewer, Maxton, near Dover, and his under-tenant, T. Stickells"*. It sold later that month for £300.

In May 1868, the licence was transferred to David Simpson on condition the landlord would be watched very closely as he had previously been refused licences in Canterbury and Sandwich. By March 1869, Simpson had left the pub but the licensing authorities initially refused to transfer the licence to George Cawthorn since not only did he have a record for assaulting police but neither could it be proved he was a married man! However, in June 1869, Mary Cawthorn was described as being the wife of George Cawthorn, *"landlord of the*

OS map 1873.

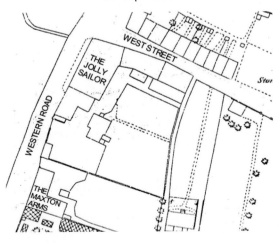

Maxton Arms", when she was charged with attempting to commit suicide by throwing herself in a pond somewhere in *"Middle Deal"*. A contemporary report added: *"She was given kindly words of advice by the magistrates, and resigned her to the care of her husband"*. Later that month, a poster advertised: *"To Be Let – The **Maxton Arms** – Apply: Robert Worthington, Maxton Brewery, Dover."*

In May 1870, the Mercury reported that *"On Saturday last an inquest was held at the Guildhall, Deal to enquire into the circumstances by which Thomas Christy, aged 45, landlord of the **Maxton Arms**, had come to his death. After the evidence, the Jury returned a verdict of Manslaughter against Francis Gimber, for whose apprehension a warrant was issued, and the witnesses bound over to prosecute at the next Maidstone Assizes"*. In July 1870, R Worthington, a *"Dover brewer"*, applied for possession of the *Maxton Arms* and, in August that year, Gimber was found to be not guilty of the murder of Thomas Christy.

William Parker was landlord in 1870, followed by John Bass in 1871, James Lines in 1873 and William James Davis in 1874.

Another report dated 3 October 1874 stated that *"Mr Langley ... applied for a certificate for the transfer of the license of the '**Maxton Arms**' – the previous landlord, James Lines, having absconded, leaving the license in the house. Permission was now sought on behalf of William Davis, recently in the employ of Mr Wright of Dover, to carry on the business until next transfer day"*. In July 1876, it was reported that the pub had been shut *"for several months"* and that the landlord had left *"clandestinely"*. Later that month, Herbert Wright of Maxton brewery applied for the licence to be transferred from Davis' name to Charles Hamilton but it was refused since Hamilton had a record of petty offences.

Later landlords included Henry Gunner in 1878, William Bax in January 1887, William Dixon in November 1887, John Young in January 1890, John Thomas Jackson in July 1890, Charles Fagg in 1892, Walter Spinner in 1893 and Alfred Pilcher in March 1894.

In November 1894, the Mercury reported that *"Mr Pilcher, landlord of the **Maxton Arms**, complained the Royal Marines had put his pub out of bounds because it was a rough house harbouring prostitutes. He argued his pub was not like that and called Inspector Chaney to confirm this, which he was able to do.*

The magistrates could not order the Royal Marines to change their ruling but Mr Pilcher was happy with the public vindication". Maria Walsh was landlady in 1895, followed by Frank Hart in January 1896. In February of that year, the Mercury reported that Hart was accused of selling alcohol outside of licensing hours. He was found guilty but, as it was his first offence, he was fined £1 and 8 shillings (40p) costs. The licence was subsequently transferred to George Naylor in September that year.

He was followed by George Marsh in February 1898 and his widow, Agnes, in May 1900, John Fox

Caleb later that year, Alfred Ward in February 1901, Benjamin John Mantle in November 1901 and Thomas Latter in 1904 (until closure). In 1906, the *Maxton Arms* was referred to the Compensation Committee for closure since magistrates reported that there were *"4 [other] pubs within 270 yards, including the Jolly Sailor next door, and does a bad class of trade"*. The pub shut down later that year and became known as Maxton House. The building was certainly there at least until the 1930s, but was subsequently demolished, and private housing now stand on its site.

MDs, 32-36 Queen Street, Deal

See entry for the *Academy Sports Bar.*

Mermaid
(exact location unknown) Deal

The *Mermaid* was mentioned in 1680 and sketchy evidence may perhaps locate the pub to the Middle Street/Farrier Street area of Deal (according to the late local historian, Les Cozens), although this cannot be confirmed.

Writing for the Mercury, Les Cozens told the story of

how a pewter pint tankard complete with domed lid came to light via a Chester antiques dealer. Made of 'Britannia metal', the inscription read *"Ye Mermaid Inn Deal"*. The Mermaid was a much-used pub name throughout Tudor times, especially in coastal locations. No other documentary evidence has come to light.

Military Tavern 5 (4) (1) Canada Road
(1 Albany Terrace/Military Road), Walmer

In October 1856, the Leith Estate granted a 63 year lease of the *Military Tavern* to William and GH Denne. Joseph Mercer was landlord in 1858, followed by Joseph Mercer in 1862, Robert Jefford in 1874 (paying an annual rent of £12), Francis Goss in 1878, Thomas Sutton in 1881 (when the pub's address was known as 5 Canada Road), Mrs Anne Sutton in 1882 and, later that year, Staff Sergeant Francis Rowe, a *"Musketry Instructor"*, Henry Hall in 1887, Charles Parker in 1891 (when the address was known as 1 Albany Terrace, Canada Road and the brewers were George Beer), Arnold James in 1903, Walter Percy Hinkley in 1905, Henry Taylor in 1908 and George Jennings junior, *"Butcher"*, in 1909.

The Mercury reported in March 1910: *"The house*

2009.

is structurally sound but sanitary conditions are in much need of improvement. On the right of the property is a butcher's, formerly a coach house. People would go to the butcher's shop, buy a chop and go to the pub and have it cooked and enjoy a glass of beer with it."

A magistrates' report later that year recommended the *Military Tavern* and the *Cinque Ports Volunteer* for closure to the Compensation Committee, and the *Military Tavern* subsequently closed down on 31 December 1910. Pain's street directory recorded that Arthur Desmoreaux, *"Hairdresser"*, was resident at the former pub in 1918. Desmoreaux was the former landlord of the *Harp* in Middle Street, Deal.

The *Military Tavern* is now a private house.

Mill Inn
78 Mill Hill (Mill Road), Deal

Together with the nearby *Yew Tree*, the *Mill Inn* catered for the residents of the new estate that had been built mainly for the miners and their families.

In March 1930, brewers, Thompson & Son Limited, offered to surrender the licence of the *White Horse* pub in order to build a new pub in the *"Miners'*

2009.

Settlement of Mill Road" (now Mill Hill) but the application was opposed by the landlord of the nearby *Yew Tree* pub, FT Beale.

In March 1932, Thompsons bought the land for £800 and, according to contemporary reports, were expected to pay between £4,000 and £4,500 for constructing the new pub. The pub was duly built and it was granted a full licence in March 1933 and opened up for business in February 1934.

JG Taylor, Secretary of Thompson's brewery at the time, temporarily held the licence until the first landlord became available. This was transferred to John William Haglington (a former Yorkshire miner) in 1935 who had previously run a fish and chip shop in Mill Road. He complained that there was not enough trade and left, swiftly followed by Sidney Hagger later that year. He was granted a one hour extension when the Cymric Male Voice Choir performed at the inn in 1936.

CJ Uden and Norma L Robinson were landlords of the pub in 1939 and, in January 1941, the licence was transferred back to Thompson's brewery (BC Dredge, Secretary), probably signifying a temporary closure during WWII. Edith Smith was installed as landlady of the newly reopened pub in 1942 and was granted a licence allowing music, singing and dancing to be performed on the premises. An advertisement in 1943 publicised: *"Mill Inn lounge – dancing to the Swingtette of The Royal Marines'*

Band – every Friday and Monday: 7.30 to 10.30".

B Creasey was registered as landlord in 1953 until at least 1956, the Morgan family in the 1950s, AE Bryant in 1966, followed by - according to Dover Magistrates' records - Peter Stevens and Alexander Walker in 1972, Stewart Workman in 1975 (when it was a Charrington's outlet), Kathleen Garton in 1977, Robert Shervill in 1985, Steven Molyneux and David Evans in 1992, Ian Sparshatt, Christopher Hammerton, Alexander Aston, Richard Morrish, Brian Johnson and Theresa Morrish all in 1993, Peter Laidlaw, Philip Cox and Nicholas Evans in 1998 and Alan Hicks, Julie Scott and Harold Scott in 2000.

The *Mill Inn* is currently owned by Admiral Taverns. In November 2009, John Townsend took over the running. The pub is situated on a very large plot and includes 8 private rooms upstairs and a beer garden. The *Mill Inn* has three darts teams, two pool teams, and boasts satellite television, and is a very popular live music venue.

c1937.

Moon (location unknown) "Deale"

This pub was mentioned in the Deale Payments for Signs list of 1662 but otherwise remains untraceable.

Monks Head

See entry for the *Fountain* (south) (2).

Mount Pleasant
Rectory Road (Park Road/Pond Lane), Upper Deal

The beerhouse made news in 1863 when Edward Matthews, a Private in The 1st Battalion 23rd Regiment, *"stole a silver watch and wearing apparel from Henry Walker of the Mount Pleasant Beerhouse, Upper Deal. Police Constable Shelvey Cox [stated that] 'the prisoner walked from Upper Deal to the lock-up and bled freely from one ear and was very drunk'. Matthews was committed for trial at the Sessions."*

The name 'Mount Pleasant' was still in use as a road or row of houses in the 1881 census, and as row of houses until at least 1936.

The site of the beerhouse is located on the actual road at the junction of the present day Rectory Road and Brenchley Avenue.

From the Police Court – 14 January 1862:

Richard Margeson, 23, fishmonger, and Henry Clements, mariner, were brought up, after having been a night in the lock-up, charged with being drunk, creating a disturbance, and interrupting Mrs Prior, landlady of the Park Tavern, in her business, on Monday evening last, and not leaving the premises when desired to do so. James Shelvey Cox, sworn: "I am a Police Constable. Last night I was sent for to go to the Park Tavern. Margeson and Clements were both drunk and refused to leave the premises. I conveyed them both to the lock-up. Fined 5/- (25p) each and 1/- (5p) each for gaol fees, which was paid.

Naggs Head, "Deale"

This was mentioned in Laker's list of 1680 inns for Deal but otherwise remains untraceable.

Napier Tavern (Lord Napier Tavern)
196 (5) (4½) (4) Beach Street, Deal

Sometimes also referred to as the *Lord Napier Tavern*, Sir Charles John Napier (later Admiral Napier) after whom the house was undoubtedly named, lived from 1786 to 1860.

The property was believed to have been the last building constructed on the east side of Beach Street (ie on the beach) and the pub opened up in 1855 shortly after its construction, with Onesiphorus Sneller, *"Builder and Publican"*, as landlord. He had previously been landlord of the *Scarborough Cat* pub which was situated more or less opposite the *Lord Napier*.

At the Petty Sessions held in January 1868, it was reported that William Cribben was charged with assaulting Sneller. At the hearing, it was discovered that the landlord had got the wrong man and William Cribben was awarded 2 shillings (10p) damages for his trouble. A Police Constable was sent to collect the right person, ie John Cribben, and bring him to justice. The court heard that Cribben had abused Mrs Sneller and Onesiphorus Sneller had thrown him out of the pub. John Cribben was fined 8/6d (42½p) and 12/6d (62½p) costs or seven days in Sandwich Gaol.

At the Petty Sessions held on 7 July 1870 *"Thomas Obree, boatman, was charged with using abusive and threatening language towards Onesiphorus Sneller, landlord of the Napier Tavern in Beach street. O Sneller, sworn – I have been abused and threatened by Thomas Obree for the last 15 months, in consequence of some difference existing between us as regards some boats of which we are part owners; he wished me to join in procuring a new one, this being the worse for wear. Obree was bound over to keep the peace for three months."*

Sneller sold the property in 1873 for £55 to William Thomsett Nicholas. A legal document that year stated: *"7.1.1873: Undertaking by Alfred Leney of Dover, Brewer, that he would pay to Onesiphorus Sneller (aged 61) and his wife, Eliza Ann (aged 63), an annuity of 25/- (£1.25p) a week (or 20/- (£1) on the death of one or other) on the understanding that they would not directly or indirectly sell beer, ale or porter in Deal."*

Later documents contained the following references relating to the pub:

"1876: The transfer of the licence of the "Napier Tavern" from Robert Flint to William Wilkins Bushell was sanctioned."

"1885: Onesiphorous Sneller died."

In 1895, Edward Hanger was registered as landlord *"with boat shop"*, and, in 1906, he was listed as the local agent for The Sea Anglers' Association.

"15.3.1897: Alfred Leney of Dover, Brewer, sold to Alfred Leney & Co Limited for £102,000 various properties, including the Napier Tavern and Capstan Ground."

"16.3.1897: Alfred Leney & Co sold to Richard Henry Fremlin of Wateringbury, Brewer, Henry Hayward of Dover, Estate Agent, and Arthur Harby of Dover, Gent., for £90,000, various properties including the Napier Tavern and Capstan Ground."

"13.6.1898: Eliza Ann Sneller died and her brother, William Henry Hayman, of 23 Victoria Road, Deal accepted £9.16.6d (£9.82½ p) in final settlement of the annuity."

"14.10.1909: Agreement between Alfred Leney and Edward Hanger, Boatman, for the lease of the Capstan Ground adjoining the Napier Tavern (on the

Map showing Napier Tavern and nearby pubs c1860.

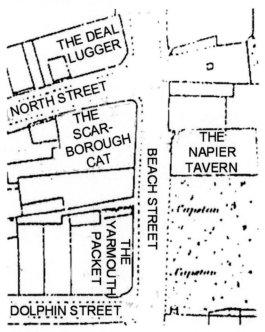

south side), with the storeroom under the verandah of said Inn for £2 pa."

Henry Brown was landlord in 1910 and, in March 1911, Clarence Walton was in charge when the pub came under threat of closure since there were "6 public houses within 161 yards, 13 customers on 5 visits [by police for licensing purposes]. The only pub to have a verandah overlooking the sea, looking for vessels in distress, causing the last seven launchings of the North Deal lifeboat." The pub shut down on 31 December 1911.

"23.10.1913: Alfred Leney & Co and Fremlin & Co sold to Deal Corporation for £400 no 196 Beach Street, formerly the Napier Tavern, and Capstan Ground abutting to property formerly of Joseph Wallis and now of Annie Leeds Crook and Mary Jane Crook to the North and to a Capstan Ground of the East Kent Brewery Company to the South."

A recent local history article from the East Kent Mercury, entitled 'The Last To Be Built', stated: "The Napier Tavern was built in 1855 to the order of its first landlord, Onesiphorus Sneller. His gravestone is to be found in the Deal Municipal cemetery ... the inscription is in Hebrew. The Napier Tavern was acquired by Deal Corporation in 1913 and demolished soon after."

The site, now covered by the promenade, lies practically opposite the turning into North Street from Beach Street.

Navy Coffee House
Beach Street, Deal

Scant documentation exists for the *Navy Coffee House* (which was likely to have also been licensed to sell alcohol) but, in 1723, it was described as being *"over against* (ie opposite) *The East India Arms"* and mention was again made in the form of an advertisement from 1730: "To be Sold in Deal, the *Navy Coffee House, lying in Beach-street next the Sea"*.

The owner at the time was Mrs Jelley. It was still called the *Navy Coffee House* in 1739.

As the description implies, the site of the *Navy Coffee House* would appear to have been on the present day promenade, north of the pier and opposite the amusement arcade (ie the former *India/East India Arms*) on the corner of Beach Street and King Street.

New Commercial Inn

See entry for the *New Inn*.

New Inn
(Carpenters Arms, Compasses, Three Compasses, New Commercial Inn, possibly Blakes Head)
32 High Street (48 & 194 Lower Street), Deal

The *New Inn* is an ancient and fairly well documented house. However, to be historically accurate with this one is impossible. Available information is full of inconsistencies and, so far as possible, the authors have left out many of the uncertain parts but have nevertheless included others if they felt them to be sufficiently interesting!

The property was seemingly established in 1605 and started life as the *Carpenters Arms*.

In 1662, the Deal Payments for Signs list refers to *"the Compasses"* which may possibly have referred to the *Carpenters Arms*, especially if three compasses had been painted on the sign hanging outside the pub (given the illiteracy of much of the population at the time). Three compasses were used on the arms of the Carpenters Guild (although the compasses could have also referred to those used by mariners).

By 1672, "William Cavell innkeeper and Mareene Stor Deyler [sic] of The Beech was resident at the *Capennters Arms, Lowere Street"*. (This was the same year that King Charles II visited Deal).

The *New Inn* was the alleged setting for the tale of Ambrose Gwinnet in 1709 (or 1723, depending on the source). Although a number of other local pubs boast this claim to fame, the *New Inn* is perhaps the mostly likely candidate (even though it may possibly have been known as the *Blakes Head* at the time, although no licensing records can be found to confirm this). However, despite information held at the British Library, it is still difficult to be 100% certain whether or not the events surrounding the

1904.

story did ever actually take place or whether it is just a piece of entertaining fiction. Nevertheless, the tale is an interesting one and is such a big slice of Deal folklore that it is perhaps worth outlining a concise version of it here.

A weary traveller called Ambrose Gwinnet stopped overnight at the pub en route to visit his sister who lived locally. He shared a bed with a stranger called Richard Collins (as was the custom of the day if money was short) and, the following morning, Collins had disappeared, but a heavy trail of blood led from the bed to the beach. The landlord summoned the authorities and Ambrose Gwinnet was tried and found guilty of Collins' murder as it was assumed that Gwinnet had robbed and killed him, and disposed of the body by throwing it in the sea. Gwinnet was hanged from the gallows that were rumoured to have stood near the beach at the North End of town, and his body was left to rot. After the crowds had dispersed, however, his sister came to pay her last respects and, to her amazement, she found that he was still breathing. She immediately got her brother down from the gallows and took him home to nurse him back to health in secret. Because there would still be a price on his head if he was found to be alive, his best option of escape was to leave the country.

He joined a ship moored in the Downs and sailed the world as a ship hand for very many years, getting caught up in numerous adventures along the way, including being captured by the Spanish! At some faraway port, he eventually crossed paths with a very familiar looking person who turned out to be Richard Collins! Collins told Gwinnet that, on the night of his disappearance from the pub, he had awoken feeling unwell since he had visited a local barber for some blood letting earlier that day and his wounds had reopened in the night and had started to

bleed. He left his bed and went outside in order to wake up the barber to redo the dressing but, before he could get there, he was jumped on by a press gang patrolling the dark streets of Deal looking for drunken victims, and he was bundled onto a passing ship, and had been unable to get back to England ever since. Needless to say, the pair did eventually return home together, Collins let the authorities know what had really happened that night at the pub and Gwinnet was pardoned. Many years later, or so the story goes, Ambrose Gwinnet ended his days as a vagrant road sweeper in the Charing Cross area of London. (Anyone interested in this story can see excerpts of a re-enactment staged by the Deal People's Theatre company in 2008 on You Tube - http://www.youtube.com/user/ DealPeoplesTheatre - the scenes taking place in St George's churchyard and the old streets of Deal, with local lad – and author – Jerry Vyse, playing the title role of Ambrose Gwinnet).

According to the pub's own potted history, 1763 saw extensive refurbishment taking place when the pub was renamed the **New Inn**. By 1783, it appears to have been known as the **Three Compasses** (even though, according to the Principal Inhabitants and Traders list of 1792, Bethel Wyborn was recorded as being landlord of the "**New Inn**"). However, it was certainly called the **Three Compasses** in 1804 when John Cavell was landlord, and he was still serving there in 1824. By 1828, the pub had reverted to its original name, the **Carpenters Arms**, with Frances Isabella Cavell in charge and, in 1829, the pub went back to its previous former name of the **New Inn** when Isaac Chandler was at the helm.

Later landlords included Davis Frampton in 1830, David Spice in 1831, Lucy Spice (widow) in 1841, William Rae (who married Lucy Spice) in 1843, William Mills in 1844 (from 1840 to 1884, the **New Inn** doubled up as a local excise office) and Thomas Kidner from 1847 to 1876 (during whose time the pub was briefly known as the **New Commercial Inn** in 1862).

2010.

An article in a local newspaper, headed *"A Wedding Supper"*, dated 29 April 1876, read: *"Mr Olds, with his usual liberality, invited all the men employed in his establishment at Deal and Dover to a sumptuous supper on the occasion of his wedding. The supper was supplied by Mr Kidner at the* **New Inn**, *Deal, where it was partaken of by 17 guests, who were liberally supplied with all they could desire and who drank the healths of the newly-wedded pair in bumpers."*

Alphonso James Redman was landlord in 1888, followed by Frank Endicott Russell in 1893, Arthur Bassington in 1894, Henry Vallom Wood in 1896 and Thomas Laird in 1903. In May that year, external alterations were approved, giving an entrance at the southern end of the public bar. Horace Boncey was at the helm in 1910, William George Wareham in 1929 and T Hutchings from 1935 until at least 1940.

During WWII, in the spring of 1944, it was reported that the driver of an American Jeep swerved and crashed at Oxney Bottom after the serviceman seemingly witnessed the apparition of a horse and rider that promptly disappeared into thin air. Many years previously, a highwayman had been hanged at the very spot, his father being the owner of the **New Inn** at the time. During repair works carried out at the pub in 1965, workmen found a secret compartment containing what appeared to be a highwayman's black outfit and pistol!

Later landlords included G Armstrong in 1948, B Miller in 1953, BB Perez in 1966, Michael Allan Griggs in 1974, Martin Burgess in 1986 and Steve Carter and Debbie Doyle in 2007.

The pub as we see it today clearly encompasses what would have at one time been two separate dwellings but unfortunately it is not known when the buildings were amalgamated.

The pub is still open for business, retaining some original features in its bars, and it is a popular eating establishment and live music venue. The **New Inn** was voted Mercury Pub of the Year in March 2010 under the landlordship of Debbie Doyle and Terry Bailey.

New Plough
33 Middle Deal Road, Deal

Ernest Ferdinand Redsull was landlord from September 1869, the **New Plough** becoming a fully licensed alehouse in 1870. Robert Edward Redsull, whose occupation was listed as *"Landlord and Shoemaker"*, took over in 1879 and he made the local news in 1883 when his pet monkey, Jenny, unfortunately died from eating cork dust.

Mrs Mary E Redsull followed in 1891 and, by 1904, the owners were listed as George Beer brewery. William Redsull took over in 1913 and remained at the pub until 1921. He had been a councillor, later Alderman and then Mayor throughout WWI. A dinner to celebrate his fifth successive year in office was held at the *Royal Hotel* on 9 November 1918, and later Redsull Avenue in Mill Hill was named in his honour.

Herbert Charles Archer took over in 1921 until 1938, followed by R Carrot in 1953 (when it was owned by Fremlin's brewery), George Boys from 1965 until 1978 when John Tobin took over, Graham Webb and Anita Horrigan in 1991 (when owned by Whitbread) and Kevin and Lisa Mitchell in 1999.

The pub closed for business in 2008 and the building has since been converted into residential accommodation.

c1920.

c2005.

Noahs Ark
Ark Lane/Peter Street, Deal

Throughout its existence, the address of the pub was variously referred to as being either in Ark Lane or in Peter Street as the building was located in between the two roads.

The *Noahs Ark* had a reputation for being a 'receiving' pub for smuggled run goods, although no written record of any such misdemeanours can actually be found. It was however ideally placed for such activity, given that it was situated at the edge of town amidst open fields and orchards. A modern-day report in the Mercury revealed the existence of a previously unknown wooden tunnel measuring 6 ft x 8 ft which was discovered in the vicinity by workmen for Southern Water.

In 1724, Joanna Codd, together with Nathaniel Yarnold, purchased *"a messuage known as Noahs Ark"* for £150, although no location was given.

In 1730, a local newspaper reported that the pub would be auctioned for sale, together with *"water-house and buildings."*

In 1755, the premises were empty until August 1756 when William Brown took over.

An extract from an article in a 1761 edition of the Kentish Post mentioned *"... James Cullen living near the sign of Noahs Ark."*

In 1804, Richard Piper was landlord, followed by William Stoker in 1808, who, later that year, was charged with pouring short measures into a 2 pint pot. By 1821, Richard Cory was at the helm when the property was described as including *"stables, sheds in front and land."*

Other landlords included Bethel Wilson in 1828 (when Ash & Co brewery were the owners) and Thomas Wilson in 1842. (Interestingly, an unnamed beerhouse ran by a Mr Shelvey was also in operation a few yards away, according to the 1841 census. This was situated in the building now known as Windy Nook which can still be viewed from both Ark Lane and Peter Street).

Stephen Henry Atkins was landlord in 1850, followed by Stephen Brown junior in 1859 and

William Langley in 1863.

In 1875, Walter Roberts, aged 12 years, stole three shillings and sixpence (17½p) from landlord, William Langley. He was sentenced to 10 strokes of the birch rod.

Thomas Charles Tilly was landlord in 1877, followed by Mark Henry Funnel who, in February 1881, received a 3-month gaol sentence with hard labour for assaulting his wife, Fanny Stuart Funnel.

Later hosts included Maria Spicer (widow) in 1879, Margaret Spicer (spinster) in 1880, Benjamin Robert Spillet in 1886, Robert Ogilvie Williams in 1887, Louis William Ballard in 1888, William Humphries in 1889, Thomas James Bowman also in 1889 (until at least 1899), William Harvey in 1908 and WM Barter in 1914.

In February 1920 (by which time the pub held a full licence), the *Noahs Ark* was recommended for closure to the Compensation Committee. It was reported that it had *"been licensed since at least 1771; 7 bedrooms for lodgers giving accommodation for 33, average recent occupation 14; house generally in poor state of repair; customers low C class, dealers, labourers, gypsies and women of the peddling class; complaints from neighbours; in the summer months the landlord supplements his income by attending fairs, fetes, etc, with swings and roundabouts, so is only there in the winter; owned by Ash & Co, brewers, since 1825, repairs had been impossible during the war, but were now being carried out."*

FH Kitton was the last landlord when the *Noahs Ark* shut down on 31 December 1920.

The pub was divided up and converted into accommodation called 'Wellington Flats'. A 1930s report stated that the building suffered from overcrowding, and it later fell into disrepair before finally being demolished in the 1960s.

Private houses numbered 24 to 27 (inclusive) Peter Street now mark the approximate site of the old pub's premises.

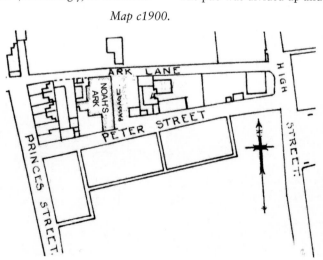

Map c1900.

Noahs Ark
(exact location unknown) Middle Street, Deal

The only mention of this pub can be found in a Will dated 24 March 1700: *"Middle Street – a messuage or tenement formerly called the Noahs Ark, now in two dwellings in the occupation of George Hulk and Gabriel Pettit, bequeathed to daughter, Johanna, in the Will of Thomas Stone of Deal, Pilot"*. Stone apparently also owned *"the Sampson and a malthouse and brewhouse attached to a windmill and windmill bank at Northwall"* as well as other local properties."

A possible location for this pub could be next door (north) to the **Tally Ho** – see separate entry.

Norfolk Arms

See entry for the **Jolly Sailor.**

North Foreland
(exact location unknown) Beach Street, Deal

This was a beerhouse and the only mention of it was found in an 1858 local newspaper report concerning a beer-flap that was considered to be a danger to the public, but the North Foreland otherwise remains untraceable. It is, of course, possible that the report was erroneous and that it should have referred to the **South Foreland** instead.

North Infantry Canteen
(location unknown) Walmer

These premises were mentioned in the Walmer Alehouse Keepers' Book of 1813 with Ralph Pittock as landlord, followed by Thomas Bunce Simmonds in 1814.

Although its location is unknown, it was possibly an on-site drinking establishment for the military situated within North Barracks since there was a similarly named concern called the **South Infantry Canteen** which, by implication, may have been located in South (Cavalry) Barracks.

North Star (possibly Plough)
12 The Marina, (185) Beach Street, Deal

The pub was possibly called the **Plough** in 1804. Although a plough would automatically conjure up visions of an agricultural appliance, it does of course also refer to the constellation of that name. It might therefore follow that the **Plough** was indeed a forerunner of the **North Star** (or could just have referred to 'ploughing' for anchors on the seabed).

However, the first mention of the **North Star** by name appeared in Hancock's Journal when it stated that the crew of the 'Ship on Sands' was drinking in the **North Star** pub on 5 February 1838. SW Elliot was landlord in 1837, followed by Samuel M Fitall from 1841 to 1889. (The pub became fully licensed in 1840).

c1955.

The 1841 census showed Fitall listed as a "*Victualler*", aged 30, and residing at the premises with his wife, "*Mary F Fitall (nee Hawkins or Petty)*", aged 35, and Rebecca F Ladd, aged 30, whose status was not listed but who was presumably an employee. By 1861, Samuel was a widower, aged 52, and still resident at the pub, together with spinster, Rebecca, also 52, who had by then become recorded as "*Housekeeper*". There was also a house servant aged 21 by the name of Elizabeth Sneller living on the premises.

Robert George Compton Wilds became landlord in 1863. (He was also coxswain of the North Deal lifeboat from 1865).

The property was put up for sale in 1869 when it was described as including a "*bar, bar parlour, tap room, kitchen, club room, two bedrooms and cellar and yard behind. Available at low yearly rent of £14*". It was on the same lease as Thomas Hight's brewery next door and both pub and brewery were for sale together.

In 1878, Wilds appeared in court on behalf of his wife who was accused of assaulting Rebecca Nicholas, the landlady of the nearby *Lifeboat* pub. She was found guilty and bound over to keep the peace. A document dated July 1876 may have been the start of the troubles: "(Due to) *Certain evil*

2009.

disposed persons having freely circulated through the town, I give notice to the Excise authorities [of accusations] made at a neighbouring house ... that whoever will inform me who the party or parties are that have raised such an infamous slander about myself, wife and daughter, much to the damage of my house and business, so that offenders may be prosecuted ...*" etc. Wilds died in 1885.

In 1886, landlord Edward Hanger was fined 15 shillings (75p) for keeping the house open on a Sunday morning, and his three customers present were each fined five shillings (25p). In 1895, he had his photograph published in The Fishing Gazette for "*promoting fishing in Deal and looking after the comforts of fishermen.*"

Later landlords included WT Baker in 1904, Ralph Erridge from 1913 to 1933, Mrs SE Erridge in 1934, followed by Sarah Brown in 1936 until at least 1956 when the pub was a popular venue with members from the nearby Deal Rowing Club.

GG Harris was landlord in 1966, and it is believed that the pub closed down around 1970. In May 1971, an application was submitted to turn the old *North Star* into flats.

However, the exterior of the building at least remains intact and it is now a private residence.

1887: Incapable of Driving: William Paramor was charged with being drunk whilst in charge of a horse and cart in Clanwilliam-road, on the 20th inst. Prisoner, who acknowledged he was a little worse for liquor, was fined 10/- (50p), including costs.

Oak & Ivy (Crown)
58-60 (11) Blenheim Road (South Sandy Lane), Deal

The *Oak & Ivy* was originally called the *Crown* beerhouse. In 1847, John Ricketts was landlord, followed by Benjamin James Ricketts in 1865. In September that year he applied for a full licence but was refused on the grounds the house was in an unfinished state so he was advised to apply again the following year.

By February 1867, the house had been renamed the *Oak & Ivy* when the Mercury reported that Mr Wraight, a resident of

Above c1920.

South Sandy Lane (now Blenheim Road), complained of noise coming from the *Oak & Ivy* and that the landlord had been summonsed to appear in court.

Daniel Shelvey was landlord in 1869 (the year when South Sandy Lane was renamed Blenheim Road), remaining at the helm until 1901 when he was listed as *"Brickmaker & Beerhouse Keeper."* Later that year, his son-in-law, George Thatcher, took over the reins and applied for a full licence as well as permission to rebuild the house (which was carried out later that year), following which the full licence was granted. In 1903, the brewery, George Beer & Sons, owned the property.

The Mercury reported in 1910 that the Blenheim Bowling Club had a Grand Opening on 26 May that year. The Club had been founded by Dr Barnes Hughes and consisted of 45 members who used the *Oak & Ivy* as their HQ. The Club was situated on the grounds east of the railway line, on the western side of Blenheim Road, opposite the pub, although it subsequently shut down in April 1946. (Garages now stand on the site but, pre railway, the site was open ground which was used for the storage of anchors).

George Thatcher's stay had been a long one until he was replaced by Tom Frere in 1929, followed by Frederick Oliver in 1938. Mr Oliver died the following year when his widow took over the licence, remaining

Above c1990.
Below: Roget sketch c1885.

at the pub until 1948. In the interim, in October 1940, the pub was damaged during enemy action during WWII and subsequently repaired.

Later landlords included Winifred Owens in 1956, Alfred Stock in 1962, GR Stock in 1966, Frederick Bacon in 1974 (when the owners were Fremlin's brewery), John Arnold in 1982, William Arthur Rogers in 1987 and Keith Stewart in 1989. Whitbreads owned the *Oak & Ivy* in 1992, and John Hoyle and Mary Shillett were the landlords in 1994. The pub closed in 2004.

Oak Tavern

See entry for the *Royal Oak Inn*.

Oak Tree (location unknown) Deal

According to Sandwich Licensing Recognizances lists, John Elenor was listed as landlord of the *Oak Tree* in 1750 and 1751, Thomas Ladd in February and November 1754 and Joseph Scarlett in December 1754. No location was given, and the pub does not crop up in any other documentation so it unfortunately remains something of a mystery.

Oddfellows Arms

See entry for the *Friendly Port*.

Old Kings Head

See entry for the *Kings Head*.

Old(e) Victory (Victory, Clarendon Tap) 38 (190A) Middle Street, Deal

The building was situated on the north side of Short Street, on the corner of Middle Street. It was originally a tap house for the nearby *Clarendon* but, in September 1866, it became a pub in its own right called the *Clarendon Tap* (later known as the *Victory*, and, after that, ye *Old(e) Victory*).

An advert from the early 1900s reads: "*Ye Old(e) Victory. For Thompson's Celebrated Walmer Ales, Double Stout & Porter, Wines & Spirits of the best quality, Tobacco, Cigars and Cigarettes of the finest Brands, Court's Pure Mineral Waters, Holbrook's Draught Cider, Sarson's Pure Malt Vinegar, all at moderate charges. Mr Scovell wishes to call attention to a special Old Scotch Whiskey, the same blend as was supplied to Lord Nelson while serving on board the old Victory. C Scovell, Proprietor.*"

Licensees included Charles Scovell from 1903, Thomas William Jezzard from 1913, Henry Rickwood from 1914, Mrs Ada J Corn from 1922 and James E Miller from 1938.

In EC Pain's '*Deal and the Downs in the War of Liberation*' he referred to '*Black Friday*', 4 October 1940, when an raid hit Deal at 1.20pm. The pub, together with four houses on the other side of Short Street, was destroyed. Despite this, its licence was renewed in March 1941 (probably with the intention of rebuilding the pub), although magistrates stated they

Landlord Henry Rickwood c1915.

"*could express no opinion as to the validity of the renewal if it was challenged elsewhere*". The pub was never rebuilt, and its site now forms part of Middle Street car park.

Olive Branch (location unknown) "Deale"

The *Olive Branch* only gets a mention in the Sandwich Licensing Recognizances list for September 1662 when it was recorded that 6/8d (33p) had been received for 'payment for signs', with £5 surety. It otherwise remains untraceable.

Paragon

See entry for the *Empire*.

Park Tavern
(21) Park Street, Deal

The *Park Tavern*'s early history paints it to be something of a 'den of iniquity' but it was probably not so different from a number of other local pubs of the time.

In October 1858, when Thomas Hutchins was landlord, it was described as being *"a common beerhouse"* when complaints were received from local residents *"begging"* magistrates that the place be shut down following accusations of *"lewd women"* exposing their breasts to passers-by from their rooms in the *Park Tavern*!

In 1860, William Betts Wellard was charged with assaulting, and threatening to shoot, Hutchins. *"He pleaded drunkenness and regretted what he had done and begged for lenient treatment … and was sentenced to 6 months in Sandwich Gaol or to be bound over for 6 months in the sum of £20 and two sureties of £10 each, which were forthcoming and Wellard was liberated."*

Benjamin Richard Estes took over in March that year and advertised in the Deal & Walmer Telegram: *"Now Open On Strictly Respectable Principles – 'Park Tavern', Deal. BR Estes. Proprietor"*. He did not stay very long at the helm, however, since Charles Prior took over in October 1860, by which time the pub was fully licensed. Later that month, four soldiers from The 2nd Battalion of the 7th Fusiliers were charged with stealing Prior's cash box containing £16 in gold, and, in 1862, Richard Margeson and Henry Clements were accused of being drunk and causing a disturbance at the pub.

Richard Hobbs and John Langley were listed on the licence in 1864, followed by John King in 1865

1944.

and Benjamin James Ricketts in 1872 (when T Ash, a brewer from Ash, owned the pub). In 1876, a Marine called Moore stole a canary bird from Ricketts worth 4/6d (22½p), was found guilty by the court and sentenced to three weeks hard labour. It was also reported that Ricketts was divorcing his wife following her apparent seduction of his 18 year old brother and indulging in *"improper intimacy"* with him!

Henry Edward James Webb took over in 1876 and, during his long residence at the *Park Tavern*, he appears to have been successful in overturning its previous tawdry reputation. An article from a local newspaper from the 1880s, headed *"Dinner at the Park Tavern"* reported that: *"The annual dinner in connection with the fortnightly smoking concerts held at the Park Tavern, took place on Thursday evening. There were 51 persons present, Mr G Jennings and Corporal Jones, RM, occupying the ends of the table. The bill of fare consisted of fat pigs, roast beef, turkeys, leg of pork, corned beef, vegetables, plum pudding and mince pies, and was served in a manner which reflected great credit upon the host … Songs were contributed by Messrs Miller, Sturgess, J Page, J Erridge, Dottery, Thomas, Denton, etc … and Mr Marshall on the cornet."* Another article dated 9 January 1886, headed *"Whist Players Supper"*, reported: *"Mr Webb, the respected host of the 'Park Tavern', Park-street, Deal, gave his annual whist supper on Thursday night. About 40 admirers of the silent game sat down to a splendid repast, after which, under the melting influence of Mr Micawber's fragrant*

Site of Park Tavern 2009.

beverage, the evening was spent in the most enjoyable conviviality, the steaming bowl being filled again and again. By the kind permission of the Magistrates the usual time was extended until midnight, when with three times three for the popular host and hostess, the party was brought to a prompt and orderly conclusion."

Webb died after having served at the pub for 55 years in July 1931 when the licence was transferred to Henry Frederick Theobald. He remained there until the outbreak of WWII when Miss Ellen Elizabeth Wheeler took over in 1939, followed by Ernest Adams (at an unspecified date) who was to become the *Park Tavern*'s last landlord.

On 20 January 1944, the air raid siren started up at 5am and did not sound the all clear until some four hours later. In the interim, and following continuous shelling, the pub received a direct hit and unfortunately Mr Adams and his wife were killed in the blast. It was reported that their baby daughter, Joy, survived, albeit seriously injured, as well as the family dog. The pub remained closed as the building was damaged beyond repair. In March that year, the licence was transferred to BC Dredge, Thompsons brewery's 'outdoor manager', and what remained of the building was demolished soon afterwards. In September 1950, the *Park Tavern*'s old licence was one of several transferred to Mr D Anderson of Thompsons brewery.

By all accounts, the pub had been a very popular watering hole up until its abrupt closure and was very much missed by local people.

The site was bought by Seeboard in August 1961 for £600 plus costs. It remains a vacant plot (now partly owned by EDF), situated between the 'Leaps and Bounds' shop and the access road leading to the rear of Marks & Spencer's premises and the pay and display car park.

Paxton Arms
(exact location unknown) West Street, Deal

Whether this pub actually ever existed is very much in doubt since the only mention of it appeared in an 1870 directory listing James Lines as landlord of the *Paxton Arms*. Given that a James Lines could also be found serving at the nearby *Maxton Arms* around the same time seems too much of a coincidence and the pub's name was probably a typographical error.

However, this scant piece of information regarding the *Paxton Arms* does fall into the right era since Sir Joseph Paxton (1803 to 1865) became famous for creating the 'Crystal Palace' that housed the Great Exhibition of 1851 held in Hyde Park. (The Palace was disassembled after the Exhibition and rebuilt on land at Sydenham Hill – then a hamlet in the Kent countryside, but now part of Greater London – before being burnt to the ground on 30 November 1936).

Pelican (1) (Pilican, Fleece, Golden Fleece, Prince of Orange, Fountain, Fountaine, Fountayne Tavern)(44) Beach Street, Deal

The pub had many different names, as will be seen below, the last of which being the **Pelican** – see entry for **Pelican** (2) for a possible explanation of the name.

Like the other pub of the same name, this particular **Fountain** (also sometimes spelt **Fountaine**) was sited on the shoreline in Beach Street. However, this one lay north of the present day **Royal Hotel**, practically opposite the turning into Oak Street, a lane which, at the time, continued on to the beach, separating the **Fountain** from the **Royal Hotel**.

In 1661, Robert Smyth was landlord of the **Fountayne Tavern**, which was leased by John Burrowes, *"A Citizen and Cloth Worker of London"*, from the Archbishop of Canterbury. By 1674, the pub was called the **Prince of Orange** and leased by *"Morgan Lodge of Deal, Chirurgeon [surgeon]"*, and, in 1719, it was called the **Fleece** (or **Golden Fleece**) and leased by James Godden, a butcher. It is believed that the **Pelican** moved from Lower Street to this site in the mid to late 1770s.

Thomas Oakley, brewer, was owner in 1789. In 1792, the Sessions Book recorded *"proposals to widen Beach Street"* and the purchase from John Iggleden, brewer (aged 22) of *"the west end of a certain storehouse adjoining the publick house or alehouse called the Pelican."*

In 1804, Edward Gibbs was landlord when the **Pelican**'s location was described as being in *"Beach Street – east side – 11 houses north of the Royal Hotel and 3 houses south of the Rodney"*. An 1821 lease confirms the site as being just north of Oak Street. It also mentioned a well and a pump to the south, hence the name **Fountain**. However, the site does seem to have moved very slightly over the years.

In early 1821 the landlord was William Yates when the rates book mentioned him as owning the *'Pelican and capstan ground'*. Later that year, Thomas Higgins took over and he was listed at the *'Pelican and capstan ground, with garden in West Street'*. The pub leases ran out in 1838, which was the year when Deal's ill fated wooden pier was being built opposite Oak Street. However, the pub's name still appears in Pigot's Directory and the Licensing Book for 1839.

According to Hancock's 'fly proprietor's' journal for that year, it was documented that he *"tooked [sic] the passengers from Pelican to Ramsgate"*. The pub was not licensed in 1840. However, in 1843, the **Pelican** was documented again as being in arrears with rates to the tune of £1/7s (£1.35).

The building was sited on the beach and was one of many demolished to make way for the wide promenade that we see today.

Pelican (2), (Harp) 153 (159) Beach Street, Deal

The first documentation the authors have found for this house operating as a pub was in 1804 when it was called the **Harp**, with William Russell in charge. John Lawrence Prescott was registered as landlord in 1824, followed by Zachariah Thompson in 1826. Prescott was back at the helm when the **Harp** closed in 1828 and it was auctioned off, together with some other public houses in the sale of the Manor of Chamberlain's fee.

In 1840, the house was registered as being an *'unlicensed alehouse'* and, in 1841, local brewer, Edward Iggulden, bought the *"capstan ground opposite the Harp."*

The 1851 census documented that Mary Philpott was resident, with George Philpott, her *"husband at sea"*. In 1852, he was listed as a *"Beer Retailer"* but no pub name was given but, by 1858, according to Melville's Directory, the premises were known as the **Pelican** beerhouse. The Pelican was one of Sir Francis Drake's ships and the pub was possibly named in commemoration. (A pelican was also a symbol for the Virgin Mary, because of the bird's reputed devotion to its young).

Interestingly, in August 1866, brethren from the wonderfully named *'Lodge of Enlightened Cottagers'* (see also entry for the **Port Arms**) celebrated their 72nd anniversary. *"They assembled at the Pelican, Beach Street, and afterwards proceeded in carriages, some of which were decorated with flags, for a drive in the country, exhilarating tunes being played on the cornet by a good musician who accompanied the party."*

In 1867, landlord, Morris Langley, applied for a spirit licence but the application was postponed as the premises were very old and about to be rebuilt on the same site. In 1868, Mr Sharpe applied for a licence *"for the Pelican, a public house newly erected opposite the North Esplanade – which was not objected to, the old premises having been licensed for many years."*

William Wicks became landlord in 1872, and, in September that year, William Irvine was charged with assaulting Mrs Wicks and giving her two black eyes. Mrs Irvine was employed as a *"charwoman and servant"* at the *Pelican* and had asked for permission to watch the fireworks display on the evening of the annual regatta. When this was refused, Irvine carried out the assault against Mrs Wicks. He was fined, and duly paid, 10 shillings (50p).

Israel Claringbold took over in 1874, followed by Frederick Augustus Smith in 1875, Morris Langley in 1877, William Henry Deacon in 1878 and 1879, Henry Smith and G Philpott in 1881 and Alfred Weston in 1882. (Up until the 1890s, the pub's address was 159 Beach Street but, due to street renumbering, it became known as no 153 Beach Street, even though the building remained the same).

In April 1884, the case of The Dover Brewery Company v Esther Annie Sparkes came to court. According to records: *"The claim was for £10/1/5d (£10.07p) for beer, etc, supplied to Mrs Sparkes when residing at the Pelican. She stated that it was actually supplied to her daughter, Miss Leadbetter, but she had made herself liable for the debt by agreeing in writing to pay for it. Ordered to pay £2 forthwith and the remainder by £1 per month."*

In 1885, local auctioneers, West & Usher, were instructed by the pub's proprietor, James Allum, to sell the premises, together with *"the trade and bar fittings, also valuable furniture, etc, etc."*

In 1886, Thomas Leach was in charge, followed by Charles Smith in 1887 and 1893, Joseph Benjamin Crick in 1894, Edith Jarvis also in 1894, Joseph Reed in 1896, Charles Hayward in 1898, EW Horner in 1904, Arthur Terrell from 1910 to 1913,

c1955.

William Herbert Porter from 1914 to at least 1922, George Lloyd in 1924 (when the pub was known as the *Pelican* Hotel) and, on her husband's death, Mrs EK Lloyd in 1932.

In 1934, Mrs Lloyd's son-in-law, Albert Thomas Caffy, a boot-maker, of 12 Allenby Avenue, Deal, was found shot dead in the kitchen at the pub, and a verdict of *"accidental death was returned as there was no reason to suspect suicide"* (or, presumably, foul play). At the time, the house was considered to be a high-class hotel. Later that year, the licence was transferred to Albert Morton Whiteley (who was still registered there in 1938). Other landlords included CL Burtwell in 1948 and Richard Vernon Betts in 1953.

Notably, landlady, Olive Roberts, retired after 13 years' service in 1966, having apparently baked and sold 40,000 of her famous 'Pelican Pies' since 1953. In Douglas Tubbs' 1966 book entitled *'Kent Pubs'*, the *Pelican* is described as *"A pub of tremendous character, whose landlady, Mrs Olive Roberts, treats her customers as guests. The walls are painted all over with a mural by local artists showing a pretty good party going on [where] you would expect painters, students, critics, Chelsea jazzmen perhaps too. You would be right on all counts. But in the Pelican, you also meet sailing people, golfers, sportsmen, professionals, the lot, and the pies made by Mrs Roberts that contain more meat than you would think possible, set in gravy that can be likened only to the bits at the bottom of the dripping bowl that you are never allowed to have."*

John P Pollard took over in 1970 and ran the *Pelican* with his partner, Arthur. He placed the following advertisement for the pub in the Mercury which read: *"Good Food, Wine & Hospitality. Hirondelle Gourmet Lounge. Noon – 2pm. 7 – 9.30pm. Closed Sundays"*. Indeed, *"haggis and tatties"* were regularly served at the *Pelican*'s annual Burns Night celebrations. The pub was a popular one, and John and Arthur obviously ran a very happy house. Having taken the decision to retire, they rang the bell for the final time in June 1987

Landlord John Pollard and assistant c1980.

with the cry of *"Last trip around the harbour, boys and girls!"* Tragically, John Pollard and former landlady, Olive Roberts, both died within a couple of weeks or so after leaving the *Pelican*: Mrs Roberts in a motor accident in Scotland and Mr Pollard of a heart attack. It was probably these incidents, together with Mr Caffy's death in 1934, which gave it the local reputation of being an unlucky pub.

Michael and Rita Little bought the pub as a free house from the brewery, Charringtons, when Mr Pollard retired in June 1987. Anthony and Anne Butler took over as landlords in August 1988, remaining there until the *Pelican* closed down and its licence was revoked on 16 May 1990.

Since the pub's demise, a number of local residents have claimed the pub used to be 'heavily haunted'. However, since spirits are no longer served on the premises, it is to be hoped that all is now quiet within its walls!

The building is now a private home although the pub's name can still be seen impressed at the top of the parapet wall.

Pelican (3)
77-79 High Street (Lower Street), Deal

See entry for **Pelican** (2) for a possible explanation of the pub's name. The **Pelican** had its origins in at least the early 1600s. According to Laker's '*History of Deal*', the Earl of Portland arrived in Deal in 1636 and, on arriving at the **Pelican**, he was met by a Spanish gentleman who complained he had been robbed by the landlord, Robert Smyth.

The Earl spoke with the landlord and offered to pay the man's bill but, in a very uncivilised manner, Smyth refused to accept payment from him. When the landlord was taken to one side and told by John Denne of Deal that he obviously did not know that he was being rude to an Earl, he replied that: *"I care for never a lord in all Christendom"*. According to Denne, it appeared the **Pelican** suffered from a very bad reputation at the time anyway and he had been told by Smyth's servants the landlord regularly

"robbed more in his house than any thief could do upon the highway". (It appears that the Earl was a Diplomat, in more ways than one, and would often be sent on missions to France and Italy, so he was possibly en route to one of these destinations when the encounter occurred).

The inn and its gardens and orchards covered an area of around two to three acres. About 1700, a malthouse and brewery were built on the site of one of its orchards and the inn itself was converted into a terrace of four houses (one for the head brewer). In 1740, brewer, Anthony Ffasham was in occupation when all the buildings and land, together with brewery equipment, were put up for sale.

Under the heading of *"Travelling Exhibitions"*, the 25 July 1750 edition of the Kentish Post advertised: *"'The Grand Microcosm of Subterranean Ford' for the 'entertainment of the speculative virtuoi and all true*

Site of Pelican 3 2009.

sons of natural and experimental studies' (rock & grotto work collected by the owner in several years travel in petrified caverns 255 fathoms perpendicular & some miles long) at the **Pelican**, Deal."

In September 1750, the Kentish Post ran an advertisement which read: "*Societies – Deal Friendly Society to meet at Thomas Reynolds'* **Pelican** *on Feast Day, Oct 3, to settle affairs: John Clements, Abraham Walker, John Cavill. (Stewards)*".

In 1769, according to the *Kentish Gazette*, part of it was sold again: "*William Wood (brewing trade) to be sold at fair appraisement the quarter part belonging to Mr William Wood, a commodious well-accustomed brewhouse with messuages (one of them a public house), malthouse, storehouses and a piece of land enclosed adjoining thereto, situate near the Market Place in the town of Deal and used by Messrs Sole Adams & Wood or their tenants and also his quarter in two other public houses to the said brewhouse*". (The **Rose** would have been one of them).

Another sales advertisement appeared in a 1772 edition of the *Kentish Gazette*: "*To be sold by auction on Monday the 6th day of July next at 2 o'clock in the afternoon at the* **Pelican** *in Deal. The brewhouse, millhouse, malthouse, vaults and other offices of Messrs Sole Adams & Wood, late brewers of Deal, aforesaid; also the enclosed lands together with three tenements or messuages thereunto adjoining and now or late in the several occupations of Mrs Elizabeth Wood, John Knott and William Wood. For further particulars, enquire of Messrs Sole & Co aforesaid, and all persons in indebted to* the said partnership are forthwith desired to pay their respective debts on or before the 5th day of August next or they will be sued for the same and all persons whom the said partnership is indebted are desired to send in their accounts immediately that they may be discharged."

It is likely that brewer, Thomas Oakley junior, took over ownership of the premises from 1774 (until 1803). In the January 1775 Assizes, Richard Adams was mentioned as landlord of the (probably wrongly spelt) "*Pilican*", and, in 1776, landlord, John Knott, was documented as refusing to billet dragoons. It is believed that, at some point in the late 1770s, the **Pelican** closed down on this site and it moved its premises to no 44 Beach Street – see entry for **Pelican** (1).

From 1823 to the early 1850s, brewer, Edward Iggulden owned the building (having previously owned the brewery which was situated on the south side of Water Street at the junction with Lower Street). From 1852, the property was owned by Hill & Sons brewery which it in turn sold on in September 1901. According to the *Country Brewers' Gazette*: "*At a public auction mart in Deal on the 1st instance, an important brewery property was offered for public sale. It consisted of the Deal brewery and the modern brewery at Mongeham, along with 63 tied houses. It was sold to Mr Matthews representing (brewers) Messrs Thompson & Son of Walmer for £93,000*". Two of the previously converted houses fronting the High Street (formerly Lower Street) were demolished soon afterwards when Stanhope Road was being laid out.

The pub, together with its pastures and orchards, had, as mentioned above, originally covered an area of around two to three acres, including the present day Stanhope Road down to West Street. Some of the pub buildings remain to this day, one of which is attached to the rear of butchers, JC Rook & Sons' premises, in George Alley off the High Street.

Deal Post Office (now the Sorting Office), the Astor Hall (previously called the Stanhope Hall, the Winter Gardens and now the Astor Theatre) and a roller skating rink (now the Astor Theatre's car park) were built on the sites of the old brewery and the remaining pub buildings and gardens. Interestingly, the current dental practice in Stanhope Road has informed the authors that a condition in its title deeds stipulates that the brewing of beer must not be carried out on the premises!

Pewter Dish (location unknown) Deal

The only documentary evidence found for this pub was found on Laker's 1680 list of Deal's inns, but it otherwise remains untraceable.

Phoenix, 145 High Street, Deal

See entry for the *Queens Arms.*

Phoenix (Laurel Tree)
188 High Street (121 Lower Street), Deal

This beerhouse was located on the site of the first house north of Griffin Street and the junction with High Street. The *Laurel Tree* was a symbolic evergreen shrub in Greek mythology, denoting fame and prosperity.

In 1864, two soldiers were charged with assaulting the landlord, Edward Austen, but the case was dismissed. The same year, the house was refused a spirit licence but gained a full licence in 1865. However, Annual Licensing Day in 1866 saw Mr Austen almost lose his licence following reports that he harboured girls of *"loose character"* on the premises. In 1872, John Bax took over.

By 1874, a mortgage document for that year mentioned *"John Pettet Ramell of Deal, grocer ... all that messuage or tenement with outbuildings yards and appurtenances being No 121 Lower Street and now known as The **Laurel Tree** late in the occupation of Edward Austen and now of John Clinch Payne abutting Lower Street West and by an alley or passage leading to Griffin Street East formerly in two separate properties the easternmost yard having been the site of a messuage subsequently pulled down."* This merely referred to a building at the rear of the pub which had been damaged by fire.

Joseph Woodham and Thomas Riley were two of the many landlords in 1875, by which time the house had been renamed the *Phoenix* (probaby because of the earlier fire). Despite its new name,

2009.

the pub closed in 1876, although the premises were described some years later in a lease as being *"formerly the **Laurel Tree**."*

The house is now an antiques shop.

Pier Hotel

See entry for *Dunkerleys.*

Pier Refreshment Rooms

See entry for *Goodwins*.

Plough, Beach Street, Deal

See entry for the *North Star*.

Plough, 38 & 40 Albert Road, Deal

This pub dated back to at least the mid 1840s. Alice Bedwell was landlady in 1847 when the *Plough* was listed as a *"Beerhouse"*, followed by John Bedwell, *"Farmer & Beer Retailer"* in 1861 until at least 1867 (when the pub was last documented). Bedwell apparently owned a large acreage of agricultural land surrounding the *Plough*.

The building was demolished and pre WWII houses (numbered 38 and 40) Albert Road now stand on its approximate site.

Plume of Feathers (location unknown) Deal

A plume of three feathers was originally depicted on the crest of the Black Prince (1330 to 1376) and has been associated with the title of Prince of Wales ever since. Leases for the *Plume of Feathers* ran from 1661, which showed Mary Ayler as landlady that year, and Nicholas Goff, *"Pilot"*, and his wife, Mary, in 1680. It is not clear how long it was a pub but leases for the property itself continued until 1851. Despite the legal documentation, the whereabouts of this pub remain a mystery.

Pooles (location unknown) Deal

The only mention of this tavern appeared in Samuel Pepys' diary on 30 April 1660: *"So we took boat and first went on shore, it being very pleasant in the fields; but a very pitiful town Deal is. We went to Fullers (the famous place for ale) but they have none, but what is in the vat. After that to Pooles, a tavern in the town, where we drank and so to boat again."*

The whereabouts of this establishment remain unknown.

See also entries for *Flying Horse* and *Red Crosse*.

Poor Dog (location unknown) Deal

The *Poor Dog* was documented in Sandwich Licensing Recognizances lists for Deal in 1680, and again in 1751 showing John Hodgeman as landlord, but no location was recorded.

At other times, the names *Dog(g)* and *Black Dog(g)* appear in documents of the same era, although neither can reliably be connected to the *Poor Dog*.

Popes Hole, Popes Court, Mongeham Road, Deal

According to the Parish Overseers Book of 1772, it was recorded that landlord, Mr Wise, was paid 3/- (15p) for some ale. In 1863, the Poor Rate Book stated that *Popes Hole* was then owned by the executors of CJ Hills, brewer, with Rebecca Wanstall as landlady. She was joined on the licence by Robert Gibbs in 1865. In 1904, Alfred Hambrook and George Oliver were listed as residents.

In 1914, *Popes Hole* was by then known as Pope's Court Tea Gardens, according to a town guide directory for that year. It advertised *"3½ acres to explore, ivy-clad cliffs, wooded walks, dells and nut grove. Strawberry teas, crab teas and prawn teas. Tennis lawns for clubs and private parties"*. (The gardens were actually created out of an old chalk quarry on the site, which had been operational in the 1540s during the building of Walmer, Deal and Sandown Castles).

By 1915, Mrs B Wilson was the registered proprietress.

Unfortunately, further information is sketchy since very little documentary evidence has survived concerning **Popes Hole**. However, it is believed that the building itself was demolished some time during the first half of the 20th century, and a magnificent detached private house known as Popes Court now stands on its site. Lord Hore-Belisha (of Belisha Beacon fame and a former Minister of Transport) was an early resident. The house is situated opposite no 18 Mongeham Road, and is surrounded by what appears to be the original beautiful gardens belonging to **Popes Hole**.

Port Arms
10 (8) (75) Beach Street, Deal

c1920.

This ancient pub stood literally on the beach until around 1893 when the road was laid down in front of it, thus separating the building from the shingle. Located close to the entrance of the old Naval Yard, it would have been a busy, bustling maritime house where news would be exchanged, wages paid (and spent!) and swashbuckling stories told. Local legend has it that it is one of the oldest pubs in Deal.

It is not clear when the **Port Arms** first claimed its name but, according to local historian, the late Gertrude Nunns, from her researches at Lambeth Palace Archives, a lease of the '*Archbishop's Waste and Sea Valley*' states that William Mullett was resident there in 1672, listed as "*Pilot, with Capstan and Tenement.*" He was followed by his widow, Elizabeth, in 1699.

Samuel Ffasham, a local brewer, appeared on the lease in 1721, followed by Thomas Oakley, brewer, in 1759 and his son of the same name in 1783.

The first documentary evidence of the **Port Arms** by name was in 1776 when Charles Hutchings was landlord and it appeared on the '*Refused To Billet Dragoons List*' of hostelries.

Other landlords included John Trevegan in 1804, brewers John Fowle and John Hoile in 1817, Henry Fitzgerald in 1824, Ann Fitzgerald from 1828 to 1839 and Thomas Trott, a famous local mariner, in 1851.

The 'Brethren of the Enlightened Cottagers' (see also entry for the **Pelican**) met there in 1861 when apparently '... *the viands were first rate, and much credit is due to Brother Thomas Trott*'. Mr Trott stayed at the pub until 1873 when, in the August, he was fined 10 shillings (50p) for opening outside of licensing hours. The same year, customer, Thomas Middleton, was summonsed for threatening Thomas Files with a poker at the pub. He was bound over to keep the peace for 3 months.

c1900.

of the darts competition! He remained at the pub until January 1983 when it was reported that he had sadly died on the same day as retiring from the business, just hours later.

Later hosts included Michael Schmid and Peter Burr in April 1983, Frank Hagger in September 1983, David Smith in 1985, Lee and Shirley Deacon in 1993, Colin and Jane Jones in March 1994, Steven and Stephanie Dempsey in October 1994, Christopher and Susan Murley in 1995, William and Lorna Prime in 2001, William and Lorna Prime and Frances Sweeney in March 2002, William Prime, Frances Sweeney and MJ Carthy in December 2002, William Prime, Michael Carthy, Lorna Prime and Shaun Barker 2004 and Brian Pitchford in 2007. The *Port Arms* closed down for a few months and its future at the time looked uncertain. However, the Mercury reported the pub's reopening at 4pm on 5 December 2008 when Mike Prime returned as manager.

Amelia Hall, *"Licensed Victualler"*, was landlady in 1881, followed by John Sharp in 1882, William Robert West Meakins also in 1882 to 1897 and long-serving Henry (aka 'Harry') John Miller Meakins in 1898 until 1940.

In November 1911, it was reported that the Annual Dinner & Smoking Concert was held in celebration of Mr and Mrs Henry Meakins' wedding day 13 years earlier and that 100 guests were entertained at the pub.

Henry Meakins owned a 'hovelling boat' called the 'Lady Haig' and another called the 'Lady Brassy' that were always beached on the shingle in front of the pub. They were both used for pleasure trips from the beach during the 1930s but, during WWII, the 'Lady Haig' took part in the 'Little Ships' evacuation of Dunkirk in 1940 and, although damaged during the mission, she was towed back to Deal almost in one piece!

On October 12 1940, the pub shut down and Meakins applied for a protection order in favour of Wilfred Martin of George Beer & Co, brewers of Faversham, on the grounds of ill health. On 9 September 1944, the pub reopened when the brewery transferred the licence to Mrs Edith Crystal. She remained there until at least the mid 1950s and was followed by Harry and Joyce Franks in 1959, John Wood in 1960, AT Reeve in 1966 and Robert Witcher (a former Royal Marine) in 1967. A Mercury article in June 1969 stated that Witcher, *"the 42 year old landlord of the Port Arms"*, had made it through to the final

The *Port Arms* comprises two bars, as well as guest accommodation upstairs. The outside terraced area to the side of the pub is shared with the nearby *Kings Arms* and *Dunkerleys*, and is a very popular venue on balmy summer days.

The *Port Arms* briefly closed again in early 2010, and the licence was taken over by Nicola Pooke, on 15 March, who organised a grand reopening ceremony on 24 April. At the time of writing, the guest accommodation was being refurbished.

According to the current licensee, there is definitely a friendly presence around as she feels certain she catches a glimpse of something out of the corner of her eye when the pub is empty. The playful entity also takes great pleasure in moving around the precisely positioned beer mats on the tables in the bar!

The pub is currently owned by Enterprise Inns.

Port Merchant, Beach Street, Deal

The *Port Merchant* appeared on the *"Refused to Billet Dragoons"* list in 1776, and, in 1780, it was described as being situated next door north to the *Watermans Arms* at no 41 Beach Street (on the beach in between the turnings for Oak Street and Brewer Street, off Beach Street).

It was sold in 1836 for £160 to Deal Pavement Commission at the same time as the *Watermans Arms* to make way for the building of the present day promenade which now aligns the beach.

Pound, Wellington Road/Blenheim Road (Mill Road, Flax Street), Deal

Pound site c1920.

Site of Pound 2009.

The **Pound** was so called after the 'stray animal' pound that was situated at or near the pub and located at the edge of town.

The first mention of this pub appeared in the Poor Rate Book of 1786 showing John Noakes as landlord, followed by Thomas Friend in 1799 until at least 1804. There is some doubt that it continued as a pub after this date. However, Friend was still registered at the house as late as 1830. In 1851, Thomas Ottaway, *"Market Gardener"*, was resident at the property and, by the mid 1850s, the house was described as comprising *"the Pound Houses"* (see entry for **Ramsgate Harbour**) straddling the junction between the former Sandy Lane South (now Blenheim Road) and what was then known as Mill Road.

The site of the pub is now a private car park for St Thomas of Canterbury Catholic Church situated on the western corner of Wellington Road and Blenheim Road.

Prince Albert, 187-189 Middle Street (189, 92 Middle Street), Deal

The **Prince Albert** is sited on the south-east corner of Alfred Square, at the junction with Middle Street.

The house was initially addressed as 92 Middle Street. Following renumbering of the main streets of Deal in 1893, it became known as 189 (now 187-189) Middle Street.

The pub's title deeds start in 1717, although records show a building on the site since 1710,

c1900.

and the cellars date back to the 1600s when it is believed a beer and general provisions shop operated from what was probably then just one unit in a single storey building. The shop would have supplied provisions to ships anchored in the Downs, as well as to the townspeople of Deal.

If the lack of court records or reported misdemeanours in local newspapers is anything to go by, save for two or three incidents, the pub appears to have mostly been a fairly well run and respectable establishment in what had been in early times a very down at heel and particularly lawless part of town. Alfred Square itself was once a bustling turning point for horse drawn coaches, as well as being full of shops, so the immediate locality would have been a busy one.

Thomas Hayward, aged 35, his wife, Louisa, aged 40, together with their ten children, were resident at "92 Middle Street" in the 1840s. (Interestingly, the houses which adjoin the premises, now numbered 9 and 10 Alfred Square, were built around 1824 on the orchard garden formerly belonging to the pub. William Thomas Hayward was one of the residents in 1827, followed by Edward Hanger, *"Beerhouse Keeper"*, aged 30, with wife, Louisa, 25, *"living in one of two cottages, known as 9 & 10 Alfred Square"* in 1841. According to the census for that year, no 10 Alfred Square was an unnamed beerhouse, although whether or not it was in any way connected to the **Prince Albert** is unknown).

A chronological list of notable dates, together with registered innkeepers, reads: 1855 and 1859: According to the Poor Rate Book, William J Riley of Middle Street was the registered *"Beer Retailer and Shopkeeper"*. No pub name was mentioned, (although its owner, Mrs Louisa Hayward, was recorded as living in Alfred Square).

1861: The census for that year states that William Samuel Riley, 33, *"Retailer of Beer (Grocer Shop and Beerhouse)"*, was resident on the premises, together with his wife Ann, four children and a house servant.

1864: The premises had by then become known as the **Prince Albert** by name.

1866: According to Kelly's Directory, William J Riley was proprietor of the *"house and shop"*. (The *"shop"* was probably run from the pub building itself, although Riley was known to have had another shop opposite the **Prince Albert**, then addressed as 126 Middle Street but now known as 19 Dolphin Street. A blocked up doorway in the present day residential house indicates its former entrance in Middle Street).

1881: William Samuel Riley was listed as *"Publican and General Dealer."*

1890: William Riley appeared before magistrates in an attempt to transfer the licence. However, they deemed him to be *"a lunatic"* and the hearing was adjourned. Margaret Baker took over the licence later that year and she remained at the pub until at least 1898. Her husband's occupation was given as *"Carpenter."*

1891: Frederick Baker, *"Licensed Victualler"*, was at the helm, together with his wife, Margaret, and their two children.

1898: According to the April 16th edition of the Mercury, Baker was charged with selling *"… adulterated whisky. Fined 10 shillings (50p), with 9 shillings (45p) costs."*

1903 & 1904: Henry Burville was registered landlord.

1905: Walter T Jefford was landlord until May 2010.

when the licence was transferred to George J Castle, who in turn transferred it to Christopher Craig in the October.

1907: According to The Deal & Walmer Telegram dated January 12: *"The license of the **Prince Albert**, Middle-street, was temporarily transferred from Christopher Craig to George Ralph Erridge, formerly of the **Deal Lugger**, now closed under the order of last year."* 'Cash' Erridge as he was nicknamed remained licensee until 1940.

1940: A protection order was taken out in March and, in May, the licence was transferred from Erridge to W

1906.

Martin who was company secretary at George Beer & Co, brewers. A transfer to the brewery often, but not always, meant a pub closure.

1944: In July, Thomas Barlow applied for a protection order and, in the September, W Martin transferred the licence over to him.

1947: In July, Barlow was charged with receiving coal from WA Gates, a Royal Marine, which had apparently been stolen from the RM depot. The landlord was found guilty and was fined £25. Hot on the heels of this verdict, the licence was transferred the following month to Alfred Potter.

1948: An application was approved in the January for alterations *"so that the 3 downstairs' rooms can be supervised. The bar will be moved back and the door replaced with a half door"*. Later that year, R Casswell was registered as landlord.

1949: In February, Alfred Potter applied for a protection order to Richard Henry Parker and, in the March, the licence was transferred to Parker.

1952: The licence was transferred in February to Stanley DA Andrews who was also granted a music and singing licence.

1953: In May, the licence was transferred to Thomas Christopher Johnson. In December, it was reported that *"Stanley Andrews, former landlord of the **Prince Albert**"* had been sent to prison.

1954: The music licence was transferred in March from Andrews to Johnson. In May, the pub licence was transferred from Johnson to James Albert Thomas Norkett and transferred once again in December from Norkett to Walter Edwin Mason.

1956: Structural alterations were approved in May. The house next door at no 187 Middle Street (which had already been in the ownership of George Beer & Co, since around the 1880s) was incorporated into the existing pub building (no 189), with interior walls being knocked through to create one larger building.

Later landlords included George Frederick Reiger from April 1960, Francis Walter Smith from May 1961, RW Fenn in 1966, Mr and Mrs Philpott from 1968 to 1972 and Harold H Willis from 1973 to 1976.

Until the 1980s, the **Prince Albert**, like so many other pubs at the time, also had its own off-sales (or 'jug and bottle') counter. Alcohol would be sold from behind an interior half door, which was accessed via the side entrance in Middle Street.

Sidney and Sheila Whitehead took over in 1976 (when the **Prince Albert** was owned by Whitbread), remaining there, together with their children, Jackie, Jenny, Paul and Colin, until 1981. Sid and Sheila have recently confirmed that the downstairs accommodation was divided into two completely separate bars, ie the saloon and the restaurant. Next door neighbour, Bill Cory, was the pub's piano player, and a tunnel apparently once led from the cellars of the **Prince Albert** into the basement of his house at no 185 Middle Street. During the great storm of January 1978, the sea spilled over the beach and flooded into Alfred Square and beyond, but completely bypassed the pub itself, although shingle several feet deep completely filled the cellars of many nearby houses. Sid and Sheila opened up the pub as a soup kitchen and took coffee and brandy up to the fishermen on the beach. (Black and white photos showing the aftermath of the storm can still be seen on the wall of the passageway outside the ladies' lavatory). They added that the **Prince Albert** was a real community pub, with its own darts team and regular coach outings to places such as Chatham. At the time, there were a lot more old Deal families living in the North End of town than there are nowadays, and it seems that, if they took a dislike to a certain pub for any reason (the **Prince Albert** excluded!), the word would be spread and the unfortunate landlord could be assured of a permanently empty bar!

Robert Woodward took over in 1981, followed by Anthony ('Tony') Peter Hopkin in 1982. Together with his wife, Christine ('Chrissie'), who joined him on the licence in 1989, they bought the pub from the brewery. They were both very keen motorcyclists and used to be joined every Easter by a number of other enthusiasts – all in fancy dress – for a sponsored motorbike ride in aid of local children's charities. The Hopkins sold up and retired in 2002, and Michael Harlick and Colin Vurley became the new owners on 25 September 2002 and remain as landlords until the present.

"Cash" Erridge, landlord at the beginning of the 20th century, was so-nicknamed because of the vast amounts of money he used to keep in a large safe at the pub, and current owners, Michael and Colin, confirm that his huge Victorian safe is still in situ. However, nothing of value is stored in it nowadays since the lock could apparently be picked with a hairpin and they consider it to be just an interesting piece of furniture. They also confirm the presence of occasional poltergeist activity, especially on the upper floors of the pub, something that the previous owners also used to experience. Whatever it is seems harmless and only manifests itself by moving small items which often do not turn up until sometimes months later in different places, although one of the current owners thinks he has also caught sight of the presence. These manifestations usually only occur when alterations are being made to the building, as well as when some of the old pub photos on display in the bar and the dining room are moved about. A cleaner working in the pub during the 1990s also reported that an unseen hand had pinched her bottom as she went about her duties!

The **Prince Albert** is situated on a corner plot and celebrates its nautical associations with a smart external navy blue and cream livery. It also boasts a typical smugglers' window at the front giving views to surrounding streets and the sea. The current owners have confirmed that, according to old deeds, there used to be an orchard behind the pub running down to the High Street before the properties in Alfred Square were built on that side (as mentioned earlier). The present day interior remains unspoilt and comprises one ground floor bar (in the original premises – no 189) overseen by Michael, and a restaurant area in the building converted in 1956 (no 187) run by chef, Colin. There is a small courtyard garden to the rear, and the upstairs accommodation includes three beautiful Georgian style en suite letting rooms.

The pub is a free house and remains open.

Prince Alfred Inn
77 College Road (98A & later 99 Lower Street) Deal

The following appeared in the Deal and Walmer Telegram dated 7 June 1862: *"HRH Prince Alfred landed at Deal yesterday afternoon and visited Sandown to indulge in a game of cricket, accompanied by several officers of the fleet"*. Prince Alfred (1844-1900) was the second eldest son of Queen Victoria and it seems likely, therefore, that the pub was named in his honour following this visit.

The pub first appeared around 1864 when Mr T Culvus was registered landlord at no 98A Lower Street. The premises were subsequently rebuilt in 1866 and the building renumbered no 99.

In 1867, the pub advertised: *"The Prince Alfred Inn – Fine Airy Beds and Sitting Rooms."*

The following year, the pub was in the news because Richard Adams and John Ashington threatened the life of Culvus and broke a pane of glass and caused other damage, with a fine of 30 shillings (£1.50) each or 21 days imprisonment. The fines were paid.

In 1871, the premises advertised: *"To Let – Income Moderate – Apply to R Worthington, Brewer, Maxton, Dover."*

2006.

Other landlords included Miss Cole in 1871, Mrs Saxby in 1872 and Mr Sharpe (formerly of the **Pelican 2**), also in 1872.

The pub closed in 1873 and the following auction details declared: *"**Prince Alfred Inn**, Deal. Messrs West and Usher are instructed by Mr T Cattermole to offer for sale by auction, 30 September, at the north-end, on the premises as above, the whole of the bar fittings, including a metal-top counter and a Warne's 5 motion beer engine (quadrant action). Also a quantity of surplus household furniture, etc."*

During recent renovations of a downstairs fireplace, the present owner found a quantity of clay pipes and old bottles. The pub is now a private house.

Prince of Orange

See entry for the *Pelican (1)*.

Prince of Wales
177 (86) Middle Street, Deal

The first mention of this pub was in 1845 when Henry T Wood was landlord of what was then a beerhouse. He was followed by George Norris in 1852 and George Thomas Jarvis in 1859. The **Prince of Wales** became fully licensed by 1864 when CT James was at the helm. Isaac Moore was landlord in 1869 and Albert Parker in 1870.

In May 1871, it was reported that William Cribben assaulted the landlord and maliciously broke three panes of glass and one quart pot. He was also charged with being drunk and noisy in the street. Cribben was sentenced to 21 days' hard labour in Sandwich Gaol.

Thomas Hornsby Finnis was registered landlord from 1872 until 1875. By 1883, the pub was owned by brewer, Alfred Kingsford, whose landlord was Edward Bolton. Bolton was followed by William Thompson in 1878, Robert William Butterwick in 1885, Henry Hill in 1886 and Henry Howgego in 1891 when the licence renewal was refused as the pub possessed *"no requirements for the wants of the neighbourhood."*

The pub is now a private house.

2009.

Providence Inn (Boatswain)
Market Street (1 Fish Market/Market Place, 1-3, 1 King Street) Deal

The early history of the **Providence Inn** is unfortunately rather sketchy. The pub appears to have been known as the **Boatswain** in 1699 when lessee, Joseph Nicholls, *"Chirurgeon"* (surgeon), was in residence, followed by William Gardner, *"Blacksmith"*, and his wife, Martha, in 1720. John Underdown, Cornelius Smith and Stribblehill Norwood, brewers, held the lease in 1738, followed by Thomas Oakley, brewer, in 1763 and Thomas Parker Oakley, *"Son of previous lessee"*, in 1783.

By 1803, the pub was called the **Fleur de Luce** (see

separate entry, before transferring its licence – and name - to new premises in Union Row around 1804). What the old pub called its premises when the *Fleur de Luce* moved is not known but it was described that year as being *"the next building north of King Street."*

In 1826, Robert Edwards. *"Gentleman"*, was listed as resident and again in 1832. He was followed by Edmund Thompson *"of the Walmer brewery"*, who held the lease in November 1839. According to the 1841 census, John M Prescott, *"Victualler"*, aged 55, was resident in *"Fish Market, Deal"*, together with his wife Jane, 55, and children Samuel, 13, and Elizabeth, 11, as well as another child called Elizabeth Waugh aged 6. In 1847, Henry Darby was listed as landlord of an unnamed beerhouse in the *"Fish Market"*, and it was not until 1854 that it was first referred to as the **Providence**. Darby remained there until his death when the licence was transferred to Alphonso James Redman in 1874, followed by Edward Trott in 1891.

In May 1892, it was reported that the new landlord, William Matthew Piercey, committed suicide by cutting his throat while temporarily insane, and his widow, Elizabeth Ann Piercey, took over the licence. She was followed by J Logan in 1908, CF Anderson in 1910 and Gilbert Frederick Martin in 1911.

In 1913, the pub was referred to the Compensation Committee for closure, together with the **Liverpool Arms**. The magistrates' report at the time stated that *"Trade was increasing and visitors' book produced showed satisfaction of the theatrical companies staying at the **Providence** appearing at the Theatre Royal* [opposite the pub]. *The landlord and his wife had turned **Providence** into a cheap hotel"*. The **Providence** survived the cull but the **Liverpool Arms** did not.

In 1914, Martin was fined 16/- (80p) plus 9/6d

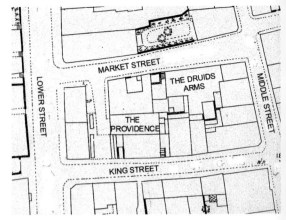

1872 map showing Providence and Druids Arms.

(47½p) when he was found guilty of selling watered-down rum.

In the early 1920s, Martin opened up the Providence Dining Rooms at nos 1 to 3 King Street which adjoined the **Providence** pub. By 1926, he was recorded as being resident of the Dining Rooms while Albert William Bartlett was resident landlord of the pub. In 1929, the Dining Rooms' premises were then listed as a *"Confectionery"* but still with Martin in residence.

The last landlord of the pub was Edward Pinks who took over in 1936. During his landlordship, the pub's private bar entrance was described as being in King Street and the entrance to the public bar in Market Street. Pinks remained at the helm during WWII until the pub was badly damaged on 1 September 1944 when a shell exploded on nearby Catt's restaurant, and what remained of the old pub building was eventually demolished in 1948.

Public conveniences are now situated on the site of the **Providence**.

From the Police Court - 8 October 1887:

Edward Williams was fined 7/6d (37½p) or 7 days, for being drunk and disorderly in the High-street, and William Frost was ordered to pay the same amount for being drunk and incapable in a public passage leading from King-street to Customer House lane.

Queen Adelaide
22 Church Street, (St Mary) Upper Walmer

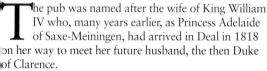

c1900.

2006.

The pub was named after the wife of King William IV who, many years earlier, as Princess Adelaide of Saxe-Meiningen, had arrived in Deal in 1818 on her way to meet her future husband, the then Duke of Clarence.

The story goes that she landed at the Naval Yard and proceeded to the *Three Kings* (now the *Royal Hotel*) accompanied by Sir Edward Owen, Lord Keith and several other luminaries. Much impressed by the warm welcome received from the people of Deal, she later contributed generously towards the cost of the building of the public baths that used to stand on the beach. Local people were equally impressed and named the public baths in her honour, as well as several other buildings. Queen Adelaide died in 1849, having outlived her husband by 12 years.

Elizabeth Knott, aged 70, was listed as *"Publican"* of the *Queen Adelaide* in the 1841 census, followed by James Knight, *"Widower, Chelsea Pensioner and Licensed Victualler"* in 1847, Edward Longley in 1862, William Canham in 1866 and George Knight in 1867. Birth records showed two sons born to Knight, one on 19 May 1868 and another on 3 October 1869. Sadly,

Mrs Knight died in 1870 aged 31 years. Knight remained at the pub and he presumably remarried since twins were born there in 1873, one of whom tragically dying in 1874 aged seven months.

Later landlords include George Timmins in 1887, George Parsons in 1879, James Henry Hogben in 1891, John Mellows in 1895, Frederick Durtnall from 1903 to 1912, followed by Walter Crittenden until the pub's closure on 8 March 1913.

It was reported that Phillips of Malling, the brewers, did not attend the Compensation Committee meetings and that it was left to the landlord to plead the case for a licence renewal. The Committee heard that the *"premises were old and not of very sound construction but in a very fair state of repair. The public house had a respectable working class trade"*. A new licence was subsequently refused.

The *Queen Adelaide* was auctioned (at the same time as the *Greyhound*) by Worsfold & Hayward on 18 February 1914 at the Fleur de Lis in Sandwich and was sold to John Turner for £125.

The property, now a private house, is a listed building.

Queens Arms (Phoenix)
145 High Street (38 Lower Street), Deal

This pub was situated in the High Street opposite the turning into Farrier Street. Old leases dating back to 1708 refer to one part of the premises being held by Samuel Harris and Richard Smith and the other to John Fuller *"of Deal"*. In 1765, Richard Smith and John Gurney appeared on the lease and, in 1776, Gurney sold to Israel Wellard, *"Carpenter"*, for £147, the premises being *"formerly two – now in four dwellings"*. In 1804, Samuel Ffasham Roby and Thomas Hayman junior took a lease for one year. (The Hayman brothers ran a brewery for a short while on the premises at the turn of the 18th to 19th centuries).

Landlords included Matthew Brown junior from 1821 to 1829 (by which time the pub was known as the *Phoenix*), Robert Thomas Martin in 1838 (by then called the *Queens Arms*, presumably to honour Queen Victoria's accession to the throne), John Hookham in 1842, Robert Ramell Lownds, *"Tailor"*, in 1853, Catherine Sherlock in 1859, William Morris in 1861 and William James Marshall in 1863.

In August 1867, David Price was found guilty of stealing a pint tumbler, being the property of landlord, William Marshall, and sentenced to seven days' hard labour. In December 1870, Ann Symes, a tramp, was arrested by the ever vigilant PC Shelvey Cox and charged with being *"drunk and riotous and refusing to leave"* the *Queens Arms*. She was discharged on condition that she promised to leave town.

Richard Henry Robinson was landlord in 1873 followed by Edward Thomas Robinson in 1884. In November, he was charged with *"supplying Thomas Brown with liquor while drunk"*. William Henry Ramell, in giving evidence, stated: *"I reside at 10 Napier-terrace. On 7 November, I was passing the Queens Arms Inn soon after 1 in the afternoon,*

c1955.

when I heard a voice that was familiar to me. I saw Tom Brown with a glass in his hand. Tom was drunk and swaying to and fro – I passed to look for a police constable, but could not find one, and went to the station and stated the case to Supt. Capps. He went to the house, when within 20 yards of the house we saw Tom come out. He staggered across the street. Supt. Capps saw both the landlord and landlady. The landlord remarked that Tom Brown had not had any beer, nothing but a glass of water. I said, if so, it was coloured water." The local newspaper reported that: *"At this stage, the case was withdrawn, on the ground that there was no evidence to prove that Brown was drunk."*

Richard Henry Robinson (brother of Edward) was landlord in 1894, Edward Harris Robinson in 1915, William Gladwish in 1916 and Charles Henry Solly in 1919.

In October 1924, Clara Kitson was charged with being drunk and disorderly at the pub and was fined 10/- (50p) for being drunk and 10/- for refusing to leave licensed premises.

By 1929, Mr Haddock, an officer of the Deal & Walmer Licensed Victuallers Association, was listed as landlord. During his time at the pub, he applied for licences to supply alcohol for various outdoor events including ones for 'Gordon's Restaurant' and the Winter Gardens (the latter now called the Astor Theatre).

William Charles Bragg became landlord in 1934. He was charged with serving alcohol at 11.30 on the night of 5 December 1937. He pleaded innocent, stating that the drinks were served in his living room to five customers and that it was a private after hours birthday party. Bragg was fined £10 and his customers £2 each. In January 1938, the licence was transferred to Harry Rayner. On 25 August 1939, a local newspaper reported: *"An outing for the children of the Maple Leaf*

Glade, no 48, took place on Wednesday, when 34 children with 24 adults, proceeded to Deal by train, leaving Dover at 1 o'clock. At Deal they went to the beach where, after spending a very enjoyable afternoon, all went to the **Queens Arms** for tea, catered for by Sister and Brother Rayner. After tea the children spent a happy time at the fair. Prima Jones gave each child an ice cream, Prima Booker apples and Dame Hornsey sweets. Fruit was also given to them from the proceeds of the children's funds. The day came to an end too soon, the party arriving at Dover at 9.30."

In 1941, it was reported that "Harry Rayner, outgoing landlord at the **Queens Arms**, which was being reopened, applied for a protection oder in favour of BC Dredge [of Thompson's brewery]."

In 1942, the licence was transferred again to Harry Brown. Later landlords included Mrs R Hewett in 1943, George Rowley from 1944 to at least 1948 and F Goldsmith in 1953. A former customer described the place, in the last years of its opening, as: "like going into someone's front room."

In February 1965, the Mercury reported that a number of properties in the High Street, including the **Queens Arms**, were due to be demolished to create a car park. Presumably, demolition followed soon afterwards.

In October 1966, Barbara Collins, in an article for the Mercury, quoted a description of the pub from a history of the **Queens Arms** written by PE Robinson recalling her grandparents' time at the pub in the early 1900s: "1 of 4 common lodging houses in the town, having a small frontage, cobbled yard housing stables. Lodging rooms at rear of building, which had great depth, and an alleyway to Duke Street. Outhouses and lockers in yard for lodgers' possessions, along with a huge copper, sink and water butt for clothes washing. Open from 6am to 11pm. Landlord Mr Robinson. All beds to be vacated by 9am. 12 bed dormitories, and 4 bedrooms. 3 bedrooms at front occupied by family, with a living room behind the bar. No seats in the bar, but tables and chairs in the tap room."

The history also described an arched vault in the beer cellar under the pavement leading both north and south, even though after some yards, the passageway had apparently been bricked up, although, at the rear, there was "a huge cellar."

The site of the old pub now lies beneath the large car park in the High Street.

Queens Head (British Tar, Fleur de Lys)
Queens Head No 1: Alfred Row (1 Bridge Road/Row/Street/British Tar Lane, Devils Row, The Drene, The Drain)
Queens Head No 2: 95 (11) Sandown Road (Middle Street, Lower Street), Deal

The pub was originally called the *Fleur de Lys* but the authors have unfortunately been unable to find any documentary evidence to pinpoint any exact dates. What is known for sure is that it was called the **British Tar** from around 1802 to 1816. In 1804, landlord, Henry Wood, paid £7 per annum rental for the pub. Its address at the time was described as being in the *"North End – 11 buildings from Alfred Square in Lower Street"*. Wood also paid 15/- (75p) rent for the stable, and 10/- (50p) for the garden. In 1808, he was accused of selling 2 quart pots containing short measures but the outcome is unknown.

By 1821, the pub was called the **Queens Head** when its premises were described as comprising *"rooms, stable and yard"* at no 1 Bridge Row, with James Walsh as landlord. (Walsh appears twice in the rate book for that year since he was landlord of the *Saracens Head* at the same time). The house was situated on the south-eastern corner of the present day Alfred Row and Bridge Road and probably had an entrance in both streets.

James Marsh was registered landlord in 1823, followed by Thomas Wood in 1828 and Richard Ditton in 1834. According to the 1839 records of fly proprietor, Hancock, he met a horse dealer in the **Queens Arms** and bought a gelding from him *"to replace old Samuel."*

In 1845, H Gardener, *"Boat Builder"* was landlord (he had previously been at the **Good Intent**) at a time when the premises were also used as a boat yard. The pub was sold by brewery owners, John Hatton, in 1872 to Daniel Mackintosh Hills, brewer, for £650. The licence was transferred from Gardener to Thomas Marsh in 1876 when the pub's address was given as Bridge Row. Edward Jell was

c1955.

landlord in 1880, followed by Daniel McKay and William Featherstone Bass both in 1881 and Alfred Valentine White in the early 1880s and John Prior in the mid 1880s. He was followed by Thomas Smith in 1886, Harriet Elizabeth Watts, widow, in January 1887, Alice Madelaine in July 1887, George Brown in 1889, Thomas May in 1890 and William Botton in May 1891. It was reported that year that the landlord had applied to open the pub early for the sale of tea and coffee to workers at the local fish factory.

In July 1891, William Black took over as landlord, followed by Henry Wright in January 1892.

In June 1892, the Deal Fire Brigade arrived at 11.30 one morning after being alerted that the pub was ablaze, as well as other adjoining cottages. The **Queens Head** was completely gutted but the pub's 'clubroom' (being of brick construction) remained more or less intact apart from slight damage to the roof. The clubroom was apparently connected to the main pub building by means of a staircase covered in by a wooden building and, together with a store room, they were described as being located *"some 8' to 10' to the rear of the pub."*

In September 1892, the old pub's licence was transferred to its newly built premises in Middle Street (now 95 Sandown Road) and William Dawson took over as landlord.

Later landlords included David John Petty in 1895, Harry Blacklocks and John William Gallaway both in 1910, Frederick Charles Careford in 1911, Thomas Henry Tucker from 1911 until at least 1948, H Green and James Arendell both in 1953 and J Gagan from 1966 to 1968. It is assumed that the *Queens Head* closed down around this time, although unfortunately no evidence can be found to support this.

Despite heavy bombing during WWII, the original pub's clubroom still exists and is now a private house (at 11 Alfred Row), and a wooden garage stands on the site of the actual pub building. In fact, no 11 is a unique address since it is now the only one in Alfred Row!

The pub's later home (at 95 Sandown Road) is now a private house.

2009.

Queens Head (Kings Head)
37 The Strand (Walmer Road), Walmer

Stephen Carter was the first landlord in 1797, and, in 1799, Edward Smith was licensee. It was first documented as being called the *Kings Head* by name in 1804.

By 1811, William Dawes was at the helm, and Mary Ann Dawes took over in 1824. She was still there in 1837 when the house became known as the *Queens Head*, probably coinciding with Victoria's accession to the throne. Mary served there until at least 1847, and, in 1852 and 1862, Edward Dawes was listed as landlord.

On 10 October 1860, a Deal & Walmer Telegram report entitled *"Local Intelligence"* stated that *"The body of William Ford was found floating in the Gull Stream on Thursday last, and was landed at Walmer in the evening, and an inquest held on the following day at the Queen's Head, Walmer."*

Other landlords included Edward Elliot in 1866, Horace Hills in 1867 and Samuel Pearson senior from 1874 (until 1882).

Another local newspaper story, this time dated 5 October 1878, reported that *"On Wednesday evening a large fish, known as the 'Thrasher', was captured in a herring net, about half a mile from the*

shore opposite the *'Queen's Head'*, Walmer. By means of ropes it was got into the fishing boat, and brought to the shore. It measured 10 feet 10 inches long and weighed about 4 cwt. It was exhibited on Thursday and Friday in a booth erected for the purpose, and we hear that about £10 was collected, which sum will help defray the costs of repairing the nets which were much damaged."*

In 1883, a local newspaper advertisement read: *"WJ Hopper, (late Samuel Pearson), 'Queen's Head', Walmer Road. Wine Beer & Spirit Merchant. Stout On Draught. Apartments To Let."*

Hopper was followed by George Band in 1898, Samuel Jones in 1904, FW Holland in 1910 and Harry William Savage in 1913.

In March 1914, when William Russell was landlord, the pub was referred to the Compensation Committee for closure. Thompson's brewery offered no objection since the licensing magistrates argued that there were six other public houses nearby. It shut down on 31 December 1914 under the Licensing Consolidation Act.

On 1 May 1915, a large advert appeared in the local paper *"Ex-'Queen's Head' Inn, 37, The Strand,*

1931 – Old Comrades' Club gather outside the former Queens Head.

Walmer. Sale of Antique and Other Furniture. Messrs West, Usher & Co are instructed to Sell by Auction, on the above premises, on Tuesday, 4th May, 1915, the whole of the Useful Household Furniture and other Effects, comprising: Iron French brass-rail bedsteads, spring and flock mattresses, feather beds, bolsters and pillows, counterpanes, blankets, bed and table linen, painted and mahogany marble-top washstands, chamberware, towel airers, stained dressing tables, mahogany and birch toilet glasses, fine mahogany Cheval ditto, SATIN WALNUT BEDROOM SUITE of Cheval Panel Wardrobe, dressing chest and marble-top tiled-back washstand, grained and antique mahogany chests of drawers, gilt-framed pier glasses, American walnut overmantels with mirror panels, pictures in gilt, oak, maple and other frames, china and glass ornaments, TWO SPANISH MAHOGANY SIDEBOARDS, American walnut cheffonier with mirror panels, couches and settees, antique mahogany, Chippendale and inlaid ditto Sheraton chairs, wicker, bentwood, stuffed, spring-seat, folding, easy and other chairs in mahogany, walnut and oak frames, upholstered leatherette, plush and tapestry, fenders and firesets, UPRIGHT PIANOFORTE IN WALNUT CASE (by D'Almaine & Co), piano stool, music stand and music, grandfather's clock with ormolu dial in oak case, marble mantel ditto, mahogany Chippendale, walnut, rosewood and oak, card, loo, dining, stand occasion and hall tables, MAHOGANY CHIPPENDALE BOOKCASE, table covers, curtains and poles, iron deed box, umbrella stands, rugs and mats, the trade glasses and utensils, scales and weights, dinner and teaware, the usual kitchen utensils in tin, iron and earthenware, and numerous other useful articles. On view the day previous to the Sale from 1 till 5 o'clock. SALE AT HALF-PAST TEN O'CLOCK. Further Particulars may be had of the Auctioneers, at the Deal Estate and House Agency, Victoria Town, Deal, & Cliffe-road, Kingsdown."

In May 1917, it was reported that three separate fire engines (from Walmer, Deal and the Royal Marines) attended at the former **Queens Head** after a fire broke out but that unfortunately most of its outbuildings were lost. This was the first call out for Walmer fire brigade.

By 1921, the premises had reopened as the Old Comrades Club and, in 1923, they were being run by Herbert G Newing. In 1936, the club secretary was listed as CH Sweet and steward was C Maybanks. By 1938, it had become known as the Royal Marines Association Club and it remains open to the present day run by stewardess Yvonne Stewart, ably assisted by husband Ray. The club, now simply called the RMA (Deal branch), is a free house owned by a trust made up of former Royal Marines from Deal.

Queens Hotel (1)
Prince of Wales Terrace, Deal

The **Queens Hotel** fronted Prince of Wales Terrace, and was situated between Sondes Road and Stanley Road. The first documentation found concerning the hotel dates back to a local newspaper report on 8 June 1878: *"This commodious and splendid hotel on the Prince of Wales' Terrace is drawing near completion – it is being fitted up with every modern improvement and in a style of elegance somewhat in advance of what has been the usual mode of hotels at Deal. We wish Mr [John] Willoughby, the spirited proprietor, every success"*. The hotel was licensed on condition that *"the premises remain in one as they are"*. The owner of the hotel was registered as

2009.

being the Conservative Land Society of Norfolk Street, Strand, London.

In the 1879 Licensing List, the hotel does not get a mention. However, in the Poor Rate Book of 1881, the hotel's rateable value was £165 (compared with £80 for the **Royal Hotel**). The hotel crops up on later Licensing Lists up to and including 1888 when Willoughby was fined for allowing out of hours drinking but, after that, nothing more is documented.

The building later became known as Amherst House and its corner plot operated as tearooms for several years during the first half of the 20th century. The entire building was later converted into a block of flats.

Queens Hotel (2) (South Eastern Hotel)
Prince of Wales Terrace, Deal

The **South Eastern Hotel** was constructed between 1896 and 1898 on part of the site of the old Naval Yard that became known as Victoria Town, and its owner was the South Eastern Railway Company. Holidaying at British seaside resorts 'for one's health' was becoming increasingly popular and it was envisaged that many well to do summer visitors would be queuing up to stay there.

Contemporary photos show it to be a handsome looking building, constructed of red brick, with facings of Ancaster stone, overlooking the seafront, situated on the corner of Prince of Wales Terrace and Deal Castle Road. It prided itself with having *"electric lighting throughout"* and apparently *"presented a magnificent appearance when lit up at night."*

The hotel boasted two glazed conservatory rooms overlooking the sea, situated either side of the ornate metal and glass canopied main entrance. Former Royal Navy and Merchant Marine stokers were employed in the boiler room to keep the boilers

stoked. There was also *"A commodious wine cellar, well stocked with the choicest vintages"*. The Mercury reported in its *Now And Then* column on 15 October 2009: *"The building was imposing, with an impressive sweeping staircase from the pavement leading to a big lobby which featured a huge chandelier."*

The internal fittings consisted of oak doors, dark walnut furniture, mosaic floors, sumptuous fireplaces with overmantles and stone pillars and arches. A contemporary report on the opening of the hotel also added: *"… the fireproof ornamental asbestos ceilings are a fine specimen of decorative art [sic]."*

The late local historian, David Collyer, writing in his Those Were The Days column for the Mercury on 16 September 1999 noted: *"The South Eastern … boasted 62 bedrooms (36 of which had private baths), electric lighting and a lift to the upper floors."*

A provisional licence was granted to John Sparke

c1970.

who was appointed in 1895, even before the first foundation stones had been laid. He was followed by Charles Sheath in 1896 who stayed there until at least 1910. Hotel managers included Thomas C Smart (formerly of the Charing Cross Hotel in London) from 1904 until 1915. C Lavanchy was licensee in 1936 and, in June 1937, he transferred the licence to Frederick Hefft (a nationalised British subject of German Swiss origin) who, at the same time, bought the freehold. In September 1939, Charles Henderson was fined £10 with £10 costs for shouting offensive words concerning Mr Hefft. Around that time, Miss Anderson, a guest, was found dead at the hotel and the coroner was informed.

In December 1939, Sofia Vanandjan, described in contemporary reports as being a '*White Russian and a former barmaid of the hotel*', was charged with being an alien and prohibited from working at the hotel. It appears she had been found to be illegally employed there "*on 1 November*" of that year "*and at miscellaneous other dates between 14 June and November*". Mr Hefft and his wife Elizabeth, as proprietors, were charged with aiding and abetting Vanandjan to commit an offence by employing her.

The Heffts were fined £2/10s (£2.50) each and Vanandjan was bound over for a year.

The hotel temporarily closed and, on 6 October 1945, the licence was transferred from Frederick Hefft to AS Hobart. It reopened on 22 October that year when it "*... was renamed The **Queen's**, the manager being a Mr Richwood* [see below], *who had ambitious plans to redevelop the car park at the rear for an indoor bowling club. Despite several attempts to obtain planning permission, this scheme came to nought – had it gone ahead Deal would have had its own indoor bowling facility, and an asset to the town.*" [Captain ED Richwood].

In January 1946, Mrs BR Boyden was Manageress. In February, the hotel was granted permission to serve alcohol to persons having "*substantial meals*" up to 1 hour after normal licensing hours. Between 40 and 60 dinners were served daily midweek, 70 to 100 daily at weekends, rising to 250 and 300 in season.

In 1947, it was announced that "*Starting Easter Saturday, April 5th, **Queen's Hotel** will be offering a first-class dinner-dance, cabaret, with leading BBC artistes booked, tickets £1/1s (£1.05)*". In May of that year, the hotel was granted a protection order

c1970.

under the proprietorship of George Charles Brown and his manager Herbert E Williams.

In October 1953, Creasey Brothers purchased the hotel and Frederick Creasey was the resident proprietor and Herbert Williams transferred the licence to Frederick and Walter Creasey. The hotel temporarily closed before Christmas 1954 and it was sold in March 1955 to a London hotelier for £6,500 plus fixtures and fittings. In May, the licence was transferred from the Creaseys to Geoffrey H Warr (formerly of the *Star & Garter* in Deal) and, in June, it was transferred from Warr to George J Garside. In September 1956, FD Richmond of the **Queens Hotel** paid £2,500 for Marine Court, Deal Castle Road.

In 1960, the basement dance hall was turned into a cocktail bar and, in 1961, Captain Richwood had plans to turn the hotel into the finest establishment of its kind on the south-east coast. He planned a banqueting hall for 500 on the car park, 40 two-room suites with kitchenettes and a rooftop garden and heliport, for an estimated cost of £100,000, although these plans were never carried out.

The *Now and Then* column of the Mercury dated 15 October 2009 reported that the conservatory rooms *"were often hired for wedding receptions and big events organised by local clubs and societies. There was once a basement nightclub called The Dive Bar, with an entrance in Deal Castle Road.*

Later, in 1966, the new owners, Stephen and Stephanie Lis, also had major changes planned, starting with a refurbishment of the Dive Bar in the basement, followed by a new lounge and dining room. Future plans also included *"a beautiful ballroom."* Again, none of these plans were ever instigated.

c1910.

c1970.

FW Creasey became Manager in the mid 60s followed by Joseph Stryczek in the late 60s and early 70s. In October 1970, Stryczek publicly denied that the hotel was up for sale (later leaving to look after a hotel in St Margaret's). The basement bar was still referred to as the Dive Bar, despite being relaunched as the Blue Bar.

In February 1972, the then owners, CW Investments, sold the hotel to Adam Weinreb for £120,000. The following month, plans were submitted for a new banqueting hall, a grillroom adjacent to the Blue Bar and the addition of a soda fountain, for an estimated cost of £250,000. A new chef from Geneva by the name of Alfred Zaghlowl was installed. In May of that year, the cost of dining at the hotel was £1.20 for a four course luncheon and £1.50 for a five course dinner. Double vodkas, whisky and gin were all priced at 30p and a double brandy at 40p.

On 9 March 1974, the new Stable Grill and Restaurant Room was opened and advertised grilled Dover sole for £2.15, scampi £1.15, rainbow trout £1.50, sirloin steak £1.50, T-bone steak £2.20, sherry trifle 30p, fruit salad 35p, assorted ices 25p, apple pie and cream 30p, coffee and cream 15p and a table cover including snacks of £1 per person.

In June 1974, the owners, A&A Weinreb Hotels, called a meeting of creditors and, in August, the company went into voluntary liquidation. It had 12 hotels in its group but only five were considered profitable. Although the **Queens Hotel** remained open, it was put up for sale.

In July 1975, Gem Hotels of Chislehurst bought the hotel. According to local newspaper reports, no major changes were anticipated but the new owners hoped to attract small conferences and seminars. However, cabaret dinner dances with international artistes were planned for an exclusive 'niterie' in the basement, and readers were invited to think up a new name for the bar in the hope of winning a bottle of champagne. Presumably, entrants were thin on the ground since the basement 'niterie' became known as Downstairs. It was advertised as *"Deal's newest nightspot … a sophisticated and exclusive buffet bar"*. There was also the **Queens Hotel** annexe from the 1950s onwards which was situated at no 10 (now renumbered 11) Deal Castle Road.

Despite all the numerous refurbishments, the hotel's days were definitely numbered, not helped by the 1970s upsurge in holiday package tours to the Mediterranean. After all, why holiday in England with its changeable weather and shingle beaches when Spanish sunshine and sandy beaches could be guaranteed for a similar price?

In October 1976, extensive alterations were made at the hotel to meet fire regulations but, a year later, it was announced the hotel would be closing *"and may never open again"* since it was still unable to comply with them.

In November 1977, the **Queens Hotel** applied for planning permission for fire escapes but blamed Dover District Council for inefficiency and Kent Fire Brigade for demanding expensive changes to meet the regulations.

By February 1978, the hotel was vacant and awaiting yet another new owner. In July, the building and contents were put up for auction but it was not until March 1979 that it was bought by V Melvani for £110,000. He stated at the time that he wanted to reopen the hotel but, only a few months later, in August 1979, it was back on the market again. In November, it was purchased by Thanet hotelier, Alan Kesterton, who planned to convert the building. In January 1980, he and John Richardson submitted plans for a luxury private members' club with apartments and flats, with additional annexes in Deal Castle Road and Ranelagh Road. Outline plans were welcomed but no formal plans were invited.

However, in August 1980, the **Queens Hotel** was back on the market yet again. In October, it went to auction but failed to reach its reserve price of £150,000 so was withdrawn. In November, it was proposed to demolish the building and build flats on the site, but it was announced in December that the Department of the Environment had plans to list the hotel as *"a building of historical or architectural interest."*

In January 1981, the future of the hotel was still in doubt since refurbishment and demolition plans had been stopped owing to the building being granted listed status. Despite this, in February, an application was received to demolish the building and, in March, the new owner, Arthur Letheren, submitted plans for luxury flats with sauna and squash courts to be built.

In April 1981, Dover District Council deferred its decision on the future of the by now derelict hotel and, later that month, the building was destroyed by fire. An enquiry in May concluded the blaze was caused by vandalism. In January 1982, the decision was taken for the hotel to be demolished and, in August of that year, the demolition was completed, the same week as its former manager, Joseph Stryczek, sadly died.

In January 1983, the council rejected plans submitted for the site but agreed to meetings with the proposed developer and architect. In April, the site was sold and, after very many further comings and goings, construction work on the new flats started in February 1987. The building was named The Queens. However, it was not until November 1992 that *"31 luxury apartments and 3 penthouses"* were ready for sale, costing between £4,000 and £15,000. Seven of the 34 flats were sold at auction the following month.

The Queens now comprises 55 flats but there is no longer an entrance on Beach Street, the main door now being situated in Ranelagh Road.

c1970.

Quern (location unknown) Deal

This pub was mentioned in the 1674 Will of John Jenkins as being *"at the sign of the Quern (or Kurn)"* in Deal.

A quern is a stone handmill used for grinding grain. Quern Road is situated at the top of Mill Hill, close to the site of the old Upper Deal Mill so this pub may have been located nearby.

Railway (Railway Station Hotel, Station Hotel)
85 Station Road (Broad Lane), Walmer (Gt Mongeham)

As its name would suggest, the pub is situated on the approach road to Walmer station.

On 25 September 1878, a provisional alehouse licence for the "*Station Hotel, Great Mongeham*" was granted to John Matthews, owner of Thompson' brewery, and landlord, George Marley. The licence was confirmed on 15 October. (The *Station Hotel* was the early name for the *Railway Tavern/Hotel* and, although the building remained the same, its address was then listed as being in the district of Great Mongeham, until a later boundary change to Walmer).

Other landlords included William Watts in 1880 (by which time it was called the *Railway Station Hotel*), John Tomlin also in 1882, John James Filmer in 1883, Stephen James Redman in 1886, Alphonso James Redman in 1887, Edwin Hills, William Carlton and James Cooper in 1888, Richard Morley and Edward Sills in 1891, Stanley Parker in 1892, William Parker in 1897, John William Minter in 1898 and John William Hinkley in 1901. The licensing authorities then changed from Wingham to Walmer District. E Leaver (who was licensed to sell beer only) was landlord in 1903, followed by John

c1900.

2009.

William Minter (again) of the *Railway Hotel* in 1904.

In 1913, Henry Joly was charged with assaulting John Fill Byng at the pub but the case was dismissed.

Later landlords included E Leaver (again) in 1915, Joseph Best in 1923, William Mockett in 1933, Albert Charles Pilcher in 1934, Henry Bygrave in 1942, HA Fenner in 1948, E Taylor in 1952, AG Burden in 1955, JA Lilley in 1957, WG Wilson in 1966 and John Jones in 1973.

The Mercury reported in 1974, when Jack and Betty Jones were in charge, that customer, Jack State, aged 62, of Mayers Road would get a free pint at the pub every day for the rest of his life since he had drank there continuously since the age of 18 in 1930 (when beer cost 4d a pint as opposed to 14p in 1974). He was also presented with an ornamental silver tankard from which to drink it.

John Leeson followed in 1982 and Peter Dowsett in 1989. In May 2003, after a £50,000 refurb by the brewery, the pub reopened with landlords, Kerry and Ann Woodward, at the helm (who had been in situ since the January). The Mercury reported the pub was affectionately known as the 'Chimney Pot Pub' because of its setting among other houses. The paper stated the pub had originally been a hotel *"dating from the mid 19th century."*

The *Railway* remains open to the present day and is owned by Shepherd Neame with S Hopkinson as its licensee.

Railway Inn/Hotel, 63 & 65 Queen Street (63 Albion Place, 9 Upper Queen Street/9 Albion Place/Queen Street West), Deal

John Hills was landlord in 1847, the year the railway came to Deal, and the inn was situated on the approach road to the newly opened station. In 1852, an advertisement proclaimed: *"J Hills – Railway Inn (near the Station), Deal – Choice Wines and Spirits and Well-Aired Beds – Guinness' Dublin Stout and London Porter."*

A later advertisement appeared in the 30 May 1860 edition of the Deal, Walmer & Sandwich newspaper: *"Old's 'Times' Omnibuses leave Hills' Railway Tavern and the Walmer Castle Deal for Dover each evening at 5.30. Fares inside 2/- (10p), outside 1/6 (7½p)."*

The Hills family remained at the pub until 1868. In 1875, Oswald Puckeridge was in charge, followed by Osmond Beer in 1878.

In 1881, the property was bought by the Deal and Dover Railway Joint Committee for possible demolition in order to make way for the railway line that was to be extended to Dover. However, it was eventually decided that demolition was unnecessary and the pub remained open.

In the 1890s, William A Bassett was licensee, followed by Frederick Mansfield in 1898 and Stephen George Hood in 1899.

In February 1905, landlord, Mr A Wadoux, was charged with selling spirits below the legal strength and was fined £1, with 9/6d (47½p) costs. Licensing magistrates reported: *"He did not rely on the bar trade but on the hotel. 30 to 40 Gravesend Pilots on his list, and he could turn out at any time to receive them. His business was increasing. When Leneys' [brewery] lease expires shortly, it would be an absolutely free house. Belongs to Railway Company."*

Later licensees included Henry John Lovell in 1911, George Elliot from 1921 to 1923 and another six landlords from 1924. Hubert Overall was the last landlord serving from March 1933 until 1934, the year the pub closed and when it was referred to the Compensation Committee. The pub's entire furniture and equipment were put up for sale on 12 October that year.

In 1944, the property was severely damaged by a bomb and remained derelict until it was finally pulled down in January 1954. Two private houses were later built on the site, now addressed 63 and 65 Queen Street. The old street name of Albion Place still appears on the Georgian terrace of properties.

c1920.

Railway Station Hotel

See entry for the *Railway,* Walmer.

Railway Station Refreshment Rooms
Railway Station, Deal

The *Refreshment Rooms* were situated on both platforms and, although not strictly pub premises, they held an alehouse (ie full) licence and were open to any members of the public and therefore qualify for an entry in this book.

Henry Brett was Manager there in 1883, Charles Sheath from 1899 to 1909, Amos Piper in 1927 and Thomas Harry Rowe from 1930.

According to the Mercury in 1939, Rowe, *"Controller of Southern Railway Refreshments Department"*, applied for improvements. Southern Railway planned to close the refreshment room on the 'down' platform as it was considered that it *"did not serve a useful purpose"* and build a new, more commodious one on the 'up' platform, 100-feet to the south of the one that was already there. They claimed that *"it would be bigger, better, more comfortable, really up-to-date, and an asset to the company and the borough."*

Permission was granted, but there is no evidence that it was ever actually built, probably due to the outbreak of WWII later that year. The *Refreshment Rooms* were subsequently demolished at an unknown date.

Ramsgate Harbour (exact location unknown)
Blenheim Road/Wellington Road (1A Cottage Row, Wellington Place, Albert Place), Deal

During the early days of the harbour at Ramsgate, it was considered to be a 'safe haven' for ships, and the pub may therefore have been deliberately named in order to attract seafaring people to its door.

Albeit as a brief incarnation, it is hard to know whether this pub was actually and conclusively part of the *Pound* (see separate entry). It should be noted that the numbering in Cottage Row (now Wellington Road) changed as new houses were built in the mid to late 1880s.

According to the 1851 census, Thomas Ottoway was resident at *"the Pound House"* and William Allen was *"Beerhouse Keeper"* of an unnamed beerhouse situated at 1A Cottage Row. Confusingly, according to various rate books, in 1855, Allen was registered as a beer retailer at *"The Pound Houses"* (as well as in South Sandy Lane that year), and in 1856 and 1857, and, in 1858, on *"the corner of Albert Place"*. Melville's street directory places him as being landlord of *"the Ramsgate Harbour pub in Wellington Place"* (now part of Blenheim Road – possibly no 13, but this cannot be substantiated). This is either a case of a moving pub or a moving Pound House!

An article entitled *'Charge of Assault'* appeared in the Deal, Walmer & Sandwich Telegram on 8 September 1858: *"Mrs Allen, of the 'Ramsgate Harbour' public house, was charged by Mrs Macey, of the 'Bricklayers Arms', with entering her house, and knocking her down in the passage; breaking some panes of glass and a tumbler. The magistrates suggested that the parties should come to an amicable arrangement out of court, which was acted upon by the defendant paying all expenses, 10s 6d (52½p)."*

In November 1858, Allen left his wife and four children and consequently served a term at Sandwich Gaol, his family becoming dependent upon the Parish. He reappeared in 1861 living at what was later to become the *Alhambra* public house.

A further documentary reference to a *'pound house'* in Cottage Row appears in 1863 although no accompanying landlord or resident is mentioned.

As may be seen from the confusion above, the authors have unfortunately been unable to discover the true identity or complete history of the *Ramsgate Harbour*!

Ranelagh House, 15 Prince of Wales Terrace, Deal

As with the *Refreshment Rooms*, although *Ranelagh House* was a short-lived boarding house and not strictly a pub, it held an alehouse (full) licence. Emily Childs was landlady between 1872 and 1874. The building later became known as the Wellington Club before being converted into flats.

Rattling Cat (possibly Victoria Commercial)
277 Dover Road, Walmer

c1900.

A 'cat' was an old nautical term, sometimes referring to a flat-bottomed boat, but more usually describing a rope, cable or chain. In the latter instance, therefore, a 'rattling cat' would describe the noise a chain made when raising or lowering the anchor over a beam. (See also definitions of 'cat' under *Globe* - formerly the *Scarborough Cat*).

So much local folklore has been attached to the *Rattling Cat* property over the years but whether it was ever actually a pub or a coaching inn remains a mystery since the authors have been unable to discover any concrete documentary evidence to confirm it being either! However, the large detached building is certainly sited well enough to have been an inn, being set back from the road and positioned on possibly one of the old Deal-Dover-London coaching routes. The name of the house appears on the building, together with the inscription *"Circa 1700"* beneath it. At first glance, it does indeed appear to be of some age, although the curious thing is that no building of any description is indicated on the 1801 Ordnance Survey map of the site. The first documentary evidence of any sort of structure being there at all shows up on an 1844 tithe map.

Nevertheless, the story attached to the place is worth telling. A different explanation for the name of the house supposedly harks back to the days of the smuggling trade. Various tunnels apparently led from the cellars beneath the house where contraband would be stored. Cats wearing collars around their necks made of linked bones were kept there and, if

they were disturbed by excise men searching the tunnels, they would provide the smugglers with an 'early warning system' since the bones would rattle together as the cats took flight, thus giving the smugglers time to move their illicit goods – or so the story goes!

There does, however, appear to be evidence of such tunnels since one of the authors visited the house some years ago and saw what seemed to be blocked off gothic shaped archways in one of the cellar walls.

The shape of the arches mirrored the external frontage of Gothic House next door to the *Rattling Cat*. It is rumoured that the tunnels used to lead to the old St Mary's church nearby and also to Walmer Castle itself. According to a local expert, if the tunnels did or, indeed, do still exist, they would have to have been long steady slopes, or shaft drops, because the sea level is about 100 feet lower than the *Rattling Cat*. They would also have to have been ventilated and supported to prevent the roofs from collapsing, and would need to have been dug in deep in order to avoid the cellars and foundations of the large house opposite the *Rattling Cat*, or at least have been diverted around them.

What is known for sure is that, before the house was called the *Rattling Cat*, the building formerly comprised three separate cottages, certainly up to at least the 1840s (which, again, causes doubt as to whether the *Rattling Cat* could ever have been an old coaching inn), although it had become one residence (originally known as Clare Cottage) at least by the latter part of the 19th century. It may have been used as a vicarage at some point. It was

2009.

not until 1948 that the *Rattling Cat* by name appeared on any Land Registry documentation.

It is possible that, if the *Rattling Cat* was indeed ever an inn, it could have been known as the *Victoria Commercial* (see separate entry). Unfortunately, however, this cannot confirmed.

According to Paul Skelton on his Dover Kent Archives website, a visitor to the house in 2005 was informed by the then occupant that the owner (who did not live on the premises) had told him that the house had indeed once been a coaching inn (although no

explanation was offered as to the origins of the owner's knowledge on the subject). He continued that the inn had provided overnight accommodation and that, in one of the upper rooms, metal rings could still be seen attached to opposite walls through which a line would be tied in order for poorer travellers to hang their arms over to go to sleep. The occupant also added that the date *"1600 and something is carved somewhere on the building."*

The *Rattling Cat* is now a private residence.

Redan

See entry for the *Clifton Inn/Hotel.*

Red Crosse (possibly Pooles) (exact location unknown) east side Middle Street, Deal

The pub may have been so-called after an expedition made by Sir Walter Raleigh in 1595 to what is now part of Venezuela. He wrote in his journal that his ship sailed along a tributary of the River Orinoco but, not knowing its name, christened it the 'Red Crosse River'.

The first documentation found for the *Red Crosse* was dated 12 September 1662 when it appeared on a list of Deal pubs which had each paid 6/8d (33p) plus a £5 surety for a new inn sign.

In 1663, the resident proprietor was John Poole, a Deal merchant and brewer. (Samuel Pepys referred in his diary to visiting the Poole family of Deal so possibly John was related. He also wrote about drinking at a tavern called *Pooles* in Deal but whether or not this had

been a previous name, or possibly a nickname, for the *Red Crosse* or was in any way connected to John Poole is not known). On 3 November that year, Poole took out a lease for £9 to include *"two messuages or dwelling houses ... commonly called The Flying Horse and the other The Red Crosse in Lower Deal"* from Gilbert, Archbishop of Canterbury, for 21 years at a rental of 9/- (45p) a year.

The two pubs were mentioned again in 1664 title deeds: *"Commonly called the Flying Horse and the other commonly called the Red Crosse lately erected in the Sea Valley, being part of the Archbishop's Waste."*

By 1683, Nicholas Eaton was named as landlord of the *Red Crosse* (although there is no further mention of the *Flying Horse*).

Red Ensign (exact location unknown) Deal

Local folklore recalls an inn of this name, possibly in the location of Oak Street, but no licensing or other records can be found to confirm this.

Red Lion (Deal Shallop, Bluebell, Royal Oak), 80 (56) Beach Street, Deal

This pub was one of many buildings situated on the beach in Beach Street, opposite the turning for Market Street and described in 1804 as being sited *"two houses south of the Fountain."*

The name **Red Lion** can either refer to an association with John of Gaunt (in the 14th century) but more usually with King James I (who reigned from 1603 to 1625). James was a Scot and proclaimed that the symbol of a red lion should be displayed in public places (it being an heraldic association with Scotland).

The earliest documentary evidence found for the **Red Lion** was on 12 September 1662 when it appeared on a list of Deal pubs which had each paid 6/8d (33p) and £5 surety for a new inn sign. It was also mentioned in Laker's 1680 list.

The pub did not appear documented by name again until 1737 when it was known as the **Royal Oak** but, in 1769, it was called the **Bluebell**, by 1789, the **Deal Shallop** (a 'shallop' was a type of boat), and, by 1796, it had reverted to the **Red Lion**.

In 1804, J Meers was landlord, followed by James Hoile in 1821. In 1853, the Archbishop of Canterbury sold to the Hills (brewing) family *"All that messuage*

*heretofore known as the **Red Lion**"* for £149.

In the Great Storm of 1881 (when many ships were lost on the Goodwin Sands), the house, having sustained roof damage, was described as being *"The old **Red Lion** working mens liberal reading rooms."*

On 17 January 1902, the Hills family conveyed *"all that messuage formerly known as the **Red Lion** with capstan ground now known as Acacia House"* to James Elson, a *"Deal Licensed Victualler"* of the **Roxburgh Castle Inn** for £460.

The building was demolished in the mid 1920s to make way for the promenade alongside the beach.

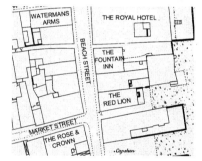

Map of Red Lion and nearby pubs c1870.

Red Lion (location unknown) Walmer

The first mention of this pub appeared in 1810 when Henry Maxted junior was listed as landlord. By 1821/22, Thomas Hunt was in charge, although the pub's proprietor, Richard Hopper, also owned the **Drum** and the **George & Dragon**, both in Upper Walmer.

Red Lyon (location unknown) Deal

The only mention of this pub appeared in owner, Constant Woodman's 1679 Will when it was described as *"a messuage called by the sign of the **Red Lyon** at or near the sea valley occupied by Goodman Jenkin."*

The area around the present day High Street (formerly known as Lower Street) was known at the time as the *"sea valley."*

Red Lyon (location unknown) Middle Deal

Very little is known about this pub, save for a few documented references. A diary entry dated 8 July 1720 recorded the day as being *"spent at Mr Fuller's with Mr Mayor ..."*, and, on 16 September 1739, a letter was addressed to Mr Richard Fuller at *"the **Red Lyon** at Middle Deal."*

The Fuller family were local brewers from at least the mid 1600s. Pepys' Diary of 1660 recorded that he *"went to **Fullers** alehouse but they had no ale so went to **Pooles**, a tavern in the town* [Deal] *and drank there."* However, whether Pepys was referring to this particular family of Fullers can only be guessed at.

Rink (Alcazar)
South Street, Deal

The ***Rink*** was granted a wine licence on 4 April 1876 and was licensed as a skating rink in September 1877, with John Austen Long in charge. By around 1900, it briefly became known as the ***Alcazar*** before reverting to its former name.

In June 1903, the ***Rink*** advertised 'Promenade Concerts'.

A Schedule of Articles and Effects dating back to 1904 when the property was sold (from East Kent Archives) reads as follows:- *"99 armchairs, 400 small chairs, 16 iron-framed 7-feet garden seats (2 faulty); 1 damaged ditto, 40 iron Deal-framed seats, 11 x 20" round iron stand tables, 4 x 15" framed shaped bath seats, 2 x 4' marble top tables on iron frames (faulty), 6 iron lamp columns, 6 lanterns glazed with opal tops, 5 x 2-light arc lamps with levers and chains, 3 small galvanised pails, 1 flagpole 28' long, Deal framed ticket box on east front with 2 doors and matchboard inside and out with small sash and frame and corrugated iron roof 4'8" x 3'8" x 7' high, with 1' boarded floor, lamp and wrought iron scroll suspended over gateway, the Deal framed stage match-boarded at back 20' x 14' with 2 dressing rooms, with Gents on north side of stage, framed and match-boarded, 10' x 12' x 8'6, with 2 x 1' shelves fixed 22" wide x 7' long, 2 x 4-tred stepladders, 2 gas brackets with wire guards, Ladies' dressing room on south side, 1 x 8'6" trestle table (faulty), all gas supply piping to **Rink**, footlights, stage dressing rooms and skeleton building, 2 small cannons on carriages with wheels, lattice-framed screen 5' x 6', 3-fold screen and 2 side wings in 4 parts, piece of skeleton frame, 16 wood framed music stands, large lantern over South Street entrance with wrought-iron scroll bracket and circular gas illumination, 25 step ladder in 2 parts, the uniforms comprising 5 coats, 2 pairs of trousers, 3 caps and 1 felt belt (faulty)."*

In June 1906, Deal Council agreed to buy *"the **Rink**, including hotel, shop and stabling"* from Thompson's brewery for £6,000. In 1922, the ***Walmer Castle*** pub next door took over the site of the ***Rink*** and advertised it as their *"Palm Court – Illuminated Grounds for Dancing"*.

The ***Rink*** was partly situated on the site of the present day Regent, as well as on the area now occupied by the car park and public toilets in South Street.

Advert for Alcazar 1900.

THE
ALCAZAR
Adjoining
THE WALMER CASTLE HOTEL, DEAL.
Proprietor - - MR. ALF. ABRAHAMS.
OPEN FOR THE SEASON.
MONDAY, JULY 9th, 1900,
And every Afternoon and Evening during the Week.
The following Artistes will appear:—
MADAME CLARA DOWLE,
The celebrated Soprano Vocalist, from the Albert Hall, and St. James' Hall Popular Concerts.
FRANK NEWBURY,
Comedian, Whistler, and Mimic.
FLO MAJILTON, the Popular Burlesque Artiste
LEOTY,
Continental Juggler and Equilibist, from the Alhambra, London, and other principal Theatres.
EMILY PARKES,
Serio, Comedienne, and descriptive Vocalist.
W. E. GILLIN, Society Ventriloquist.

Advert for Rink 1903.

THE RINK, DEAL.
SOUTH STREET.
Lessee and Manager - MR. GEORGE SHARP.
HIGH-CLASS
PROMENADE CONCERTS,
TWICE DAILY throughout the Season.
Afternoons at 3. Evenings at 8.
Artistes for Week commencing JUNE 15th, 1903:
MISS KATE WILLEY, Soprano.
MISS BELLE GREEN, Comedienne (late of Walter George's Light Opera Company).
MR. WALTER KEAST, Tenor.
MR. FRANK WOOD, the celebrated Humorist and Mimic.
Accompanist and Stage Manager - Mr. JAMES HALLE.
BIJOU ORCHESTRA. Musical Director, Mr. GEORGE SHARP.
Front Seats, 1s. Other Seats, 6d. Promenade, 3d.
NOTICE.—On those Evenings when the Marine Band plays, the Concert will commence at 9 o'clock.
The Rink is well sheltered from wind and rain, and a most enjoyable evening may be spent there.

Rising Sun (Sunn Inn)
5 George Street (Sun Alley), off Griffin Street, Deal

John Dillon was listed as landlord in 1804, followed by John and Mary White in 1821, but, by 1832, Mary was there on her own. Other landlords of the period included William Rogers in 1842 and Thomas Castle in 1845 and 1852. During that period, the pub was sold for £352 in 1849. Robert Clayson was landlord in 1855, followed by James Taylor in 1866 when the pub had a skittle alley upstairs, much to the apparent annoyance of the neighbours, according to contemporary court reports!

In 1871, landlord, John Bax, was summonsed for kicking banjo player, Samuel Glover, in the eye, and the same year, it was reported that three Royal

2009.

Marines had caused a "disturbance" at the pub.

Later landlords listed included John Hurren in 1875 and 1879, Edward Jordan in 1880, William Barrett also in 1880, Thomas Marsh in 1882 and, following his death in 1894, his widow, Mary, was listed in January 1895. Another Thomas Marsh was landlord in 1904.

In March 1906, the pub was considered to be *"badly situated for police supervision"* and, in 1907, Thompson's brewery sold it for £185, and the premises were delicensed.

The property is now a private house.

Rising Sun Inn, 2 North Barrack Road
(Cambridge Place/4 Rope Walk), Walmer

In 1855, Henry Thomas Wood was registered landlord of the *Rising Sun* in Rope Walk. In 1858, a local newspaper story reported on his inquest after he had shot himself, at the age of 42. Described as being the proprietor of the *Rising Sun*, an accidental verdict returned. His widow, Sarah, was listed as licensee in 1859. In 1861, that part of Rope Walk became known as Cambridge Place.

By 1862, Simon White was *"Landlord and Billiard Table Keeper"* until his move to the **Lord Warden** pub opposite in 1867. John Ffasham was installed by 1870, succeeded by another Henry Wood in 1871, William Fenn in 1874 and Thomas Phillips in 1876. In November 1879, Phillips was fined 20 shillings (£1) for refusing to admit two police constables into the premises. He was still there in 1881 when, confusingly, the address is referred to again as being Rope Walk (no 4).

Other licensees included G Beer in 1889, Frank Margraves in 1891 and 1895 (during which time the address had changed to North Barrack Road around 1893), John Mercer in 1898, Alf Clarke in 1908 and James Lee in 1911.

In March 1911, a licensing magistrates' report described the premises thus: *"Considered by Royal*

Map showing Rising Sun Inn and nearby pubs 1872.

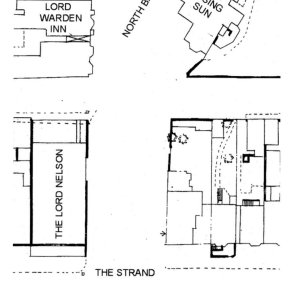

Marines to be good for a late drink as the barracks bar/canteen closed at 9.30. There is a large tap room in which it is considered no self-respecting person would want to sit. Used by a lot of fish people. No stables."

There was also a large clubroom upstairs that was used by The Royal Ancient Order of Buffaloes (no 1157 Lodge) consisting of 60 members.

Despite alterations being made to the pub's frontage in 1908, the pub closed on 30 December 1911.

By August 1912, the premises had been rebuilt on the same site and became known as the Kings Hall Kinema. A contemporary description stated that *"The auditorium seated 344, mostly in relaxing seats, with a single row of green velvet ones behind them. The décor was a sandwich of chocolate to dado level, pale green and then deep crimson from the plaster moulding to the roof."*

It later became Kings Cinema and then a dance hall called the Strand Palais. The management later became famous for turning down the Beatles, even though the Rolling Stones performed there in 1963!

The building now houses a retail outlet called Cyclelife.

Rising Sun (exact location unknown)
Mill Cottages, Mill Hill, Deal

This beerhouse was only mentioned in an 1851 document when it was described as being situated at *"Mill Cottages, near the old windmill at the top of Mill Hill"*, although its exact location remains unknown.

Rodney

See entry for the *Admiral Rodney*.

Rose & Crown, 79 Beach Street, Deal

See entry for the *Admiral Penn*.

Rose & Crown (location unknown) Deal

The name of this establishment appears on a list of 1680 Deal inns but, other than that, it remains untraceable. It cannot be taken for granted that it refers to the *Rose & Crown* – later known as the *Admiral Penn* – in Beach Street since no documentary evidence exists.

Rose (location unknown) Walmer

The only reference to this pub by name was found in the Walmer 'Payment for Signs' list of 1678, but no location was given.

Rose
91-93 High Street (29 Lower Street), Deal

The *Rose* is situated on the west side of the High Street and lies immediately south of St. George's Church. The building itself probably dates back to the mid 1700s or earlier although the authors have been unable to find any documentary evidence to support this.

The *"Widow Hinds"* was listed as landlady in 1804, followed by Joseph Ralph in the 1820s and Henry White from 1832 until the mid 1850s.

A local newspaper story from 1858 reported that *"two rival 'sweeps' were involved in a fight in the tap room"*. In 1859, John Boakes was landlord, followed by David Almond in 1874. The *Rose*, in common with a lot of other pubs at the time, was often used an auction house, as well as a meeting place for local societies and clubs (and originally started life as an hotel). The Lord Palmerston Lodge of Oddfellows used to meet there quarterly in 1880, for example. In 1882, Almond was fined 5 shillings (25p), with £1 costs, for *"selling whisky below the standard."*

In 1885, the brewery company, Hills & Sons, advertised for persons willing to tender for alterations and additions to the house. Shortly afterwards, a further storey was added above the pub. At the same time, an annexe was constructed

c1904.

next door south of the original pub building (although it no longer forms part of the pub and now comprises two retail shops). It is believed that the building was perhaps used as the offices of Hills & Sons at some point.

In 1887, Percy Alfred Frost, the then incumbent, advertised the **Rose**: *"Family and Commercial – Well-Aired Beds – Bait and Livery Stables – Large Room for Dinners and Banquets – Commercial Stock Room."*

A later but similar advertisement read: *"The **Rose** – Family and Commercial Hotel and Posting House, Deal – Stock Room and every convenience for Commercial Gentlemen – Spacious Hall for Public and Trades' Dinners, Concerts, &c – Special Attention and every comfort for Golfers, Cyclists, Anglers, &c – Good Stabling – F.A. Oxley, Proprietor, late of the Sussex Hotel, Bognor."*

In 1893, landlord, George Edwards, was fined 40 shillings (£2), with 7/6d (37½p) costs, for selling ½ pints of whisky and gin *"not of the substance and quality demanded"*. He was followed by Frederick Augustus Oxley in 1899, Arthur E Clarke in 1908 and JC Cleminson in 1914.

In 1915, the landlord, Samuel Thomas Dodsworth, was charged with *"failing to comply with the Defence of the Realm Act 1914"* whereby soldiers were only allowed to drink lemonade or ginger beer until 10pm. 50 soldiers were found to be consuming alcohol on the premises and the landlord was found guilty and fined 40 shillings (£2).

Later landlords included GW Case listed in 1936 and 1948, W Dale in the mid 1950s when the pub was a Charrington-owned house. WE Thompson was landlord in 1966 and, according to a local newspaper report dated 13 November 1969, 'Tubbs', a cat belonging to landlady Margo Thompson got stuck in the rafters of St George's Church next door and had to be rescued by the RSPCA!

More recent landlords included Stewart Workman in 1975, John Forster in 1981, Philip Dodd in 1986 and Stan and Min Dale in 1988. During their time, Charrington artist Bill Pierce painted a new sign for the **Rose** that hung outside the pub. The Dales were followed by Shirley Walsh in 1991 and Paul Fieldon in 1992.

The **Rose** now comprises two bars and a beer garden. The landlords are Peter and Josie Fielden.

Rose Tree (exact location unknown)
Blenheim Road (1A South Sandy Lane), Deal

The *Rose Tree* was a short-lived beerhouse as the only documentary evidence found was in the Deal census for 1851 listing Thomas Young as *"Beerhouse Keeper and Carpenter"* at 1A South Sandy Lane. The present day address for the building is unknown but it would be situated somewhere at the north end of what is now Blenheim Road.

Row Barge

See entry for the *Fountain (south) (2)*.

Roxborough Castle (Roxborough Arms, Roxburgh Arms, Roxbury Arms, Roxbury, Richborough Castle, and also incorporating Pier Hotel) 12 (5) Broad Street, Deal

This pub was situated on the south east corner of Middle Street and Broad Street. The *Roxborough Castle* possibly took its name from a 600 ton barge of the same name. It was used as an emigrant ship to Australia from about 1838 to 1868. (Apparently, the journey to Melbourne in 1855 under Captain John Adams took three months).

The first mention of this establishment is found in Melville's Directory of 1858 when Richard Husband Collins was landlord at the *Roxbury* beerhouse.

In September 1863, the local newspaper reported a street disturbance involving eight to ten drunken men emerging from the *Roxburgh Arms* at 1 o'clock in the morning, *"fighting, swearing and cursing."*

In 1869, the beerhouse was granted a licence to also sell wines. In 1872, landlord, Daniel Kirkaldie, was fined 5 shillings (25p) for opening on a Sunday and his two customers were fined 2/6d (12½p) each. On 21 November 1872, a report from the Petty Sessions stated: *"Daniel Kirkaldy [sic], landlord of the*

1904.

Roxborough Castle in Broad-street was charged with having his house open for business purposes on Sunday 17th November and George Epsley and Thomas Newing were charged with being on the premises. Epsley said his milk was left at the Roxburgh [sic] Castle by the Mongeham dairyman and he had merely called there for it. The Magistrates observed that the case was rather weak – no proof of drinking having been given; it was evident that the policeman was rather too quick for them. The landlord was ordered to pay the costs of 5/- (25p) and Epsley and Newing 2/6d (12½p) each."

It was reported that the Deal Boatmen Club held its annual dinner there on 8 January 18 73 when permission was granted to stay open until 1am.

Daniel Kirkaldie died on 3 August 1874 and the pub was transferred to his widow, Mary Ann. On 1 January 1880, Stephen Edward Watts took over as licensee and, later that year, brewers, Hills & Son, spent £310 on alterations and additions to the premises. A spirits' licence was applied for but refused.

By 1886, Stephen's widow, Harriet Elizabeth, was running the pub and, on 5 May 1887, she handed over the reins to Robert Berridge.

Berridge stayed at the helm for almost three years when, on 27 March 1890, he transferred the pub to Ursula Sands, wife of Henry Sands. She in turn transferred it to Charles Setterfield on 3 March 1892, followed by Catherine Almond on 5 January 1893 and John William Setterfield on 4 May 1893. Later that year, when Isabella Setterfield was landlady, the *Roxborough Arms* was classed as a beerhouse with a wine licence. She left in 1898 and, in 1899, the premises were granted a full licence and were being run by Alfred William Castle, followed by George Henry Dawson in 1913 and Frederick W Hood, *"Freeman"*, from 1914 until at least 1923.

c1955.

In January 1933 Louis Welton, the landlord of the nearby *Pier Hotel* took over the *Roxborough Castle* using the same as an annexe. This remained the situation throughout the 1930s, and was a very successful business. In July 1940 both pubs, along with several other Thompson houses, had their licences transferred to B C Dredge, the brewery company secretary. This was due to voluntary evacuation and wartime conditions.

Later landlords included Mrs M Collins in 1948, R Worman in 1956, W J Bonney from 1956 to 1957, R H Wing in 1957 and N R Neale in 1966. The house closed on 6th May 1971.

The ground floor of the *Roxborough Castle* is now Millards Insurance and the *Pier Hotel* is now part of *Dunkerleys* – see separate entry.

Royal Arms

See entry for the *Berry*.

Royal Canteen
(location unknown) Walmer

The only record of this pub related to John Francis registered as landlord of the *Royal Canteen* in the Alehouse Keepers' Book for Walmer in 1805. (He later went on to run the *Bathing House Tavern* – see separate entry). (It was also mistakenly referred to as being called the *Royal Courtesan* at some point).

Royal Clarendon

See entry for the *Clarendon*.

Royal Courtesan

See entry for the *Royal Canteen*.

Royal Exchange
183 (175) Beach Street, Deal

The *Royal Exchange* was situated on the north eastern corner of Exchange Street at the junction with Beach Street.

A 'for sale' advertisement from the Kentish Gazette, circa 1728, stated: *"The **Royal Exchange** being an old well-accustomed house situated on the beach, the front being sashed and with a full prospect of the Downs, and the back part looking into the country with lane and stables and yards. All other necessary conveniences. Enquire of the said house of Mr Primrose of Deal".*

A later advertisement appeared in the Kentish Gazette in 1751: *"Sale – 40-ton Folkestone built hooker. John Doorn, Master at the Sign of the **Royal Exchange**".* Doorn was still registered there, as *"Victualler"*, in 1792 (and 1804).

On 22 November 1793, it was reported: *"21st. About 2 o'clock on Tuesday morning a stranger arrived in the diligence from Canterbury and went to bed at the **Royal Exchange** Inn. In the course of the forenoon he shifted his quarters and went to the **New Inn** where he requested a private room and bed. The waiter recognised him as one Lyons who was wanted for forgery and who had escaped from an officer of Police in London."*

On 26 September 1799, the Deal Borough Sessions Book recorded that: *"Under Act 39 Geo. 3, C. 79 - An Act for the effectual suppression of Societies established for Seditions & Treasonable purpose and for better preventing Treasonable and Seditious Practices mentions - Royal Navy Lodge no 157 meetings usually held at the **Royal Exchange** Inn in the town of Deal on the 1st Monday of every month, 24th June and 27th December."*

Charles Lord was recorded as landlord in 1804, followed by Robert and Hannah Birch in 1814, Charles Warman in 1819 and Thomas Atkins in 1828.

In 1828, the *Royal Exchange* was again advertised for sale: *"All that messuage, tenement and established inn called or known by the name of the*

c1955.

Royal Exchange' in Beach Street, with the yard, stables, outhouses, buildings and extensive premises thereunto belonging and now used therewith - to other with a Dwelling House and premises in Exchange Street adjoining thereto - and also Four Storehouses and a large Yard and Warehouse adjoining, as the same are now in the several occupations of Charles Warman and others.

These premises are subject to a lease granted to Edward Iggulden Esq. for 21 years from 29th September 1819 at the yearly rent of £5.1s.0d (£5.05p)."

John Wanstall was landlord in 1834, Daniel Cork in 1837 and Sarah Cork, widow, in 1839 until her death in 1864 when a local advertisement publicised: *"**Royal Exchange** Family and Commercial Hotel. Anne Donoghue, successor to the late Mrs Cork"* (although her husband, Antonio James Donoghue, was actually the registered landlord at the time).

In February 1869, a local newspaper report, headed 'Tradesmens' Annual Supper', reported that: *"The annual supper of the Deal & Walmer Friendly Society was held on Monday evening last at the 'Royal Exchange' Hotel, Deal, when between 20 and 30 members sat down to an excellent repast provided by Mrs Donoghue."*

By 1872, the hotel was owned by Hill's brewery, and later landlords included J Dolford in 1878, Catherine Ann Neary in 1875, Miss S Turton in 1882 and Stephen Kent Winkworth and Mary Ann Edwards in 1876.

On 5 May 1886, an article in the Mercury reported: *"We are pleased to notice the resuscitation, so to speak, of what used to be one of the most, if not the most, comfortable of our small hotels – we allude to the 'Royal Exchange' Hotel, lost to the visitors of Deal for some years, entirely through mismanagement – it is now in good hands, and from what we hear and see is in a fair way of recovering … The present landlady, Mrs Edwards, is improving the house – and we wish her every success."*

Edward Gardner took over in 1887, followed by Elizabeth Ann Kirby in 1888, Thomas John Chandler in 1893, George Richard Crick, *"Hotel Proprietor"*, from 1894 to 1899, Mrs Ella Bullock in 1905 (when Thompson's brewery owned the house) and Charles Edward Snowdon in 1910. Around this time, he was fined £1 and 18/2d (91p) costs for permitting drunkenness on the premises. Snowdon was followed by Arthur Wadoux from 1913 to 1922, David Currie Ross in 1931, Mrs Dorothy Gladys Hagger in 1938, D Case in 1936 and C Tucker in 1953 (by which time it had become a Charrington's house).

The *Royal Exchange* closed its doors in 1965 and the building was later converted into flats which remain to this day.

2009.

Royal Exchange
20 Dover Road, Walmer

The *Royal Exchange* was a beerhouse, first mentioned in 1858 when William Bushell took a 63 year lease from the Leith Estate on the property. He was followed by William Adams as landlord, and then by William Dewell who was documented there in 1875 and 1878 when the property was recorded as including a *'public house and shop'*. The shop was situated next door south of the pub.

By 1887, John Mercer, *'beer retailer'*, was landlord when, at the Cinque Port Petty Sessions, he was charged with being drunk on (his own) licensed premises and for using threatening, abusive and disgusting language. Police Constable Stuart was called to the house by the landlord's son and found *"the accused very drunk and swinging his arms about"*. Mercer was fined £1 but it was reduced to 10 shillings (50p) and he was given a week to pay. It was noted that he was applying for 'owner-and-driver' licences for two x four-wheeled carriages.

In 1895, Amos Marks was listed as landlord, followed by T Knight in 1898 and Daniel Charles Knight in 1906. The *Royal Exchange* was owned by Thompson's brewery who offered no opposition when the decision was taken to close the house on 31 December 1906.

The *Royal Exchange* is now a private house.

2009.

Royal George
56 (51) High Street (Lower Street), Deal

This pub was situated on the north eastern corner of Water Street and High Street. Igguldens' brewery had stood on the south eastern corner in the early part of the 19th century.

The *Royal George* was probably named either after a ship of the same name which sank on the Goodwins in 1763 or, alternatively, another one which sank off Spithead, Portsmouth in 1782 with the loss of 800 lives.

In 1804, *"Widow Anderson"* was in charge, with George Clark taking over the following year. In November 1806, it was reported that some soldiers from the Buffs had started a brawl at the pub and the Mayor summoned his constables to deal with the disturbance.

George Millgate was registered landlord of the *"Royal George and storeroom"* in 1821, followed by George Noakes in 1832, Isabel Noakes from 1838 to 1845 and Joshua Mockett in 1847. By 1851, the address of the pub was known as no 56 Lower Street (previously no 51). Mrs Mary Usher was landlady in 1859.

In July 1862, one of the most violent storms ever witnessed descended on Deal and the *Royal George* was one of many buildings to have had its windows broken by the wind, rain and hail.

Foreground site of Royal George 2010.

James Baldwin Ball was landlord in 1865, followed by George Barne in 1868 and William Wardrop in 1869.

In June 1869, a lengthy report, headed *"The 'Royal George' Public-House Burnt Down"*, appeared in a local newspaper. It is worth reproducing it in full to compare the style of writing, language and the minute detail given, in comparison to similar modern day newspaper reports:

"About half-past twelve at midnight, on Sunday last, a fire broke out at the above old established public-house. It appears that the landlord, Mr Wardrop, his wife and son had retired to rest and about half-past twelve the landlord had occasion to go downstairs to his bar to procure some brandy, and while engaged replenishing a spirit lamp had the misfortune to upset it, and on striking a lucifer a spark fell from it and ignited the spirit and quickly enveloped the room in flames. The readiest means at hand it appears was the beer engine, and this the landlord availed himself of as long as the heat and smoke would permit, when on finding his efforts useless, he ran off to the police station for assistance. Superintendent Parker, together with the whole of the police, were on the spot with their apparatus recently purchased for use on such occasions, within a quarter of an hour. On examining the premises the police found that the inmates had all left.

On opening the front door they found that the fire was confined principally to the passage and a room on the left called the parlour. The smoke and heat rendered it impossible for any one to enter further. Not more than a dozen persons were on the spot when the police arrived. They proceeded to attach their apparatus to the Water Company's main, when it was found that they had not a sufficient length of hose, and the water was not full on, or there is little doubt the fire would have been easily subdued had proper means been at hand for extinguishing it at that time. Parker then dispatched some of his men to procure the fire engine attached to the brewery of Messrs Hills and Son, which arrived at 1.45 and was soon got into play, but by this time the flames had ascended to the roof of the building and was [sic] rushing from all the windows. Attention was then, of necessity, given to the houses on the opposite side of the street which were momentarily threatened, and but for the arrival of the brewery engine would no doubt have ignited. This danger having been averted the engine was brought to play on the burning premises, and about two o'clock the roof fell in. About the same time the garrison engine arrived from Walmer, with a number of marines, under the command of Captain Le Grand, they got to work in a few minutes and a plentiful supply of water being by this time obtained, they rendered very efficient service, and by the aid of the two engines the fire was quickly subdued; but not until the premises and contents were entirely destroyed.

The Royal Marines, with their engine, had a very narrow escape from a serious calamity, a moment after they had cleared the burning premises in passing towards the fire plug, in Alfred Square, the roof fell in, forcing a portion of the front wall into Lower-street. Had the Marines been but a minute later they could not have avoided being struck by the mass of brick work as it fell. It was fortunately a calm and still night, had there been any wind nothing could have prevented the fire communicating with the opposite houses.

The premises belong to Messrs Poulter, brewers, Dover, and are insured in the "Guardian". The contents, we understand were partially insured in the North British office but a short time since."

(Deal fire and police stations were both based at the Town Hall in the High Street at the time).

The pub was demolished after the fire and, despite initial plans to rebuild it, the **Royal George** never reopened.

The pub's site is now open ground and is used as a car park by M&D motor garage. The garage's workshop on the north side of Water Street possibly also formed part of the pub's premises (and their workshop on the opposite side of Water Street may have comprised part of the former Iggledens' brewery premises).

Royal Hotel (Three Kings Inn/Hotel, Kings Arms), Beach Street, Deal

2009.

The present day architecture of the **Royal Hotel** suggests a build date of around 1720, replacing an earlier building, with the northern part added in the late Victorian era.

According to Laker, Humphrey Bigglestone was charged with receiving goods stolen from ships in 1656. He took a lease of the building in 1661, and which had become known as the **Kings Arms** by at least 1662. The first mention of the inn as the **Three Kings** was in 1699 when Mary Watts, "*Widow*", was in charge. In 1720, the lease stated that it was "*hereafter leased with the Bell*" (another inn in Beach Street). John Paramor was owner that year, followed by Hercules Baker in 1732.

Throughout the 1700s, the inn was used as a courtroom and many references to mayors, justices, juries, hearings and examinations have been documented. It was also a place where clubs and societies would meet.

An extract from the Kentish Post dated 21 March 1750 stated: "*Three Kings Society, Deal – 'for the better maintenance of their widows' – to meet at Three Kings, where anyone under 40, healthy & not belonging to the sea may be made a member."*

Thomas Baker was registered landlord in 1751, followed by Elizabeth Baker in 1763, John Baker in 1771 and Richard Knocker, "*Vintner*", in 1779.

A 1785 advertisement in the Kentish Gazette stated: "*The Three Kings Inn, together with the stables and coach house adjoining, to be sold with post chaises and other effects."*

In 1794, it was reported that the Austrian, Colonel Mack (later famous for surrendering to Napoleon's army at Ulm in 1805) stayed at the inn. Thomas Fenner and Thomas Flint, local brewers, held the lease in 1795, and, in 1795, landlord, Richard Knocker, was described as being an "*Inn and Excise Office Keeper."*

Another notable guest included Lord Craven, the Duke of Portland, who arrived from Dover in a post-chaise and four, and stayed at the inn in 1799 before embarking with his troops for the Helder.

Lord Horatio Nelson was also a frequent visitor to the inn and a suite of three private rooms linked by a gallery overlooking the beach was always made available to him in which to entertain. He wrote to his friends, Sir William and Lady Hamilton, in 1801 urging them to come Deal, adding that: *"The Three Kings, I am told, is the best house. It stands on the beach …you can bathe in the sea that will make you strong and well … I hate the Downs but if my friends come it will be paradise"*. Nelson would come ashore to dine with them there on their subsequent visits to Deal while his ship was anchored in the Downs.

According to late local historian, David Collyer, in the 9 September 2004 edition of the Mercury, the ghost of Lord Nelson's paramour, Lady Emma Hamilton, can occasionally be seen in the corner of the lounge bar at night.

In 1801, the Kentish Gazette reported: *"William Myers respectfully informs the inhabitants of Deal that*

2009

*he intends to open a school at the **Three Kings Hotel** for the education of both sexes in reading, writing and arithmetic. Applications to be made to him at Mr Saffrey Sayers, Boatbuilder, in Deal"*. Later that year, the hotel was referred to as also being a *'Coffee House'*.

In 1804, the **Three Kings** included a *"tap room, and stable, etc, in Custom House Lane"* when Thomas Cross was landlord. By 1808, the owner was Edward Iggulden, brewer. In 1815, the inn was leased with the **Three Kings** tap (a building situated to the north of the property). It was again described as including a *"tap/inn"* in 1821 under the auspices of J Rickman. It boasted *"stables with room over, coach house with room over, wash house, laundry and garden in Lower Street and land."*

In July 1818, Princess Adelaide of Saxe-Meiningen was a guest at the inn and, by all accounts, made a big impact on the town – see separate entry for **Princess Adelaide**.

In 1828, Robert Gibbs was registered landlord of the **Three Kings**, followed by Michael Elwin, a *"Gentleman"* from Dover, who leased the building (excluding the stable) in 1829 (as well as leasing the **Swan** the same year).

Charles Bladen, James Gaby Breach and William Potts Bathe *"of Bishopsgate Street, London"* became licensees of the newly named **Royal Hotel** on its reopening in 1837 (no doubt in celebration of Queen Victoria's accession to the throne that year). They entered into a 99-year contract the following year for *"The **Three Kings**, **Three Kings** tap and adjoining tenement and capstan ground. Premises now known as The **Royal Hotel**."*

They were followed by Thomas Bathe Jeffery in 1840, George Quiddington in 1841, Francis Breton in 1849, Sabina Bentley in 1860, Charlotte Rhodes Grellet in 1861, Hermann William Whitlaw in 1865 and Robert Allen in 1865. The Mercury reported in December of that year: *"Mr Allen, the worthy and kind-hearted proprietor of the **Royal Hotel**, distributed 80 basins of soup among the poor of that neighbourhood on Saturday last. A 2lb loaf accompanied each basin."*

In 1869, the inn advertised an *"Annual Haunch of Mutton Festival"* which apparently continued for a number of years.

In 1878, Robert Allen's widow, Alice, was landlady, followed by John Ashley Foster in 1879, Samuel Watkins Hiscocks in 1886, Lettice Betsy MacDermot in 1890, Arthur Spencer Vincent in 1894, James Gardiner in 1897 and Florence Hannah Meinhardt in 1910.

In 1914, a local newspaper, headed *"The Spy Menace - A Suspicious Incident"* reported: *"Friday. At mid-day to-day an incident of a suspicious nature occurred in Deal which has aroused considerable excitement. There is situated on the seafront at Deal a fine commercial hotel which commands an uninterrupted view of the Downs and the coast beyond. From this hotel – which is managed by a lady whose name is not an English one – there proudly floats from the eastern and western portions of the building the 'Union Jack of Old England'. Suspicion was aroused this morning when a fairly large pigeon, whose plumage was not of the ordinary colour, was seen to enter the building by one of its open windows, and more remarkable still, the window was immediately closed. A gentleman who happened to be passing at the time, witnessing the extraordinary occurrence, immediately did his duty and gave information to the preservers of the law. Some few minutes later two blue-coated officers visited the hotel mentioned, and, after an interview with the manageress, the little feathered visitor, whether friend or foe, was carried away by its captors. The whole occurrence was also witnessed by several Deal boatmen who happened to be on the spot, though as a rule the suspicions of our boatmen are not easily aroused."*

It later became clear that the hotel in question was the **Royal Hotel** and the *"lady whose name is not an English one"* was, in fact, its landlady, Florence Hannah Meinhardt (who later changed her surname to Fryer). In 1915, she was fined 10/- (50p) for failing to shade or obscure the window of a ground floor lavatory so that no light could be shed outside at night, and, in 1917, she was charged with being *"unlawfully found drunk and incapable on licensed premises"*. She was given a £5 fine and ordered to pay 10/6d (52½p) doctor's fees.

In 1929, Captain EH Symonds was landlord. In April 1932, it was reported that, while he was at the helm, a fire broke out on Good Friday in one of the top back rooms of the servants' quarters which were *"full of smoke and the room well alight."*

During WWII, Sir Winston Churchill

2009.

and Dwight Eisenhower were visitors to the hotel, no doubt discussing battle plans. (Photos of one of Churchill's visits to Deal can be seen on the wall of the lounge bar above the fireplace).

In November 1968, an advertisement proclaimed: *"Wine, Dine and Dance at the Royal. Dinner 7.30 to 10.30. Dancing till 11.45. 30/- (£1.50) each."*

On January 30 1969, it was reported the Pelican Company Unlimited (a club formed at the **Pelican** pub) held its first annual dinner and dance at the **Royal**.

In May 1971, it was announced that managers, Michael and Barbara Calverly, would be leaving the hotel after four years and that Eric Hodge would be taking over. At the time the **Royal** was owned by Crest Hotels, a division of Bass Charrington (and before that, was owned by the Trident Hotel group). Hodge's stay, however, was not a long one since Robert and Jane Pryce took over in the September when Michael Gregory was its managing director.

The **Royal Hotel** was owned by Mermaid Hotels from 1971 for some years. (The company also owned and ran the famous smuggling inn, the

Mermaid in Rye, at the same time).

Other notable dates and occasions gleaned from local newspaper reports included the appointment of a new manager, Victor Millard in October 1975; Pat Hollis, manager, spent £5,000 replacing carpets in March 1978 after the recent sea water flood; Bruce Lee became manager and Ian Dunkerley head chef in September 1982; Ian Dunkerley became manager in November 1983 and, in July 1986, he left to manage Abbots Barton Hotel in Canterbury (see also separate entry for **Dunkerleys**); Keith and Julie Clarke were appointed managers in May 1986, followed by Barrie and Jennifer Smith in February 1990; and Andrew and Amanda Wedl and Peter Highfield become the new owners in February 1996, with Peter Highfield also taking on the role of head chef.

During refurbishment works at the hotel in October 1996, a Regency fireplace was discovered in one of the guest rooms; Peter Highfield was announced as chef/proprietor in October 1997; the Wedls moved on to the Cliff Inn (now the White Cliffs Hotel), St Margaret's at Cliffe, and new owners, Shepherd Neame, brought in a temporary manager, Paul Ribbons, in October 2002, followed by permanent managers, Paul and Sheila Patterson in November 2002 and Denise Copley in November 2003.

In 2003, the **Royal Hotel** was given a £450,000 revamp by Shepherd Neame and in January 2004 it was officially reopened by brewery chairman Robert Neame who pulled the first pint, together with Cllr Sue Delling, then Mayor of Deal. As well as a total interior refurbishment, the outside areas overlooking the sea were also given a facelift.

The **Royal Hotel** today remains in the ownership of Shepherd Neame and is one of Deal's top hotels, being the only building left remaining on the beach from the many that stood side by side until the 1830s (since when all were demolished). The large building housing the **Royal**'s former lock up garage for guests' cars is situated in Chapel Street behind the hotel. The hotel's smart fixtures and decor allude to its former nautical history which can be found in its bedrooms, restaurant and airy bar overlooking the beach.

Royal Marine
36 (15) Gladstone Road (South Ropewalk), Deal

The *Royal Marine* beerhouse was first mentioned in 1861 when Samuel Barber was landlord. At some point during its history, it also included a stable/coach house at the rear. It was located next door to the *Wheatsheaf* beerhouse (later the *Victoria Inn* – see separate entry). The Royal Marines came to Deal in 1861 so presumably the beerhouse was so called in commemoration of this event.

By 1881, Samuel Maxwell was in charge when he was described on the census for that year as being aged 47 and a *"Royal Marine Pensioner, Londonderry, Ireland, Royal Marine Hospital Nurse and Beerhouse Keeper"*. The beerhouse got its last documented mention two years later.

The *Royal Marine* is now a private residence.

2009.

Royal Marines

See entry for the *Berry*.

Royal Oak, Deal

See entry for the *Red Lion*, Deal.

Royall Oak (location unknown) "Deale"

The *Royall Oak* appeared in the Deale 'Payment for Signs' list of 1662, with landlord, Bryan Maygreve, but, other than this reference, the pub remains untraceable.

Royal Oak Inn (Blewbore/Blue Boar and possibly Oak Tavern) 41 Middle Street, Deal

These premises stood on the corner of Middle Street and Bear Pump Lane (now Oak Street) and apparently had vast cellars.

Leases dating back to 1661 showed a pub on the land called the *Blewbore*. The site was referred to in 1710 as *"land on which a malthouse stood"* when it was sold by the heirs of Peter Bridger (son of Deal brewer, Richard Bridger) to Samuel Silkwood. He in turn willed it to his nephew, Richard Silkwood, in 1711.

In 1722, Henry and William Silkwood, who were brothers of Richard *"late of Betteshanger, husbandman, deceased"*, sold it to maltster, William Friend, of Deal. William married Sarah Gilbert in 1724 and, by 1742, he had acquired the northern and southern parts of a tenement which adjoined the land already acquired. He pulled these down and built a new brewhouse on the site. (The northern part was freehold and in the Manor of Chamberlain's Fee, while the southern part was leasehold and in the Manor of Court Ash).

By 1742, William had died and John Friend acquired the premises from William's widow, Sarah, and her son, William, but because there were now no marks to distinguish the leasehold from the freehold, he bought the freehold from John Dilnot who was the Lord of the Manor of the Chamberlain's Fee. In 1782, John Friend assigned the southern part to William Otley who took a new lease of it from the Archbishop of Canterbury in 1783.

William sold the northern part (his title to this was not included in the deeds seen) and assigned the lease of the southern part to John Tatnell, who mortgaged both parts to John Hollams.

In 1786, John Tatnell sold the northern part of the building *"now called or known by the name and sign of the Royal Oak"* to Messrs Fenner &

Royal Oak on right c1920.

Flint, brewers of Canterbury, who, on the same date, assigned the mortgage in trust for them to *"Edward Sole of Deal, gentleman"*. By 1786, it appears that this part eventually covered the whole site.

In 1794, John Holl, Lieutenant of the Deal Castle Company of Volunteers, was elected Mayor of Deal. On the occasion, *"... the Company assembled and fired three volleys in honour of the event and marched to the Royal Oak Inn where the Mayor and Corporation were banqueting and there mounted a sergeant's guard."*

The house boasted a concert room where local societies and tradesmen held meetings and elegant balls. The celebrated Catch Club would also convene there.

A list of landlords included Thomas Rickman in 1804, Henry and Eliza Epps in 1820, John Epps in 1826, Henry Epps, *"Excise Officer"*, (again) in 1832, Henry Holt Lowin in 1839 and 1845, Thomas Gambrill in 1852 and Frederick Kent in 1855.

An 1861 advert for the **Royal Oak Inn** announced: *"Professor Jilley – The Great Wizard of*

Site of Royal Oak 2009.

the East – Grand Entertainment on 9th/10th December. Admission: front seats – 15 shillings (75p); back seats – 6d (2½p)."

In 1865, W Brooks was licensee of the **Oak Tavern**, Oak Street which, presumably refers to the **Royal Oak**, although no definitive proof can be found to substantiate this.

The pub closed down and it was put up for sale in May 1873 when an advertisement stated: *"The whole of the household furniture, 5 motion beer engines, gas chandeliers and other fittings will be sold by Mr M. Langley on Friday, 13th June, 1873"*. However, it is probable that the pub did not sell since Langley applied for and was granted a licence for *"the Royal Oak and two other* [unnamed public] *houses"* on 6 September of that year, although it appears unlikely that the pub ever reopened since, by 1875, it was noted that he did not apply to relicence.

By the early 1900s, the property variously housed the Minerva Printing Works, Denne & Joce Printers, East Kent Advertiser office, Deal and Walmer Angling Society HQ, Deal & Walmer Chamber of Commerce, and the last mention of it appeared in Pain's Local Street Directory of Deal in 1939/40 when it was referred to as a Christian Mission. A title deed around this era also referred to the conveyance of *"smugglers passages, if any"* with the property. (Tunnels underground supposedly linked the **Royal Oak** to the **Harp** pub opposite – which is now the Middle Street fish and chip restaurant and takeaway – as well as to a building in the High Street).

The building was completely destroyed by a shell during WWII on 21 June 1944, although the cellars apparently survived intact. The site of the pub building remained open ground until the 1960s when an H bomb fall out shelter was built within the pub's old cellars by three local businessmen and exhibited to the public as a kind of 'show home'! It was reported that, as a result, two people from Ashford had agreed to have similar shelters built (on different sites) by the company at a cost of £1,000 and £1,200 respectively.

Whether or not the original 'show home' shelter still exists somewhere beneath Oak Street car park which now stands on the site is anyone's guess!

Royal Standard
Dover Road (Walmer Road), Walmer

The building housing the first incarnation of the *Royal Standard* hotel was situated near the junction of Liverpool Road and Dover Road. Its earliest mention was in 1810 when Stephen Blythe was landlord. On 5 February 1813, in an article entitled '*Cocking*', the Kentish Gazette advertised: "*A Main of Cocks and Stags to be fought at the Royal Standard, Walmer Road on Wednesday 10 February for Five Guineas a battle between the gentleman of Dover and the gentlemen of Walmer Road – also two pair of Great Cocks to be fought; one Shak Bag to fight before dinner, and one after dinner. An ordinary will be on the table at a quarter before one o'clock.*"

Blythe was succeeded in 1821 by Henry Snelling (who later enjoyed a long stay as licensee of the *Stag* in Walmer) and Joseph Kopetsky (formerly of the King's German Legion) in 1826. It was reported in 1829 that a 'Mr Bailey' was found hanging from the *Royal Standard* signpost, although the circumstances surrounding his death are unknown. Thomas Pearce became landlord in 1832, followed by Thomas Nash from 1839 (to at least 1855).

At this time, Lower Walmer was in the process of being built up and the area would have been a busy one. Plans for the construction of St Saviour's Church were first proposed around 1842 and building started round about 1848. A consecration ceremony took place on 2 July 1849 at the Church, followed by a celebration at the *Royal Standard*. (The pub was rebuilt about 1865 on a plot slightly further up Dover Road from its previous site, albeit on the same side of the road).

In 1855, the hotel was owned by Valentine Hoile, "*Brewer of Sandwich*", and Thomas Barnes was registered landlord in 1858 and William Laws in 1859 (by which time auctions had become a regular feature of the house), followed by John Jennings Attwood in 1865.

A local newspaper story from December 1866 reported that "*The Third Cinque Ports Artillery Volunteers held a general meeting* [at the pub] *to distribute prizes and for important business. Full dress, no side arms.*"

On 18 January 1867, Walmer Catch Club held a concert there.

The pub closed about 1870. The building then became a home for the clergy and the Rev Charles Elvin (author of *Records of Walmer*) was a notable resident. Until around WWI, the building comprised private residences variously known as Wexcombe House and The Grange. The Fair Maid of Kent tea rooms were later housed there (in nos 2 to 10 Dover Road) up until around the end of WWII.

The *Royal Standard* now forms part of the Wellington Court apartment buildings.

c1925.

2009.

Saint George (location unknown) Deal

This pub was mentioned in Laker's list of pubs in 1680 but, because its location is unspecified and nothing more is known about the place, it cannot reliably be connected in any way to the *Royal George* in Lower Street.

Salisbury Arms (location unknown) Walmer

This pub was mentioned in passing in Langridge's research documentation in 1977 but otherwise remains undetectable.

Salutation

See entry for the *Friendly Port*.

Sampson/Sampson & Three Cups (location unknown) Deal

This pub got a mention in Deal pilot, Thomas Stone's 1700 will when he left the *"messuage and premises"* to his wife, Mary, but, other than that, it remains untraceable. The *Sampson* and *Sampson & Three Cups* are assumed to be one and the same establishment.

Sandown Castle Hotel (Castle Inn, Good Intent) 241-247 (approx) Sandown Road, Deal

Originally called the *Good Intent* when it was first mentioned in the 1805 valuation list, the pub was renamed the *Castle Inn* in 1863 and the *Sandown Castle Hotel* by 1910. The building was formerly used as a canteen for Sandown Castle itself before becoming a public house.

Landlords included John Broker of the *Good Intent* in 1821, Mary Broker in 1830, Henry Gardner in 1836, Daniel Jarvis in 1845, Luke Jarvis in 1852, Archibald Hewitson of the *Castle Inn* in 1863, Elizabeth Ann Hewitson (widow) in 1864 and Henry Terry Pettit in 1865.

A report from October 1869 stated that *"The gale at Deal was no doubt sallied by the exertions of the landlord who had a few days previously driven a quantity of wooden piles in front. The [sea] water completely surrounded the old inn which seems sooner or later to be doomed for demolition."*

Thomas Cattermole became landlord in 1870, followed by John Marsden Redman also in 1872. There were four landlords in 1873, namely Thomas Hay (who was fined 8/6d (42½p) for opening the pub during prohibitive hours on a Sunday), followed by George Richard Redman in March, John Oxley in July and Thomas Hayshaw in September. Later landlords included George Ramsden in 1874, John

Marsden Redman (again) in 1875/6 and Thomas Sladden from 1876 (to at least 1880) who was charged with serving drinks out of hours, but the case was dismissed.

In October 1885, police records reported that *"James Knight, 30, and William Taylor, 29, labourers, were charged with breaking into the Castle Inn, Sandown and stealing therefrom about 27 pint bottles containing ale, nine drinking glasses, a jug and six pewter measures … the property of Messrs Hills and Son, on the 2nd inst. Thomas Cattermole said he lived near the Castle Inn, and on looking through a telescope the previous day he saw three men, whom he recognised as the two prisoners and another named Gimber, coming from the back of the Castle Inn. They looked bulky … After evidence the three prisoners were committed for trial at the next Quarter Sessions, to be held on the 16th inst."*

A late Victorian advertisement publicised the *"Castle Inn Recreation Grounds – Trap Bat Rounders, Drop Handkerchief, Dancing on the Green and a Variety of Other Sports. Wednesday Nights – June"*. (There had also been a horseracing track on the sandhills very close to the pub for a brief time).

John Robert Macey Tandy was landlord from 1886 (until at least 1901) who, in February 1887, *"was charged with having his house open during prohibited*

c1930.

hours on Saturday last … Fined 20 shillings (£1) and 9 shillings (45p) or 14 days. The fines were paid."

In 1892, the old building was demolished and a new pub erected very close to the original site. Edwin Davis was landlord in 1904 when it was still known as the **Castle Inn** but the name had changed by 1905 to the **Sandown Castle Hotel**. Frederick Brice took over in 1909, followed by James George Taylor in 1911, George Cranwell in 1936, AA Attwood in 1956, Michael Hollingsworth in 1966 and Mr and Mrs Wally Burnell from 1971 (formerly at the **Mill Inn**).

In July 1987, the Mercury reported: *"A buyer may have been found for the **Sandown Castle** pub which*

has been on the market since Christmas, price £140,000. The boarded-up pub is under offer." However, in October 1988, it reported that the *"Kent Fire Brigade attended a mystery blaze at the derelict **Sandown Castle** pub, on Monday (3 October) night. A small bonfire seemed to have started the fire which caused serious damage to the bar".* The building was subsequently demolished.

Private houses, numbered 241 to 247 Sandown Road, mark the approximate site of the pub and its car park, and a keen eye can spot the change in kerbstones marking the area of the former entrance into the old pub.

c1870.

Sandown Hotel (exact location unknown)
Harold Road/Godwyn Road, North Deal

It is doubtful whether the *Sandown Hotel* was ever built but is included here since the authors cannot be 100 per cent certain that it was not!

According to the 3 September 1892 edition of the Mercury, Henry Stephen Chapman was the owner of a piece of ground in North Deal which was bounded on the east by the new parade and, on the west, by the road leading to Sandown Hills. He applied to build a bungalow-style hotel on the site of the old windmill, with a frontage of 100-feet, and he actually held a provisional licence at least until 1897.

The *Sandown Hotel* was going to fill the gap that existed at the time between the present-day location of Harold and Godwyn Roads, and the windmill used to stand roughly at the top of Godwyn Road.

According to later reports, the proposed hotel was to be situated "*on the north, by property of Mr DM Hills and on the south by the roadway adjoining the enclosure known as Stony Park*". The plans produced showed "*the frontage to the ground next to the parade which he* [Chapman] *asked might be licensed was 279 feet.*"

Unfortunately there is no evidence to suggest the *Sandown Hotel* ever actually became a reality.

Sandwich Arms

See entry for *Dunkerleys*.

Sandwich Hoy (location unknown) "Deale"

The *Sandwich Hoy* was only mentioned once, on the Sandwich Recognizances List of Deal pubs in 1680, but otherwise remains untraceable.

Saracens Head, 1 Alfred Square, Deal

A Saracen's head would often form part of noble families' coats of arms whose members had taken part in the Holy Land Crusades.

The *Saracens Head* is situated on the northwest corner of Alfred Square with College Road.

In 1806, the building was described as comprising a "*Carpenter's shop and tenement*". The first known landlord of what was by then called the *Saracens Head* beerhouse was James Walsh in 1821 (who was also landlord of the *Queens Head* the same year), followed by Laura Smith in the 1830s and Richard Resker Hammond from 1845 until 1869. The Hammond family also used to run the coal merchant's business next door according to Pigot's Directory of 1824.

The Mercury reported: "*The 87th birthday of Mr Charles Tomlin, tailor, was celebrated* [at the pub]. *The much-respected gentleman, in vigorous health, sang a song for the entertainment of the assembled company.*"

William Licence was landlord from 1869 (until 1896) and, during his time at the helm, a local newspaper reported on 15 January 1887 that: "*An inquest was held at the Guildhall on Wednesday morning on the body of James Redsull, who was found dead at his house on the previous morning. Edward Henry Snoswell, of 162 Middle-street, swore: 'I have known the deceased for many years,*

2010.

and was in his company on Monday evening at the Saracens Head. It was his birthday – he was 81. He had three pints of beer during the evening ... I went home with him because of a nasty curb and some steps leading to where he lived in Alfred-row... The old man was 'cherry merry', but no more than usual ... He did not drink any spirits. He said he was born

c1905.

on 10 January 1806'. Dr Mason [stated that] *in falling down stairs, his head got caught in the corner at the bottom and he was unable to extricate himself … Verdict: Accidental Death."*

Towards the end of the 19th century, it was reported that Thomas Constance, a 'pensioner' aged 55 and *"a notorious offender"* having had 48 previous convictions, was charged with being drunk and disorderly, as well as causing wilful damage to two panes of glass at the pub amounting to £1/15/0d (£1.75p). He was sentenced to one month's hard labour on each charge, to run consecutively.

The *Saracens Head* was a busy community pub in the Victorian and Edwardian era and many outings were organised with its customers meeting inside for a few drinks before boarding the charabanc. The outings continued up until at least WWII.

Henry George May was licensee in 1896, followed by Edmund Joshua Pain in 1901, Arthur Edmund Pain in 1913, JH Cullen in 1914, John Hobday in 1922, Henry George Bridger in 1935 and Richard Frederick Thompson (from the brewery) in 1940. According to the 1950s' liquidation assets of Thompson & Son, the building next door to the pub in Alfred Square had also belonged to the brewery (and various coal merchants' businesses, as mentioned above, had operated from it

since at least 1824).

Later licensees included Paul Sayle from 1943 to about 1955, BM Dobson in 1966, John Frame in 1970, James Powell in 1983, John Kemp in 1985, Martin Burgess in 1990, Kenneth Woodcock in 1991, William Kember also in 1991 and Franz Feeburger and Christine Feeburger (née Dalton) from 1994. Franz Feeburger sadly died while 'in office' and a commemorative plaque can be seen attached to the tree and bench opposite the *Saracens Head* in Alfred Square. Kevin and Pamela Canale took over the reigns in 2000.

A previous landlady told the authors that the *Saracens Head* was haunted by a female spirit but whether or not she still puts in the odd appearance is unknown. During internal renovations in 2009, an original fireplace was discovered in the bar. Unfortunately, as it was impractically situated behind the bar counter, it was covered up again. The pub's exterior was attractively repainted in 2010 in a smart new livery reminiscent of a bygone age.

The pub remains open for business and is now owned by Shepherd Neame and comprises one large open plan L-shaped bar with pool table, and a small, attractive paved garden to the rear. The current incumbents are John and Marianne Steward.

Sawyers Arms (location unknown) Deal

The only reference to this pub was in a birth announcement dated 23 February 1863: *"To the wife of Mr Lawrence, Sawyers Arms, a daughter"*. It could possibly have been a misprint and may have referred instead to the *Sandwich Arms* since its landlord, John Edward Lawrence, was also a sawyer by trade.

Scarborough Cat

See entry for the *Globe*.

Scotch Armes (location unknown) Deal

The only mention of this pub was found in the 1679 Will of Robert Mumford, a pilot, which stated that he wished to leave *"To his son Samuel Mumford all that my messuage called The Scotch Armes with appurtenances and the one half of the yard thereunto belonging which messuage is* built on the land lately lying waste belonging to the Archbishop and now occupied by William Anderson or his assigns together also with my half of the Capstan standing near the house where I formerly lived in Deal."*

The pub otherwise remains untraceable.

Seagull

See entry for the *Clarendon*.

Seagull (exact location unknown) Beach Street, Deal

Not to be confused with the other *Seagull* (now the *Clarendon*) in Beach Street, this pub only had a passing mention in a 1743 document and otherwise remains untraceable.

Seven Stars

See entry for the *Greyhound, Middle Street*.

Shah (Fishing Boat, Hovelling Boat)
139 (68) Middle Street, Deal

The pub was located next door south of the *Ship* and a tunnel reputedly led from one pub to the other.

James Beal was landlord of the *Hovelling Boat* in 1861, followed by his widow in 1865. The house became known as the *Fishing Boat* certainly by 1869. It was reported in 1870 that its landlord, John Gilbert Smith, while out for an evening's shooting on the marshes, accidently discharged one barrel of the gun through the top of his right arm while attempting to recover a wounded jackdaw from a ditch! Henry J May, a professional bricklayer, took over in 1871, followed by Harry Chitty in 1872, James Galley Grigg in 1873 (when the pub was renamed the *Shah*) and David

House on right 2009.

Philpott in 1879.

In 1881, William Adams was charged with causing wilful damage to the door of the *Shah* on Christmas night and landlord, Richard Morris Hayman, gave evidence against him. Adams was subsequently sentenced to 14 days hard labour.

It was reported on 8 November 1884 that *"Mr M. Langley applied for a new licence for 'The Shah' Inn, Middle-street in the name of William Thomas Maben. Mr Hayman, the late tenant, had not renewed the license at the last annual licensing meeting. Supt. Capps said the house had for some time past been a resort for soldiers. People in the neighbourhood had complained. The Magistrates refused to grant the new license. There* were four licensed houses within a stone's throw from this, and they did not think it was required."

The **Shah** subsequently closed down and became a lodging house. Although now unlicensed, a local newspaper report, entitled "*A Desperate Fight*", from the Deal Police Court dated 11 June 1887 makes interesting reading: "*Kate Gillard, a tramp, was charged with being drunk and disorderly in Middle-street, Deal, on the 4th inst. PC Mercer said that on Saturday night about 8 o'clock, he was called to the house, formerly called the 'Shah', in Middle-street. When he arrived he found several persons fighting in the passage, and some were bleeding very much … There was a very large crowd in the street, and he requested the four people he had turned out to go away quietly; two of them did so, but prisoner and her husband stopped there. The house was a lodging-* house for tramps. He advised prisoner to go away several times but she refused, and he was obliged to take her into custody … He was called to turn them out. He thought there would be murder done, as they were bleeding profusely. The husband, who was present, said he went outside to get his wife out … when he was struck violently on the head with a poker or thick piece of wood. They were fruit picking and pea-picking at Deal last year, and had come again for the same purpose this year, but it was too early. On promising that it should not occur again and to quit the town, prisoner, who appeared to be deeply affected, was dismissed, the Bench taking into consideration that she had been locked up since Saturday. Prisoner: God bless you, sir, I am truly thankful.*"

The **Shah** is now a private house.

Shield of Marshall Blucher (location unknown) Walmer

The only mention of this pub appeared in Walmer Alehouse Keepers' books for the years 1816 and 1817 when Christopher Andrews was landlord, followed by William Gambor in 1818, Edward Sharpe in 1822 and Andrew Wright Baker in 1823.

It is possible that the name of the pub was a corruption of (or indeed just a straightforward misnomer for) the *Field Marshal Blucher*. (German Field Marshal Gebhard Leberecht von Blucher, 1742-1819, made his name during the Napoleonic wars).

Ship, Beach Street, Deal

See entry for the *Clarendon*.

Ship, 141 (69) Middle Street, Deal

In 1694 (at a time when there were already 78 licensed victuallers in Deal) "*10 perches of land or beachy ground with appurtenances abutting to Middle Street to east, to a certain pond there towards the west…*" were leased for 21 years at an annual rent of half-a-crown (12½p) to Susanna Wood from Richard Gookin who was the Lord of the Manor of Chamberlain's Fee.

By 1702, Susanna had died and the lease was transferred to Israel Claringbold, "*a husbandman of Sholden*" and his wife, Margaret (née Wood). "*A messuage now in two dwellings*" was in the occupation of Joan Scarlett and Ann Wood, both widows. Later that year, Claringbold mortgaged the property, including a stable, to a Deal pilot.

In 1707, George Larkin, a mariner, bought the freehold of the whole and left all his real estate to his two sons, George and Stephen. In 1713, the property was described in a lease as containing "*All that now erected messuage or tenement in two dwellings divided with the yard garden and land thereunto*". In 1764, it was transferred to Dr George Lynch of Canterbury, who in turn conveyed it to Mrs Elizabeth Hooper, widow of Lieutenant Hooper. She later went on to marry Henry

Mackeson of the Hythe brewing family and placed the building in trust for her two sons, Edward and Henry Hooper. After her death in 1768, it was advertised in several of the July editions of the Kentish Gazette that the property was "*To be sold to the highest bidder. On Thursday 14th day of this Instant at the House of John Foffey called the* **Blacksmiths Arms** [later the **Hope**] *in Deal. All that freehold messuage (now in two dwellings divided) with the Yard Garden and Land belonging with the appurtenances lying and being in the Middle-street; now in the several tenures or occupations of Henry Mackeson and the Widow Middleton. For particulars enquire of Samuel Roby, Attorney, at Deal*". In fact, Mackeson bought it and continued to live in one part with Elizabeth Bean.

In June 1771, a lease referred to the "*building in Middle Street*" abutting to "*lands of John Dilnot Esq (formerly a pond called the Sand Pit Sole) demised to Daniel Jarvis there towards the West …*". The Sand Pit Sole (now known as Ivy Place) was the name of a pond and piece of land that stood behind the pub and a 1784 lease described its position as being "*bounded on the West by Lower Street, on the North and East by the other part of Sand Pit Sole* and on the South by Sand Pit Sole Lane". A narrow passageway leading into the Lane from Middle Street used to run between the pub and the **Shah** next door (no 139 Middle Street) but it has since been blocked off. However, from the street outside the pub, evidence of its location can still be detected behind the small wooden doorway that separates the two buildings.

In a 1792 directory, Mackeson was listed as a "Wine Merchant" but there is no mention of the **Ship** by name. A Certificate for Redeemed Land Tax in 1799 referred to "wine vaults and a stable". On Mackeson's death, his four sons inherited the property but faced a challenge from one of Lieutenant Hooper's daughters who "has or pretends to have a claim under the will of her father". They paid her £15 for "quieting and extinguishing the claim."

The property was sold again in 1812 to Captain David Ross, RN, for £527.10s.0d (£527.50p). In 1833, he acquired land opposite the pub "now used as a Drying Spot" and remained at the house until his death in 1835.

In 1856, Thomas Hight was owner/brewer of the unnamed pub, with John Ralph as landlord, followed by Gardners, owners/brewers, in 1858, with Charles Hinds as landlord. The pub got its first name-check in 1865 licensing records when it was "relicensed as the **Ship**" and John Forest was landlord. The brewery owner in 1869 was John Omer when a local newspaper that year, reporting an 'Accident', stated: "As a man named Oliver, waggoner to Mr John Omer, Star Brewery, Sandwich, was engaged yesterday afternoon in lowering a barrel of beer into the cellar of the **Ship** Inn, Middle-street, his foot slipped and sent the cask down with a jerk, which snapped the bone of his leg."

Frederick Chapman was landlord in 1870, Henry Stephen Chapman in 1877, David Clay in 1878 (when the pub's address was given as 69 Middle Street), Frederick Pullen in January 1879, John Oliver Terry in May 1879 and John Galley Grigg, "North Sea Pilot", in July 1879.

2006.

In July 1886, another local newspaper article, headed 'Pleasure Parties', reported the following: "On Saturday last a pleasure party consisting of twenty three of the employees of Messrs Bligh Bros, coach-builders, of Canterbury, visited Deal in waggonettes and put up at Mr Grigg's, the **Ship** Inn, Middle-street. Here they dined and had tea and after a pleasant evening, departed at 11pm. On Monday a party to the number of sixteen hailing also from Canterbury, being the employees of Messrs Court Bros, visited Deal and made the **Ship** Inn their headquarters."

Mrs Anne Murray Grigg was landlady in 1892, followed by Charles Quinton in 1897, Charles Frederick Boore in 1898 (when, due to street renumbering which had taken place around 1893, the pub's address was given as 141 Middle Street) and Frederick Brice in 1902 (the same year that Hill's brewery sold the pub to Thompson's brewery for £750). In February of that year, the Deal, Walmer & Sandwich Mercury recounted a Police Report which stated that the pub had "… too many entrances [in] Middle Street, New Street and High Street. If the back door was kept locked during opening hours, the Police would withdraw their objection."

Frederick Brice was landlord in 1904, followed by Henry Thomas (a previous landlord of the **Hope**) in 1907, Henry Thomas in 1910, Mrs E Thomas, widow, in 1914, George Alfred May from 1921 and Mrs Elizabeth Catherine May in 1931 (until at least 1948) when Thompson's brewery owned the pub. During the 1930s, the **Ship** was in danger of closing as it was described in a magistrates' report as containing "4 ground floor licensed rooms, basement cellar, rear kitchen and six bedrooms and boxroom, 2 working-class tenants, tap room or saloon very little used; within 210 yards are 8 other licensed and 1 off-licence. Police visits to the **Ship** (54)". It went on to say that the pub's sanitary conditions were "only fair" and that, compared with the nearby **Pelican** (which was described as a "high-class hotel"), the **Ship** was "practically a lodging house". Decrease in local trade was blamed on the nearby Constitution Club since, as well as its bar and billiard facilities, its concerts and dances were patronised by miners who would otherwise have drank in the *Ship*. Despite a poor inspection report, however, the pub's licence was renewed.

Charrington's brewery took over the *Ship* in 1951 and SFG Barnes was landlord in 1955, Jim and Laura Collett in 1963 (for 11 years), Victor Thomas in 1974, John and Diane Turner in 1983 and Patrick

and Vicky Foley in 1984. Raymond Dennis and Penelope Handley (now Dennis) took over on 18 October 1985 and they remain the owners/landlords of what is now a very agreeable free house.

The interior of the present day *Ship* remains charmingly authentic, having retained much of its historic nautical fascination and comprising a large double fronted bar and a snug at the back, together

Ship (location unknown) Deal

The *Ship* was mentioned in passing in an 1806 article when its landlord, Mr Michener, spoke about Lord Nelson, Sir William and Lady Hamilton entertaining in a room with a sea view.

Unfortunately, no evidence of the landlord's name can be found in any directory, and neither the pub's name nor the date of the article tallies with the two other pubs of the same name in Deal at the time.

Ship & Castle

See entry for the *Sir John Falstaff*.

Sir Colin Campbell, 36 Campbell Road (1, 5 Campbell Street, Back Road), Walmer

Sir Colin Campbell was the original title of Lord Clyde (1792 to 1863). He was a distinguished Field Marshal, mainly remembered for the relief of Lucknow in India. He became known as Baron Clyde of Clydesdale in 1858.

John S Holtrum took a 63-year lease from the Leith Estate for the building in 1856. Thomas Marsh was landlord in 1858, followed by James Knight in 1859 and William Rayner Holness in 1867. He was fined 5 shillings (25p) with 8/6d (42½p) costs for opening the house *"during the hours of divine service"*. Lewis Worrels followed in the 1870s. By 1889, the property was owned by James Knight, with George W Finnis behind the bar until at least 1898.

2009.

In July 1924 (by which time the pub had become full licensed), it was reported the annual charabanc outing visited Kearsney, the Alkham Valley, the Duke William pub in Ickham and finished up at the Black Pig public house in Barnsole for an open air concert. The landlord at the time was Frank S Adams.

Other licensees included FJ Thompson from Thompson's brewery in 1903, James Percy King in 1910, AJ Banks in 1922, GR Heard in 1934, James Quigley in 1954 and George Davenport in 1956.

The pub closed down on 6 June 1962, and the premises operated as a fish and chip shop for a while before becoming the private house that stands there today.

Sir John Falstaff (Ship & Castle)
199, 199a & 201 (52, 57 Lower Street) High Street, Deal

The beerhouse was situated just north of Water Street, next door to the **Royal George** pub (which was on the corner plot).

It was first documented in 1804 when Stephen Pritchard was landlord, followed by Zachariah Selth from 1821 to 1840. An entry in Hancock's *'A Fly Proprietor's Diary'* of 1838 recalled that, on 9 July, *"for stealing the lead from Selth's Ship & Castle, Brown was whipped and Larkin was not"*. He also noted that a new coach house had been built for the house that year and that, further, two labourers in the employ of Mr Welland, a farmer from Great Mongeham, were charged with *"taking manure at an improper hour"* contrary to an Act of Parliament from the rear of the **Ship & Castle** and were both fined 1 shilling (5p) each as it was their first offence.

Edwin Danby Darby was landlord in 1847, followed by Francis S Leggett in 1858 and his widow, Elizabeth Jane Leggett, in 1861. In 1863, a police report described the property as being a common lodging house with two tramps living there.

On 21 July 1865, a local newspaper article from the Court Sessions reported: *"Wednesday - Before W.M. Cavell, Esq, Mayor and J. Iggluden Esq - John Donovan and Ann Donovan, husband and wife, and members of the medical fraternity, were placed at the bar on two charges of assault and two also of committing wilful damage. The nature of the charges is disclosed in the following evidence:*

Elizabeth Jane Leggett - I am landlady of the Ship & Castle beer shop. Last evening, shortly after eight o'clock, a man came to the house to see the male prisoner. He had been there a few minutes when I heard a noise in the tap-room, and on going thither I saw Donovan dancing on the table with only his trousers on, and offering to fight his visitor. I sent for a constable, and Seeth came. At that time some crockery ware had been broken in the tap-room. I

2009.

told Seeth that I wanted Donovan removed from the house, and he said he would fetch Cox to assist him. During his absence the male prisoner forced himself into the bar-parlour, striking me with his hand as I stood at the doorway to obstruct his progress. He was followed by the female prisoner. When in the parlour Donovan seized the poker, and with it broke the table and the gas-fitting; and his wife broke other articles in the room. Donovan also knocked down with the poker another tramp who attempted to enter the room. I estimated the damage at 15 shillings (75p). Donovan was drunk at the time, but his wife was sober; and both left the house before the police returned.

Police-constable Seeth, who deposed to being sent for, as stated by the last witness, and also to seeing Donovan in the condition named, with his wife clinging to him, said - I went to fetch Cox, and on returning the prisoners had left the Ship & Castle. We afterwards saw them in Water Street, and there took Donovan into custody. The man offered much resistance, but the woman went quietly to the station. The Bench sentenced the male prisoner to 21 days imprisonment in Sandwich Gaol with hard labour, and the female to seven days, also with hard labour. The offence constituted by Donovan's knocking a fellow tramp down with a poker was not investigated, the party injured (Henry May) withdrawing the charge on the plea that the man was 'too drunk to know what he was about.'"

James Siddens took over the **Ship & Castle** in 1871 and applied for a change of name in December that year. Permission was granted but Siddens was told that its current name had to remain until the next licensing day in 1872. The premises were owned by Flint brewery of Canterbury at the time. The pub was subsequently renamed the **Sir John Falstaff** (after one of William Shakespeare's most popular characters). Siddens appeared in court in June that year to give evidence against a young teenager called William Mackay who was charged with ill-treating and torturing a cat *"on the site of the old* **Royal George.**"

Edward Henry Snoswell was landlord in 1873. In 1877, Richard Wraight Crickett, a chimney sweep (together with his wife, Esther Elizabeth) was charged with being drunk and disorderly and breaking a pane of glass worth 7 shillings (35p) at the **Sir John Falstaff.** While on duty, PC Curtis said that he saw a crowd opposite the pub and heard screams of *"Murder!"* while Crickett was *"struggling with a man and making a great noise".* Crickett's wife was apparently lying on the steps of the pub. The prisoners were drunk and were transported to the police station, the woman on a barrow. Both were sentenced to 14 days' hard labour at Sandwich Gaol. (Presumably Esther Crickett was not the only customer unable to use the pub's steps since it was reported in April 1882 that Deal Borough Council had paid for their removal in the sum of £15, probably as an early health and safety measure!).

1876 saw more trouble at the pub when a tramp called William Giles was charged with being drunk and riotous on the premises and for insulting Edward Snoswell at 1.10am Christmas morning, as well as striking PC John Batt Annall. (Interestingly, Annall later went on to run several pubs of his own). Giles told the court that he was a maker of boats for toyshops by profession, before being discharged with a caution.

Later landlords included Thomas Perry in 1878, Thomas Akehurst in 1879, Elizabeth Penn (Akehurst's daughter) in 1884 and James Oliver in May 1887. An entry dated 24 August in the Deal Licensing Register for 1887 noted: *"Application to transfer license refused as applicant (licensee) owed Poor Rates of £1 4s 9d (£1.28) and Town Rates of £3 14s 6d (£3.72½)."* However, on 7 April 1888, the opposition was withdrawn and the application granted.

Alfred Maynard took over the licence in March 1890, which in turn was transferred to Andrew Edward Chambers in March 1891. The pub closed two months later, on 5 May 1891, and was subsequently refused a new licence in the September since it was maintained that there were *"no requirements for this house, the* **Rising Sun** *being 190 yards distance and the* **Prince Albert** *112 yards."*

The property is now a private house and the pub's old coach house, stables and yard still remain and form part of the premises owned M&D Repairs garage in Water Street.

Sir Sydney Smith, 115-117 (117) Beach Street, Deal

This pub was situated on the southeast corner of Beach Street and Brewer Street and opposite the Adelaide Baths – the Baths were later demolished in the 1880s, never having been a great success. The pub was named after naval hero, Sir William Sydney Smith (1764-1840).

The pub was first mentioned in an 1821 rate book showing John Wanstall as landlord, followed by Ralph Pittock in 1828 and 1839.

Jonathan Capon was licensee in the 1840s and 1850s and who, by all accounts, ran a respectable house, followed by John Marsh in 1860. However, all that changed when Joseph Maxted took over in 1861 when he managed to secure a 4am opening licence.

The pub became quite a den of iniquity, frequented by the most unsavoury of characters. In ensuing years, police were called on several occasions to

FULLY LICENSED. Phone : Deal 531.
CENTRAL POSITION ON SEA FRONT.
Noted House for Golfers and Anglers.
Accommodation for 20. Proprietor–E. T. GEORGE.

1936.

"quell riots within". There were frequent complaints of fighting, with obscene and filthy language being used, and accusations of a brothel being operated on the premises. Evidently, Maxted and his wife were heavy drinkers and fights between them were a regular occurrence. He was locked up on at least one occasion after they had exchanged blows.

In 1868, boatmen William Cribden and Edmund Hall were charged with maliciously damaging the property.

In October 1869, a local newspaper entitled *"Maxted v The Justices of Deal"* reported: *"This case came on for hearing at the East Kent Quarter Sessions at Canterbury, on Tuesday, before Lord Fitzwalter and a large number of county magistrates. It was an appeal by Joseph Maxted, landlord of the '***Sir Sydney Smith***', Beach-street, Deal, against a decision of the Mayor* *and Magistrates by which they withheld his license to sell exciseable liquors. Mr Barrow, who appeared for the respondents, said he had been instructed that the house in question was the worst conducted public-house in Deal, that the appellant and his wife were nearly always drunk, and that a girl named Maria Marsh had been kept there for the purpose of prostitution. The justices upheld the decision of the Magistrates, the appeal was dismissed, with costs against the appellant".* (The licence was however subsequently renewed on a later occasion).

2009.

Other landlords of the era included John William Reely in 1870 and Robert Jones in 1878.

In 1886, it was reported from the Deal Petty Sessions that three boys named James Frederick Friend, Alfred Buttress and Henry Constant were charged with stealing 2/7d (13p) from the till at the **Sir Sydney Smith**. *"The landlord, Mr Jones, stated that he heard a noise in his bar, and saw Friend outside the door and two other boys running down Brewer-street. PC Farrier said he took Friend and Constant into custody, and they told him that Buttress was also 'in the swim'. He went in search of him and found him at home in bed. Buttress' sister gave the witness 1/5d (7p), which she had taken from his pockets. PC Farrier took the boy into custody. Supt. Capps said that Friend had been before the Court and birched on several occasions, and Buttress was also an old offender. Friend said that Constant went into the house and knocked, and as no one came, he got on the counter, leaned over to the till and took the money, giving him (Friend) 9d (3½p), Buttress 1/4d (6½p) and keeping 6d (2½p) to himself. The magistrates ordered Constant to receive six strokes with the birch, Buttress nine strokes, and Friend twelve, the latter to be sent to St. Augustine's prison* (in Canterbury) *for 14 days, and afterwards to a reformatory for two years. They hoped the sentence would have the desired effect of teaching certain boys in Deal that they must not give way to habits of theft."*

GT Pledge was the landlord in 1908 and, in 1910, the pub was threatened with closure when G Harlow was at the helm. However, it was decided that its *"expanding trade should be encouraged"* as it was reportedly selling 2½ barrels of beer and between 2 and 3 gallons of spirits every week. He also provided coffee, cheese and small loaves for *'halfpenny lodgers'* between 6am and 7am.

By 1911, however, the pub was still struggling to keep its licence since it was reported that there were five other public houses within 147 yards of the premises, excluding the **Royal**, with its main clientele comprising boatmen. Francis Stag Adams, the owner of the sea bathing machines sited opposite the pub, stated that *"the Sir Sydney Smith provided a service to bathers who often needed reviving after bathing."* While the nearby **Napier** and **Horse & Farrier** pubs closed, the **Sir Sydney Smith** managed to survive, even though it had the smallest premises of them all at the time.

In April 1916, landlady, Ada Jane Redman was charged with serving out of hours (while her husband was evidently serving on HMS Newmarket during WWI). She was fined £2.

By the 1930s, the pub had expanded to encompass the next door property at no 115 Beach Street to accommodate the ever increasing tourist trade. Ernest Thomas George was landlord from 1935 to 1944 when, it appears, the pub shut its doors for the last time after the pub was seriously bomb damaged.

Deal Borough Coucil asked the Thompson & Son brewery to transfer the licence to the Astor Hall, which was duly carried out, so long as the transfer contained a covenant (left over from the days of Hill's brewery) that alcohol was not to be made or sold on the premises. Thompsons agreed to sell the licence for £400, provided all malt liquors were bought from them. The bar and other fixtures and fittings were sold for £400.

The pub has now reverted to two separate residential houses.

OS map 1872.

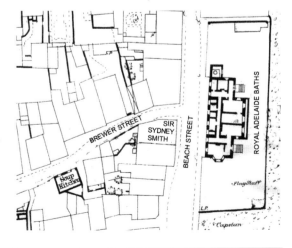

South Eastern Hotel

See entry for the *Queens Hotel* (2).

South Foreland, 1 (80) Beach Street, Deal

2009.

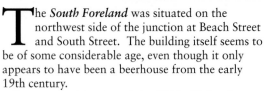

2009

The *South Foreland* was situated on the northwest side of the junction at Beach Street and South Street. The building itself seems to be of some considerable age, even though it only appears to have been a beerhouse from the early 19th century.

From some time around the 1830s, Richard Redman ran an unnamed beerhouse on this spot and remained there until at least 1852. HW Spears was the landlord in 1854 and 1855 but, the following year, the pub was unlicensed. In 1858, James Knight was licensee, followed in 1859 by Mrs Ann Baker, the former landlady of the *Ship/Seagull* in Beach Street (see entry for *Clarendon*). While in office, the theft of her shawl was considered newsworthy enough to make the local paper! The following year, she was charged with selling spirits and fined £12/11 (£12.55), with £1/17/6 (£1.87½) costs, and her licence to sell beer was made null and void.

The property was sold by auction at the *Walmer Castle* pub in March 1861. The particulars described it as *"A beer shop called the South*

Foreland in Beach Street, facing the street and near the Naval Yard. Parlour, Bar, Sitting Room, Kitchen, Four Bedrooms and Large Yard with back entrance to Crown Court in rear. Annual rent £15 (for 21 years), plus 2 shillings (10p) *and 4/9d* (23½p) *for redeemed Land Tax in 1857"*. Edward Austen took over the helm later that year, and it was last mentioned by name in an 1869 local newspaper.

At some point during its history, the house also operated as a brothel. According to recent information, there used to be a booth on the ground floor where it is thought clients would pay the 'madam' before ascending the stairs. A two way mirror was affixed to one of the internal walls. It's possible the 'madam' also entertained customers herself. It appears her ghost is still up to her old tricks. Apparently, overnight male guests at the now very respectable and private home claim they have been *rudely* awoken from their sleep by her presence!

The *South Foreland* is now a private house. See also entry for *North Foreland*.

South Infantry Canteen
(location unknown) Walmer

These licensed premises appeared in the Walmer Alehouse book so therefore qualify for insertion in this book. The *South Infantry Canteen* was named in directories in 1811 with Thomas Carter as landlord, John Marshall in 1812, Thomas Simmons in 1813 and Ralph Pittock from 1816 to 1817.

Although its location is unknown, it was possibly an on-site drinking establishment for the military situated within South (Cavalry) Barracks since there was a similarly named concern called the *North Infantry Canteen* which, by implication, may have been located in North Barracks.

Sovereign
off Primrose Hill, Deal

The *Sovereign* was situated in a courtyard leading out of Broad Street and into the alleyway known as Primrose Hill, according to 1675 documentation.

In Constant Woodman's Will of 1679 she bequeathed *"To my niece Susan Bourne wife of Sampson Bourne all that messuage called by the name of The Sovereign together with stables etc now occupied by Sampson Bourne ... Also all that other messuage near the Sea Valley occupied by William Pierce"*. It was still documented as being a pub of this name in 1699 when an accompanying stable also comprised part of the premises.

A Conveyance dated 8 May 1750 described the property as *"all that tenement (then and now divided into three parts) commonly known by the Name of the Sign of the Sovereign with*

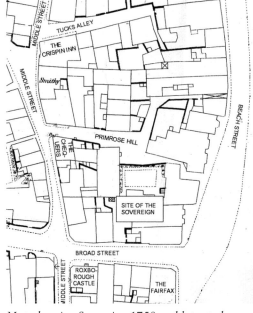

Map showing Sovereign 1750 and later pubs.

appurtenances (being part of the Archbishop's Waste)". This was the last documentation indicating the use of the building as licensed premises.

One of the three tenements was later used as a primary school in 1802 and another had become a printers by 1885. Giraud ran the printing business initially, later followed by the Pain family.

The entire premises were bought for £650 by Deal Corporation in 1930. The accompanying conveyance stated that *"there is some vestige of a blocked-up vault or passage. The vendors would be willing to convey all subterranean vaults, passages and smugglers holes, if any, which are now vested in them and enjoyed by them as appurtenances to the property."*

The three buildings were demolished after WWII and their sites are now covered by Middle Street car park, although it is difficult to pinpoint their exact location.

Spread Eagle (exact location unknown)
High Street (Lower Street), Deal

This pub only had a passing mention in an 1852 document but otherwise remains untraceable.

St George

See entry for *Saint George*.

Stag (Duke of Wellington), 7 The Strand, Walmer

According to the pub's history displayed on the wall of the *Stag*, the building was erected in 1715, originally comprising two separate dwellinghouses, both owned by Isaac Vincent, a Captain in HM Royal Navy. However, confusion abounds since, according to contemporary maps, there did not appear to be a building on the site during the first half of the 18th century. It was originally known as the 'Stagg Ayle Shoppe' and most of the early proprietors were pilots as well as having other occupations.

The first documentary evidence found by the authors dates back to 1815 when the pub was known as the *Duke of Wellington*, with William Beal (formerly at the *Good Intent*, Walmer) as landlord.

EDWARD BURKE. "STAG HOTEL" Facing the Sea Apartments
Proprietor. Strand, Walmer

1906.

Other licensees included Thomas Davies in 1819, Christopher Goodwin in 1821 and Henry Snelling from 1822 (until 1847). What had originally been two properties united in to one building in 1832. It was referred to as being *"at the sign of the Stag"* in 1835. A vessel called 'The Stag' sank off the coast of Deal in 1728 which may explain the, albeit much later, name for the pub.

Later landlords included John Reynolds in 1855 and James Mackins in 1858. On 7 October 1860, it was reported that three soldiers forced open the door and entered the *Stag*. A coastguard secured the door and went for help. The soldiers were sent to Sandwich Gaol and then on to Maidstone Assizes. In 1867, Mackins was charged with keeping the pub open *"during the hours of Divine Service."* However, the charge was dropped when it was explained that the customers at the time were fishermen who had just landed 11,000 mackerel and were therefore in great need of refreshment!

By 1871, the landlord's name was listed as John Thomas Mackins (and he remained at the pub until 1882).

In September 1876, the Mercury reported the

"Sudden Death of a Marine: An inquest was held at the *Stag* Inn, Walmer, on 4th October, to enquire into the circumstances attending the death of Stephen Tole, aged 26, a private in the Royal Marines stationed at Walmer, who died on Monday evening as he was being conveyed by the picket in a drunken state from Deal to the Royal Marine Barracks. After lengthy evidence the Jury returned as their verdict 'Death from natural causes', and accompanied the same with a recommendation that the Military authorities have a proper stretcher provided with straps, etc, for use on such occasions, and that it be kept at the police station or some other suitable place in the town where it could be got at with facility, also that in future no picket should be permitted to carry a man with face downwards."

The *Stag* was owned by John Hatton, *"Brewer and Maltster"*, in 1877, followed by brewer, George Beer, in 1882. The Mercury reported in March that year that Mackins and three other local men had been released from St Augustine's Prison in Canterbury after a three month period of incarceration following sentences for bribery. The article continued: *"They were met by a large number of their friends, and proceeded by train to Deal. A number of flags were hoisted in different parts of the town and guns were fired on the beach as they reached their homes. Flags flew from the masts of all the boats at Walmer, and a cannon gave Mr Mackins a thundering salute as he reached the portals of his house, the Stag Inn."*

William Jenner was landlord for a few months in 1887. However, by the December, a local newspaper advertisement read: *"To Let with immediate effect – Stag Inn, Lower Walmer. Apply Dover Brewery Company"*. The advert was repeated in the January and February 1888 editions. The licence was subsequently transferred from William Whitcombe (of the Dover Brewery Company) to James Trollope in March that year.

Later licensees included John Mercer in 1890, Thomas Nash in 1898 and Horace Young in 1902. In 1906, a shy and retiring Edward Burke announced in the local newspaper that he *"wishes to notify his numerous friends that he has re-taken possession of The Stag Hotel, Walmer, and would be glad to meet them."*

By 1908, FJ Gillespie had taken over, followed by Robert Gallway the same year, and Edward Thomas Hill in 1909.

2006.

In February 1913, the *Stag* was referred to the Compensation Committee for possible closure. It was argued that, although there were five other pubs nearby, the *Stag* was *"in a good state of repair, with good sanitary conditions. Good class of trade, mainly tradesmen. Rear entrance used for Jug & Bottle [off licence] trade, access to the front of the pub only possible through partition where landlord served customers. Bar accommodation greater than that of True Briton and the Alma. Trade as good as other pubs in area. Present landlord, ET Hill … Stabling for landlord's use only. Pub belongs to Messrs Ash & Co, brewers, Canterbury. Bar trade 124 barrels per year, 128 gallons of spirits, 20 gallons of wine. Only Ash house in Walmer. 1½d (1p) per glass beer, 5d (2p) a quart."*

William Upton was landlord in 1914, followed by FW Holland in 1915, Mrs Minnie Cooke in 1918, Sidney J Bottle in 1923, Herbert Harcourt Smith in 1924, John William Fellows in 1930, Charles F Castle in 1934, Jesse Butcher in 1937, James Butcher in 1938 and Henry Edward Tomkinson also in 1938. The pub temporarily closed from August 1940 until November that year when the licence was transferred to the Company Secretary at Mackeson & Co.

Thomas Newton Stammers took over the licence in 1944. In June 1948, Charles Ribbands, landlord of the *Antwerp*, was charged with threatening behaviour towards Stammers at the *Stag*. Ribbands was bound over for 12 months and ordered to pay the sum of £5.

Ronald Lawrence Barker was landlord in 1949, followed by James E Bridges in 1954, Charles Douglas Moonlight in 1954 and Saxon Johnson in 1957. A Mercury article dated 8 June 1967 reported that Saxon and Jennie Johnson were moving on after ten years at the *Stag*. *"Smugglers would meet their women who would hide goods under their crinolines, all in the Stag and disappear via a secret passageway to the house next door, now Lukeys [off licence], to vanish again into York Road and disappear again to the Old Forge. The Walmer mail coach used to be housed in the yard."* (Lukeys off licence is now called The Strand Wine Shop). The article posed the question: *"Why is the saloon bar floor a double one and why is the 6 inch space in between packed with broken glass?"* It may have been a form of soundproofing to deaden any 'unusual' noises from the cellars below.

According to Dover magistrates' records, Stanley E Hall became landlord in 1967 and, in January 1975, it was reported that customers had formed a human chain in order to put out a fire in the garage which had started at the rear of the pub. The contents of the garage contained old chairs, crates and paper but the customers managed to extinguish the flames before the fire brigade arrived.

John Pettit was landlord in 1976, followed by Roger Cook in 1979, John Baker in 1987, Michael Barber in 1990, Carl Reed and Sharon Bailey in 1992, Graham Ward in 1993, Stephen Johnson in November 1995 (by which time the pub was a Whitbread's house), Michael and Penny Barnes in September 1995, Michael Wood, Jane Wood and Albert Finnis in June 1999 and Anthony and Jane Willis and Albert Finnis in September 2003 (until 2010).

According to recent landlords, the pub has, or had, its own resident ghost, described as being a tall man dressed in long heavy weather clothing, perhaps reminiscent of a boatman from a bygone era. He sometimes appeared in the early morning and, at other times, last thing at night, while walking through a wall downstairs and across the bar before disappearing through another wall. Occasionally, he would take a different route and walk through the arch at the back of the pub before vanishing. The landlords also confirmed there was further activity in the cellar.

After the last landlords left in early 2010, the pub temporarily closed, but reopened again on 11 April that year. The *Stag*'s current licensees are Anthony and Jennifer Bessants and the owners are Punch Taverns.

Star

See entry for the *Empire*.

Star & Garter, 17 Oak Street & 101 & 103 (101-103/101) Beach Street, Deal

c1910.

The early history of the pub is unfortunately rather sketchy but the deeds date back to the 1780s when the property was owned by John Moore, Archbishop of Canterbury. Charles Denne (who was also licensee of the nearby *Crown*) bought the building in 1862 which he named the *Star & Garter* (signifying the highest order of knighthood in Britain) in 1864. Denne lived on the premises and ran the business as a family and commercial hotel and bottled his own spirits.

As with many other inns along the seafront, the *Star & Garter* was a popular rendezvous for local fisherman who would cook their freshly caught sprats on the open fire there while supping a few pints. The pub was also used as a meeting place for the Deal Clergy Society for over 40 years. Elizabeth Denne took over as proprietress on her husband's death in 1881 (and ran the pub until she

died at the age of 90 in 1921). In 1915, the hotel's address was recorded as no 101 Beach Street.

During Elizabeth's time there, she made the news when she prepared a *"special meal"* for Captain Matthew Webb who famously became the first person to swim the English Channel between Dover and Calais in 1875.

Elizabeth was succeeded by her eldest son, William Herbert Denne, and her daughter, Elizabeth Anne Denne. William died in 1924 and his sister carried on the business on her own until she too died in 1940. A protection order was obtained for the licence until Sarah Denne and Edward John Denne took it over later that year. Sarah died in 1946, leaving Edward as sole proprietor until he surrendered the licence in January 1948. He moved to a house called 'Bellavista' which adjoined the *Star & Garter*. Reminiscing over old times in the

Mercury in August 1948: *"Mr Edward Denne remembers the great storm in 1881, when the shutters of the hotel were blown right across the old Pier Yard – the site of Deal's first pier, a wooden one – and tiles were blown off roofs, and during the blizzard tremendous seas came up the beach, and it was a mercy the hotel did not suffer more than it did. Its firm resistance to the worst that the memorable storm gave was a fine tribute to the skill of the builder. With a smile, Mr Edward Denne recalled the days when, as a boy, he picked the barnacles off the old Deal pier, as he said good-bye to the 'East Kent Mercury' reporter who had interviewed him."*

2010.

The following advertisement also appeared in the Mercury in 1948: *"The 'Star & Garter' fully licensed residential hotel, 101 Beach Street, Deal. Now reopened to residents. Full board. Bed and Breakfast. Special Terms [for] Permanent Residents. Mrs L O'Donnell, Proprietress."*

Arthur W England was landlord in 1949 when it was reported that a former Arsenal and Scotland footballer assaulted his wife, Laura, at the premises and was fined £5 and £8/9/0d (£8.45p) costs.

By February 1952, GH Warr was landlord when he advertised *"Westerham Ales, Wines & Spirits, with First-Class Food and Well Stocked Bars"*. In December 1956, another advert appeared in a local newspaper publicising a three course business lunch for 4/6d (22½p) *"for food lovers"* daily from 12.30.

VH Monro was landlord in 1958, followed by Lionel PB Huth in 1959, Mr and Mrs Victor Filmer

in 1965 and ND Agnew in 1966, by which time the hotel's premises had been extended since its address was then known as nos 101-103 Beach Street. Graham Griffiths was landlord in 1974 (when the brewery owners were Bushell, Watkins & Smith of Westerham), followed by Glynis McKenna in 1983. The Mercury reported that year: *"Former stockbroker, Nick Tremayne, and his joint licensee, Glenys McKenna, have taken over the Star & Garter public house, on Deal's seafront. Glenys' established reputation in catering is already reflected in the menus for both restaurant and bars which feature seafoods and range from traditional Sunday lunches to bar snacks. Accommodation at the Star & Garter is fully booked for the Open golf championship, and arrangements are now being finalised to cater for a party of visiting Belgian anglers."*

According to the late David Collyer, one of the landlords told him that David Croft and Jimmy Perry, writers of (among other things) the BBC comedy series Dad's Army used to drink at the pub and did a lot of preparation work there, including writing some early episodes. It was rumoured the local area was the envisaged setting for the 1960s/1970s TV series and that the fictional name of Walmington-on-Sea was deliberately chosen to sound like a cross between 'Walmer' and 'Birchington-on-sea' (although much of the actual exterior filming took place in Thetford, Norfolk).

The late Charles Hawtrey, a local resident and 'Carry On' actor, was a frequent customer at the pub. He was not the only

c1960.

regular however, since, according to landlady, Glenys, the place also boasted its own resident ghosts. One was nicknamed 'Mrs Sullivan' who sometimes appeared in the bar area, but more often in the lobby, smartly dressed in brown tweed and "*looking stern*"! Another female apparition was seen in the kitchen, wearing a long grey-blue dress with her hair in a bun.

Glenys believed that the rear bar area was once the stable block belonging to the nearby **Swan** pub (see separate entry) that used to stand to the south of the **Star & Garter** in Beach Street.

The hotel and pub closed their doors for the final time in 2004 after Glenys decided to retire. An article headlined '*Pub Landlady Calls It A Day – But Won't Be Raising A Glass!*' appeared in the 1 April edition of the Mercury: "*Landlady Glenys McKenna has pulled her final pint and locked the bar for the last time at the **Star & Garter**. 'I will be sad to move on and I will miss all the regulars, but I had lots of good times'. Glenys is now settling into retirement*

*and missing the panorama from her old bedroom at the pub. For she enjoyed uninterrupted views of the sea from the **Star & Garter**, on the corner of Beach Street and Oak Street*". She continued: "*'I don't drink [as] I had to stay in tune behind the bar and had to be sharp, so didn't bother with alcohol'. Glenys and her late husband shared a history of running pubs and bars in Deal and Sandwich ...*".

The article went on to mention the pub was also the base for a variety of clubs and charitable groups including the Deal Chess Club, Deal Folk Club, the Hoodeners and the Guide Dogs for the Blind Association. The hotel boasted 10 bedrooms and many visitors returned each year.

Glenys added: "*The **Star & Garter** was a talking pub. We had quiet music so people could chat and there was always a bit of laughter.*"

Shepherd Neame took the decision to sell the building after Glenys' departure and it has since been divided into private houses now numbered 17 Oak Street, 2 Wood Yard and 101 Beach Street.

Star(r) (exact location unknown) Beach Street, Deal

A lease dated 1 August 1679 stated: "*William Archbishop of Canterbury to John Banks of Deal cordwinder on surrender of former Lease made to John Brames of Deal deceased, dated 13 November 1661, and 20/- (£1), tenement or dwellinghouse in Lower Deal abutting to Beach Street east to the tenement called the **Starr** north, to Edward Swaines' yard west and to the tenement demised to Ann Wakes south in the occupation of Samuel Orbell for 21 years at 1/- (5p) pa. Witnesses: T Snow and Richard Watts.*"

The **Star(r)** otherwise remains untraceable.

Station Hotel

See entry for the **Railway**, Walmer.

Strand (Black Horse Hotel, Dolphin) 36 (192) High Street (Lower Street), Deal

A potted history of the **Black Horse** prepared for the hotel went back to 1618. However, because of various inconsistencies, the authors' findings and documentary evidence "only" stretch as far back as 1658 when the hotel was called the **Dolphin** and Thomas Fitch, was registered "*Landlord and Tallow Chandler*". In 1661, he leased the premises, together with the tenement next door, from the Archbishop of Canterbury and renewed the same in 1679. Later that year, there was a **Black Horse** in the present day Broad Street – see separate entry. In 1679, there were two tenements, one called the **Dolphin**. John Moore was recorded in Sandwich Licensing Recognizances in 1661 at the **Black Horse** although no address was given so its location is unknown.

In 1720, Samuel Ffasham leased the pub. In 1727, according to the pub deeds, the **Dolphin** was still in place, with alleyways each side of tenements as before (and one at the rear). In 1735, victualler, John Baker, leased for 21 years "*a tenement or inn*" called the **Black Horse**, with the tenement used as its tap and stables in Lower Street.

To summarise, the main house appears to have been called the **Dolphin** and, in 1735 or thereabouts, it then became known as the **Black Horse**. In 1750, Sarah Friend, widow, was on the lease, followed by Edward White in 1756. The following appeared in the Kentish Post in February that year: "*Notice: To be lett at Lady-Day, the Sign of the **Black Horse** by the Market Place in Deal, being many years a Public House and now in the occupation of Edward White.*"

Mariner, William Spong, was landlord in 1788, followed by Richard Barton who had a long stay at the house from around 1792 (until 1830). The Valuation List of 1821 showed annual rates payable for the pub were £12/10/0d (£12.50p), the stables at the rear £2/10/0d (£2.50p) and chaise house opposite £2. (A 'chaise' was a type of open carriage for two people, with just a canvas type cover over the occupants). The house was a major coaching stop and a very bustling place since coaches arrived and departed at all hours of the day. Brewer, John Iggulden, owned the pub until 1822.

William Bax was landlord from 1830 (until 1845). The 1839 Pigot's Directory showed trade was still brisk, with coaches and post chaises still operating, although the advent of the railway would eventually put paid to this side of the business. (Nevertheless, as travelling further afield had become easier, the hotel later concentrated on the tourist holiday trade).

Wanley Holton was landlord from 1847 to 1855 (during whose time brewer, Edward Iggulden, was owner in 1851 when the leases came to an end), followed by George Walter Smith in 1859. From the earliest days, meetings and auctions were a feature of the inn. On 1 January 1863, the Telegram reported a *"Sale at the Black Horse – freehold house and butchers in Lower Street at corner of Duke Street. Slaughter house in Duke Street contiguous. Sold for £350 (formerly the property of J. Knoll Parker)"*. Later that year, John Thomas Outwin owned the licence (also running the **Clarendon** and later other houses including the **Walmer Castle** inn), followed by landlady, Mrs Emily Punnett in 1874, and landlord, Henry Spurrier in 1882. Major work was undertaken in 1887 when Mr Hart was proprietor. A new wing was added at the rear incorporating a 40-foot dining room seating between 60 and 70 people, amounting to 23 rooms in total. The work was undertaken by WT Denne.

Later landlords included Alfred Ernest Banfield in 1891, John Edward Spicer in 1898, Edward David Rickard senior from 1908 to 1916 and A Gormie in the

1989.

1930s. The pub was owned by Davy & Co from the 1940s. J Barnett was landlord in the early 1950s.

According to the Mercury in September 1963, extensive alterations were carried out at the **Black Horse Hotel** and a new dining room was created from the former kitchen. During the works, a huge iron range, believed to be an original fitting, was discovered and it had been restored and placed on show. The article added that the building was believed to be over 500 years old (although this seems rather unlikely).

In February 1964, the newspaper reported that the new bar was then in its fourth and final stages of reconstruction and the former public bar, old dining room and pilots' bar had been knocked into one. Further, that a glass panel inserted in the floor showed the cellars beneath what had formerly belonged to the old Customs House (which had been sited in the building next door north for some time). The oak-framed pine carved door which lead to the cellar originally came from Deal Manor House and was also thought to be about 500 years old.

S Bushell was landlord in 1966, according to the Regency Directory. In the 1974 Deal Official Guide booklet, an advertisement appeared publicising the house: *"Black Horse Hotel, High Street, Deal. Telephone: Deal 4074. Resident Manager: Mr J. Bunyan. Free House. AA**. RAC. Central Heating. 13 Bedrooms with All Amenities, 3 with Private Bathrooms. The Black Horse offers the atmosphere and character associated with the best of English Inns. Old World Restaurant and Bar Renowned for Good Food and Good Wine. Visit the Tavern Bar. Ports and Sherries served from the Wood. The Wine Shop (attached to hotel) offers a fine selection of Wines. Davy's Wine Merchants and Shippers since 1870. London: Exeter: Hythe: Deal."*

In June 1976, the Mercury announced that Keith and Eunice Collins, together with Keith's mother, Grace, had bought the **Black Horse** from Davy & Co, and intended to give the pub, *"once Deal's Customs House"*, a new look. They hoped to reopen the 13 bedrooms and the restaurant that had been closed. In August, the Mercury was advertising *"A good night out with the Collins family"* at the **Black Horse**.

In September 1980, the Mercury reported that Keith Collins had submitted plans to demolish the **Black Horse**, which were refused, and the hotel was subsequently listed as being a building of architectural importance. Sadly, however, the interior was not listed and was changed out of all recognition. Local people remember the original bar as being low-beamed and having tremendous character.

The **Black Horse Hotel** closed in 1997 and was subsequently bought by Jays Leisure Group with the intention of keeping the ground floor as a pub and restaurant but turning the many upstairs rooms into flats. However, their application to convert the upper rooms was withdrawn since the property was Grade II listed. Following a change of name, an article in the Mercury in December 1998 stated: *"The Strand opens tonight, Thursday 10th December 1998, at 8pm. Manager, Jim Feeney. Work is underway on 16 ensuite bedrooms and the manager's flat should be completed in the New Year."*

The **Strand** comprised a modern open plan interior and was a popular late night venue for youngsters on weekends. It unfortunately closed down in 2009 and, at the time of going to press, the upstairs rooms are being converted into private residential flats for sale and part of the ground floor has become an amusement arcade-cum-coffee shop.

Sun (Three Roebucks, Three Bucks) (exact location unknown) Beach Street, Deal

Thomas Lily was the first documented landlord in 1699. In 1709, *"the sign of the Three Bucks in Lower Deal, part of the Archbishop's Waste abutting to the sea"* was mentioned in title deeds. In 1720, Anthony Glover was registered landlord of *"the Sun formerly the Three Roebucks."*

Leases continued until 1851 but how long it operated as a pub is unknown.

Sunn Inn (exact location unknown) Brewer Street, Deal

The only mention of the **Sunn Inn** appeared in Melville's 1858 Directory showing Robert Harvey as landlord. The pub otherwise remains untraceable.

Sunn Inn

See entry for the **Rising Sun**, George Street, Deal.

Swan, 93-99 (129) Beach Street, Deal

The **Swan** is historically and regularly confused with a pub of the same name in what was called Five Bells Lane (see separate entry for the **Hole in the Roof**).

The first documentation found about this pub was in 1678 when it was mentioned in the Will of Bartholomew Marsh, *"Gentleman"*, as *"all that messuage called the Swan in Deal."*

In 1681, *"John Pierce James Neale held one tenement known as the Swan and three tenements in Burn'd Alley comprising stable, etc."*

According to a lease dated 24 August 1686 from Lambeth Archives *"William Archbishop of Canterbury to Tobias Bowles of Deal, Merchant, on surrender of Lease to William Watts and Mary, his wife, and £3, tenement or dwellinghouse and garden in Deal abutting to a wagon way south, to the stable and yard of John Kerby north and to the tenement of Sarah Banes, widow, west, now or late in the tenure of Thomas Bowles and that brewhouse, storehouse, waterwell and cove in the yards called The Swan Yard abutting from the northernmost part of the Swan brewhouse to the northernmost part of the storehouse and cove and to an alley there called Burn'd Alley south and to the Middle Street west, together with the use of a wagon or court way from the corner of the Swan brewhouse up to the Beach street there east between the Swan house and the back part of the houses in Burn'd Alley (the said Tobias Bowles having a wagon or court way from the northernmost part of the Swan brewhouse up to the Swan house and so to the Beach Street there towards the east and also a 3ft way to Burn'd Alley and from there to the brewhouse towards the north)*

For 21 years at 3/- (15p). Witnesses: R Snowe and William Verrier."

By 1720, the premises also comprised a house and adjoining shop abutting Chapel Street, with Daniel and Margaret Pope as licensees, followed by John Bell in 1735, lessee, Thomas Oakley in 1736, William Pope in 1737 and lessee, Hercules Wyborn in 1777.

There were numerous residents or landlords listed in later years but it is unclear for how long it actually remained a pub (although it was still referred to in documentation as *"the Swan"* until the 1850s). Michael Elwin, a *"Gentleman"* from Dover, leased the house in 1829 (at the same time as leasing the **Three Kings**), and Stephen Pritchard (a local Justice of the Peace and author of Pritchard's History of Deal) held the lease from 1858.

The pub was demolished and the present day block encompassing 'Rhoda Houses' was built on its site in 1863 (according to the date on the front of the building). The present building now comprises various private flats.

Swan Inn

See entry for the *Hole in the Roof*.

Swans

See entry for the *Hole in the Roof*.

Swipping Boat (location unknown) Deal

The only mention of this pub appeared in Mariner, Peter Bryant's 1671 Will when he left *"to my brother Nicholas Thoroughgood the spot of land around and adjoining to the messuage called the Swipping Boat. Also to my brother Humphrey Bryant £20 and his debt of £100."*

Until the 19th century, "swipping" meant the salvaging of anchors from the seabed. However, the word fell out of use and probably the term sweeping (as in mine sweeping) was later used instead.

Sydenham Green

See entry for the *Lord Warden*, Mill Road.

April 1864: The Town Clerk produced a petition for signature in favour of closing public-houses on Sundays. Councillor Kelsey said if carried into effect the people would not be deterred from having their beer, but would get in two gallons on Saturday and get tight on Sunday. Someone suggested that the petition be laid under the table.

Tally Ho (Frederick William)
118 (144) Middle Street, Deal

The term 'Tally Ho!' brings to mind the famous cries of foxhunters when their prey is in sight. This explanation may well have something to do with the naming of the pub but, in this instance, the authors believe it not to be the case. On 8 May 1830, newspapers reported that *'The Independent Tally-Ho'*, a four-in-hand coach, broke the record for travelling 109 miles between Birmingham and London in seven hours and 39 minutes, averaging a speed of 14mph. This might explain why the first mention of the **Tally Ho** alehouse by name appeared on a transfer deed dated shortly thereafter, on 25 January 1831, from Thomas and Elizabeth Pain when selling *"the messuage and premises in Middle Street"* to Henry Elvery and James Wise, a builder.

2009.

However, an earlier street directory from 1812 showed Henry West (a mariner), his wife Sarah, William Elvery, John West (a butcher) and Henry Gammon West (also a mariner) all living at 144 Middle Street in what was probably then just a private residential house. Local artisan, Charles Finn discovered the name *'Valentine West'* and the date *1747* inscribed in the lead while undertaking repairs to the roof in 2007, together with the outline of a footprint and the initials *RW* written alongside and a date of *'1779'*. RW may possibly have been another member of the West family.

George Turner was listed as a *'Beer Retailer'* at the property in an 1830s' street directory, but no pub name accompanied the listing (although, as mentioned above, the building had become known as the **Tally Ho** alehouse by 1831). By 1859, Turner had added *'Shop Keeper'* to his title and, in 1861, he was registered as a *'Greengrocer and Beer Retailer'*.

In 1865, A Taylor took over the licence, followed by Mrs Anne Turner in 1866 and John Marsh in 1872 until at least 1879. The pub was sold for £175 in 1882.

On 10 January 1884, licensee, Michael Kelly, changed the pub's name to the *Frederick William*. Prince Frederick William had lived a century earlier and was the youngest brother of King George III so the pub was possibly named after him, although it may equally just have been the name of a Kelly family member. Perhaps the most logical explanation, however, is that it was named after the famous 'Prince Frederick William' mail steamer from the 1850/60s. Whatever the reason, the pub was only known by that name for two months (surely something of a record!) since, on 6 March 1884, a new landlord, Mr Simmonds, changed the name back to the **Tally Ho**. In February 1886, the premises were advertised as a *"Small beerhouse to let. The **Tally Ho**. Rent: £10.00. Comfortable House. Income: from £50 to £60. Apply on the Premises or to Messrs Gardner's Ash Brewery."* Alfred Miller was at the helm when he transferred the licence to Frederick Newing Moat in October 1886. In 1887, Moat transferred it to Priscilla Hardy and she in turn passed it to Edward Richardson in 1888. Later landlords included Grove Ralph Norris in 1889, John Jordan in 1897, Georgina Emily Jordan later the same year, James Edwin Redman in 1904 and Frederick W Mills in 1905. The Mercury reported in December 1909 that a fire broke out in a private room at the pub. Thanks to a newly installed electrical alarm system, the fire brigade soon arrived and were able to extinguish the flames before too much damage had been done.

John Roberts took over in 1910 when it was noted that the rateable value of the premises was £12/10s (£12.50) and the annual rent was £12.

The pub closed on 30 June 1910 when it was referred to the Compensation Committe after becoming another victim of the 1904 Licensing Act.

The **Tally Ho** is now a private house.

Tangier Arms

See entry for the *Margate Hoy*.

Telegraph
1 Hamilton Road (Cemetery Road), Walmer

In May 1903, the Thompson brewery proposed the building of a pub on the corner of Cemetery and Telegraph Roads at a cost of £1,120. A licence was granted on condition that those held for the **Lord Nelson** in Short Street and the **Empire** (formerly the **Paragon/Star**) in Middle Street be surrendered and that the pubs closed within one month, ie before building of the **Telegraph** had been completed.

2006.

James Vincer Pilcher was the first landlord in January 1904 and, on his death in 1912, his wife, Elizabeth, took over the licence.

In 1936, landlady, Elizabeth Ingleton, transferred the licence to Harry Ingleton, followed by Robert George Hayman in January 1937, CL Holland in November 1942 and John Leslie Bilton from 1944 to 1948.

A local newspaper article dated 30 January 1948 stated that there had only been one male person present (apart from the landlord presumably), a Mr Parfitt, the piano player, at the 'Ladies Night' which had recently been held at the pub. A Pyrex dish and a silver shield were presented to Mrs Bilton as "*a mark of the high esteem in which you are held*", and her husband, John, the landlord, apparently concurred!

Later landlords included Andrew Morgan in late 1948, John J Hanley and his wife, Annie, in 1953, DM Ruse from 1953 to 1956, Cyril and Catherine Morgan from 1961 to October 1987, Brian Mainwaring in 1987, Charles Johnson in 1990 and Malcolm Morrison in 1993.

In February 2005, according to an article in the Mercury, the floral displays of landlady, Maggie Williams, had been so impressive the previous summer that she was awarded 'Hanging Baskets/Small Garden of the Year' winner by the pub's brewery, Shepherd Neame, and was she presented with a plaque and £250 worth of gardening vouchers.

The current landlord is Robert Hutson. The pub remains open for business in the meantime and boasts a thriving pool team and four darts teams!

Thompson(s) Bell (George & Dragon)
335 Dover Road (Walmer Street, High Street, Turnpike Road), Walmer

This pub possibly started off life as an unnamed beerhouse before becoming the *George & Dragon*, when licensees included several members of the Watson family over a period of 150 years or so. Thomas Watson was recorded as landlord in 1674, followed by Thomas Simmonds and brewer, Mr Ffasham, in 1681, Mr Stringer in 1700, Sarah Watson, "*Widow*", in 1766, Henry Watson in 1780, Sarah Watson in 1797 (until at least 1839), Sarah Stringer, "*Publican*", in 1841, George Tanton, "*Licensed Victualler*", in 1845, Edward Stephen Parker in 1855, Henry Carlton, "*Pork Butcher*", in 1858, Walter Carlton in 1882, Mrs H Williams in 1891 and Robert Berridge, "*Proprietor*", also in 1891, when the house was advertised as serving "*Refreshments of the Best Quality. Dinners, Teas, etc.*"

Edward Castle took over in 1898, followed by George Herbert Ash in 1908, GW Cotton in 1910, Sylvan Woodward in 1913, Mrs Louisa Richards in 1916, Mrs George Richards in 1918, Charles Limeburner 1922 and Walter A Cole in 1930.

In March 1937, the pub was referred to the Compensation Committee for possible closure. Its accompanying report stated: "*Landlord Walter Ashley*

c1957.

Cole since September 5th 1927; 8 changes since 1902; 4 licensed rooms on ground floor; 3 large double bedrooms and a large upstairs room used as sitting room. No letting trade. Sanitary arrangements only fair". However, the pub remained open.

Mrs Edith Wilmott was landlady in 1945, followed by EE Elliot in 1956 and Frederick and Dorothy Fagg in 1964. It was announced on 21 May 1973 that the pub had changed its name to the **Thompson(s) Bell** at the suggestion of Bass Charrington (who had taken over the Thompson brewery). (The pub is variously referred to as either the **Thompson Bell** or **Thompsons Bell**).

It was reported at the time that the 90lb bell, which had originally hung in the brewery, used to be housed on the bar counter of the pub. These days, however, a smaller replica now hangs in the entrance to the bar.

(The Thompson & Son brewery was established by Edmund Thompson around 1820, although it is believed that a brewery had stood on the site for a long time before then. Its premises were situated about 100 yards south of – and on the opposite side of Dover Road from – the pub. The South Foreland lighthouse was depicted as the company's trademark on all of its bottles. Charringtons took over from Thompsons in 1951, the brewery itself closed down around 1974 and most of its buildings were demolished in 1981).

Margaret Durras took over from the Faggs in 1977, followed by Stefan Pollard and Dineke Vogels in 1984. In April 1998, the Dover Express carried an article entitled *"You're the best bar none, chuck!"* stating that

customers at the **Thompson(s) Bell** had jokingly renamed the pub the 'Free Deirdre Arms' after Granada TV's 'Coronation Street' character of Deirdre Barlow (then known as Deirdre Rashid), played by actress, Anne Kirkbride, was sent to prison for 18 months. The article stated that the landlords *"have joined a campaign to free Deirdre … by draping a banner over the pub's real sign. They vow it will stay there until Granada soap writers write her release into the scripts. Mrs Vogels, 34, said: 'When Deirdre was arrested one of the regulars asked us if we were going to campaign for her release. We decided to rename the pub The Free Deirdre Arms until she's freed.'*

James Feeney took over as landlord in 2007, and the pub is currently owned by Punch Taverns.

2006.

Three Bucks

See entry for the *Sun*, Beach Street.

Three Castles (location unknown) Deal

Butcher George Roby's 1691 Will referred to *"a messuage known as 'The Sign of The Three Castles'"* (an obvious reference to the local Deal, Walmer and Sandown Castles) but, other than this, no other mention of it can be found.

Three Compasses 129 (146) Beach Street, Deal

c1920.

2009.

Historically, on naval ships, three compasses would be located, one on each deck. However, three compasses were also symbolic of carpentry guilds and, on this occasion, an engraving for one of these guilds can be found above the entrance door.

The **Three Compasses** is situated on the corner of Beach Street and Coppin Street and a former smuggling run apparently still exists at the top of the building, which allowed contraband to be spirited away across the rooftops of neighbouring properties. It was described some years ago as being *"just one of the seafront taverns used by the smugglers as a front for their illegal activities. It possesses a large brick shaft, through which the smugglers made their way to the rooftop, and thence to freedom, hauling their spirits up after them, while the Excise men searched the building in vain"*. However, the authors have unfortunately uncovered no evidence to suggest that the building operated as a "tavern" before the mid 1860s, by which time smuggling had more or less died out.

On 15 September 1866, referring to an apparent refusal to grant a spirits licence to the pub, a letter addressed to the editor of a local newspaper stated: *"In the **Three Compasses**, I find there are no fewer than 14 beds, two modern water-closets, urinals and a supply of water commensurate with the wants of the inmates.*

*What makes the rejection of this application for a licence more striking is the fact that a licence was granted to the **Waterman's Arms** – a house every way disproportionate as to accommodation to the **Compasses**. (signed) A. Citizen."*

The Kent & Sussex Directory and Licensing Records for 1867 show that the pub was owned by *"Alfred Kingsford, brewer, of Buckland next Dover"*, and Elizabeth Richardson Myhill applied for, and was granted, a spirit licence that year. According to a local newspaper, Henry Wood transferred the licence of the pub at no 146 Beach Street to William Appleton who was landlord from 1870, followed by Harry Barrett in 1884 and John Thomas Outwin from 1886 to 1890.

In 1890, the house was closed for four to five months owing to the bankruptcy of the resident tenant. An application for a new licence was refused following complaints from local residents. One witness said, *"I live in Beach Street, immediately opposite the **Three Compasses**. The behaviour of the inhabitants of Coppin Street has been a great nuisance to Beach Street. It is from fighting and drunkenness, bad language and disorderly women. The house next to mine has been vacant for some years. The neighbourhood has been respectable since the house was closed"*. Following an adjournment of the hearing, however, the licence was eventually granted and transferred. Over the following five years, it seems that the pub was spasmodically shut for at least three of them, but the brewery usually managed to have a tenant installed in order to keep the licence 'alive'.

William Wyborn became landlord of the *Three Compasses* at what had by then become known as no 129 Beach Street (due to street renumbering) but the pub closed down on 12 October 1894. Wyborn twice applied for, but was refused, a renewal of the licence in June and August of 1895 as the neighbours opposed the application for a new tenant because of the many complaints of drunkenness and indecent behaviour received by the police. The authorities deemed that the *"house was not required by the public"*. However, when the matter was appealed at the Quarter Sessions on 3 September that year, the application proved successful and the licence was renewed.

According to Pain's Directory, John Edwards was in charge from 1898 to 1905, John W Robinson from 1909 to 1911 and Mrs Emily J Hall in 1918. An advert from that year read: *"Boats of all descriptions for hire"* (from the pub). In the April, Mrs Hall was fined five shillings (25p) for allowing a light to be seen from the road during a blackout. In 1919, the licence was transferred to her daughter, Claire Edith Johnson.

Later landlords included W Lock in 1921, JG Allen in 1933, Thomas Swift in 1936, WP Loughlin in 1938, I and JT Matthews in 1956, long-serving William and Iris Brett from 1962 until 1982 when Norman McSloy took over, Klaus and Friederika Mayr in 1989 and Nicholas Barbasiewicz in 2008.

The *Three Compasses* is a free house and remains open to this day, operating as a restaurant and bar.

Three Feathers (exact location unknown) Deal

In his 1674 Will, Stephen Pearce left to his grandchild, Mary Crossby, after his wife's demise, *"the northernmost part of the cellar or low room and chamber of the house called the Three Feathers where Mitchell Iriginne is living."* Unfortunately, nothing more is known about the pub.

Three Feathers (location unknown)

The *Three Feathers* was the heraldic symbol of Sir Edward Woodstock (1330-1376), who was the eldest son of Edward III, and better known as the Black Prince. He was the first English Prince of Wales.

In his 1674 Will, after the demise of his wife, Stephen Pearce bequeathed to his grandchild, Mary Crossby, *"the northernmost part of the cellar or low room and chamber of the house called the Three Feathers where Mitchell Iriginne is living."*

Unfortunately, nothing more is known about the pub.

Three Horseshoes
(exact location unknown) Broad Street, Deal

Three horseshoes was the heraldic symbol of the Worshipful Company of Farriers. This pub was located on land that now forms part of Broad Street. According to the Sandwich Recognizances Payments for Signs list, William Teale was resident in 1662 and, in 1664, the licence was transferred to Mary Estes, spinster. In the 1668 Will of brewer, Richard Bridger (who also owned the *Blewbore/Blue Boar*), he left to his daughter, Sarah, *"my house called the Three Horseshoes and the*

buildings, yards and appurtenances until my grandchild, Mary Estes, reaches the age of 21". This was the last mention of the pub by name.

In 1777, Thomas Peck, *"Surgeon"*, George Leith, and *"Gentleman"*, John May, were named as lessees. The leases expired in 1801 and the premises were perhaps demolished as part of a road widening exercise when Broad Street was named that year. (The street was named after a local baker called Broad).

Three Horseshoes
(exact location unknown) North End, Deal

According to a 1662 document, *"John Poole sold to Thomas Swaine, husbandman, a messuage, malthouse at or near North End* now or late of Thomas White (called the *Three Horseshoes)."* No other information could be found about this pub.

Three Horseshoes

See entry for the *Liverpool Arms.*

Three Kings (Upper Deal)

See entry for the *Liverpool Arms.*

Three Kings

See entry for the *Royal Hotel.*

Three Marines (location unknown) Deal

The *Three Marines* is mentioned in a list of 1680 Deal inns but is otherwise untraceable. (The name could possibly have been a corruption of *Three Mariners*).

Three Mariners

See entry for the *Three Marines.*

Three Roebucks

See entry for the *Sun,* Beach Street.

Three Tuns (location unknown) "Deale"

This was mentioned in Laker's 1680 list of Deal inns by name only but otherwise remains untraceable.

True Britain

See entry for the *Lifeboat,* The Strand, Walmer.

True Britannia

See entry for the *Lifeboat,* The Strand, Walmer.

True Briton

See entry for the *Lifeboat,* The Strand, Walmer.

True Brittons

See entry for the *Lifeboat,* The Strand, Walmer.

Trumpett & Banner (location unknown) Deal

This pub was mentioned in the 1662 Deal Payment for Signs List when Richard Davies was landlord, but which otherwise remains untraceable.

Tube

See entry for the *Academy Sports Bar.*

Two Brewers

See entry for the *Empire.*

Two Brittons

See entry for the *Lifeboat,* The Strand, Walmer.

Unicorn
(exact location unknown) Beach Street, Deal

The *Unicorn* was one of several public houses in Deal advertised for sale by auction at the *Three Kings* (now the *Royal Hotel*) on 17 September 1730 while it was in the occupation of Henry Hillgrove.

In August 1750, it was reported that a 'Deal Boat' would be for sale at an auction to be held *"at the sign of the Unicorn"* later that month.

It was last mentioned in 1776 when W Swift was landlord, and the *Unicorn* was one of 30 public houses recorded as 'refusing to billet dragoons'.

Nothing more is known about this pub and its exact location remains a mystery.

Union Flag, Deal

See entry for the *Watermans Arms*, 41 Beach Street.

Union Flag
12 The Strand (11 Walmer Road), Walmer

The 'Union Flag' is so-called when the British flag is flown on land (and the 'Union Jack' when flown at sea).

The first mention of this building appeared in 1805 when Francis Simmon(d)s (variously spelt) was resident at the house, but no pub name was mentioned until the following year when he was registered as living at the *Union Flag* public house (up to and including 1824). In 1825, John Pott was registered landlord.

It is not known how long the building remained a pub since, according to documents held by the Leith Estate, it had become a Post Office by 1848 with John F Simmons in residence, followed by Miss Honora Simmons in 1893 (by which time it was probably a private house).

Unfortunately, no other documentary evidence could be found about the pub so it was possibly quite a short lived affair. It is now a private house.

2010.

Union Tavern (exact location unknown)
possibly Union Road (Street Row), Deal

Mr Epps was registered landlord in 1868 when an inquest was held at the *Union Tavern* concerning the late James Tapper, a boatswain from the screw steamer, '*Clotilda*', which had been en route from London to Genoa. The verdict was *"Death from over-drinking of raw spirits"*. Captain W Pennington was advised by the jury to keep a watchful eye upon his rum stores for the remainder of the voyage.

The pub was probably located in Union Road since the old Union workhouse once stood on the site now occupied by St Andrew's church.

No other information could be found concerning this pub.

Velvet Underground

See entry for the *Academy Sports Bar.*

Victoria Inn/Tavern/Tap (Wheatsheaf)
36 (14) Gladstone Road (South Ropewalk), Walmer

This was one of two pubs situated next door to each other for a short period (the other being the *Royal Marine* beerhouse – see separate entry), both of which being fraternised by servicemen stationed at East Barracks on The Strand since there was a conveniently sited passageway opposite the pub leading out of the Barracks called Guards Passage.

2006.

The first mention of the property by name was as the *Wheatsheaf* beerhouse in September 1866 when Thomas Jull applied for a full licence, but this was refused. After several more attempts, his wife, Eliza, applied for - and was granted - the licence in 1871. By 1875, George Hunt was landlord and he renamed the house the *Victoria Inn* (sometimes also called the *Victoria Tavern*).

In 1887, the new landlord, Thomas Randall, was accused of assaulting Andrew Gilchrist, but the case was dismissed. He stayed at the inn until at least 1891. In 1893, the landlord was accused of serving drinks after hours and was fined £2, with 7/6 (37½p) costs.

In 1894, licensee, Edwin Mose, was granted a time extension for an old soldiers' dinner held at the pub.

In 1901, the pub was referred to in a directory as being called "*The Victoria Tap*", and, in 1905, the licence was transferred to William David Spears who remained until 1938. Mrs D Spears took over in 1939 until 1940 and, on her death, the licence was briefly transferred to her daughter, Miss LM Spears. In 1944, Lilian Margery Timblick was listed as landlady and she remained at the pub until 1971 when it closed. According to a former customer, the *Victoria* had become "*a quiet pub, mainly for locals*" in its latter years. The building is now a private house.

Victoria Commercial (location unknown) Upper Walmer

The site of the *Victoria Commercial* Inn is unknown but there is a possibility that it may have been a previous name for the house known as the *Rattling Cat* – see separate entry.

In 1856, the owner was Mr Gardner and his tenant was William Pierce. (Gardners was a brewery around this time and assuming it is the same person, Pierce had previously run several other pubs in the local area). The inn was mentioned in a report of a court case in the Deal and Walmer Telegram dated 16 September 1865 when it stated that a woman had been attacked by a Marine outside South Barracks. She had apparently been en route to the "*Victoria Commercial Inn in Upper Walmer*" at the time.

In a separate court case during the 1860s, the plaintiff gave his address as the "*Victoria Commercial Inn, Upper Walmer*". Once again, the name of the road is not mentioned.

According to the Poor Rate book of 1866, the landlord was listed as Robert Moore Hodgetts. The inn was owned between 1865 and 1867 by Mr Beazley (a former landlord of the *Lord Nelson* pub in Deal), and it offered overnight accommodation, and included tea gardens. Unfortunately, no other documentary evidence has been found about the inn.

Victory

See entry for ye *Old(e) Victory.*

Volunteer

See entry for the *Cinque Ports Volunteer.*

Walmer Castle, 4 South Street, Deal
(originally 2 High Street – formerly Lower Street – Deal)

The first mention of the site of what was to become the original *Walmer Castle* was found in records of land and properties owned by the Archbishop of Canterbury from 1675 to 1851.

According to a potted history to be found inside the pub, the *Walmer Castle* dates back to 1661 when Elias Mockett ran the inn, followed by the Widow Mockett in 1704 (and their son, Joshua, until his death in 1737).

The *Walmer Castle* was a coaching inn situated on the north-west corner of South Street, which was then a busy terminus for horse-drawn passenger and mail coaches (as indeed it remains so for present-day buses and coaches). In 1804, the inn also had its own tap house and although both premises were registered that year as being the same public house, they each had their own landlords: William Salmon at the inn and Francis Baynes at the tap.

Erasmus Sympson was landlord in 1812, followed by Elizabeth Sympson in 1828, Eliza Jane Sympson in 1843, George Goundry in 1853 and George Bradman in 1854 and William Cooke in 1858.

In 1860, three soldiers were fined 12 shillings (60p) and costs of 4 shillings (20p) or 21 days' hard labour for breaking up the tap room.

William Jarman was registered landlord in 1861, followed by George Harrison Rolfe in 1863. In 1867, landlord, Mr W Jewitt, advertised: *"Livery and Bait, Stables, Coaches to and from Dover 3 times a day"* at the hotel.

In October 1867, a fire broke out at the back of the pub around 3am one morning. The Royal Marines fire brigade arrived 45 minutes later but their hose caps would not fit the town mains. Deal had no fire engine of its own at the time and messengers were sent to seek assistance from those at Dover and Sandwich. By the time help arrived, the blaze had taken full control and none of the building could be saved, although fortunately no injuries or loss of life were reported. The local newspaper

Site of second building, now Lloyds TSB 2010.

reported that, although Mr Wilkins, the next door tailor, was not insured, his furniture and effects had been saved; the *Windsor Castle* pub, ran by Robert Redman, had been fully insured and was only slightly damaged; and Mr Jewitt, the *Walmer Castle*'s landlord had been fully insured but the brewery owner, Mr Hills, had not!

The new *Walmer Castle* was rebuilt on the same site – at a cost of "£1,698/19/6" (£1,698.97½) – and works were completed by 1870 when Thomas Gould became landlord.

Gould was followed by John Barrowcliffe Albury in 1871 (when the *Walmer Castle* became known as a 'commercial inn'), John Thomas Outwin in 1872 and James Adams in 1874. A local newspaper, reporting from the Petty Sessions, related that: *"Mr James Adams, landlord of the 'Walmer Castle' Hotel, applied for a temporary light refreshment licence for the Deal and Walmer Skating Rink in South-street. Agreed – the Magistrates informing the applicant that they would have pleasure in rendering him all the assistance in their power"*. (See also separate entry for the *Rink*).

In 1876, the following appeared in a local newspaper: *"It is gratifying to observe that this conspicuous building* at the South-end of the town is again occupied, and will shortly be opened for business by Mr Adams of London, to whom we wish every success."* [*This was possibly a building serving the *Rink*].

Around the same time, a local advertisement declared: *"Walmer Castle Inn, Deal. Opposite Dover Road. First Class Accommodation. Billiards, Good Beds and Stabling."*

John George Bishop became landlord in 1877.

According to the pub's own history, William Matthews was landlord from 1878. A horse apparently ran loose into the pub and careered into the bar, trampling the poor man to death. Matthews' ghost supposedly haunts the building to this day.

After a temporary closure, an application to reopen the *Walmer Castle* hotel was agreed on 25 September 1880.

Before the coming of the railway to Deal in 1847, according to a 20th century article from the Mercury, *"there was a coaching service operated by a Mr Bates, and then Mr S Olds. The coach was known as The Clarence, which used to start and finish from the Walmer Castle Hotel in South Street. In those days the … Hotel stood where there is now Lloyds Bank."*

Alfred Weston became landlord in 1882, followed by William Henry Little in 1886, Edward Brown in 1888, Paul Alex Schurig in 1891, Henry Louis Ravensburg in 1892 and Thomas Henry Denny in 1893. Later that year, an auction notice for the building stated:

"Short Notice of Sale (in consequence of the serious indisposition of the Proprietor). 'Walmer Castle' Hotel, Deal.

Messrs Richard Rowbotham & Co have received instructions to submit to Auction upon the Premises, on Monday, March 20th, 1893, at 12 o'clock punctually (unless previously disposed of), the Lease of the Premises and adjoining Shop, expiring June 24th, 1895, and an agreement for a further term of Seven Years at same rental. (The shop is let until March 25th, 1895, at a rental of £45 a year).

Together with the Goodwill of the Business, Stock-in-Trade of Wines, Spirits, Cigars, &c., Trade Fittings & Effects, Household Furniture, comprising brass-mounted iron French bedsteads, bedding, linen, marble-top washstands, Brussels and other carpets, Spanish mahogany sideboards, mahogany dining-tables, rosewood loo tables, card tables, chairs, chimney glasses, plated articles, kitchen requisites, and a variety of useful effects.

Note: The lease of the premises, together with the goodwill of the business, and the trade fittings, furniture, and effects, will first be offered in one Lot, and if not disposed of, will then be sold according to the Catalogue. Particulars and Conditions of Sale and Catalogues can be obtained upon the premises, of Messrs Lewin & Co, solicitors, 32, Southampton-street, Strand, WC, and from the Auctioneers, 11, Adam-street, Strand, London, WC, and at Guildford."

Site of present building c1932.

The *Walmer Castle* remained closed until Lloyds Bank took over the building on 7 March 1896.

A new building was erected at no 4 South Street and building works were completed by 1897, which is the date that appears on the top of the present-day *Walmer Castle.*

Robert William Bennett Jones appeared on the licence for the new hotel in 1895. In 1902, it was described in sales' particulars by auctioneers, West & Usher, as being a *"handsome, newly erected, fully licensed hotel … together with skating rink now known as Marine Terrace Gardens …"*. (The hotel also boasted its own stables at the rear – see below - which have since been converted into the Court Yard Oyster Bar & Restaurant in Sondes Road).

In 1904, later auctioneers' sales particulars described the *"Skating Rink, known as the Marine Terrace Gardens, overlooking the sea … the Walmer Castle Mews in the rear, consisting of four sets of excellent stabling and coach-houses, and part covered yard, and the Poulterer's & Fishmonger's Shop and House adjoining, situated in South Street, Deal … The Walmer Castle Hotel and the Rink are now in hand, the estimated Rental being £200 per annum; three sets of Stabling, Yard, and Coach-house, are let to Mrs Olds, at £60 per annum; the fourth Block of Stabling is let to Dr. Roberts, at £15 per annum; and the House and Shop is let on lease to Mr WC Reid, at £50 per annum. The whole having a valuable frontage to South-street of 247 feet or thereabouts, and a frontage to Beach-street and the Sea of 81 feet or thereabouts."*

RT Shepherd became landlord in 1904, followed by Thomas Powell in 1912. According to the pub's own history, Powell was another landlord to meet a sorry end by a horse. He was apparently kicked in the head by one and died from his injuries. His widow, Eliza, took over the pub after his death.

Numerous other landlords included John Logan in 1915, Ernest Tatner in 1921, Ernest Robinson in 1927, William E Purkis in 1934, N Purkis in 1953, William C Chaffey in 1974 (when the *Walmer Castle* was a Charrington's house), John West in 1975, Thomas Bradley in 1978, Michael Yates in 1983, Clifford Salmon in 1986, Robert Shervill and Anthony Downing in 1995, Robert Shervill and Sarah Bedford in 1996 and Brendan Richard Carrick in 2004 (until the present).

The former **Walmer Castle** at no 2 High Street (on the corner of South Street) remains a branch of Lloyds Bank. It was reported in September 2009 that several members of bank staff had, on separate occasions, heard someone walking about in empty upstairs' rooms after business hours (possibly former landlord, William Matthews?). Local legend also has it that a body was found floating in water in the cellar some years ago after the sea had flooded into the building.

Although the current **Walmer Castle** at no 4 South Street is no longer a hotel, it is a popular late night music venue, currently owned by Admiral Taverns. According to an albeit sceptical Pete, the barman, the ice machine in the basement has turned itself on and off several times, so maybe the presence from over the road at Lloyds Bank enjoys flitting between the two buildings to keep an eye on things!

Watercress Tavern (location unknown) Deal

The only mention of this pub appeared in 1787 deeds which documented *"Catherine Eleanor daughter of John and Sarah at the **Watercress** Tavern"* in Deal, although no clue to its precise location was given.

Watermans Arms (Hamburg Ensign, Union Flag, Cross Keys, Hamborough Arms, Hamborrow Arms, Hamborough Castle) (41) Beach Street, Deal

The **Watermans Arms** was situated on the eastern (beach) side of Beach Street, somewhere opposite the turnings for Oak Street and Brewer Street, and next door to the **Port Merchant** pub.

This pub was originally called the **Hamborough Castle**. (The pub's name was sometimes also mis-spelt the **Hamborrow Arms**). It was leased by William Woodman in 1661, along with two other pubs, the **Bell** in Beach Street and the **Lyon & Whelp** in Middle Street. After his death, the leases were passed to his widow, Constant Woodman, in 1680 (and the **Hamborough**

Arms had also been mentioned in her Will of October 1679). In 1727, a lease referred to it as being *"formerly the **Cross Keys**, now the **Union Flag**"*, in 1729 it was known as the **Hamburg Ensign** and, in 1763, *"the **Watermans Arms** sometimes called the **Hamburg Ensign**."*

In 1776, it was recorded in the *"Refused to Billet Dragoons"* list and, by 1780, its name appears to have settled as the **Watermans Arms**.

The pub was sold to Deal Pavement Commissioners in 1836 and eventually demolished to make way for the present day promenade.

Watermans Arms, 91 (128) Beach Street, Deal

The **Watermans Arms** was situated on the southeast corner of Chapel Street (at the junction with Beach Street).

It opened in 1866 with Frederick John Thomas Caspell as landlord. In 1873, he was fined seven shillings (35p) for *"opening during prohibited hours"*. By 1877, Henry James Caspell was in charge, followed by Leonard Roberts in 1898, Albert Andrews in 1904, JT Wratten in 1906, Mrs Anne Bassett in 1907 and George Charles Payne also in 1907. The pub was recommended for closure to the Compensation Committee in 1909 but remained open until 1911 when FW Holland was licensee.

Foreground showing site of Waterman's Arms 2009.

By the 1930s, the building was in the ownership of RS Newbury who ran the Wedgewood Dairy from the premises. The last mention of the property appeared in Pain's street directory for 1939/1940 when it was listed as housing *"amusements"*. Mr John Rogers, the father of one of the authors, recalls the building as being double fronted.

The property was demolished in 1954 as part of a road widening scheme. The empty site can be found on the opposite site of the road behind the **Royal Hotel** and in front of the large house on the corner of Chapel Street.

Wellesley Arms, 48-50 (44) Dover Road, Walmer

Site of Wellesley Arms c1920.

The **Wellesley Arms**, named after Arthur Wellesley, the Duke of Wellington and one-time Lord Warden of the Cinque Ports, was situated at the junction of the present day Cambridge and Dover Roads.

The first mention of the **Wellesley Arms** was in 1857 when landlord, Richard Rogers, *"Grocer & Cheesemonger"*, (together with his wife, Georgina), was fined £2 for *"keeping the house open during improper hours."*

William Brisley was landlord in 1859, followed by Mary Anne Hatcher in 1861. It was reported in 1863 that a mariner by the name of William Moss was charged with assaulting a soldier by the name of John Ward at the pub. He was fined 10 shillings (50p) and 17 shillings (85p) costs or 14 days hard labour. He paid the fine.

John Ferris took over in 1867. (He was noted as being one of the *"Noble 600"* who had taken part in

the Charge of the Light Brigade on 25 October 1854).

Later landlords included William H Knight in 1874, George West in 1878, Henry Hook in 1881, Charles Green in 1882 and James Henry Norris in 1899.

A magistrates' report in 1911 stated the pub was mainly used by Royal Marines and the working classes adding the landlord had a wife and six children and it had been recommended for closure five times since 1901. The report added that it was the only house in Walmer owned by the George Beer brewery at the time and £385 had recently been spent on it, although the report recommended the tap room should be *"matchboarded"*. Despite this, the **Wellesley Arms** closed down on 30 December 1911.

By 1913, it had become known as WH Wyborn's Garage and Cycle Shop. Maurice & Mark Green Carpets showroom now stands on its site.

Wellington Arms (exact location unknown)
Wellington Road (8 Cottage Row), Deal

Despite knowing its previous postal address, frustratingly, the authors have been unable to pinpoint the present-day building of the old **Wellington Arms** in Wellington Road, although it appears to have been a fairly short lived beerhouse.

In 1855, William Dewell was listed as a *"Beer Retailer"* in Cottage Row but neither pub name nor street number was recorded. Melville's street directory of 1858 showed William Bax at the *"Wellington Arms beerhouse, Cottage Row"*. In March 1860, the local

newspaper recorded that *"Mr Jowitt of the 'Wellington Arms' was present at the meeting of the Licensed Victuallers at the **Walmer Castle** public house."*

John Bax was registered as residing in Cottage Row in 1861 when his occupation was given as *"Retired Mason"* (previously recorded as being a *"Stone Mason"* in nearby Queen Street from the 1820s up until 1858).

Unfortunately, due to street renumbering and subsequent rebuilding, this pub remains untraceable.

West Gate Barracks (location unknown) Deal

West Gate Barracks in Deal appeared by name only on a list of public houses owned by brewers, Cobbs of Ramsgate, between 1808 and 1818. Because of its name, it is tempting to assume that it was indeed located inside or close by one of the local barracks but this cannot be confirmed.

Wheatsheaf

See entry for the *Victoria*.

Wheatsheafe (location unknown) "Deale"

The only reference to the **Wheatsheafe** appeared on the "Deale" Payment for Inn Signs list in 1678.

This pub remains untraceable since it cannot reliably be connected to the later **Wheatsheaf** in Gladstone Road.

White Hart (location unknown) Walmer

The only mention of this pub appeared in the Walmer Alehouse Keepers book which recorded Edward Sharpe as landlord of the **White Hart** in 1816 and 1817.

In 1818, Sharpe moved on to the **Marine Hotel** and then to the **Shield of Marshall Blucher** in 1822. The location of the **White Hart** remains unknown.

White Horse, 56 Middle Street, Deal

On 13 November 1661, Edward Cranbrook took a lease on the property in Middle Street. On 1 August 1679, Phineas Axtol, "*Gentleman*", and his wife, Ann, took over "*a tenement formerly part of premises leased to Edward Cranbrook*" and John Printon, "*Mariner*", took over the other part. By 1682, Axtol, by then referred to as an "*Innkeeper*", took "*Elizabeth Clark in apprenticeship*" and he was still registered at the property in the 1694 list of local victuallers.

In 1699, the property was still described as being in two tenements, with Thomas Dale occupying one part and Mark Turner and Edward Noakes, "*Churchwardens*", in the other.

By 1730, Thomas Dale appeared to be occupying both tenements, when his occupation was given as a "*Baker*", followed by Gabriel Drayson in 1738 and Simon Reynolds on 28 September 1757 when it was recorded that: "*... hereafter the two premises are leased together as one tenement and outhouse lately known as the **White Horse** at a rental of 21 shillings (£1.05).*"

John Miles was licensee from 1778 until 1787 and John Coleman was registered as "*Master of the White Horse public house*" in 1794, followed by John Iggulden, "*Brewer*", in 1799.

The Poor Rate book for 1804 showed Samuel Attensall as landlord of the pub "*and stable opposite*". He remained there until at least 1811

2009.

when the property was described as "*the White Horse with tenement opposite in Market Street*". By 1821, Thomas Castle was registered as landlord, although the pub remained in the ownership of John

Iggulden from the brewery company. (Pigot's directory of 1824 does not mention the pub at all. This could have been an oversight, however, since a lot of other public houses which are known to have been operating at the time also fail to get a mention in the directory for that year). 1828 Magistrates' records for the *White Horse* show a line drawn through the section where the landlord's name should have been inserted, and, in 1829, the pub is not mentioned at all in their records. It therefore seems likely that the *White Horse* closed down around that time. The final recording of the *White Horse* building by name appeared in

Hancock's Fly Proprietor's journals for 1838 and 1839.

Later businesses that operated from the building included an outfitter's shop in 1904 in the name of AS Taylor. By 1936, GS Bulbeck was proprietor of a secondhand furniture shop there, and it was later occupied by John Fish, a builders' merchant, in 1966.

The building is now occupied by Milaad Tandoori. Pillars inside the restaurant possibly suggest the property's previous incarnation as a pub, as well as the old beer flap on the pavement outside. The interior of the ground floor is also on two separate levels (indicating the original two tenements of the building).

White Horse 46 Queen Street
(1 Upper Queen Street/Queen Street West), Deal

c1955.

This pub was situated on the right hand corner of the present day Queen Street and West Street, at the junction of the approach road to Deal Railway Station.

John Castle was registered as innkeeper of an unnamed beerhouse on the site in 1847, followed by Richard B Orrick in 1849 (who gained a full licence that year).

An advertisement from 1852 read: *"Richard Orrick, White Horse Inn (near the Railway Terminus). Licensed to Hire Open and Closed Carriages. Net and Commodius Gigs, Clarences, Landaus. A Pair Horse Omnibus, etc, on the Most Reasonable Terms. Post and Saddle Horses to Let. Orders sent to the White Horse or to no 13 Middle Street will meet with immediate attention."*

c1955.

Henry Butt was landlord for most of the 1860s, followed by JH Phillips around 1869 and William Wilkins Redman in 1871 (until 1895). Redman was fined £1 for serving out of hours in 1879. He was followed by George R Withall in 1898, H Taylor in 1904 and George Henry Walker in 1908.

A Magistrates' report in March 1911 stated: *"On 5 visits by Police, they found only 20 customers. A clean house, well furnished, with respectable tenant, Alfred Ward. Trade was common travellers, cyclists, travelling trade and tradesmen. Bar was used by a great number of married people and trade was increasing."*

Mr and Mrs Charles L Hume were landlords from 1916 until 1922.

In 1926, an application was made to redevelop the *White Horse* when Bert James Hunt was landlord. This was subsequently refused. In March 1930, it was again threatened with closure since it was argued that demolition of the building would *"enable improvements to dangerous area for traffic"*. Thompson & Co, the brewery owners, applied to transfer the licence to proposed new premises to be built within the miners' estate in Mill Road (later to be called the *Mill Inn* in

what subsequently became known as Mill Hill). However, FT Beal of the nearby *Yew Tree* in what was then Mill Road (now Mill Hill) opposed the request, as did the local Temperance Society, and the application was refused.

Frederick Charles Young took over as landlord of the *White Horse* in May 1931, followed by Mrs Davis in 1944 (until 1967). Actor Roger Moore had a holiday home in Middle Street in the late 1950s/early 1960s, in his pre Bond days, and was a frequent customer.

The *White Horse* closed in 1967 and Mrs Davis campaigned (successfully, as it turned out) against objection by the police to her taking over the licence at the Sportsman in Sholden on the grounds of her advancing years (69) and the fact there had been underage drinking problems at the *White Horse*.

Douglas Tubbs describes the *White Horse* in his 1966 book *'Kent Pubs'*: *"For a warm, friendly, working class atmosphere in an old fashioned pub where the beer is good and people talk racing at lunchtime, Mrs Davis will make you welcome."*

The pub stood next door to the present day Deal Garden Centre in Queen Street and was demolished in August 1968 for road widening purposes.

White Lyon

See entry for the *Queens Arms*.

White Posts Inn

See entry for the *Fawn*.

Windmill (location unknown) Deal

According to the Sandwich Borough Records, licensed victualler, Edward Haw, paid 6/8d (33½p) plus a surety of £5 for a new inn sign for the *Windmill* in Deal in September 1662.

As no other records have been found for this pub, its location remains unknown.

Windsor Castle
6 High Street (205 Lower Street) Deal

This pub was located next door but one to the original *Walmer Castle* public house (which is now a branch of Lloyds Bank). The building used to have two stone steps from the pavement up to the entrance door.

The *Windsor Castle* opened its doors in 1855 when Robert E Redman was landlord. In 1872, the house was owned by Thompson & Co, brewers, and, in 1873, the licence was transferred to William Wilkins Redman, followed by John William Hayman in 1874, who remained there until at least 1882.

In 1885, Alfred Goslett (previously from the *Crispin Inn*) became landlord. Later that year, local butchers held their first supper at the *Windsor Castle.* By all accounts, it was a great success and it was decided to make it an annual event.

By 1899, Mrs Rosanna H Goslett took over the reins (remaining there until 1922). She was fined £1 with 8/6d (42½p) costs later that year for selling gin at four per cent below the legal strength. The *Windsor Castle* remained in the Goslett family up

c1955.

until around 1948, when it was variously run by Rosetta Goslett and George E Goslett.

Mr E Way became landlord in 1954, followed by J Ryan in 1955 and Bernard Creasey in 1956. In January 1958, the Mercury reported the unfortunate death of a soldier when he tripped and fell to his death on the steps of the pub. In March 1960, the licence was transferred from John Pearce to Jack Goodwin.

According to a report in the Mercury dated 23 July 1964: *"A man who bends 6-inch nails, hammers them through a 2-inch piece of wood and who used to introduce J Arthur Rank films with the gong, Carl Dane OBE, entertained customers at the *Windsor Castle* Hotel Friday lunchtime. Landlord, Jack Goodwin, recognised him when he called at the pub and he returned the next day."*

Goodwin remained at the pub until it closed in 1966. It was demolished around 1967 and a branch of Vye's grocers opened up in the new building erected on the plot. Part of the local Superdrug store now stands on the site.

Wine Shades, 53 (108) Beach Street, Deal

According to the dictionary, the word 'shades' describes a cool, shadowed and secluded retreat.

Wine Shades shared its history with the *Clarendon* which was located immediately next door.

The registered owner was John Thomas Outwin (formerly at the *Clarendon*) and *Wine Shades* opened for business in 1870 at a time when the *Clarendon* had temporarily closed. (The building had not previously been licensed).

Wine Shades remained open for several years since

Outwin still appeared as owner in 1882. By 1884, a licence transfer was recorded from *"Miss Mackenzie to Edmund Hartwood Tyrell"*. In 1886, *Wine Shades* became incorporated into the reopened *Clarendon*.

The former *Wine Shades* is now encompassed within the central (and lower part) of the present day *Clarendon* building.

For more background information concerning *Wine Shades*, please refer to the entry for the *Clarendon*.

Winter & Richards (exact location unknown)
High Street (Lower Street), Deal

Winter & Richards were listed as *"Retailers of Beer"* in 1832 and probably operated as a beerhouse/shop. It appears, however,

that this was a short lived operation since unfortunately no further information has been discovered.

Yarmouth Arms
(exact location unknown) Beach Street, Deal

The only mention of this pub appeared In the 1678 Will of widow, Margaret Godshon, when she bequeathed *"To Thomas Godshon my eldest son and sole executor all the messuage etc in which I now live in Lower Deal known as the* **Yarmouth Arms** *which I lease from Richard Gookin gentleman ... Also all those two capstans with the ground belonging which are standing over against my said dwellinghouse"*. (Godshon could possibly be a misspelling of 'Goodson').

Nothing nore is known about the **Yarmouth Arms** and the building is now a private house.

Possible location of the Yarmouth Arms – 2010.

Yarmouth Packet
195 (180) Beach Street, Deal

The Yarmouth Packet was situated on the northeast corner of Dolphin Street. It should be mentioned that a house several doors away to the south currently bears the name of the 'Yarmouth Packet' but no evidence can be found to suggest that this particular building did, in fact, ever form part of the pub or have any connections with it.

The earliest mention of the pub was in 1772.

The late local historian, Les Cozens, related in his Mercury column 'Not A Lot Of People Know ...' *"that at about five o'clock on June 21 1799, a Mr Sutton, keeper of the* **Yarmouth Packet** *public house, was found hanging in the privy. Once before he had attempted the same rash act, but was cut down. His father, brother and sister had put an end to their lives in a similar way. The coroner's inquest brought in a verdict that he had taken his own life. Some 70*

2009.

years later, according to the Mercury, another landlord committed suicide in a similar way by hanging himself in the privy."

In 1804 (when William Best was licensee), the location of the pub was described as being *"next on north to* **Globe***, five houses north of* **Royal Exchange***"*. (Both the **Globe** and the **Royal Exchange** were neighbouring pubs and the reference to the former referred to the previous **Globe** site, now known as Globe House, before its move to the nearby **Scarborough Cat** premises).

Benjamin Ralph was landlord in 1828 and 1832, G Prestwidge in the late 1830s, Ambrose Cullen in 1840 and Henry West in 1847 (until 1862). The pub was described in 1858 as being *"a house much frequented by North Sea pilots."*

In 1866, it was reported that a Mr Cotten had

applied for, and was granted, permission to lay a drainpipe from the pub under the road to link up to a cesspool on the capstan ground opposite.

Gillon & Co, brewers of Sandwich, owned the pub in 1873, and Edward Pooley was landlord for a short time in 1874. He was followed later that year by Mrs Amelia Kemp who remained landlady until around 1908 while it was in the ownership of the East Kent Brewery.

In 1901, the *Yarmouth Packet* was one of 21 local public houses threatened with closure. A letter in protest was signed by 35 Gravesend pilots who apparently used the pub *"night and day"* after coming ashore.

Mrs Agnes Job took over in 1911 and she was still there in 1919 when the pub closed its doors for the last time on 31 December.

The following auction particulars appeared in 1921:*"195 Beach Street (Late **Yarmouth Packet** Inn), Deal: Sale of the Household Furniture, Bar Fixtures and Effects.*

Messrs GC Allen & Co are instructed by Mrs AM Job (who is leaving Deal) to Sell by Auction on the premises, as above, on Tuesday, 25 October 1921 the Household Furniture Bar Fixtures and Effects comprising: Iron French and Camp Bedsteads, Wire and Wool Mattresses, Feather Beds, Bolsters and Pillows, Mahogany Marble-top and Painted Wash-stands, Towel Airers, Chamber Ware, Pedestal Cupboards, Mahogany Antique Commode, and three other ditto, Mahogany Antique Stained and Painted Chests Drawers, Mahogany Duchesse & other Dressing Tables, Excellent Gilt-frame Chimney Glasses, 2 Mahogany Card Tables, 4ft. Mahogany Cheffonier, Mahogany Cottage Dining, Occasional and Deal Tables, Pianoforte in Walnut Case, Mahogany Dining Lath-back Easy Rush-sent and Occasional Chairs, Hand Sewing Machine and Cover, Pair Antique Brass Candelabra, Brass Gas Brackets, Brass Tea Kettle & Spirit Stove, Walnut and Bamboo Overmantels, Bamboo Music Cabinet, Mahogany Frame Couch, Box Ottoman, Mahogany Frame Couch, Box Ottoman, Quantity Books, Dinner and Tea Ware, China and Glass, Fenders and Firesets, Rugs, Mats and Linoleum, Wringing and Mangling Machine, and the usual Kitchen and Culinary Articles, etc, etc.

The Bar Fixtures and Fittings comprise: 10ft.6in. Mahogany Counter, 3-pull Beer Engine, Piece Partitioning and Quantity Shelving, Deal Seat, Dial Clock, Lead Piping, Pewter Measures, etc.

The Goods may be Viewed the Day Prior to Sale from 11 to 4 o'clock. Sale at Eleven o'clock. Further particulars of the Auctioneers at their Offices, 9 Queen Street, Deal. Telephone 117."

The property is now a private house.

Yew Tree, 136 Mill Hill (Mill Road) (formerly sited at 142 Mill Hill), Deal

In 1878, Samuel Terry was granted a licence for 'off' sales in premises described as being *"near Upper Deal Mill"*. He later made several applications for an 'on' licence for the premises, all of which were refused, until he was eventually granted one in September 1886, when his occupation was given as *'Market Gardener and Beer Retailer'*. The property was then described as being a beerhouse in an area of *"fields and nearby lime kilns."*

Early owners were HED Trafford, brewers of Littlebourne. Numerous landlords included William Carlton in 1888, James Cooper in 1891, William Henry Gilham in 1889, William Marsh in 1906, George Goldsmith Norris in 1909 and Thomas Rogers in 1910 (until 1911). An advertisement that year read: *"Yew Tree Inn, Mill Road, Deal. Under New Management. Thomas Rogers, Proprietor. Mackeson's Milk Stout and Bottled Beers. Delivered if required."*

William Flint was landlord in 1912, followed by WJ Archer in 1914, James Webb in 1916, EB Tucker in 1921 and FT Beal from 1924 until at least 1932.

In 1931, there was an application to enlarge the *Yew Tree* and new premises were erected next door (going down what was then Mill Road – now Mill Hill) by brewers, Mackeson, the following year. (The old building – a bungalow – became known as the "old" *Yew Tree*, even though it was no longer operating as a pub and, by 1939, it had become a confectionery shop and general store run by Mr H Johnson).

Together with the nearby **Mill Inn**, the *Yew Tree* catered for the residents of the new estate that had been built mainly for miners and their families.

Henry Walton took over as landlord in 1934 (remaining until 1937) and he placed the following advertisement in the Mercury in April 1934:

"Corrona Lodge Buffaloes – Dinner and Dance – Music and Singing Licence Granted Provided Certain Structural Alterations Adhered To."
The Mercury also reported in July 1934: "A whippet handicap was run on the grounds of the **Yew Tree** Inn, Mill Road, on Saturday, June 30th. The winning dog was Mr Price's 'Coming Home'; 2nd. Mr Gilmore's 'Nanny Goat and 3rd Mr Davies' 'Miss Greaves'. The next handicap takes place on

New Yew Tree with old Yew Tree to rear c1931.

*Saturday, July 14th, distance 180 yards. Entry fee 2 shillings (10p), to Henry Walton, proprietor, **Yew Tree** Inn, Mill Road, Deal."*

Walton also advertised the *"Ladies' Thrift Club – Supper and Dance"* at the **Yew Tree** in a November 1935 edition of the Mercury.

In 1936, the address of the **Yew Tree** was given as 'Mill Road', in the district of Mill Hill, Deal, but, in 1939, part of Mill Road itself had been renamed 'Mill Hill' (ie that part of Mill Road which lay south of Manor Road).

The Mercury reported in 1947 that: *"Deal Labour Party held a most successful Smoking Concert … about 200 people attended. By kind permission of Mrs [Jane] Walton"* (who was landlady at the time). In September 1948, it wrote that: *"Yew Freshwater Angling Club held their Annual Match at the Royal Military Canal near Appledore. The winner was H Walton [landlord] with a 4lb catch."*

F Green was landlord in 1955 and Bernard Creasey from 1959 (until 1984).

In May 1969, the Mercury reported that Mayor, Councillor John Blake, tried out the latest way of drawing a pint at the **Yew Tree** – by pressing a button. Ten beer dispensers were installed at a cost of £50, apparently guaranteeing a faster and better pint of beer!

Later registered landlords included Derek Evans in 1984, Richard Morrish in 1990, Ray Stevens and Cheryl Walker in 1992, Nicholas Barnes and Glyn Marsh in March 1993, Nicholas Barnes and Julie Page in November 1993, Ben and June Granger in

August 1994 and and Robert and Judith Goodright in November 1994.

The original pub building still stands on the previous site (at 142 Mill Hill – formerly Mill Road), albeit having been converted into a residential bungalow.

The present day pub remains open and is a popular live music venue with beer garden and children's play area at the rear. It is run by Chris and Bill and owned by Punch Taverns.

Old Yew Tree building 2009.

Kingsdown and Mongeham

Conqueror

See entry for the *Victory*.

Earl of Zetland

See entry for the *Zetland Arms*.

Friendly Port
125 Mongeham Road, Great Mongeham

Uniquely for Mongeham, the *Friendly Port* was a beerhouse (meaning it was only allowed to sell beer). The village's other two pubs were alehouses and therefore had full licences to sell all types of alcohol.

Edward Cavell was listed as landlord in 1862 and, according to the Wingham and Sandwich magistrates licensing records for 1873, John Bigginton was at the helm, the pub's owner at the time being William Denne of Sandwich. John was still landlord in 1880 when William Bigginton became its owner. In 1882, Daniel Drayson took over as landlord (remaining until 1899).

In October 1891, a fire started in a cottage at the rear of the *Friendly Port* and quickly spread to the thatched roof of the pub, as well as to two nearby cottages. Although the fire brigade responded quickly, the roof was well alight by the time they had arrived and, as there was no water supply nearby, the blaze caused a lot of damage.

Russell and Co of Gravesend were the pub's brewers from 1896.

Thomas Cox became landlord 1901, remaining until his death in 1905 when his widow, Elizabeth, stepped in. She was followed by Henry Harris who took over in November 1906. After his death the following September, his wife, also called Elizabeth, held the reins until Alfred Hopper arrived in October 1909. During his tenure, the *Friendly Port* was famed for selling teas, as well as alcohol, to visitors from Deal and local villages.

In March 1919, the renewal of the *Friendly Port*'s licence was opposed by villagers, with 92 out of a population of 410 people signing the petition, and a letter from the vicar was also presented to the court.

The pub was referred to the Compensation Committee on 6 March 1919 and the *Friendly Port* subsequently closed on 3 April 1920.

The outline of the original pub sign can still be seen on the wall of the building, which is now a private house.

c1910.

Kings Head
Upper Street, Kingsdown

Today, the *Kings Head* is a thriving pub in the heart of what is also a thriving village. Its beginnings go back many hundreds of years, possibly to Tudor times, when some say the original building was a hunting lodge used by King Henry VIII when visiting his nearby castles.

Certainly it used to be a farm and dairy in the 18th century, later selling beer and other refreshments to travellers, as well as housing a blacksmith's forge.

Records dating from 1807 showed Richard Jarvis as landlord, followed by Stephen Sutton who was there from at least by 1841. He was there for at least forty years before being succeeded by his son. Len Pattison was landlord from 1913 to at least 1915. By May 1924, Albert Gifford had taken over and was still there in 1937.

On 5 February 1951, the licence was held by Alfred Watts. In August 1954, it was reported that a 'regular' at the pub had accidentally been run over and killed. The customer used to visit the pub five or six times a week to down a pint of beer. The regular was, in fact, a goose which belonged to Mr Groombridge, a local farmer. Landlord, Alfred Watts, told the Mercury the goose would stand outside and screech until given a pint, and would always drink the glass clean dry!

Later that year, Dennis Payne took over as landlord. He had served on HMS Ajax in WWII, taking part in the sinking of the German battleship 'Graf Spee'. He was tragically killed in a motor accident in Cyprus in May 1962.

Percy John Powell took over after Dennis Payne in the late 1950s. In December 1960, he was charged with dangerous driving, electing for trial by jury at the quarter sessions where he was acquitted, with £21 costs.

In November 1969, Leonard Forder became the landlord. John Garnett and Rosemary Gledhill took over in September 1976, followed in early 1983 by Barry and Bev Mallion. It was repo ed that, in a bid to *"win back the locals"*, the jukebox, pool table and video games had all been removed, and a proposed new

c1920.

restaurant was planned. After 18 months, however, they had left, with Kevin and Mandy Kerry taking over in June 1984, followed by Andrew Crook in November 1989, who remained until January 2001 when Alex C Evans and Amanda J Sumner took the helm.

In 2006, oak beams, at least 400 years old, were found behind walls of the pub.

Alex and Amanda, the current owners, confirm that there is a blocked-up tunnel which runs under the pub and into the hills behind. A skittle alley is also housed in the beer garden at the rear.

Interestingly, one of the twin tail fins of a German Dornier 217 was found on Kingsdown beach early in 2010 and was left to soak in a child's inflatable paddling pool full of water in the garden, to preserve it in the short term. The old green camouflage paint was still visible, as well as parts of the Swastika. It is hoped after restoration it will be put on permanent display inside the pub.

The present day *Kings Head* is a warm, welcoming and unspoilt free house.

2010.

Leather Bottle, 103 Mongeham Road (Sholden Bank), Great Mongeham

The current *Leather Bottle* is the third building to bear the name on the site.

The first recorded licensee was Mary Bass in 1807, followed by Thomas Chandler in 1826. It was, however, a public house long before that, possibly from as early as the 17th Century. In July 1864, Chandler's widow, Harriet, told the Deal & Walmer Telegram that, following the death of her husband, she would continue to run the pub. Teas at moderate prices were offered, and the *Leather Bottle* advertised an *"excellent bowling green and good stabling situated just 1½ miles from Deal Station."* The pub was then owned by local brewers, Hills & Son.

By 1872, Thomas Sutton had become landlord, his wife, Mary Ann, joining him on the licence the following year. During their tenure, the first fire to strike the *Leather Bottle* destroyed the pub. By September 1876, following her husband's death, Mrs Sutton was running it alone, and continued to do so until at least 1885.

Daniel Philpott took over in 1891. In August 1893, a second disastrous fire resulted in the total destruction of the *Leather Bottle*, having started in the kitchen chimney and spreading to an adjoining store and three cottages. After a rebuild, Alfred Leon Philpott became mine host in September 1897, together with Stephen William Philpott, followed by Mary Ann Hall in November 1897 and William Jefford in February 1900.

Horam Gore was landlord in 1914, Sidney Beeching in 1915 and Alfred Hoffer in 1920. The licensing authority changed from Wingham & Sandwich Magistrates to the Borough of Deal Bench on 1 April 1935. Hoffer remained there until his retirement in 1954 when Thomas Pranklinfi took over. Internal alterations and improvements were carried out around this time.

Charringtons planned to surrender the *Leather Bottle*'s licence (together with another two pubs in Deal) in order to replace it with a brand new public house to be built on a vacant site at the corner of Rectory and St Martin's Roads. However, these plans were turned down by Deal Borough Council in January 1959. The following October, Charringtons appealed against the refusal of planning permission. They argued that the corner site had been owned by the brewery since 1935 and that they wished to replace *"the tired, worn out and behind-the-times Leather Bottle"*. The then landlord, Albert Brooks,

2006.

was apparently selling 180 gallons of beer a week and it was envisaged that this amount would rise slightly at the new location. After losing the appeal, Charringtons applied, in March 1960, for permission to build shops instead but was this also refused, although houses were eventually built on the new site.

By 1966, Ronald Batson was landlord. Other landlords included Iris Batson in 1977, Michael Gunn in 1981, Paul and Ena Gravenell in 1981 and Alan and Joan Flynn in 1987. The Flynns were there for 18 years until 2005. During their time at the pub, they were involved in many activities which raised funds for local causes, including pensioners' dinners, Deal Hospital and the local school swimming pool.

Daniel Warwick is the current landlord of this popular free house.

Rising Sun
Cliffe Road, Kingsdown

In the early 1900s, the world's first bus service to run to a printed timetable ran from Deal to the *Rising Sun*, Kingsdown.

According to the potted history on the wall of the pub, the building was erected in 1692 as a *"dwellinghouse"* owned by Thomas Broadley.

The *Rising Sun* was first licensed in the late 18th century, with Richard Sutton registered as landlord in 1771. As was common in those days, he had several jobs, including fisherman,

c1910.

netmaker and ropemaker. When he died in 1801, Sutton's widow, Eliza, became landlady. She died in 1804, and their daughter, Hannah, inherited the pub, remaining there until her death in 1826. Josiah Mockett was landlord from 1827 until 1832. During his tenure, the pub was sold to brewer, Edward Thompson, for 275 guineas (£288.75). He was followed by Robert Spinner until 1839 and then Harry Saffery (formerly of the *Fleur de Lis*) until 1848.

Landlord, Richard Arnold, was charged with selling alcohol on a Sunday afternoon in May 1858, although the case was not proven. His son, William, took over in 1863, and then his own son, William John, followed him in 1881. Thirty years after his grandfather, William John was also charged with selling alcohol out of hours. However, he was found guilty and fined 5/- (25p) plus 8/6d (42½p) costs. Brewery company, Thompson & Son, owned the *Rising Sun* at the time.

Other landlords included Thomas Charles Harden from 1905 until 1929, Alick Sutton (who was apparently a descendant of the earlier Suttons at the pub) until 1936, James Hyland until August 1943 when CL Bagshaw took over. By the mid 50s, Mr P Main was in

2010.

charge, and Thompson brewery had been taken over by Charrington & Co.

In October 1969, landlords, Arthur and Pam Silbery, left to take over at the *Forester*. February 1974 saw Michael and Pixie Brunt as managers of the *Rising Sun*. By May, a building next door called the Beehive had been converted into a 40 seater restaurant for the pub.

Stewart Workman, and, later, John West and John Glaysher took over in 1975, followed by Michael Brigden in October 1977. After the floods of January 1978 the pub reopened, and, in March 1983, he revived the barrel race on the beach.

Richard Day followed briefly in 1984, when Bass Charrington sold the pub to Shaun Galley. He was followed by James Hawkins in 1986.

In April 1988, Ralph and Pam Charles took over the *Rising Sun*. Ralph had been a professional boxer from 1968 until 1972 and the British and European welterweight champion. In March 1987, he pulled the first pint at the relaunch of the *Three Horseshoes* at Mongeham (see separate entry).

The *Rising Sun* is a free house and, like the nearby *Kings Head*, has a skittle alley in the beer garden at the rear. Ralph and Pam remain the landlord owners ably assisted by John Charles.

Three Horseshoes
139 Mongeham Road, Great Mongeham

The sign outside the pub dates the premises from 1735 when it was originally a blacksmith's forge. Joseph Browne held the first licence in 1740. Shadrach Allen was landlord in 1826 and, in 1840, he was unsuccessfully prosecuted for selling alcohol out of hours. He retired in 1877, and several landlords followed in quick succession, namely John Drayson in 1877, Alfred Philpott in 1878 and William Moat in 1879. Shadrach Allen died in March 1879, aged 80 years.

2006.

company, Leney & Co of Dover. William Wraight returned to the *Three Horseshoes*, this time staying until February 1932 when Herbert Arnold took over. The licensing authority passed from Wingham & Sandwich Magistrates' Court to the Borough of Deal in 1935.

At 3.30pm on 5 December 1881, a fire broke out in the large thatched roof of the kitchen at the rear of the *Three Horseshoes*. The blaze was prevented from spreading to the main house when some forty men formed a chain with buckets and a good supply of water. Deal Fire Brigade, based at the Town Hall, attended promptly to render further assistance. The *Three Horseshoes* is the only pub in the village not to have had its main building damaged by fire. Alfred Ratcliffe took over in 1882, staying until 1897, when he was succeeded by Leonard Wraight. He was followed by William Wraight in 1898 and George Latham in February 1902.

In 1906, ownership of the pub passed from brewers, Hills & Son of Deal, to another brewery

During the 1950s, William Rolfe was landlord, and Mr J Ferguson in 1966.

By September 1978, John Ayling was at the helm when he won the local landlords' day-out banger racing competition. The following April, he successfully appealed against a decision which had turned down his application for an extension of opening times during the Deal Regatta. He argued that customers could leave his premises, walk 100 yards to the *Leather Bottle* and continue drinking there. John and his wife, Margaret, left the *Three Horseshoes* for a well earned retirement in November 1985. In the December, a new bar on the first floor was planned.

Interviewed by the Mercury in March 1987, landlord, Keith Austin and his daughter, Mandy, said that their pre-Christmas grand opening had been such a success that they planned to do it all over again! They invited former British and European middleweight champion, Ralph Charles, to pull the first pint. (See also entry for the **Rising Sun**). Norman McSloy took over in 1991, followed by Keith and Diane Checksfield in 1999 (who remained until in September 2003).

The Mercury reported that Martin and Wendy Styles raised £1,210 for East Kent Search & Rescue in September 2004, and July 2005 saw the landlords advertise the *"perfect pub garden"* by offering 'bat & trap' and barbecue facilities. In December that year,

they raised £1,450 for the hospice unit at Deal Hospital.

July 2008 saw new landlords, Sam and Sarah Rodwell, take over. A year later, the Mercury reported that celebrity chef, Ainsley Harriott, had enjoyed lunch there with his family before attending a local wedding.

Sam and Sarah are still in charge of this long-established village public house, offering a wide range of food and drink to their customers, as well as holding regular live music events.

Victory (Conqueror)
17 North Road (Middle Row), Kingsdown

According to a court report in December 1860, "William Erridge was charged with assaulting Lucy Margaret Erridge, wife of Henry James Erridge, landlord of the *'Conqueror'* public house at Kingsdown and with assaulting her daughter, Charlotte. William Erridge was fined 15/- (75p) with 13/- (65p) costs."

c1900.

The following year, Henry Erridge was registered in the 1861 census as being aged 36 and resident landlord of the **Conqueror**, with his wife, seven children and a servant. In June 1865, he appeared before magistrates charged with selling beer to three men, namely George Laming, Henry Webb and John Lilley, on Sunday afternoon, 18 June 1865. He was fined £1, plus costs.

About a year later, the **Conqueror** became known as the Victory. Claims in a local newspaper some years ago that the Conqueror was an early name for the Rising Sun can be discounted, since both pubs were in existence at the same time.

James Bingham and his wife, Ann, became the first licensees of the newly-named **Victory**. He was followed by his son, also called James, by 1882. Although the pub was sold at auction in 1897, Bingham remained there until at least 1915.

By 1937, Mr Swift was in charge. In March 1949 the sea 'paid a visit' to the **Victory** during floods, according to reports

in the Mercury. This was while George Arnold, who took over in 1946 (until 1958), was landlord.

According to a 1950s' article: *"One of the many Victory Inns in Kent, commemorating Nelson's flagship, is at Kingsdown, near Deal, where there is an interesting but fearsome head on an interior wall, which has often been mistaken for a sea serpent. It is the old figure of the royal barge of King Thebaw, the last king of Burma, and was a familiar sight in former days on the waterways of Burma. The barge was several hundred feet long and propelled by a hundred oarsmen. When the barge was broken up at Bombay, Admiral Sir John Hext kept the figurehead. A member of the Imperial Customs later purchased it and presented it to the landlord of his favourite inn, the Victory, where it is a great attraction to visitors."*

King Thebaw – 1859 to 1916 – was the last native ruler of Konbaung, Burma. After attempts to regain his kingdom from British occupation, he and his family were arrested and sent to live in exile in India for the rest of their days.

On 10 October 1958, HR Shilling took the helm. He was to become the pub's last landlord as the **Victory** closed not long afterwards.

The **Victory** building is now a private house.

Figure from King Thebaw's royal barge.

Zetland Arms (Earl Of Zetland)
Wellington Parade, Kingsdown

Large white sided building on right c1920.

The pub's original name was the *Earl of Zetland*. In 1860, a lugger of this name was taken under tow and headed for Ramsgate. The tug towing her was fully laden with goods from the ship, the Earl of Eglington, which had been wrecked at St Margaret's Bay. However, the Earl of Zetland was towed too fast, and was dragged under.

The location of the *Zetland Arms* is an unusual one, set as it is on the beach itself. Although not immediately connected to the pub, a Dover District Council information board erected in front of the *Zetland Arms* records that, in 1813, Thomas Bingham, a member of a well known local family, was killed on Kingsdown beach by Customs men during a smuggling raid.

In 1870, the pub's landlord was James Arnold, followed by Jarvist Arnold, the famous coxswain of the Kingsdown lifeboat, 'Sabrina', in 1871. He was cox from 1865 until 1888. His tenure of the *Zetland Arms* was shorter since, by 1882, he had been succeeded by William Erridge. William Wellard took over in 1910 and remained until at least 1915.

Robert Bartlett was landlord in 1936. In March 1949, the sea flooded the pub during storms. Henry Beard became licensee in 1948, followed by Percy Furnall in the 1950s.

In 1974, Bill Pierce, the Charrington brewery artist, painted a new sign for the pub. In May 1977, the Mercury reported that Frank Westby planned to introduce bar snacks, and to enlarge the bars. The pub was temporarily closed when he installed bow windows to give the pub a more historic look, as well as to improve its facade. The grand reopening took place on Friday 8 July at 6pm. Timothy Cobbett, a direct descendant of the writer, William Cobbett, took over as temporary manager.

In September 1977, TV broadcaster, David Frost and former Prime Minister, Harold Wilson, were in Deal making a television programme about Prime Ministers. After visiting nearby Walmer Castle, they called at the *Zetland Arms* for lunch, and a photograph of them both enjoying a pint hangs on the wall of the bar in commemoration of the event.

After several changes of ownership, Timothy Cobbett, celebrated his 30th year as landlord in 2007. The *Zetland Arms* is one of the closest pubs on the British mainland to France.

c1980.

A selection of additional photographs

Above: Get ahead – get a hat is the order of the day for this 1924 outing from the Five Bells, Deal.
Below: A rare view inside the saloon bar of the Antwerp, Deal, 1932.

Above: A Victorian engraving of Thompson's brewery, Walmer.

Below: Hill's brewery and the Rose Hotel, Deal, in the late 19th century.

Kingsdown lifeboat coxswain Jarvist Arnold c1870 when licensee of the Zetland Arms.

PC Shelvey Cox, the ever vigilant bobby who kept a close eye on the town's pubs and their customers.

And finally . . .

This book would not be complete without mention of a local legendary drunken reprobate, referred to as 'The Irrepressible Tom Brown' in local newspapers of the time.

Brown lived with his sister in the West Street area of Deal and regularly stole money from her to pay for his beer. He was hauled into court on no less than 90 occasions between 1847 and 1900 (and that's only when he was caught), mostly on drunk and disorderly charges.

He spent long periods of incarceration in Sandwich Gaol and was also sentenced to various correctional institutions and lunatic asylums in the hope of being cured of his alcoholism.

Nothing worked and he continued quenching his thirst in the pubs of Deal whenever he was at large. Despite a lifetime of drunken debauchery, he lived well into his 90s and is believed to have died in Eastry workhouse in 1915 – probably with a pint in his hand!

Index to landlords' surnames of Deal and Walmer

A

Abbot	Deal Hoy
Abbott	Dunkerleys
Adams	Crown Inn, Jolly Gardener, Park Tavern, Pelican (3), Royal Exchange, (W); Sir Colin Campbell, Walmer Castle
Adamson	Granville
Agnew	Star & Garter
Akehurst	Sir John Falstaff
Albury	Walmer Castle
Allen	Admiral Keppel, Deal Lugger,(Beach Street) Hare & Hounds (D), Ramsgate Harbour, Royal Hotel, Three Compasses
Almond	Fountain, Rose, Roxborough Castle
Ambrose	Granville
Anderson	Providence, Royal George
Andrews	Prince Albert, Watermans Arms (91 Beach St)
Annall	Brickmakers Arms, Hare & Hounds (D)
Appleton	Deal Castle Inn, Greyhound, (142 Middle Street) Three Compasses
Archer	New Plough, Yew Tree
Arendell	Queens Head(D)
Armstrong	New Inn
Arnold	Liverpool Arms, Oak & Ivy
Ash	Thompson(s) Bell
Ashby	Cambridge Arms, Crispin Inn
Ashton	Fountain
Aston	Mill Inn
Atkins	Fawn, Noahs Ark, Royal Exchange (D)
Attensall	White Horse (Middle Street)
Attfield	Dunkerleys
Attle	Admiral Keppel
Attwood	Royal Standard, Sandown Castle Hotel
Austen	Lord Nelson (W), Phoenix, South Foreland
Austin	Bowling Green Tavern, Jolly Sailor
Axon	Army & Navy
Ayler	Bird in Hand

B

Bacon	Oak & Ivy
Bagnall	Bohemian
Bailey	Clarendon, Eagle, Lord Clyde, New Inn, Stag, Army & Navy
Baker	Cambridge Arms, Clarendon, Fountain, Kings Head, North Star, Prince Albert, Royal Hotel, South Foreland, Stag, Strand, Dolphin (W)
Ball	Deal Hoy, Royal George
Ballard	Noahs Ark
Bamber	Eagle
Band	Alma (W), Queens Head (W)
Banfield	Strand
Banks	Sir Colin Campbell
Barbasiewicz	Three Compasses
Barber	Stag, Port Arms
Barlett	Lifeboat (The Strand)
Barlow	Prince Albert

Barne	Royal George
Barnes	Berry, Bowling Green Tavern, Cambridge Arms, Dolphin (W), Royal Standard, Ship Stag, Yew Tree
Barnett	Strand
Barrett	Lord Nelson (W), Rising Sun
Barter	Noahs Ark
Bartlett	Providence
Barton	Strand
Barty	Bowling Green Tavern
Bass	Maxton Arms, Queens Head(D)
Bassett	Railway Inn,(D) Watermans Arms
Bassington	Kings Head(D),New Inn
Baston	Anchor
Batby	Fountain
Batchell	Duke of Wellington
Bathe	Royal Hotel
Bax	Friendly Port (D), Maxton Arms, Phoenix, Rising Sun,(D) Strand
Baynes	Walmer Castle
Beal	Hole in the Roof, Shah, Stag, Yew Tree
Bear	Magnet
Beasley	Lord Nelson (D)
Beazley	Victoria Commercial
Bedford	Walmer Castle
Bedlove	Green Dragon
Beer	Railway Inn (D), Rising Sun Inn(W), Stag
Bell	Berry, Swan
Bentley	Fawn, Hare & Hounds (W), Royal Hotel
Berridge	Roxborough Castle, Thompson(s) Bell
Berringer	Clifton Hotel
Berry	Black Horse (Broad Street), Magnet
Best	Railway,(W) Yarmouth Packet
Betts	Duke of Wellington, Pelican (2)
Bilton	Lord Warden (D), Telegraph
Bing	Friendly Port,(D)
Bingham	Globe,(199 Beach St)
Birch	Royal Exchange (D)
Birchell	Alma (D)
Bishop	Globe, Walmer Castle
Black	Queens Head,(D)
Blacklocks	Queens Head,(D)
Bladen	Royal Hotel
Bloyce	Lifeboat Inn,(Campbell Rd)
Blythe	Royal Standard
Boakes	Kings Arms, Rose
Bodker	Goodwins
Bolder	Cambridge Arms
Bolt	Forester
Bolton	Prince of Wales
Boncey	New Inn, Roxborough Castle
Booker	Clarendon
Boore	Ship
Bottle	Stag
Botton	Queens Head,(D)
Bourne	Eagle
Bowbyes	Lifeboat (The Marina)
Bowman	Noahs Ark
Boyden	Queens Hotel,(2)
Boys	New Plough
Bradley	Walmer Castle
Bradman	Walmer Castle

Bragg	Queens Arms
Brailsford	Black Bull
Bramhall	Cambridge Arms
Branch	Dunkerleys, Royal Hotel
Breton	Royal Hotel
Brett	Railway Refreshment Rooms, Three Compasses
Brice	Sandown Castle Hotel, Ship
Bridger	Eagle, Saracens Head
Bridges	Stag
Bridgestone	Royal Hote
Brisley	Wellesley Arms
Broadbent	Clarendon
Broker	Sandown Castle Hotel
Brookes	Dunkerleys
Brooking	Lifeboat (The Strand)
Brooks	Deal Castle Inn, Royal Oak Inn
Brown	Bear Pump, Bohemian, Clarendon, Crown Inn, Deal Hoy, Deal Lugger, Fawn, Five Ringers, Globe, Jolly Sailor, Maxton Arms, Napier Tavern, Noahs Ark, North Star, Queens Arms, Queens Head,(D) Queens Hotel Walmer Castle
Browning	Deal Lugger, Druid Arms
Bruce	Admiral Penn
Bryant	Mill Inn
Bullen	Dolphin (W), Lord Clyde
Bullock	Crown Inn, Royal Exchange (D)
Burden	Railway,(W)
Burgess	Brickmakers Arms, New Inn, Saracens Head
Burke	Stag
Burnell	Sandown Castle Hotel
Burnett	Lord Nelson (W)
Burnville	Drum
Burr	Port Arms
Burrows	Fountain
Burton	Liverpool Arms(D)
Burtwell	Pelican (2)
Burville	Prince Albert
Bushell	Hare & Hounds (W), Lord Clyde, Napier Tavern, Royal Exchange (W)
Bussey	Bell Inn
Butcher	Stag
Butler	Admiral Keppel, Pelican (2)
Butt	White Horse (Queen Street)
Butterwick	Prince of Wales
Buttress	Crown Inn, Hope
Bygrave	Railway

C

Caleb	Maxton Arms
Callaghan	Deal Hoy
Calverly	Royal Hotel
Cameron	Magnet
Campbell	Sir Colin Campbell
Canale	Saracens Head
Canham	Queen Adelaide
Canney	Deal Cutter, Horse & Farrier
Capeling	Five Bells Inn, Greyhound
Capon	Sir Sydney Smith
Careford	Queens Head(D)
Carey	Bohemian
Carlton	Railway(W), Thompson(s) Bell, Yew Tree

Carraher	Magnet
Carrick	Walmer Castle
Carrot	New Plough
Carter	New Inn, Queens Head (W), South Infantry Canteen
Carthy	Port Arms
Case	Rose, Royal Exchange (W)
Caspell	Watermans Arms
Casswell	Prince Albert
Castle	Black Bull, Five Ringers, Prince Albert, Rising Sun, Roxborough Castle, Stag, Thompson(s) Bell, White Horse (Middle Street), White Horse (Queen Street)
Cattermole	Sandown Castle Hotel
Cavell	Five Ringers, Kings Head, Lord Clyde, New Inn
Cawthorn	Maxton Arms
Cecelin	Five Ringers
Chaffey	Walmer Castle
Chamberlain	Bowling Green Tavern
Chambers	Sir John Falstaff
Chandler	Bell Inn, Duke of Wellington
Chandler	New Inn, Royal Exchange (Beach Street)
Chanel	Alma (Deal)
Chapman	Cinque Port Arms, Cinque Ports Volunteer, Crispin Inn, Hope, Ship
Chappell	Clifton Hotel
Child	Admiral Keppel
Childs	Ranalagh House
Chittenden	Dunkerleys, Black Bull
Chitty	Shah
Christy	Lord Warden (W), Maxton Arms
Claringbold	Clifton Hotel, Pelican (2), Ship
Claris	Cinque Port Arms
Clark	Royal George
Clarke	Lord Clyde, Lord Warden (W), Rising Sun Inn, Rose, Royal Hotel
Clay	Ship
Clayson	Bohemian, Rising Sun
Cleary	Kings Head
Clements	Five Ringers
Cleminson	Rose
Cleve	Bricklayers Arms (W)
Clift	Chequers Inn, Lord Nelson (W)
Cobb	Alma (Deal)
Cole	Harp, Prince Alfred Inn, Thompson(s) Bell
Coleman	Deal Hoy, Dolphin (W), Eagle, Locomotive, White Horse (Middle Street)
Collard	Eagle
Collett	Ship
Colley	Liverpool Arms
Collins	Dunkerleys, Eagle, Five Bells Inn, Roxborough Castle, , Strand
Collis	Fountain
Cook	Admiral Rodney, Stag
Cooke	Bohemian, Stag, Walmer Castle
Cooper	Lord Nelson (D), Railway(W), Yew Tree
Copland	Greyhound
Copley	Royal Hotel
Corbett	Dunkerleys, Kings Head
Cork	Royal Exchange (D)
Corn	Old(e) Victory

Cory	Deal Hoy, Noahs Ark
Cotton	Thompson(s) Bell, Yarmouth Packet
Coucher	Clifton Hotel
Coulder	Lord Nelson (W)
Couper	Drum
Cousins	Granville
Cox	Brickmakers Arms, Mill Inn
Craig	Prince Albert
Cranbrooke	Drum
Cranwell	Sandown Castle Hotel
Creasey	Mill Inn, Queens Hotel,(2) Windsor Castle, Yew Tree
Cribden	Sir Sydney Smith
Crick	Pelican (2), Royal Exchange (D)
Crickett	Sir John Falstaff
Crittenden	Queen Adelaide
Crofts	Duke of York(D)
Cross	Royal Hotel
Crossland	Admiral Keppel, Granville
Crystal	Port Arms
Cullen	Fleur de Lis, Fountain, Saracens Head, Yarmouth Packet
Culvus	Prince Alfred Inn
Curd	Lord Clyde
Curling	Anchor, Bowling Green Tavern, Deal Hoy, India Arms
Currie	Magnet

D

Dadd	Admiral Keppel
Dale	Black Bull, Bohemian, Margate Hoy, Rose
Darby	Providence, Sir John Falstaff
Davies	Liverpool Arms(D), Stag
Davis	Lord Warden (W), Maxton Arms, Sandown Castle Hotel, White Horse (Queen Street)
Davison	Berry, Cambridge Arms, Jolly Gardener
Dawes	Kings Head, Queens Head (The Strand)
Dawkins	Alma (W)
Dawson	Queens Head(D), Roxborough Castle
Day	Jolly Gardener
Deacon	Pelican (2), Port Arms
Delahaye	Black Bull
Dempsey	Port Arms
Denne	Crown Inn, Fountain, Military Tavern, Star & Garter, Strand
Dennis	Ship
Denny	Walmer Castle
Desmormeaux	Harp
Deverill	Cambridge Arms
Dewell	Royal Exchange (W), Wellington Arms)
Deyler	New Inn
Diffey	Locomotive
Diggerson	Horse & Farrier
Dillon	Berry, Rising Sun(D)
Ditton	Queens Head(D)
Divers	Bowling Green Tavern
Dixon	India Arms, Man of Kent, Maxton Arms
Dobson	Cambridge Arms, Saracens Head
Dodd	Rose

Dodsworth	Rose
Dolford	Royal Exchange (D)
Donnelly	Cambridge Arms
Doorn	Royal Exchange (D)
Doughty	Lord Nelson (W)
Dowle	Admiral Keppel
Downing	Walmer Castle
Dowsett	Railway
Doyle	New Inn
Dredge	Lord Warden (W)
Driver	Five Ringers
Dry	Five Ringers
Dunkerley	Dunkerleys, Royal Hotel
Dunn	Lord Warden (D)
Durban	Hope
Durras	Thompson(s) Bell
Durtnall	Queen Adelaide
Dye	Cambridge Arms

E

Eason	Berry
Eastes	Lord Warden (D), Park Tavern
Eaton	Red Crosse
Edgecombe	Cambridge Arms
Edwards	Providence, Rose, Royal Exchange (D), Three Compasses
Eldridge	Clarendon
Eleanor	Oak Tree
Elgar	Black Bull
Ellen	Lord Nelson (W)
Elliot	North Star, Queens Head (W), Railway Inn, Thompson(s) Bell
Elson	Duke of Wellington, Empire
Elwin	Swan
Embleton	Clarendon
England	Star & Garter
Ensor	Eagle
Ensore	Eagle
Epps	Royal Oak Inn
Epsley	Hovelling Boat
Erridge	Crown Inn(138 Beach Street), Deal Lugger,(201 Beach St) North Star, Prince Albert
Estes	Amsterdam
Evans	Berry, Black Bull, Dunkerleys, Fountain, Jolly Gardener, Mill Inn, Yew Tree
Everett	Brickmakers Arms
Eyres	Empire

F

Fagg	Maxton Arms, Thompson(s) Bell
Fairclough	Clarendon
Farrer	Admiral Keppel
Faucheux	Forester
Feeburger	Saracens Head
Feeney	Strand, Thompson(s) Bell
Fellows	Stag
Fenn	Prince Albert, Rising Sun Inn
Fenner	Railway, Royal Hotel
Ferris	Eagle, Wellesley Arms
Ferry	Fleur de Lis

Ffasham	Admiral Keppel, Port Arms, Rising Sun Inn,(W) Strand, Thompson(s) Bell	Garrett	Anchor, Lord Nelson (D)
		Garside	Queens Hote(2)l
Fielden	Rose	Garton	Brickmakers Arms, Mill Inn
Fieldon	Rose	Gates	Prince Albert
Filmer	Railway(W), Star & Garter	George	Sir Sydney Smith
Finnis	Albion, Alma (D), Deal Cutter, Deal Hoy, Five Bells Inn, Fox, Granville, Jolly Butcher, Prince of Wales, Sir Colin Campbell, Stag	Gibbs	Liverpool Arms, Pelican (1), Royal Hotel
		Gilbert	Bear Pump, Five Ringers
		Gilham	Yew Tree
Fish	Crown Inn	Gillespie	Stag
Fisher	Jolly Gardener	Gladwell	Lord Nelson (W)
Fitall	North Star, White Horse (Queen St)	Gladwish	Queens Arms
Fitch	Strand	Godfrey	Cambridge Arms
Fittall	Eagle	Godshon	Yarmouth Arms
Fitzgerald	Port Arms	Golding	Admiral Keppel
Flavell	Academy Sports Bar, Clarendon	Goldsmith	Queens Arms
Fleming	Kings Arms	Goldup	Greyhound
Flint	Napier Tavern, Royal Hotel, Yew Tree	Goodchild	Anchor
Flower	Cinque Port Arms	Goodman	Lord Nelson (W)
Flynn	Fountain	Goodright	Yew Tree
Foat	Jolly Sailor	Goodson	Admiral Keppel
Foley	Ship	Goodwin	Stag, Windsor Castle
Folwell	Deal Lugger	Gormie	Strand
Foord	Lord Nelson (W)	Gosby	Kings Head
Ford	Bowling Green Tavern	Goslett	Crispin Inn, Windsor Castle
Forest	Ship	Goss	Military Tavern
Forester	Jolly Sailor	Gough	Kings Head
Formoy	Brickmakers Arms	Goughe	Bird in Hand
Forster	Admiral Keppel, Rose	Gould	Walmer Castle
Forth	Bohemian	Goundry	Walmer Castle
Foster	Bell Inn, Fleur de Lis, Hole in the Roof, Lord Warden (D), Royal Hotel	Grace	Dolphin (W)
		Granger	Yew Tree
Foulkes	Berry	Grant	Deal Hoy, Hare & Hounds (D)
Foulser	Bowling Green Tavern	Graves	Crispin Inn, Lord Nelson (W)
Fowle	Port Arms	Gray	Eagle
Fox	Granville, Jolly Butcher	Greatorex	Duke of Wellington
Foxhall	Magnet	Green	Hole in the Roof, Lifeboat Inn,(Campbell Road) Queens Head, Wellesley Arms, Yew Tree
Frame	Saracens Head		
Frampton	New Inn		
Francis	Bathing House Tavern, Bowling Green Tavern, Locomotive, Marine Hotel	Greenstreet	Deal Lugger
		Gregory	Royal Hotel
Franks	Port Arms	Grellet	Royal Hotel
French	Deal Hoy	Grey	Lord Warden (D)
Frere	Oak & Ivy	Griffiths	Crown Inn, Star & Garter
Friend	Alhambra, Bear Pump, Fountain, Pound, Strand	Grigg	Albion, Shah, Ship, Chequers Inn, New Inn
Friers	Fountain	Groombridge	Eagle
Frost	Rose	Grout	Alma (D)
Fry	Beachbrow	Gunner	Bowling Green Tavern, Brickmakers Arms, Maxton Arms
Fryatt	Clarendon		
Fryer	Royal Hotel	Gurney	Queens Arms
Funnel	Noahs Ark	Gutteridge	Jolly Gardener

G

H

Gadd	Lord Warden (D)	Haddock	Queens Arms
Gagan	Queens Head,(D)	Hadlow	Clarendon
Gallaway	Queens Head,(D)	Haggar	Five Ringers
Gallway	Stag	Hagger	Mill Inn, Port Arms, Royal Exchange (D)
Gambrill	Royal Oak Inn	Halford	Five Ringers
Gammon	Anchor	Hall	Anchor, Military Tavern, Port Arms, Stag, Three Compasses
Gardener	Queens Head		
Gardiner	Royal Hotel	Hammerton	Mill Inn
Gardner	Providence, Royal Exchange (D), Sandown Castle Hotel,	Hammond	Admiral Keppel, Clarendon, Saracens Head
Garner	Hole in the Roof	Hanbrook	Lord Nelson (W)

Handley	Ship
Hanger	Jolly Sailor, Napier Tavern, North Star,
Hanley	Telegraph
Harding	Lord Nelson (W)
Hardy	Tally Ho
Hargreaves	Dunkerleys
Harlick	Prince Albert
Harlington	Mill Inn
Harlow	Sir Sydney Smith
Harmsworth	Hare & Hounds (D)
Harris	Berry, Duke of Norfolk, Duke of York, Fox, Friendly Port, Horse & Farrier, Jolly Sailor, Locomotive, North Star, Queens Arms
Hart	Maxton Arms, Strand
Harvey	Jolly Sailor, Noahs Ark, Sunn Inn
Hatcher	Wellesley Arms
Hawkes	Deal Hoy
Hawkins	Cambridge Arms, Clifton Hotel, Five Bells Inn
Hay	Sandown Castle Hotel
Hayden	Dolphin (W)
Hayman	Deal Hoy, Dunkerleys, Forester, Liverpool Arms, Marine Hotel, Prince Albert, Queens Arms, Shah, Telegraph
Hayshaw	Sandown Castle Hotel
Hayward	Druid Arms, Lord Nelson (D), Pelican (2), Prince Albert
Heard	Sir Colin Campbell
Hearn	Lord Nelson (D)
Heaton	Dolphin (W)
Hefft	Queens Hotel (2)
Henley	Fox
Hewett	Queens Arms
Hewitson	Sandown Castle Hotel
Hewitt	Granville
Hicks	Fountain, Mill Inn
Higgins	Harp, Pelican (1)
Highfield	Royal Hotel
Hill	Beachbrow Prince of Wales, Stag
Hills	Queens Head (W), Railway (W), Railway Inn (D)
Hilson	Lord Clyde
Hinds	Alma (D), Alma (W), Harp, Rose, Ship
Hinkley	Military Tavern, Railway
Hiscocks	Royal Hotel
Hobart	Queens Hotel (2)
Hobbs	Berry, Park Tavern
Hobday	Bell Inn, Saracens Head
Hobson	Admiral Keppel
Hodge	Royal Hotel
Hodges	Bird in Hand
Hodgetts	Victoria Commercial
Hogben	Queen Adelaide
Hoile	Admiral Penn, Port Arms, Red Lion, Royal Standard
Holbrook	Drum, Dunkerleys
Holden	Bohemian
Holland	Kings Head, Magnet, Queens Head (W), Stag, Telegraph, Watermans Arms
Hollands	Eagle
Hollingsworth	Sandown Castle Hotel
Hollis	Royal Hotel
Holman	Five Ringers
Holmes	Deal Hoy
Holness	Lord Nelson (D), Sir Colin Campbell
Holton	Lord Nelson (W), Strand
Holtrum	Sir Colin Campbell
Hood	Railway Inn (D), Roxborough Castle
Hook	Wellesley Arms
Hookham	Deal Castle Inn, Liverpool Arms, Lord Nelson (W), Queens Arms
Hooper	Ship
Hopkin	Prince Albert
Hopper	Queens Head (W)
Horncastle	Deal Castle Inn
Horner	Army & Navy, Pelican (2)
Horrigan	New Plough
Howe	Berry
Howgego	Prince of Wales
Howland	Alma (Deal)
Hoyle	Duke of York, Oak & Ivy
Hubbard	Empire
Hubble	Eagle
Hume	White Horse (Queen Street)
Humphreys	Chequers Inn (D)
Humphries	Noahs Ark
Hunt	Victoria, White Horse (Queen Street)
Hunter	Bell Inn
Hurren	Rising Sun (D)
Hutch	Fleur de Lis
Hutchings	New Inn, Port Arms
Hutchins	Park Tavern
Huth	Star & Garter
Hutson	Telegraph
Huxstep	Drum, Harp

I

Ickham	Sir Colin Campbell
Ingleton	Telegraph
Ingram	Black Bull

J

Jackson	Deal Hoy, Dolphin (W), Maxton Arms
James	Jolly Gardener, Military Tavern, Prince of Wales
Jarman	Bohemian, Walmer Castle
Jarvis	Deal Lugger, Pelican (2) Prince of Wales, Sandown Castle Hotel
Jeffery	Royal Hotel
Jefford	Military Tavern, Prince Albert
Jell	Queens Head (D)
Jelley	Navy Coffee House
Jelly	Black Bull
Jenner	Stag
Jennings	Druid Arms, Fountain
Jewitt	Walmer Castle
Jezzard	Old(e) Victory
Job	Jolly Butcher, Yarmouth Packet
Johnson	Berry, Cambridge Arms, Deal Hoy, Five Bells Inn, Lord Warden (Mill Road), Mill Inn, Prince Albert, Stag, Telegraph, Three Compasses
Jolly	Lord Clyde, Lord Nelson (W)
Jones	Alma (D), Bohemian, Cambridge Arms, Chequers Inn Deal Hoy, Port Arms, Queens Head (W), Railway (W), Sir Sydney Smith, Walmer Castle
Jordan	Berry, Hare & Hounds (W), Hare &

	Hounds (D), Magnet, Rising Sun, TallyHo
Judd	Magnet
Jull	Victoria

K

Kavrazoni	Dunkerleys
Kebell	Bowling Green Tavern
Kelly	Tally Ho
Kelsey	Alma (D)
Kematon	Bowling Green Tavern
Kember	Saracens Head
Kemp	Brickmakers Arms, Cambridge Arms, Five Ringers, Lord Warden (Mill Road), Saracens Head, Yarmouth Packet
Kennet	Cinque Ports Volunteer
Kennett	Empire
Kent	Royal Oak Inn
Kenward	Hare & Hounds (W)
Kidner	New Inn
King	Chequers Inn, Park Tavern, Sir Colin Campbell
Kirby	Royal Exchange (D)
Kirkaldie	Roxborough Castle
Kitchen	Kings Head
Kitson	Queens Arms
Kitton	Noahs Ark
Knight	Black Bull, Queen Adelaide, Queen Adelaide, Royal Exchange (W), Sir Colin Campbell, South Foreland, Wellesley Arms
Knocker	Royal Hotel
Knott	Magnet, Pelican (3), Queen Adelaide
Kopetsky	Royal Standard

L

Ladd	Oak Tree, Hole in the Roof
Laidlaw	Mill Inn
Laird	New Inn
Lambert	Kings Head
Lamburn	Bowling Green Tavern
Laming	Granville
Langley	Anchor, Deal Cutter, Duke of York, Five Bells Inn, Fleur de Lis, Friendly Port, Noahs Ark, Park Tavern, Pelican(2)
Larkin	Five Ringers, Ship
Larkins	Horse & Farrier
Laurence	Granville
Lavanchy	Queens Hotel
Lawrence	Dunkerleys, Globe, Jolly Butcher
Law	Clarendon
Laws	Royal Standard
Leach	Black Bull, Cambridge Arms, Crown Inn, Hare & Hounds (W), Pelican (2)
Leaver	Railway (W)
Lee	Rising Sun Inn, Royal Hotel
Leeson	Berry, Lord Clyde, Railway (W)
Leggett	Berry, Sir John Falstaff
Leney	Napier Tavern
Lenham	Cambridge Arms, Deal Hoy
Letts	Hare & Hounds (D)

Lewis	Bowling Green Tavern, Cinque Ports Volunteer, Clarendon
Licence	Saracens Head
Lilley	Railway
Limeburner	Thompson(s) Bell
Lines	Maxton Arms
Lis	Queens Hotel
Little	Pelican (2), Walmer Castle
Lloyd	Pelican (2)
Lock	Three Compasses
Logan	Providence, Walmer Castle
Long	India Arms
Longley	Queen Adelaide
Lord	Royal Exchange (D)
Loughlin	Three Compasses
Lovell	Railway Inn (D)
Lowin	Royal Oak Inn
Lownds	Granville, Queens Arms
Ludford	Bell Inn
Ludwig	Fountain
Lumley	Granville
Lunn	Lord Nelson (W)
Lusted	Harp
Luther	Granville
Lynch	Hole in the Roof, Ship

M

MacDermot	Royal Hotel
Macey	Bricklayers Arms (D)
Mackeson	Ship
Mackie	Horse & Farrier
Mackins	Chequers, Stag
Mackney	Dolphin (Beach Street)
Madelaine	Queens Head
Mainwaring	Telegraph
Maker	Clifton Hotel
Maltby	Eagle
Mansfield	Railway Inn
Mantle	Maxton Arms
Marden	Horse & Farrier
Margraves	Rising Sun Inn (W)
Marks	Royal Exchange (W)
Marley	Railway (W)
Marsh	Admiral Keppel, Anchor, Chequers Inn, Crown Inn, Deal Cutter, Drum, Duke of Wellington, Five Bells Inn, Five Ringers, Lifeboat (The Marina), Lord Nelson (W), Maxton Arms, Queens Head, Rising Sun, Sir Colin Campbell, Sir Sydney Smith, Swan, Tally Ho, Yew Tree
Marshall	Queens Arms, South Infantry Canteen
Martin	Cinque Ports Volunteer, Prince Albert, Providence, Queens Arms
Mason	Prince Albert
Matthews	Three Compasses, Walmer Castle
Maundy	Bear Pump
Maxted	Lord Warden (D), Sir Sydney Smith
May	Admiral Keppel, Alma (D), Beachbrow, Empire, Liverpool Arms, Queens Head, Saracens Head, Shah, Ship
Maybanks	Queens Head (W)
Maynard	Sir John Falstaff

Mayr	Three Compasses
McFadyen	Admiral Keppel
McHayle	Clarendon
McKay	Queens Head
McKenna	Star & Garter
McKinnon	Five Ringers
McLennan	Lord Warden (D)
McLernon	Hare & Hounds (D)
McSloy	Three Compasses
Meadows	Alma (D)
Meakins	Kings Head, Port Arms
Meaning	Granville
Meers	Red Lion
Meinhardt	Royal Hotel
Mellows	Queen Adelaide
Mercer	Berry, Military Tavern, Rising Sun Inn, Royal Exchange (W), Stag
Miles	Anchor, Kings Head, Lifeboat (W), White Horse (Middle Street)
Millard	Royal Hotel
Miller	Alma (D), Granville, New Inn, Old(e) Victory, Tally Ho
Millgate	Royal George
Mills	Lord Nelson (D), New Inn, Tally Ho
Milne	Lord Warden (W)
Minter	Drum, Railway
Mitchell	New Plough
Moat	Hare & Hounds (W), Kings Head, Tally Ho
Mockett	Bell Inn, Eagle, Globe, Magnet, Railway Royal George, Walmer Castle
Molyneux	Mill Inn
Monckton	Lord Clyde
Monro	Star & Garter
Moonlight	Stag
Moore	Granville, Prince of Wales, Strand
Morey	Lord Warden (D)
Morgan	Dunkerleys, Eagle, Five Bells Inn, Fountain Mill Inn, Telegraph
Morley	Railway (W)
Morris	Queens Arms
Morrish	Mill Inn, Yew Tree
Morrison	Telegraph
Mory	Black Bull
Mose	Victoria
Mulhern	Deal Hoy, Magnet
Mullet	Port Arms
Mullett	Kings Head,
Mumbray	Crosskeys, Watermans Arms, (41 Beach Street)
Murley	Port Arms
Myhill	Fleur de Lis, Three Compasses

N

Nash	Dunkerleys, Royal Standard, Stag
Naylor	Maxton Arms
Neal	India Arms
Neale	Drum, Dunkerleys, Margate Hoy, Roxborough Castle, Swan
Neary	Royal Exchange (D)
Neeve	Five Ringers, Jolly Sailor, Magnet
Netherclifft	Cambridge Arms
Newell	Alma (D)
Newing	Queens Head (W)

Nicholas	Lifeboat (D), Napier Tavern
Nicholls	Fountain, Providence
Noakes	India Arms, Pound, Royal George
Norkett	Prince Albert
Norrington	Crown Inn
Norris	Deal Hoy, Deal Lugger, Globe, Horse & Farrier, Lifeboat Inn, Prince of Wales, Tally Ho, Wellesley Arms, Yew Tree
North	Admiral Keppel, Cambridge Arms, Fountain

O

O'Connell	Admiral Keppel
O'Grady	Berry
Oates	Deal Hoy
Oatridge	Deal Hoy
Oliver	Oak & Ivy, Sir John Falstaff
Orgill	Alma (W)
Ormston	Bohemian, Deal Hoy
Orrick	White Horse (Queen Street)
Ottaway	Ramsgate Harbour
Outwin	Clarendon, Goodwins, Strand, Three Compasses, Walmer Castle
Ouwersloot	Admiral Penn
Overall	Railway Inn
Owens	Oak & Ivy
Oxley	Rose, Sandown Castle Hotel

P

Padbury	Eagle, Kings Head
Page	Yew Tree
Pageter	Bricklayers Arms (W)
Paige	Albion
Pain	Lifeboat (The Marina), Saracens Head
Palmer	Black Bull, Forester
Paramor	Royal Hotel
Parker	Bowling Green Tavern, Deal Castle Inn, Lord Warden (D), Maxton Arms, Military Tavern, Prince Albert, Prince of Wales, Railway,(W) Thompson(s) Bell
Parmenter	Dunkerleys
Parnell	Hoop & Griffin Inn
Parrett	Clifton Hotel
Parsons	Drum, Duke of York, Queen Adelaide
Partridge	Magnet
Patterson	Royal Hotel
Payne	Five Bells Inn, Greyhound, Maxton Arms, Watermans Arms
Peaks	Lord Clyde
Pearce	Cinque Port Arms, Deal Castle Inn, Fountain, Royal Standard, Windsor Castle
Pearson	Lifeboat (The Strand), Queens Head(W)
Peckham	Clifton Hotel
Penn	Hovelling Boat, Sir John Falstaff
Pepin	Alma (D)
Percy	Bowling Green Tavern
Perez	New Inn
Perry	Alma (D), Sir John Falstaff
Peters	Albion

Petters	Lord Clyde
Pettit	Sandown Castle Hotel, Stag
Petty	Kings Arms, Queens Head
Phillips	Berry, Lord Nelson (W), Prince Albert, Rising Sun Inn, White Horse (Queen Street)
Philpot	Fountain, Shah
Philpott	Pelican (2), Prince Albert
Pickard	Admiral Penn
Pickford	Lord Clyde
Piercey	Providence
Pilcher	Hoop & Griffin Inn, Jolly Gardener, Maxton Arms, Railway,(W) Telegraph
Pinder	Clarendon
Pinks	Providence
Piper	Noahs Ark, Railway Refreshment Rooms
Pitchford	Bowling Green Tavern, Port Arms
Pittock	North Infantry Canteen, Sir Sydney Smith, South Infantry Canteen
Pledge	Sir Sydney Smith
Pluckhall	Hoop & Griffin Inn
Plumridge	Friendly Port
Pockett	Hole in the Roof
Pollard	Pelican (2), Thompson(s) Bell
Poole	Red Crosse
Pooley	Yarmouth Packet
Pope	Liverpool Arms, Lord Warden (D), Swan
Porter	Fountain, Pelican (2)
Pott	Locomotive, Union Flag
Potter	Prince Albert
Powell	Admiral Keppel, Alma (W), Fox, Globe, Magnet, Saracens Head, Walmer Castle
Prescott	Kings Head, Pelican (2), Providence
Prestwidge	Yarmouth Packet
Prime	Port Arms
Prior	Park Tavern, Queens Head
Pritchard	Admiral Keppel, Eagle, Sir John Falstaff,
Pryce	Royal Hotel
Puckeridge	Railway Inn, (D)
Pullen	Ship
Punnett	Strand
Purkis	Walmer Castle
Pygall	Bohemian

Q

Quiddington	Royal Hotel
Quigley	Sir Colin Campbell
Quinn	Clarendon
Quinton	Bowling Green Tavern, Ship

R

Radcliffe	Dunkerleys
Radford	Chequers Inn
Rae	New Inn
Ralph	Forester, Kings Head, Rose, Ship, Yarmouth Packet
Rammell	Bear Pump
Ramsden	Sandown Castle Hotel

Ran	Alma (W)
Rand	Kings Head
Randall	Five Bells Inn, Victoria
Rands	Lord Warden (W)
Ravensburg	Walmer Castle
Rayner	Queens Arms
Raynor	Drum
Rea	Fountain
Read	Admiral Penn, Alma (D), Dolphin (W), Five Ringers, India Arms
Reader	Cambridge Arms, Druid Arms
Reading	Alma (D)
Redman	Admiral Penn, Crown Inn, Deal Castle Inn, Eagle, Five Bells Inn, Lifeboat (The Strand), New Inn, Providence, Railway, Sandown Castle Hotel, Sir Sydney Smith, South Foreland, Tally Ho, White Horse (Queen Street)
Redsull	Dover Castle, Fawn, Forester, Hope, Jolly Gardener, New Plough
Reed	Pelican (2), Stag
Reely	Sir Sydney Smith
Reeve	Port Arms
Reeves	Alma (W)
Reiger	Prince Albert
Reilly	Dunkerleys
Renihan	Lifeboat (The Strand)
Rennie	Bowling Green Tavern
Reynolds	Duke of Wellington, Lord Clyde, Stag, White Horse (Middle Street)
Ribbands	Stag
Richards	Bohemian, Magnet, Thompson(s) Bell
Richardson	Tally Ho
Richwood	Queens Hotel
Rickard	Strand
Ricketts	Oak & Ivy, Park Tavern
Rickman	Drum, Royal Hotel, Royal Oak Inn
Rickwood	Old(e) Victory
Ridley	Clarendon
Rigglesford	Black Bull
Riley	Bohemian, Phoenix, Prince Albert
Roberts	Admiral Keppel, Admiral Penn, Albion, Cambridge Arms, Five Bells Inn, Forester, Fox, Hope, Pelican (2), Tally Ho, Watermans Arms
Robinson	Dover Castle, Five Bells Inn, Fox, Mill Inn, Queens Arms, Three Compasses, Walmer Castle
Rock	Kings Head
Rogers	Lord Warden (W), Oak & Ivy, Rising Sun, Wellesley Arms, Yew Tree
Rolfe	Lord Warden (W), Walmer Castle
Romney	Granville, Lord Clyde
Rooff	Admiral Keppel
Rook	Dolphin (W)
Rose	Chequers Inn
Roser	Lifeboat (The Strand)
Ross	Royal Exchange (D), Ship
Rothwell	Hole in the Roof
Rowe	Military Tavern, Railway Refreshment Rooms
Rowley	Queens Arms
Ruse	Telegraph
Russell	Alma (W), Clifton Hotel, Duke of

Wellington, New Inn, Pelican (2), Queens Head (W)

| Ryan | Magnet, Windsor Castle |

S

Saffery	Fleur de Lis
Safrey	Bear Pump
Saggs	Five Ringers
Sainsbury	Five Ringers
Salmon	Bohemian, Cambridge Arms, Walmer Castle, Walmer Castle
Sands	Greyhound, Roxborough Castle
Savage	Queens Head (W)
Sawkins	Harp
Saxby	Prince Alfred Inn
Sayers	Bowling Green Tavern
Sayle	Saracens Head
Scarlett	Oak Tree, Ship
Schmid	Port Arms
Schurig	Walmer Castle
Scott	Lord Nelson (D), Lord Nelson (W), Mill Inn
Scovell	Old(e) Victory
Selth	Deal Lugger, Dover Castle, Sir John Falstaff
Setterfield	Lord Warden (W), Roxborough Castle
Shakey	Admiral Keppel
Sharp	Crown Inn, Fleur de Lis, Port Arms
Sharpe	Marine Hotel, Prince Alfred Inn
Shaw	Alma (D)
Sheath	Queens Hotel, Railway Refreshment Rooms
Shelvey	Friendly Port, Hare & Hounds (D), Oak & Ivy
Shepherd	Walmer Castle
Sherlock	Queens Arms
Shervill	Mill Inn, Walmer Castle
Shillett	Oak & Ivy
Shipley	Alma (D)
Shrewsbury	Crown Inn
Shrubb	Alma (W)
Siddens	Sir John Falstaff
Silbury	Forester
Sills	Railway
Simkins	Lord Warden (W)
Simmonds	Lord Nelson (W), North Infantry Canteen, Thompson(s) Bell
Simmons	South Infantry Canteen, Union Flag
Simpin	Lord Warden (W)
Simpson	Maxton Arms
Sinden	Granville
Singer	Crown Inn
Sitton	Dunkerleys
Skinner	Alma (W), Hare & Hounds (D), Jolly Gardener, Liverpool Arms
Sladden	Sandown Castle Hotel
Sloper	Albion
Small	Alma (D), Greyhound
Smallbones	Alma (D)
Smart	Queens Hotel
Smith	Admiral Penn, Alma (D), Arrow, Deal Lugger, Drum, Hope, Jolly Gardener, Locomotive, Lord Nelson (W), Lord Warden (D), Magnet, Mill Inn, Pelican (2), Port Arms, Prince Albert, Providence, Queens Arms, Queens Head (W), Royal Hotel, Saracens Head, Shah, Stag, Strand, Pelican (1), Pelican (3)
Sneller	Napier Tavern
Snelling	Royal Standard, Stag
Snoswell	Crown Inn, Friendly Port, General Wolfe, Lord Warden (W), Sir John Falstaff
Snowdon	Royal Exchange (D)
Sokell	Alma (W)
Sole	Royal Oak Inn
Solley	Deal Castle Inn, Lifeboat (The Strand)
Solly	Queens Arms
Soole	Duke of Wellington
Southall	Locomotive
Southam	Dolphin (W), Five Bells Inn
Spallin	Forester
Sparke	Queens Hotel
Sparkes	Greyhound
Sparks	Friendly Port, Kings Head
Sparshatt	Mill Inn
Sparshott	Cambridge Arms
Sparshott	Lord Warden (D)
Spears	Bohemian, Deal Lugger, General Wolfe, Hare & Hounds (W), South Foreland, Victoria
Speed	Admiral Penn
Spice	New Inn
Spicer	Dunkerleys, Hope, Locomotive, Maxton Arms, Noahs Ark, Strand
Spillet	Noahs Ark
Spinner	Five Ringers, Maxton Arms
Spong	Strand
Spooner	Cambridge Arms
Springhall	Five Ringers
Spurrier	Strand
Stacey	Crispin Inn
Stammers	Stag
Stanton	Lifeboat (D)
Stapleton	Lord Nelson (W)
Startup	Dunkerleys
Steadman	Lifeboat (The Strand)
Steed	Fleur de Lis
Stevens	Academy Sports Bar, Cambridge Arms, Five Ringers, Lord Warden (W), Mill Inn, Yew Tree
Steward	Saracens Head
Stewart	Dunkerleys, Oak & Ivy, Queens Head (W)
Stickells	Maxton Arms
Stiles	Kings Head
Stills	Bowling Green Tavern
Stock	Oak & Ivy
Stoker	Noahs Ark
Stokes	Arrow, Eagle, Liverpool Arms, (D)
Stride	Greyhound
Stringer	Thompson(s) Bell
Stryczek	Queens Hotel, (2)
Stupples	Crown Inn
Sturges	Lord Nelson (W)
Styles	Bowling Green Tavern

Sutton	Admiral Keppel, Army & Navy, Dover Castle, Military Tavern
Sweeney	Port Arms
Swift	Three Compasses
Swinyard	Jolly Gardener
Sykes	Locomotive
Symonds	Royal Hotel
Sympson	Hoop & Griffin Inn, Walmer Castle

T

Tandy	Sandown Castle Hotel
Tanton	Crown Inn, Thompson(s) Bell
Tatner	Walmer Castle
Taylor	Berry, Bowling Green Tavern, Cherry Tree, Jolly Gardener, Lifeboat (The Strand), Locomotive, Military Tavern, Railway, Rising Sun,(D) Sandown Castle Hotel, Tally Ho, White Horse (Queen Street)
Terrell	Pelican (2)
Terry	Ship, Yew Tree
Thatcher	Oak & Ivy
Theobald	Park Tavern
Thomas	Duke of York, Harp, Hope, Lord Clyde, Ship
Thompsett	Fountain
Thompson	Black Bull, Clarendon, Deal Lugger, Friendly Port, Pelican (2), Prince of Wales, Providence, Rose, Saracens Head, Sir Colin Campbell
Thomson	Magnet
Thorneycroft	Clarendon
Thornhill	Hare & Hounds (D)
Tidy	Granville
Tilbury	Bohemian
Tilly	Noahs Ark
Timblick	Victoria
Timmins	Queen Adelaide
Tobin	Albion, New Plough
Tomkinson	Stag
Tomlin	Admiral Rodney, Hoop & Griffin Inn, Railway, (W)
Toms	Lord Clyde
Townsend	Mill Inn
Travis	Amsterdam
Trevegan	Port Arms
Trollope	Stag
Trott	Exchange Beer Shop, Kings Head, Port Arms, Providence
Tuck	Crispin Inn
Tucker	Beachbrow, Queens Head, Royal Exchange (D), Yew Tree
Turner	Hare & Hounds (Dover Road), Harp, Ship, Tally Ho
Turton	Royal Exchange (D)
Tweed	Jolly Gardener
Tyler	Eagle
Tyrell	Cambridge Arms

U

Uden	Mill Inn
Upton	Berry, Duke of Wellington, Stag
Usher	Royal George

V

van Zyl	Chequers Inn
Verrier	Bowling Green Tavern, Five Bells Inn, Magnet, Wellesley Arms
Vickers	Alma (D)
Viles	Crown Inn
Vincent	Royal Hotel
Vogels	Thompson(s) Bell
Vurley	Prince Albert

W

Wadoux	Railway Inn,(D) Royal Exchange (D)
Wakeham	Chequers Inn
Wakerell	Brickmakers Arms, Lifeboat Inn, Campbell Road)
Walker	Clarendon, Mill Inn, White Horse (Queen Street), Yew Tree
Wallace	Five Ringers
Wallis	Harp
Walsh	Eagle, Maxton Arms, Queens Head, Rose, Saracens Head
Walters	Admiral Keppel
Waltham	Farrier
Walton	Granville, Napier Tavern, Yew Tree
Wanstall	Royal Exchange (D), Sir Sydney Smith
Ward	Maxton Arms, Stag
Wardle	Eagle
Wardrop	Royal George
Wareham	Bohemian, New Inn
Warman	Royal Exchange (D)
Warr	Queens Hotel, Star & Garter
Watkins	Admiral Keppel, Magnet
Watson	Five Bells Inn, Thompson(s) Bell
Watt	Berry
Watts	Cambridge Arms, Deal Castle Inn, Queens Head, Railway,(W) Roxborough Castle, Royal Hotel
Way	Windsor Castle
Wearmouth	Bowling Green Tavern
Weaver	Jolly Sailor
Webb	Alma (W), Bricklayers Arms (W), New Plough, Park Tavern, Yew Tree
Wedl	Royal Hotel
Welland	Lifeboat (The Strand)
Wellard	Army & Navy, Lord Nelson (W), Park Tavern, Queens Arms
Weller	Greyhound
Wells	Duke of Wellington, Fox
Welton	Dunkerleys, Roxborough Castle
West	Tally Ho, Walmer Castle, Wellesley Arms, Yarmouth Packet
Weston	Duke of York, Friendly Port, Pelican (2), Walmer Castle
Wheatley	Garibaldi
Wheeler	Park Tavern

Whelan	Duke of Wellington
Whetstone	Greyhound
Whitall	Fleur de Lis
Whitcombe	Stag
White	Admiral Keppel, Black Bull, Globe, Kings Arms, Lord Nelson (W), Lord Warden (W), Queens Head, Rising Sun, Rising Sun Inn,(W) Rose, Strand
Whitehead	Prince Albert
Whiteley	Pelican (2)
Whitlaw	Royal Hotel
Wicks	Pelican (2)
Wilds	North Star
Willey	Lord Nelson (W)
Williams	Deal Hoy, Lord Nelson (W), Lord Warden (W), Noahs Ark, Telegraph, Thompson(s) Bell
Willington	Drum
Willis	Eagle, Prince Albert, Stag
Wilmott	Thompson(s) Bell
Wilson	Horse & Farrier, Noahs Ark, Railway, (W)
Windsor	Clarendon
Wing	Roxborough Castle
Wingate	Alma (D)
Winkworth	Royal Exchange (D)
Witcher	Port Arms
Withall	White Horse (Queen Street)

Wolwill	Locomotive
Wood	Albion, Fleur de Lis, Fountain, New Inn, Pelican (3), Port Arms, Prince of Wales, Queens Head, Rising Sun Inn,(W) Ship, Stag, Three Compasses
Woodcock	Saracens Head
Woodham	Phoenix
Woodman	Bell, Watermans Arms
Woodward	Prince Albert, Railway,(W) Thompson(s) Bell
Workman	Bohemian, Mill Inn, Rose
Worman	Roxborough Castle
Worrels	Sir Colin Campbell
Worsley	Bricklayers Arms (W)
Worth	Greyhound
Wraight	Cambridge Arms, Cinque Ports Volunteer
Wratten	Five Bells Inn, Watermans Arms
Wright	Cambridge Arms, Clifton Hotel, Liverpool Arms, Queens Head
Wyatt	Beachbrow, Jolly Gardener
Wyborn	Brickmakers Arms, Crown Inn, Five Ringers, Kings Arms, Lifeboat (The Strand), Margate Hoy, New Inn, Swan, Three Compasses
Yates	Pelican (1), Walmer Castle
Young	Berry, Maxton Arms, Stag, White Horse (Queen Street)

Index to landlords' surnames of Kingsdown and Mongeham

A

Allen	Three Horseshoes
Arnold	Rising Sun, Three Horseshoes, Victory, Zetland Arms
Austin	Three Horseshoes
Ayling	Three Horseshoes

B

Bagshaw	Rising Sun
Bartlett	Zetland Arms
Batson	Leather Bottle
Beard	Zetland Arms
Beeching	Leather Bottle
Bigginton	Friendly Port
Bingham	Victory
Brigden	Rising Sun
Brooks	Leather Bottle
Browne	Three Horseshoes
Brunt	Rising Sun

C

Cavell	Friendly Port
Chandler	Leather Bottle
Charles	Rising Sun
Checksfield	Three Horseshoes

Cobbett	Zetland Arms
Cox	Friendly Port
Crook	Kings Head

D

| Day | Rising Sun |
| Drayson | Friendly Port, Three Horseshoes |

E

Erridge	Victory, Zetland Arms
Evans	Kings Head
Ferguson	Three Horseshoes

F

Flynn	Leather Bottle
Forder	Kings Head
Furnall	Zetland Arms

G

Galley	Rising Sun
Garnett	Kings Head
Gifford	Kings Head

Glaysher	Rising Sun
Gledhill	Kings Head
Gore	Leather Bottle
Gravenell	Leather Bottle
Gunn	Leather Bottle

H

Harden	Rising Sun
Harris	Friendly Port
Hawkins	Rising Sun
Hoffer	Leather Bottle
Hopper	Friendly Port
Hyland	Rising Sun

J

Jefford	Leather Bottle

K

Kerry	Kings Head

L

Latham	Three Horseshoes

M

Main	Rising Sun
Mallion	Kings Head
McSloy	Three Horseshoes

Moat	Three Horseshoes
Mockett	Rising Sun

P

Pattison	Kings Head
Payne	Kings Head
Philpott	Leather Bottle, Three Horseshoes
Powell	Kings Head
Pranklinfi	Leather Bottle
Ratcliffe	Three Horseshoes
Rodwell	Three Horseshoes
Rolfe	Three Horseshoes

S

Saffery	Rising Sun
Shilling	Victory
Silbery	Rising Sun
Spinner	Rising Sun
Styles	Three Horseshoes
Sumner	Kings Head
Sutton	Kings Head, Leather Bottle, Rising Sun
Swift	Victory

W

Warwick	Leather Bottle
Watts	Kings Head
Wellard	Zetland Arms
West	Rising Sun
Westby	Zetland Arms
Workman	Rising Sun
Wraight	Three Horseshoes

Acknowledgements

The authors wish to acknowledge the works and findings of the following authors (other than those whose books are mentioned below in 'Bibliography/Publications') and researchers, past and present, who have either directly or indirectly assisted (or inspired!) them in the writing of this book: Samuel Pepys, William Cobbett, AJ Langridge, Harry Franks, Gertrude Nunns, Bob Collyer, David Collyer, Les Cozens, June Broady, Beryl Foley-Fisher, Charles Finn and Judith Davies, Barbara Baker, Andrew Sargent, Gregory Holyoake, David Chamberlain, Paul Skelton, Alec Hasenson and Martin Tapsell.

They also wish to thank the following organisations and individuals, be they home owners of former pubs, publicans or people with local knowledge, in providing other documentary and verbal evidence, and apologise in advance for anyone inadvertently omitted from the list: John Rogers, the late Betty Rogers, Pete the Book, John and Jeannie Gold, Carol Murray, Lynn Stockdale, Carole Smyth, Sidney and Sheila Whitehead, Arthur North, John and Donnie Farago, Marion Elliot (née Skinner), Stuart Hammond, Valerie Hambridge, Cynthia Tucker (née Marsh), Peter Stevens, John Higgins and Barry Smith, Alan and Eileen Taylor, Brenda Newton, David Warden, Ann Lyons, Frances Woodcock, Julie Deller, Peggy Frost, Janet Axbey, Stephen Misson, Jess Williams, Nick from the Tally Ho, Hilary from the Albion, Mick Ruse, Ken Cox, Jim Skardon, Alison Cable, Mick Gurney, Bruce Laird, Michael Collyer, Vic Edginton, Helen O'Sullivan, John Ling, Dave and Lyn Harrison, Brian and Sue Franklin, Steve Grant and Leona Rusk, Cathy and Ian, Mike Morgan, John Norris, Nigel Blundell, Michael Harlick and Colin Vurley of The Prince Albert, Ray and Penny Dennis of The Ship, CAMRA, Williamson & Barnes, Mowll & Mowll, Mrs J Constantine, Mr A Leith and Richard Sturt on behalf of the Leith Estate, Vyse Collection, Cavell Collection, Godfrey Davis Collection, Denise Coe and the Staff of Deal Library, Dover Library, Sittingbourne Library, the former Worshipful Town Mayor of Deal Cllr Bill Gardner, Les Bulman, Tony Higgins, the Town Sergeant, Deal Town Council, Dover District Council, Deal Society, Will Honey Collection, Frances Lancaster, Judith Doré, Deal Maritime & Local History Museum, Mark Frost at Dover Museum, Sue Briggs of the East Kent Mercury, Alan Sutton Publishing, Chalford Publishing Company, TF Pain & Co, Edward Hayward of Deal, Pearson Education, Tempus Publishing Limited, East Kent Archives at Whitfield, Whitebread Archives, Centre for Kentish Studies at Maidstone, Shepherd Neame Brewery, Catherine Lister of Coors Museum of Brewing, Canterbury Cathedral Archives, Lambeth Palace, Kew Records Office and Ordnance Survey.

Deal OS Maps: Reproduced from the 1871, 1872 & 1873 Ordnance Survey Maps with kind permission of Ordnance Survey
Walmer OS Maps: Reproduced from the 1872 and 1898 Ordnance Survey Maps with kind permission of Ordnance Survey.

Enormous thanks also to

Trevor Hatton for undertaking so much of the research work for this book behind the scenes, as well as snapping many of the original photographs; Jerry Vyse, university student and local author of 'Time To Go', for taking time out from his studies and very hectic social life to help compile the index of landlords and pub names; Steve Bell, musician and all round 'good egg', for his proofreading assistance; Nick Evans, author of Dreamland Remembered, for cracking the whip to ensure deadlines were met, advising, editing and arranging for the book's publishing and printing; Sue Carey for the gruelling task of collecting together – and the deciphering of – seemingly thousands of pieces of illegibly written pieces of scrap paper (aka research material) and for typing up the entire contents of this book.

Finally, in loving memory of Betty Rogers, Ralph & Evelyn Glover, Sydney & Imelda Jordan and Bill & Mabel Cronk, without whom this book would have proved impossible for so many different reasons.

Bibliography/Publications

Kent Pubs by DB Tubbs;
Kent Inns and Signs by Michael David Mirams;
The Local – A History of the English Pub by Paul Jennings;
A Dictionary of Pub, Inn and Tavern Signs by Colin Waters;
The Wordsworth Dictionary of Pub Names;
Laker's History of Deal;
Pritchard's History of Deal;
Deal & District at War, 1939–1945 by David G Collyer;
A History of Deal by Gertrude Nunns
Discovering Deal by Barbara Collins
Deal in Old Photographs by June Broady
Deal: Sad Smuggling Town by Gregory Holyoake
Deal: All in The Downs by Gregory Holyoake

The Life and Times of a Small House in Deal by Andrew Sargent
Saga of the Goodwin Sands by David Chamberlain
Bygone Deal and Walmer by Beryl Foley-Fisher
The Last of Our Luggers and the Men who Sailed Them by EC Pain;
Deal & Walmer and the War of Liberation by EC Pain;
Time To Go by Jerry Vyse;
Shops Remembered in Deal and Walmer by Judith Gaunt;
Kingsdown and Ringwould – A History and Guide edited by David Harding;
Reminiscences of Old Deal by EC Pain;
Elvin's Records of Walmer;
Hancock's Fly Proprietor's Diary;
Bygone Kent magazine;
Sketches of Deal, Walmer & Sandwich by John Lewis Roget, MA Hons;

Mine of Humour by George Brailsford (edited by Jerry Vyse)
East Kent Mercury;
Dover Express;
Kent Messenger;
Deal & Walmer Telegram;
Dover District Council's 'Coalfields Heritage Initiative Kent website';
Dover Magistrates' Court records;
Pike's Directories;
Pain's Directories;
Bradshaw's Directories;
Kent Service Directories;
Pigot's Directories;
Kelly's Directories;
Melville's Directories;
Regency Directory;
Deal Directory & Guide, 1721;
The Deal Scene, 1887-1977;
Various Deal Town Guides.